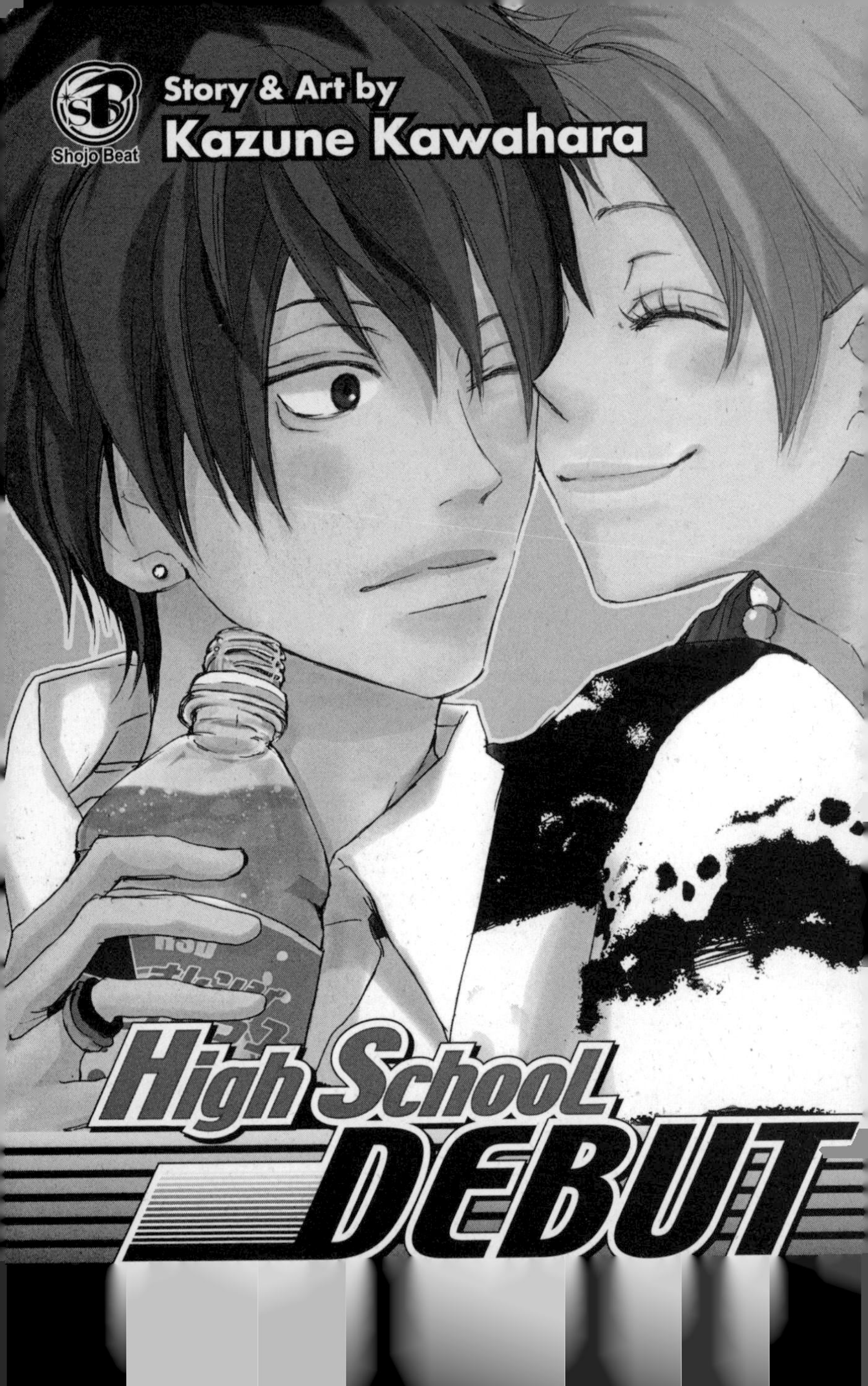
Shojo Beat
Story & Art by
Kazune Kawahara
High School
DEBUT

High School DEBUT

★★ Contents

Story Thus Far... ★★

High school student Haruna used to spend all her time playing softball in junior high, but now she wants to give her all to finding true love instead! While her "love coach" Yoh is training her on how to be popular with guys, the two of them start dating. Their relationship has its fair share of drama, but it only strengthens their bond. ♥

Haruna is now in her second year, and she is chosen to help out at the entrance ceremony for new students. For some reason, three of the freshmen boys seem interested in getting to know her better. Is there trouble on the horizon...?!

Meanwhile, Yoh is attracting attention from the freshman girls. Haruna sees how popular he is and resolves to prepare herself for a fight for his love. But Yoh holds her hand and makes sure everyone in school knows that they're an item! Yoh and Haruna are official! So what could possibly happen now...?!

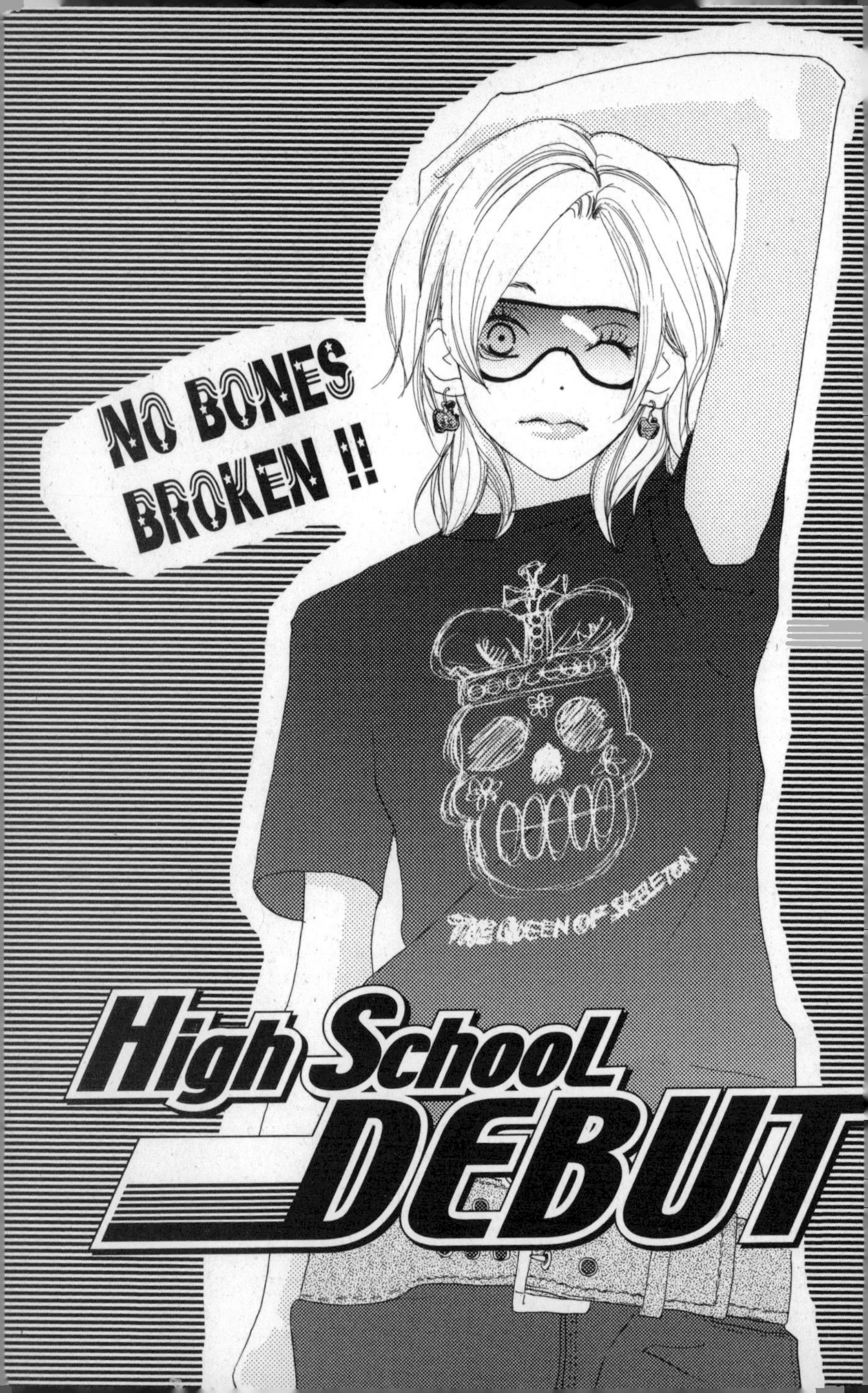
NO BONES BROKEN !!
THE QUEEN OF SKELETON
High School DEBUT

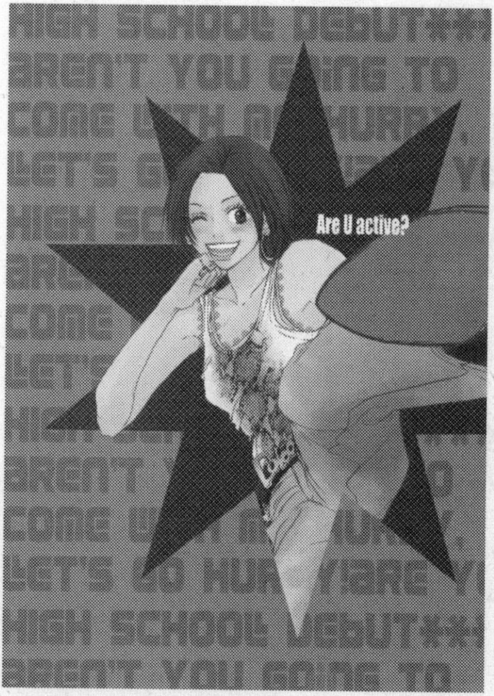
Are U active?

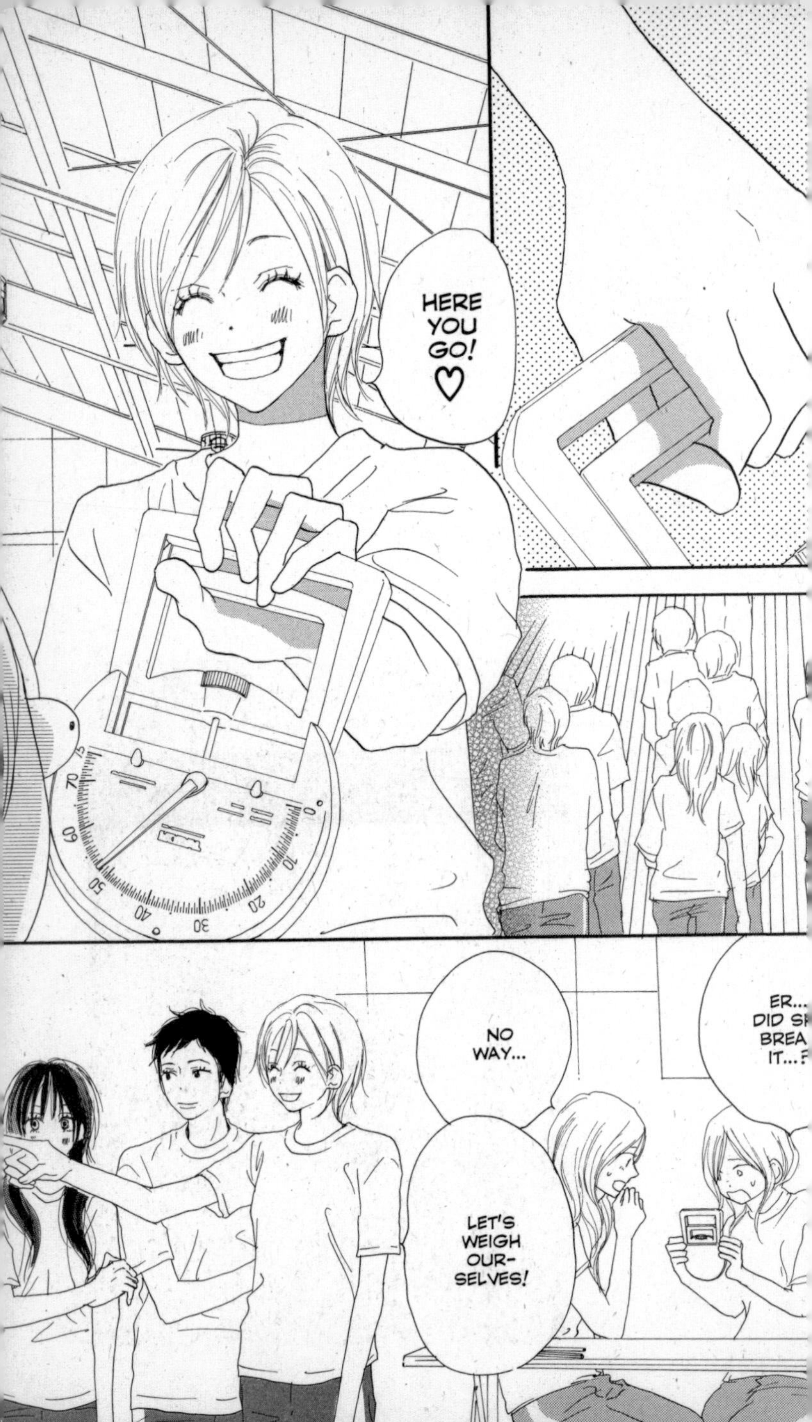
HERE YOU GO! ♡
ER... DID SH BREA IT...?
NO WAY...
LET'S WEIGH OUR-SELVES!

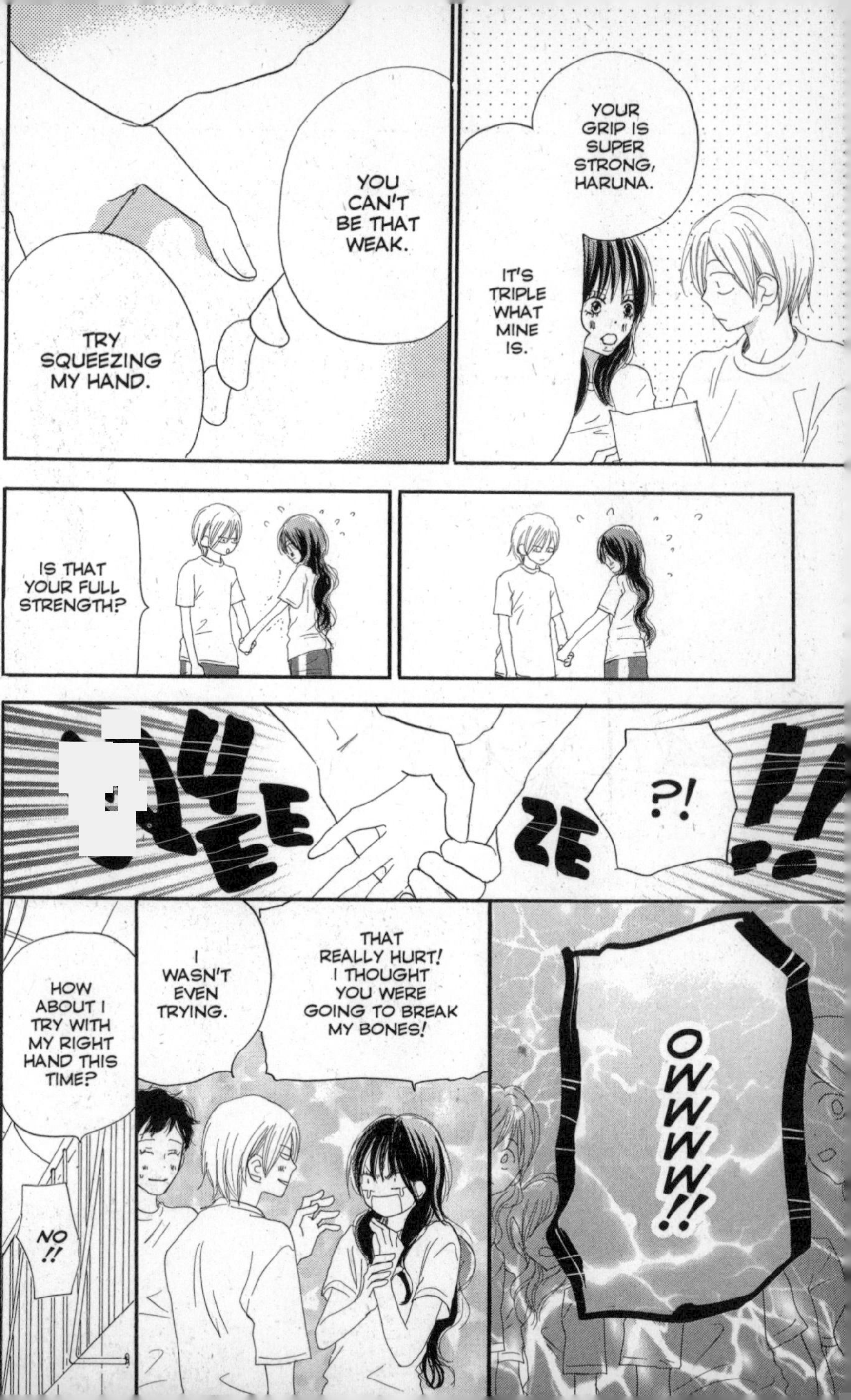
YOUR GRIP IS SUPER STRONG, HARUNA.
IT'S TRIPLE WHAT MINE IS.
YOU CAN'T BE THAT WEAK.
TRY SQUEEZING MY HAND.
IS THAT YOUR FULL STRENGTH?
?!
UEEZE!!
OWWWW!!
THAT REALLY HURT! I THOUGHT YOU WERE GOING TO BREAK MY BONES!
I WASN'T EVEN TRYING.
HOW ABOUT I TRY WITH MY RIGHT HAND THIS TIME?
NO!!

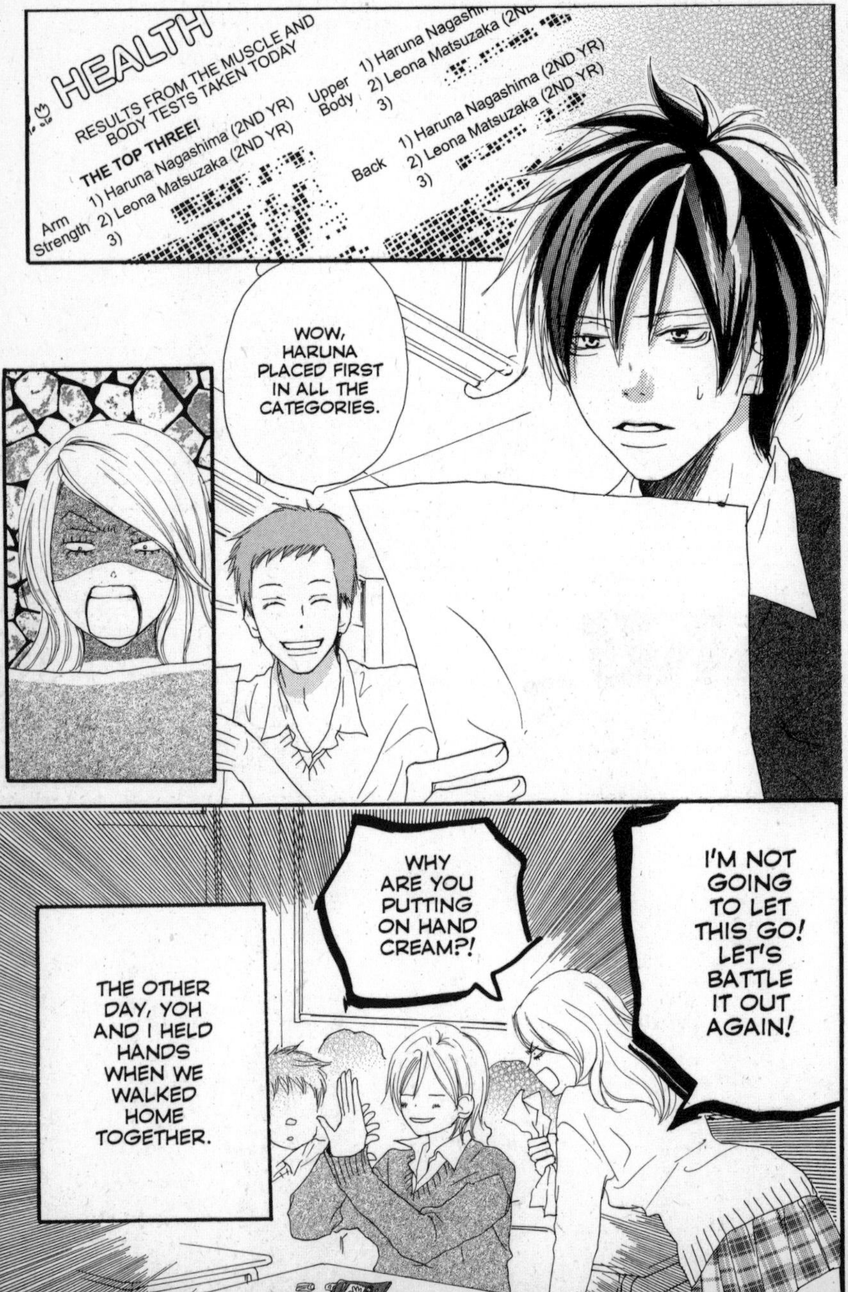

HEALTH
RESULTS FROM THE MUSCLE AND BODY TESTS TAKEN TODAY
THE TOP THREE!
Arm Strength 1) Haruna Nagashima (2ND YR) 2) Leona Matsuzaka (2ND YR) 3)
Upper Body 1) Haruna Nagashima (2ND YR) 2) Leona Matsuzaka (2ND YR) 3)
Back 1) Haruna Nagashima (2ND YR) 2) Leona Matsuzaka (2ND YR) 3)
WOW, HARUNA PLACED FIRST IN ALL THE CATEGORIES.
I'M NOT GOING TO LET THIS GO! LET'S BATTLE IT OUT AGAIN!
WHY ARE YOU PUTTING ON HAND CREAM?!
THE OTHER DAY, YOH AND I HELD HANDS WHEN WE WALKED HOME TOGETHER.

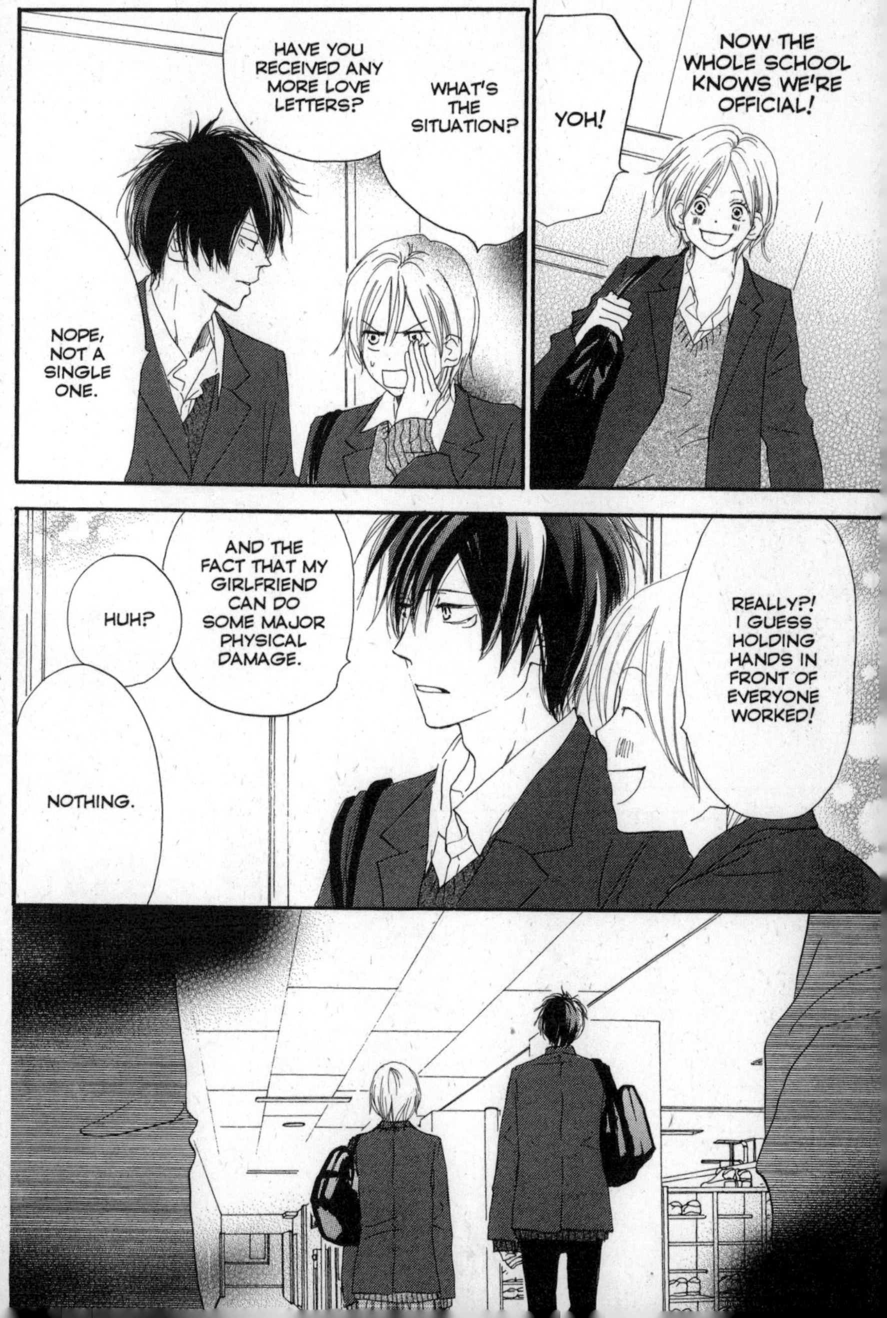
NOW THE WHOLE SCHOOL KNOWS WE'RE OFFICIAL!
YOH!
WHAT'S THE SITUATION?
HAVE YOU RECEIVED ANY MORE LOVE LETTERS?
NOPE, NOT A SINGLE ONE.
REALLY?! I GUESS HOLDING HANDS IN FRONT OF EVERYONE WORKED!
AND THE FACT THAT MY GIRLFRIEND CAN DO SOME MAJOR PHYSICAL DAMAGE.
HUH?
NOTHING.

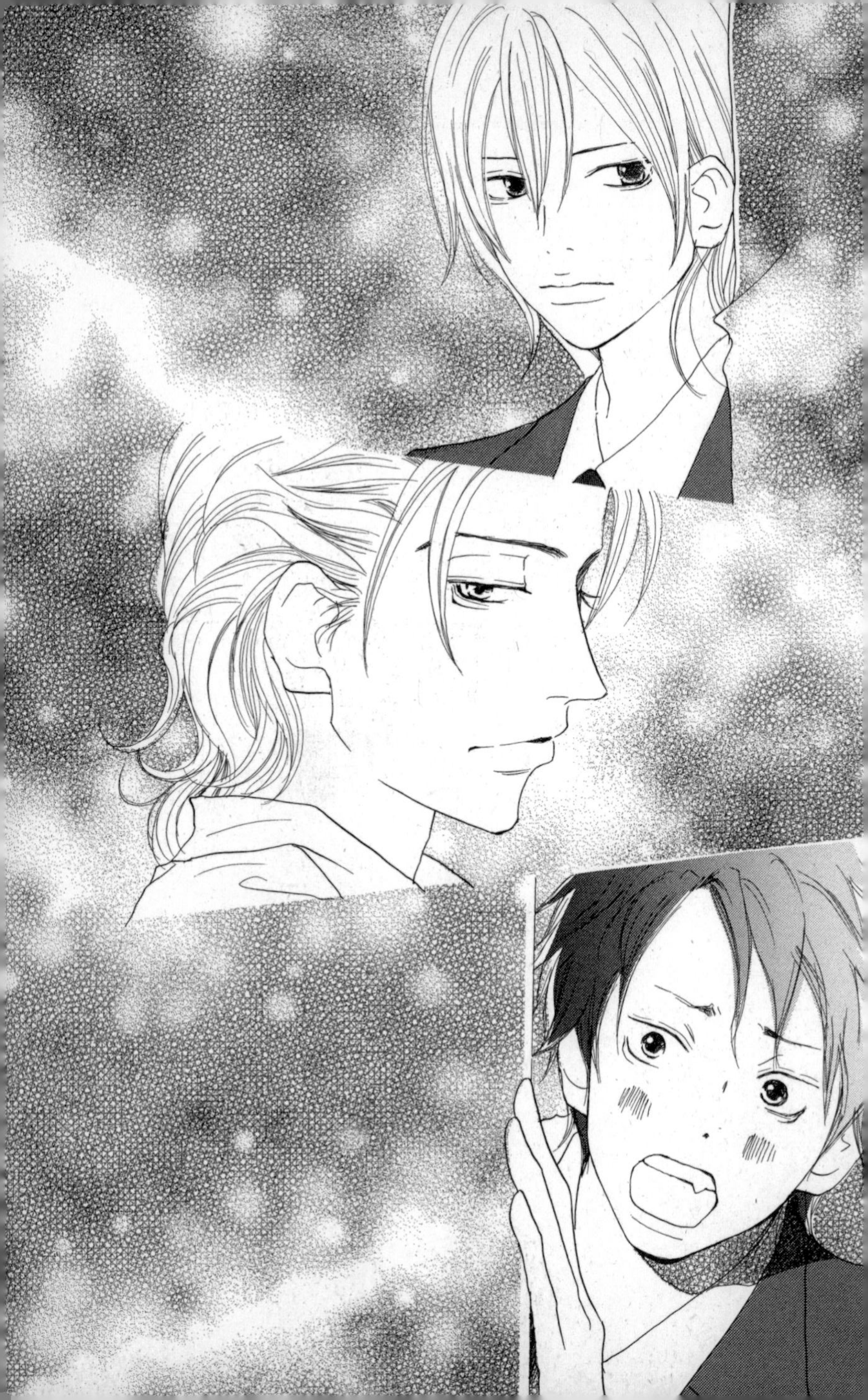

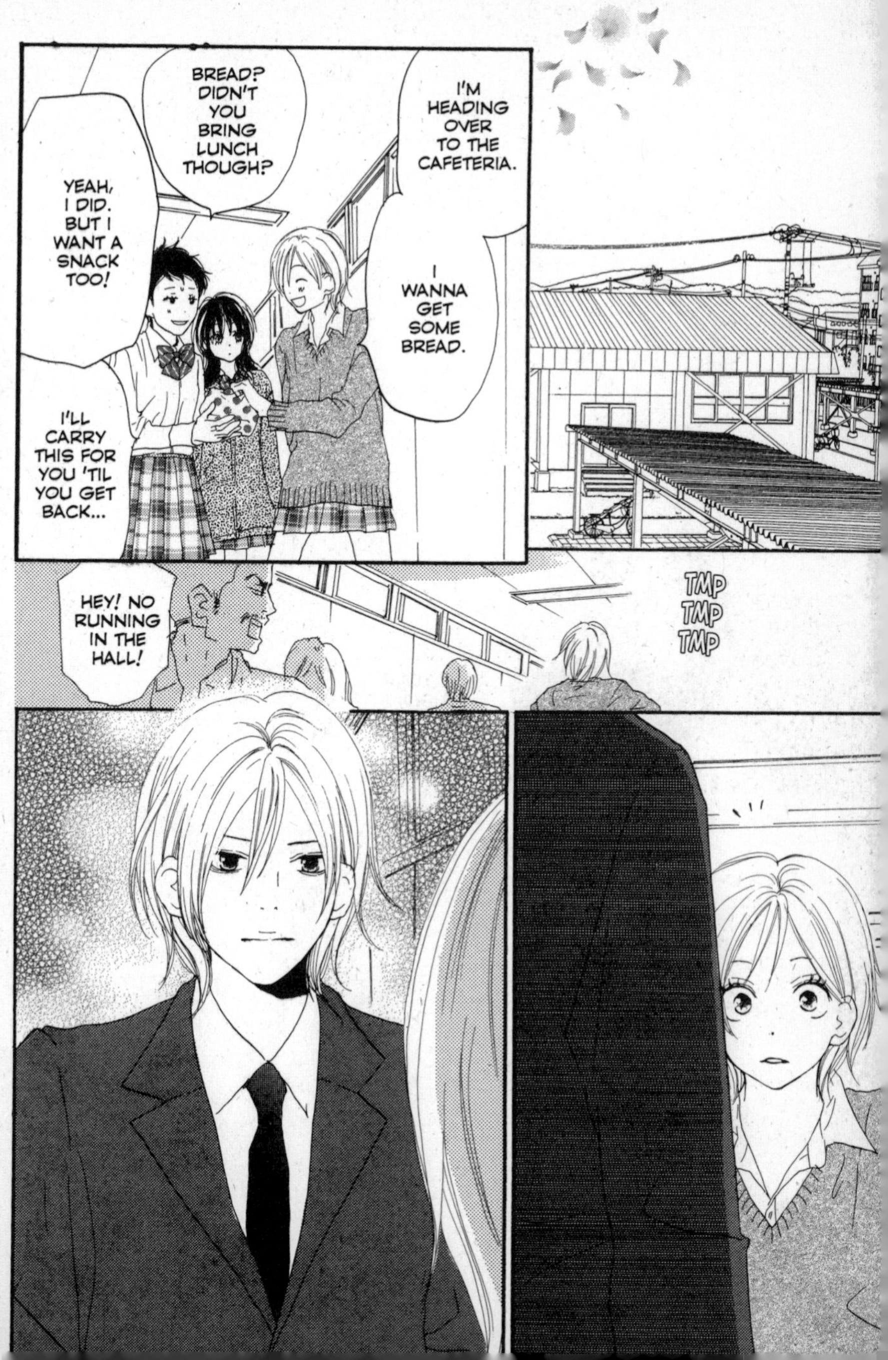
I'M HEADING OVER TO THE CAFETERIA.
I WANNA GET SOME BREAD.
BREAD? DIDN'T YOU BRING LUNCH THOUGH?
YEAH, I DID. BUT I WANT A SNACK TOO!
I'LL CARRY THIS FOR YOU 'TIL YOU GET BACK...
TMP TMP TMP
HEY! NO RUNNING IN THE HALL!

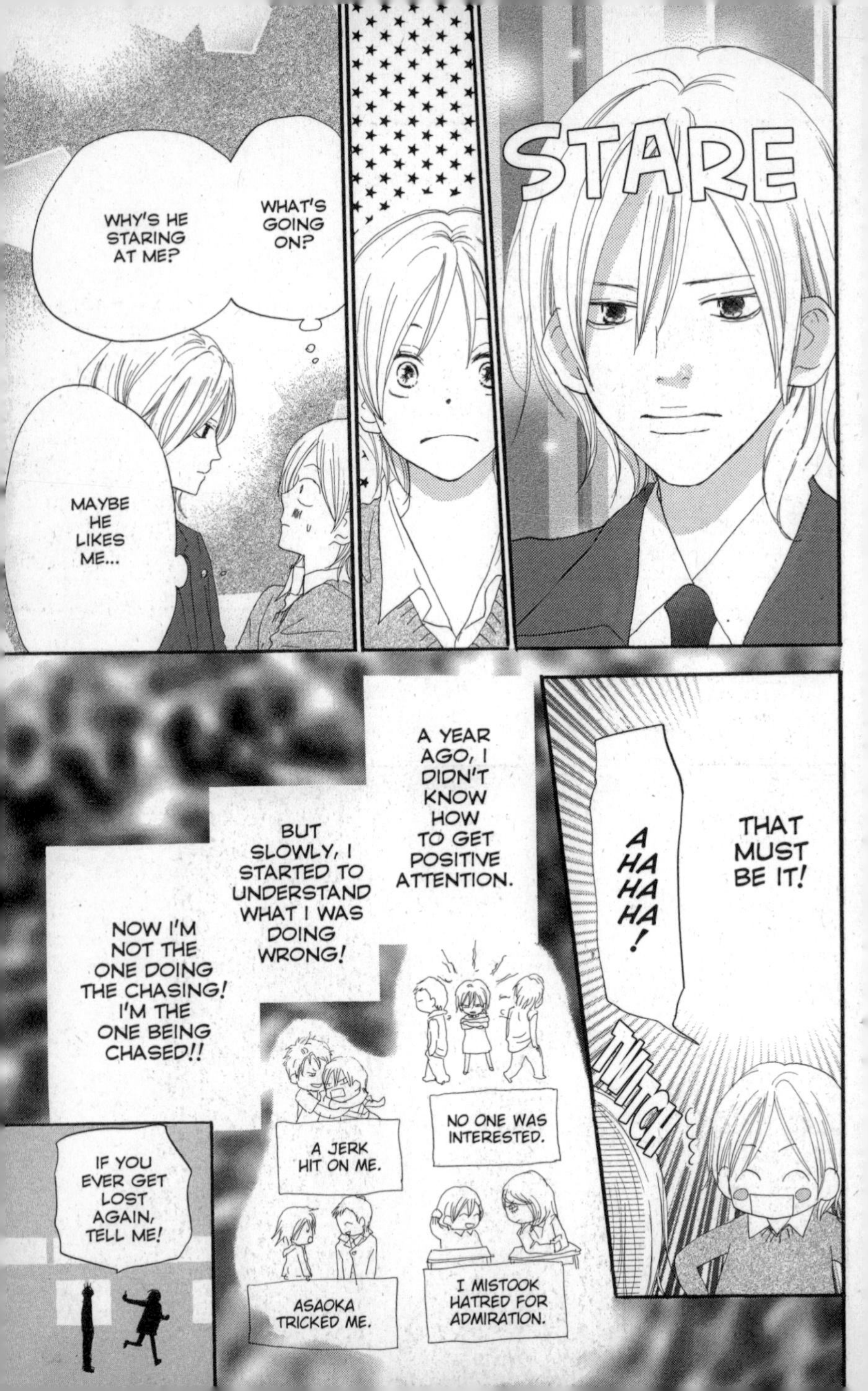
STARE
WHAT'S GOING ON?
WHY'S HE STARING AT ME?
MAYBE HE LIKES ME...
THAT MUST BE IT!
AHAHAHAHA!
TWITCH
A YEAR AGO, I DIDN'T KNOW HOW TO GET POSITIVE ATTENTION.
BUT SLOWLY, I STARTED TO UNDERSTAND WHAT I WAS DOING WRONG!
NO ONE WAS INTERESTED.
A JERK HIT ON ME.
I MISTOOK HATRED FOR ADMIRATION.
ASAOKA TRICKED ME.
NOW I'M NOT THE ONE DOING THE CHASING! I'M THE ONE BEING CHASED!!
IF YOU EVER GET LOST AGAIN, TELL ME!

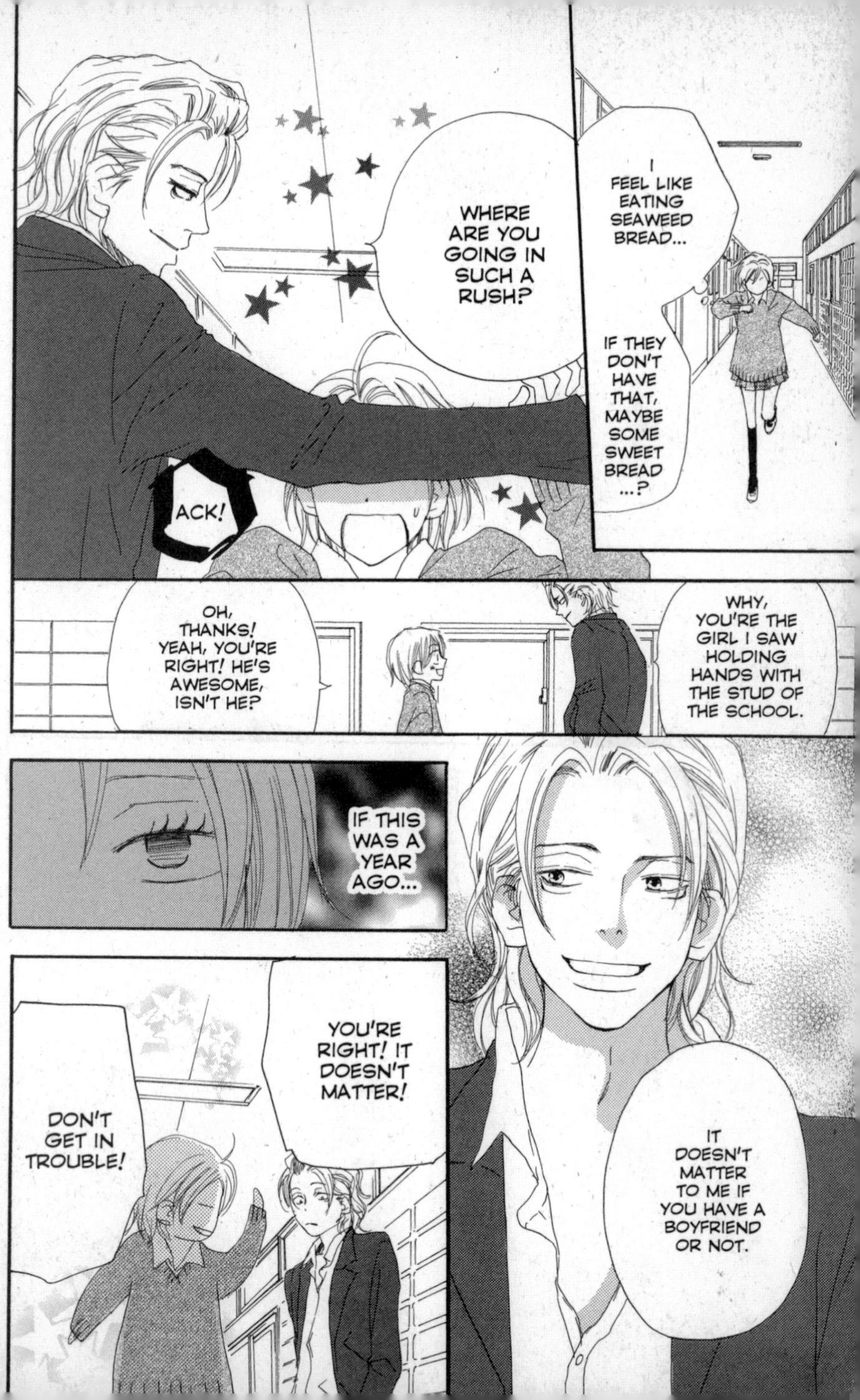
I FEEL LIKE EATING SEAWEED BREAD...
IF THEY DON'T HAVE THAT, MAYBE SOME SWEET BREAD ...?
WHERE ARE YOU GOING IN SUCH A RUSH?
ACK!
WHY, YOU'RE THE GIRL I SAW HOLDING HANDS WITH THE STUD OF THE SCHOOL.
OH, THANKS! YEAH, YOU'RE RIGHT! HE'S AWESOME, ISN'T HE?
IT DOESN'T MATTER TO ME IF YOU HAVE A BOYFRIEND OR NOT.
IF THIS WAS A YEAR AGO...
YOU'RE RIGHT! IT DOESN'T MATTER!
DON'T GET IN TROUBLE!

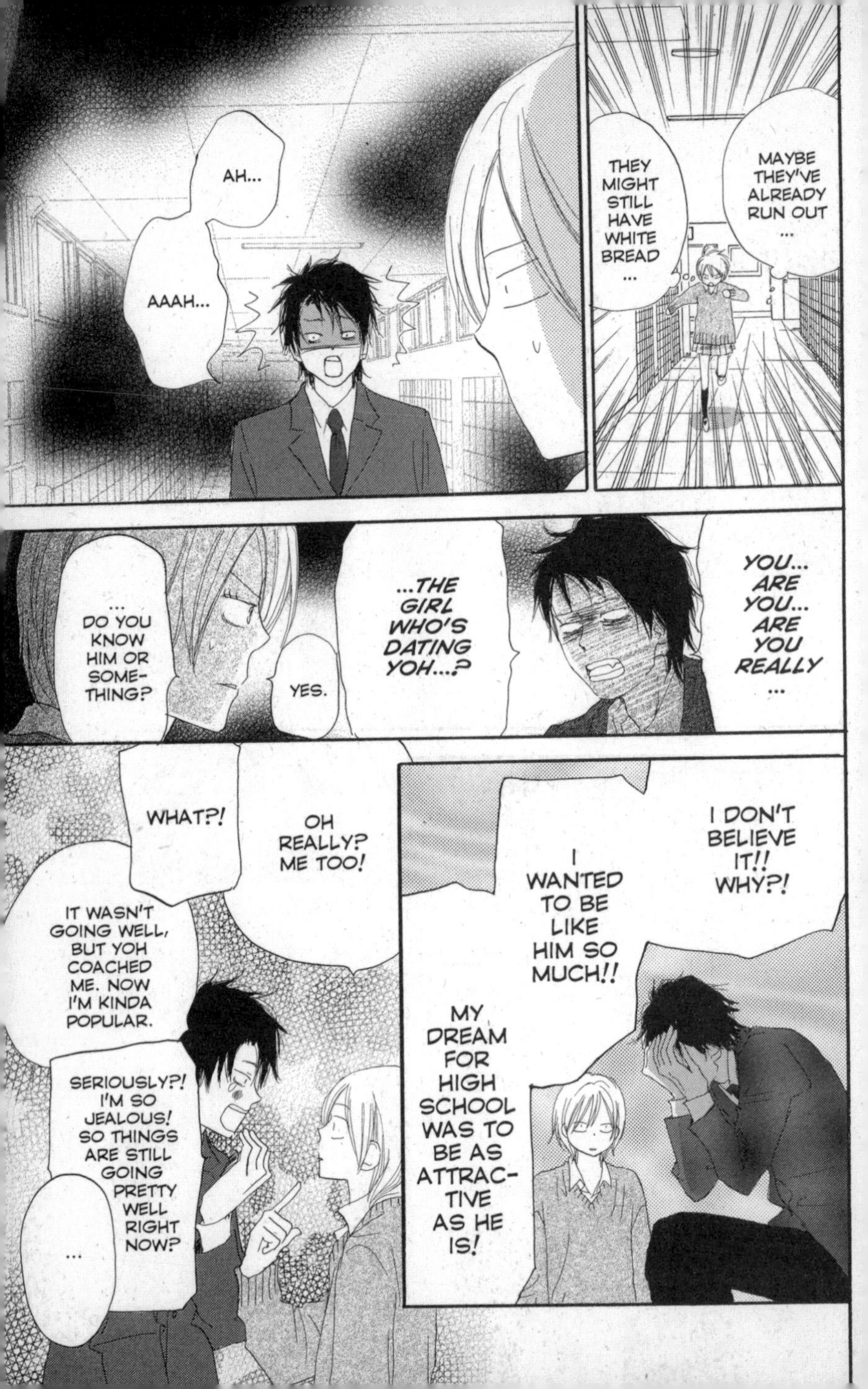
MAYBE THEY'VE ALREADY RUN OUT ...
THEY MIGHT STILL HAVE WHITE BREAD ...
AH...
AAAH...
YOU... ARE YOU... ARE YOU REALLY ...
...THE GIRL WHO'S DATING YOH...?
YES.
... DO YOU KNOW HIM OR SOMETHING?
I DON'T BELIEVE IT!! WHY?!
I WANTED TO BE LIKE HIM SO MUCH!!
MY DREAM FOR HIGH SCHOOL WAS TO BE AS ATTRACTIVE AS HE IS!
OH REALLY? ME TOO!
WHAT?!
IT WASN'T GOING WELL, BUT YOH COACHED ME. NOW I'M KINDA POPULAR.
SERIOUSLY?! I'M SO JEALOUS! SO THINGS ARE STILL GOING PRETTY WELL RIGHT NOW?
...

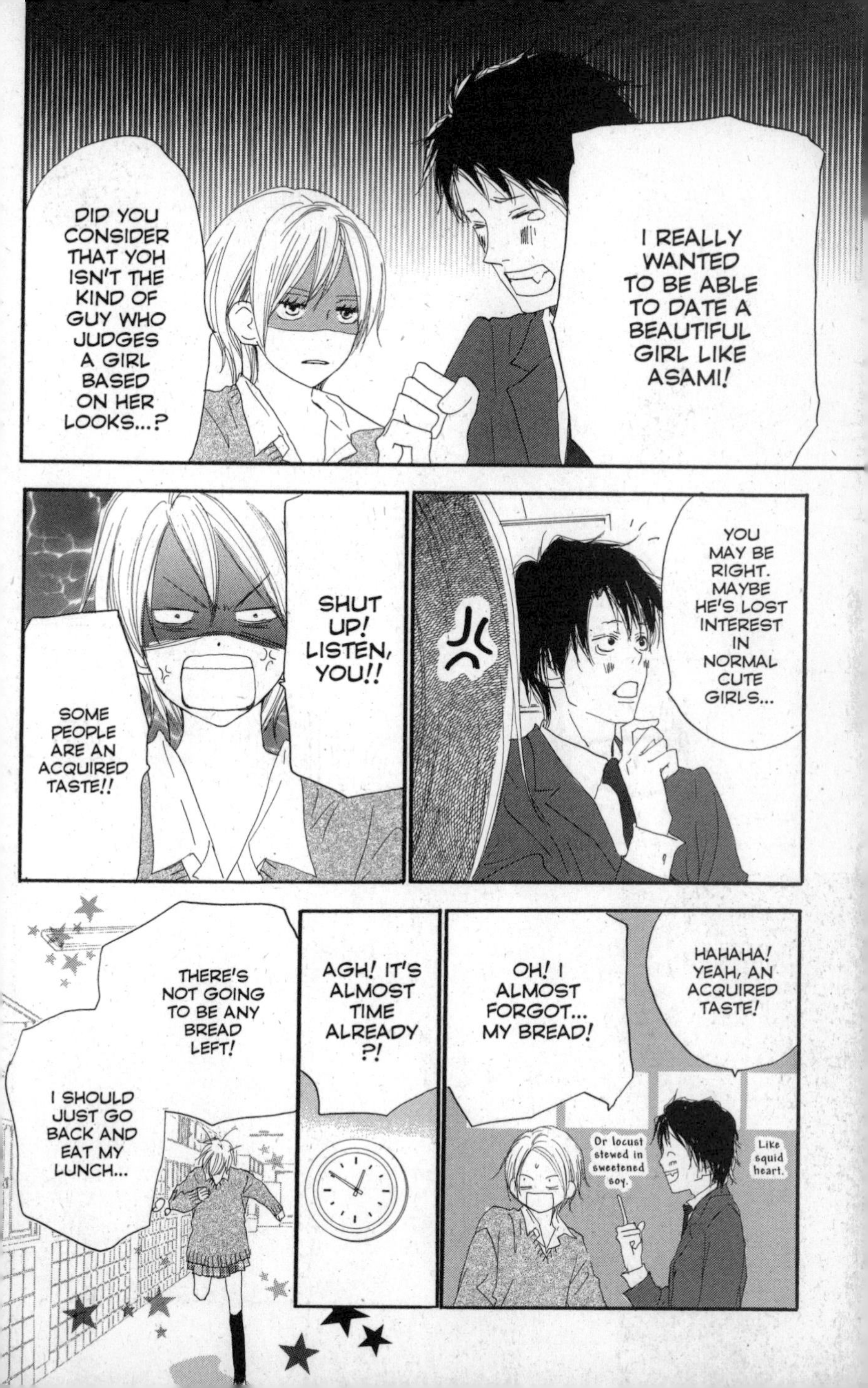
I REALLY WANTED TO BE ABLE TO DATE A BEAUTIFUL GIRL LIKE ASAMI!
DID YOU CONSIDER THAT YOH ISN'T THE KIND OF GUY WHO JUDGES A GIRL BASED ON HER LOOKS...?
YOU MAY BE RIGHT. MAYBE HE'S LOST INTEREST IN NORMAL CUTE GIRLS...
SHUT UP! LISTEN, YOU!!
SOME PEOPLE ARE AN ACQUIRED TASTE!!
HAHAHA! YEAH, AN ACQUIRED TASTE!
OH! I ALMOST FORGOT... MY BREAD!
Like squid heart.
Or locust stewed in sweetened soy.
AGH! IT'S ALMOST TIME ALREADY?!
THERE'S NOT GOING TO BE ANY BREAD LEFT!
I SHOULD JUST GO BACK AND EAT MY LUNCH...

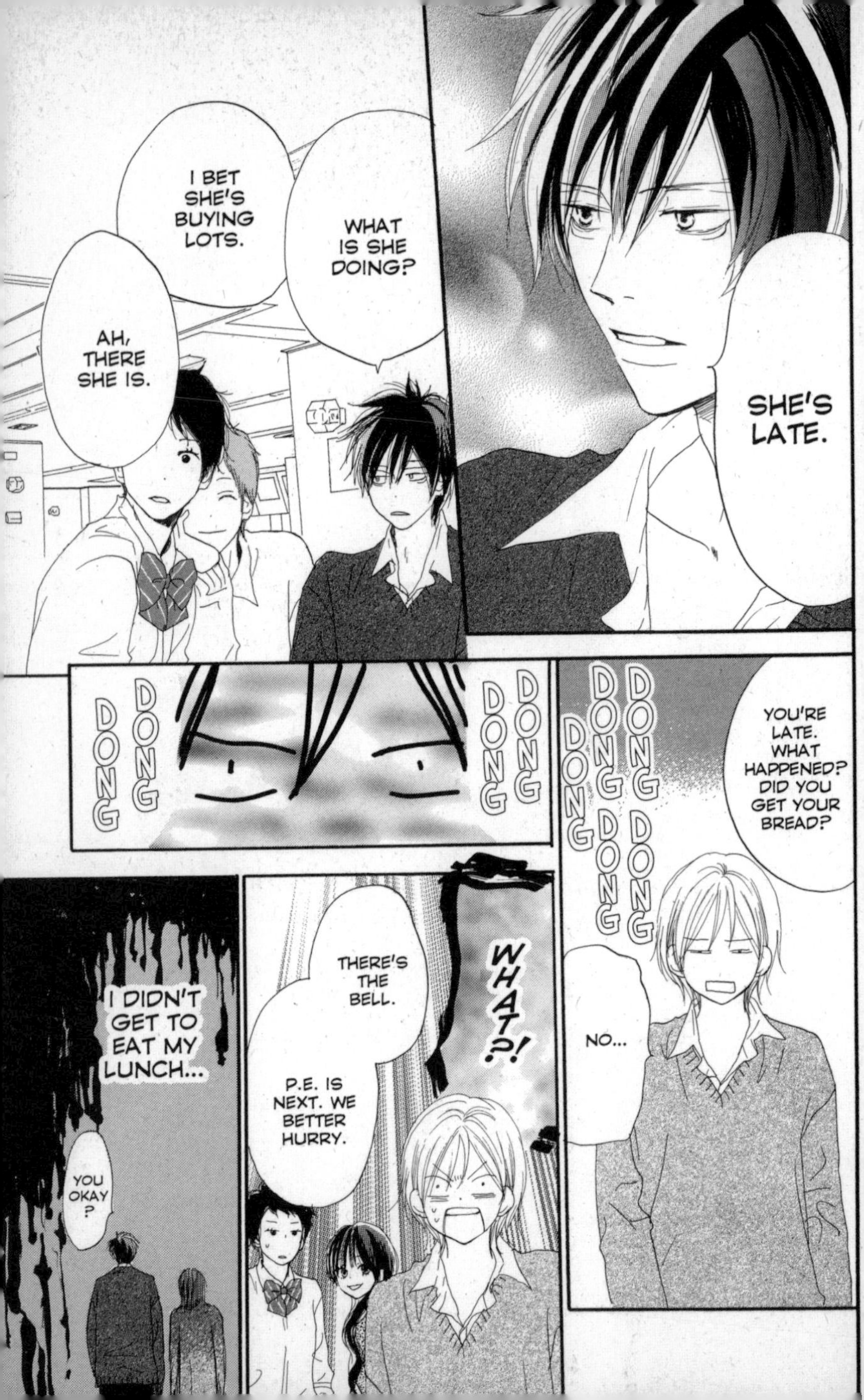
SHE'S LATE.
WHAT IS SHE DOING?
I BET SHE'S BUYING LOTS.
AH, THERE SHE IS.
YOU'RE LATE. WHAT HAPPENED? DID YOU GET YOUR BREAD?
DONG DONG DONG DONG
NO...
DONG DONG DONG DONG
WHAT?!
THERE'S THE BELL.
P.E. IS NEXT. WE BETTER HURRY.
I DIDN'T GET TO EAT MY LUNCH...
YOU OKAY?

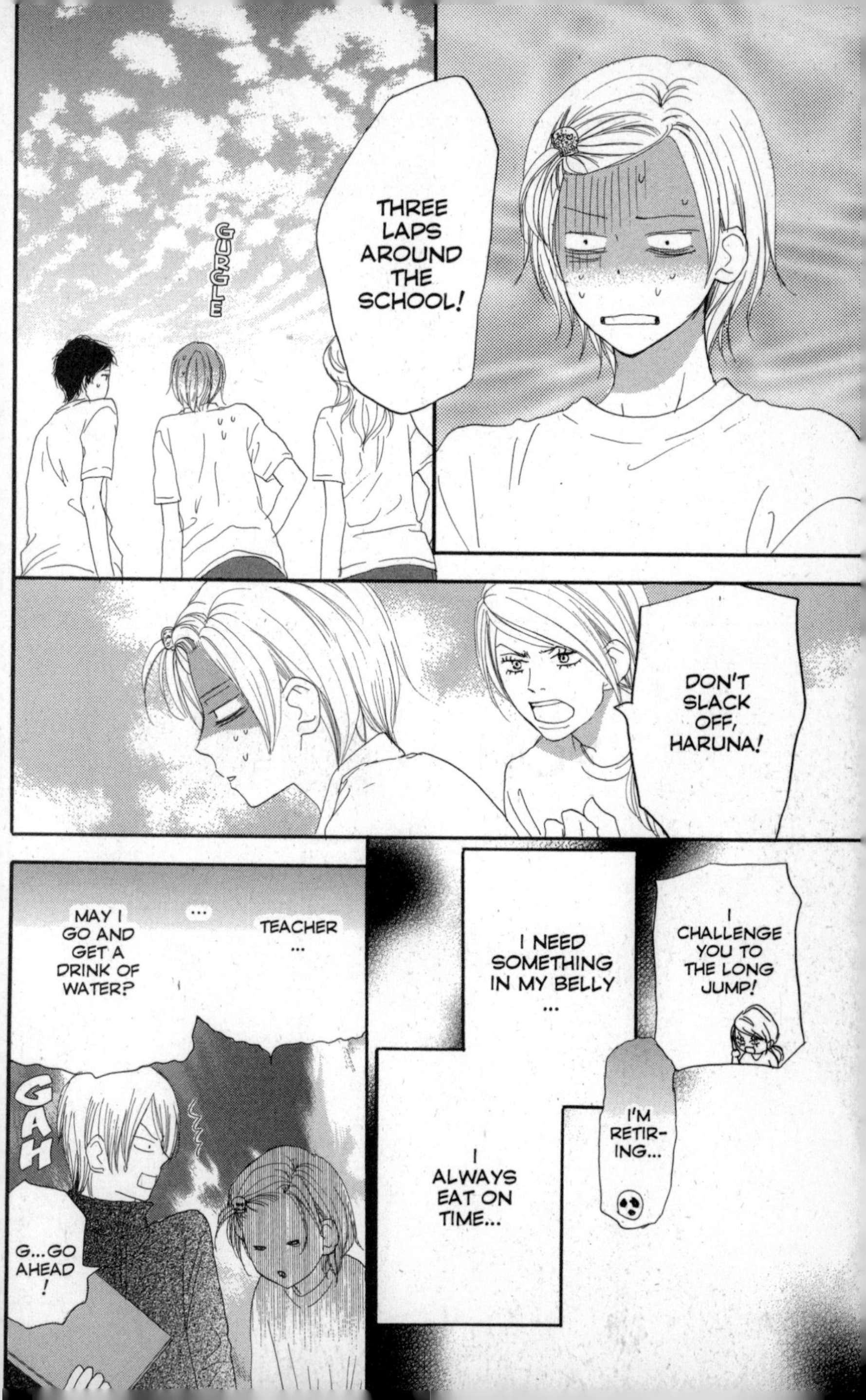
THREE LAPS AROUND THE SCHOOL!
GURGLE
DON'T SLACK OFF, HARUNA!
I CHALLENGE YOU TO THE LONG JUMP!
I'M RETIR-ING...
I NEED SOMETHING IN MY BELLY...
I ALWAYS EAT ON TIME...
TEACHER...
...
MAY I GO AND GET A DRINK OF WATER?
GAH
G...GO AHEAD!

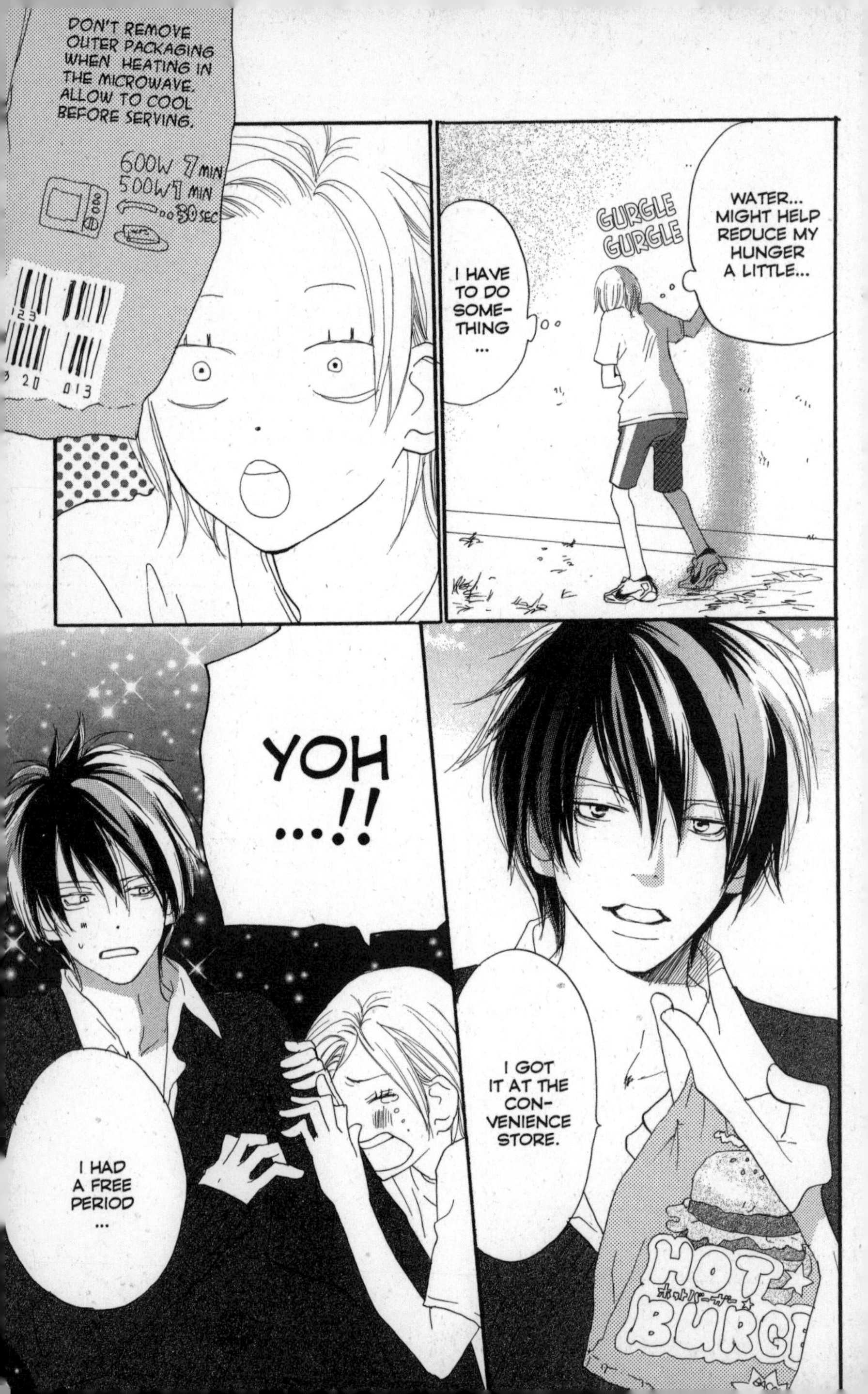
WATER... MIGHT HELP REDUCE MY HUNGER A LITTLE...
GURGLE GURGLE
I HAVE TO DO SOME-THING ...
DON'T REMOVE OUTER PACKAGING WHEN HEATING IN THE MICROWAVE. ALLOW TO COOL BEFORE SERVING.
I GOT IT AT THE CON-VENIENCE STORE.
YOH ...!!
I HAD A FREE PERIOD ...

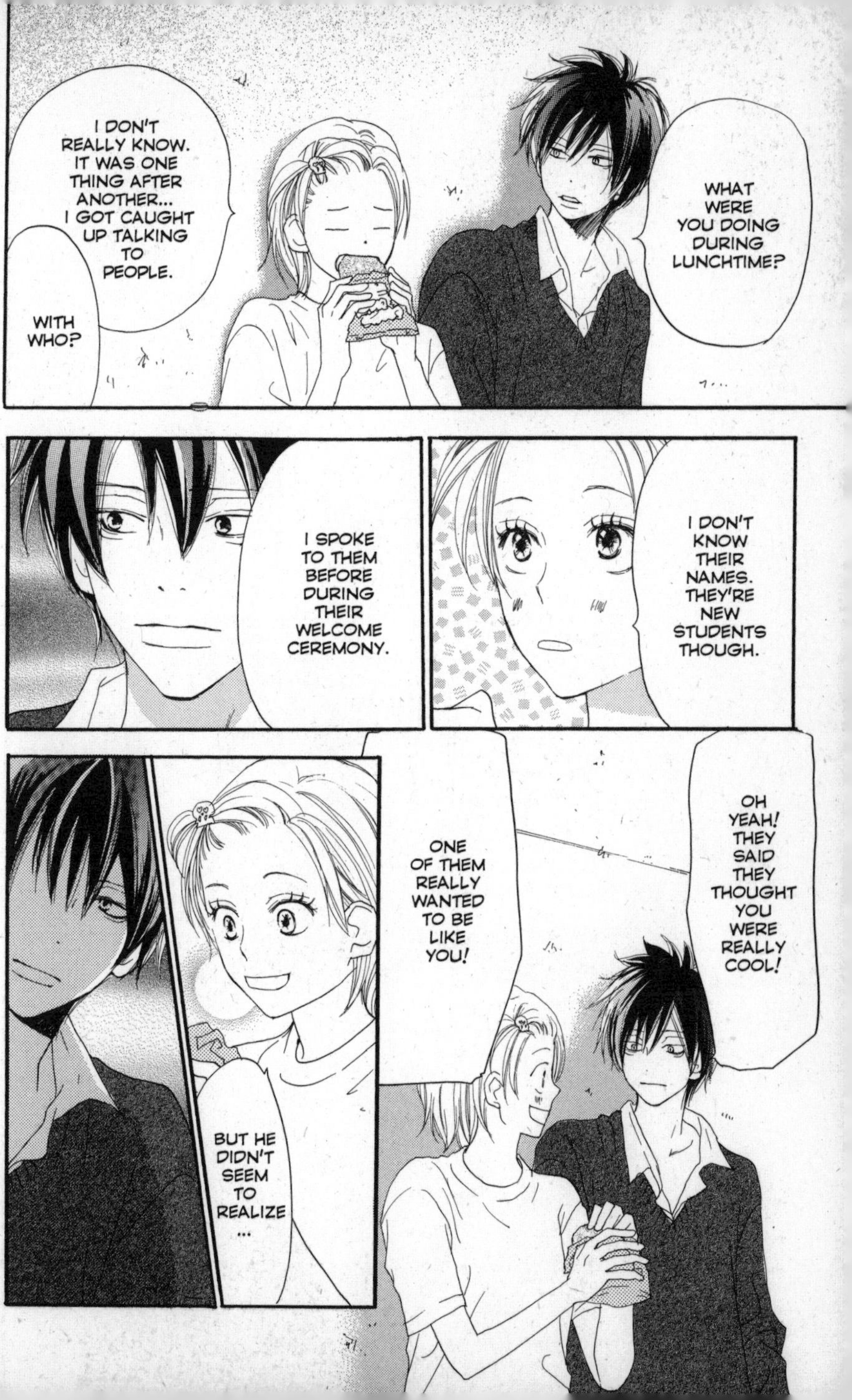
WHAT WERE YOU DOING DURING LUNCHTIME?
I DON'T REALLY KNOW. IT WAS ONE THING AFTER ANOTHER... I GOT CAUGHT UP TALKING TO PEOPLE.
WITH WHO?
I DON'T KNOW THEIR NAMES. THEY'RE NEW STUDENTS THOUGH.
I SPOKE TO THEM BEFORE DURING THEIR WELCOME CEREMONY.
OH YEAH! THEY SAID THEY THOUGHT YOU WERE REALLY COOL!
ONE OF THEM REALLY WANTED TO BE LIKE YOU!
BUT HE DIDN'T SEEM TO REALIZE ...

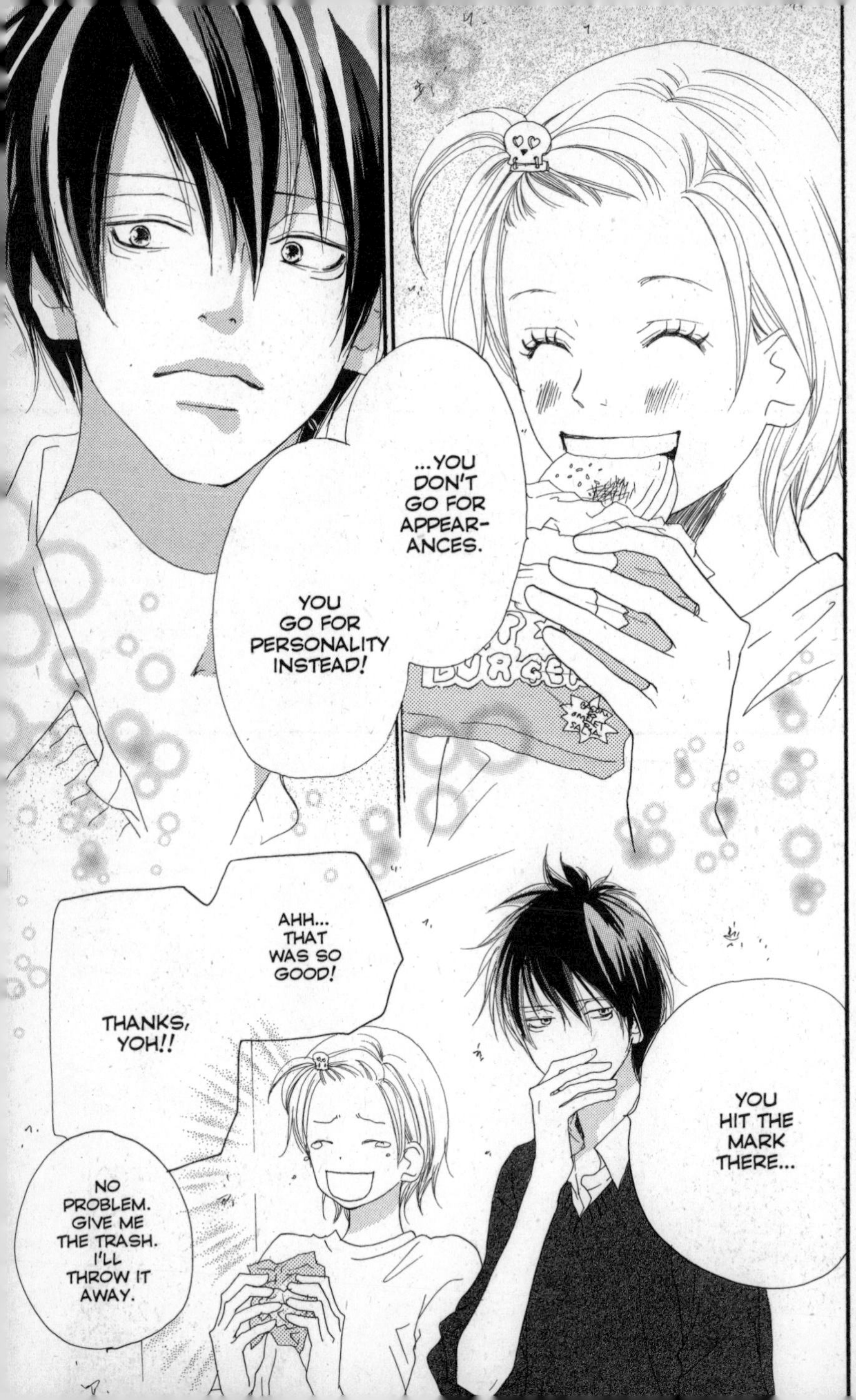
...YOU DON'T GO FOR APPEARANCES.
YOU GO FOR PERSONALITY INSTEAD!
YOU HIT THE MARK THERE...
AHH... THAT WAS SO GOOD!
THANKS, YOH!!
NO PROBLEM. GIVE ME THE TRASH. I'LL THROW IT AWAY.

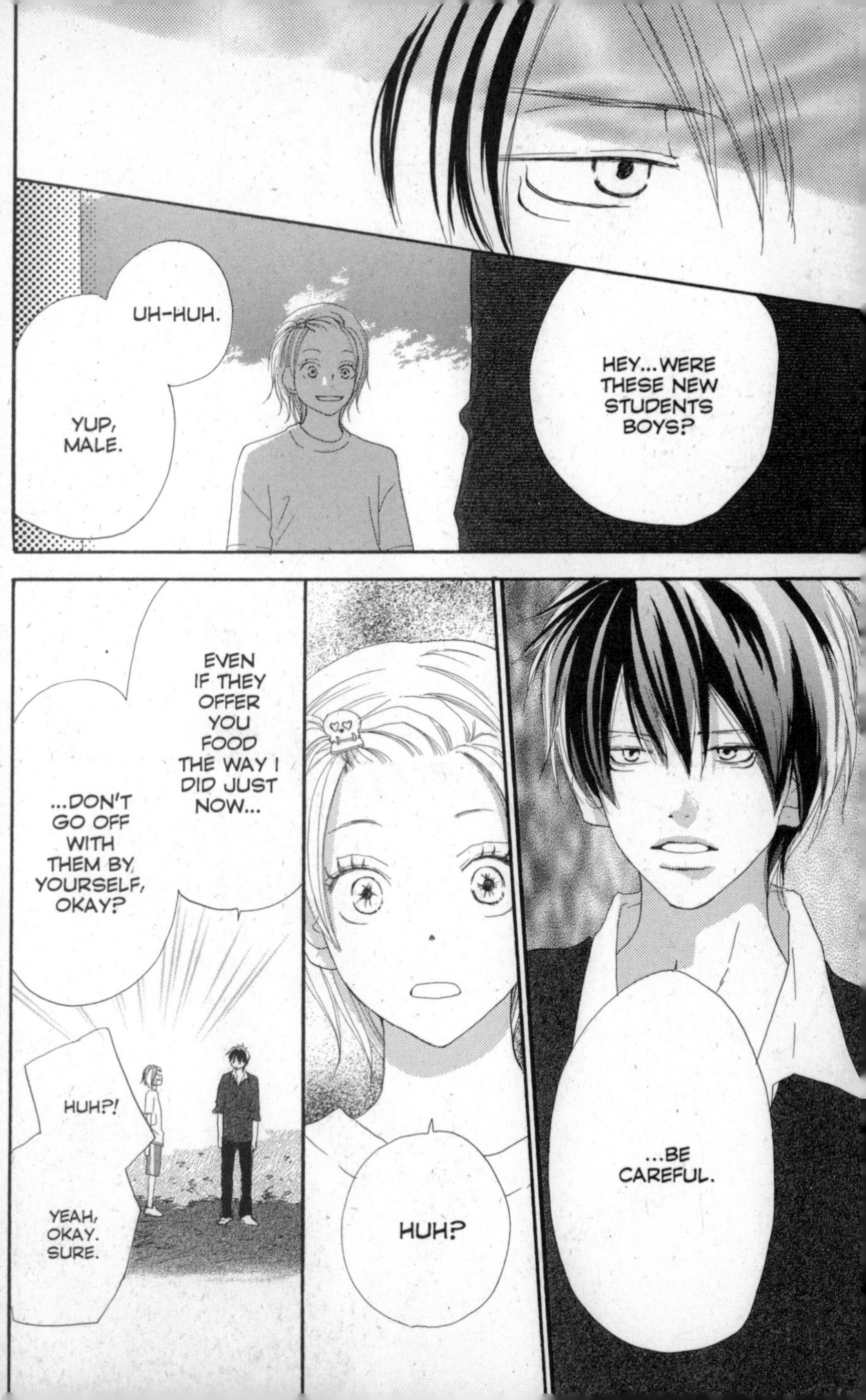
HEY...WERE THESE NEW STUDENTS BOYS?
UH-HUH.
YUP, MALE.
...BE CAREFUL.
HUH?
EVEN IF THEY OFFER YOU FOOD THE WAY I DID JUST NOW...
...DON'T GO OFF WITH THEM BY YOURSELF, OKAY?
HUH?!
YEAH, OKAY. SURE.

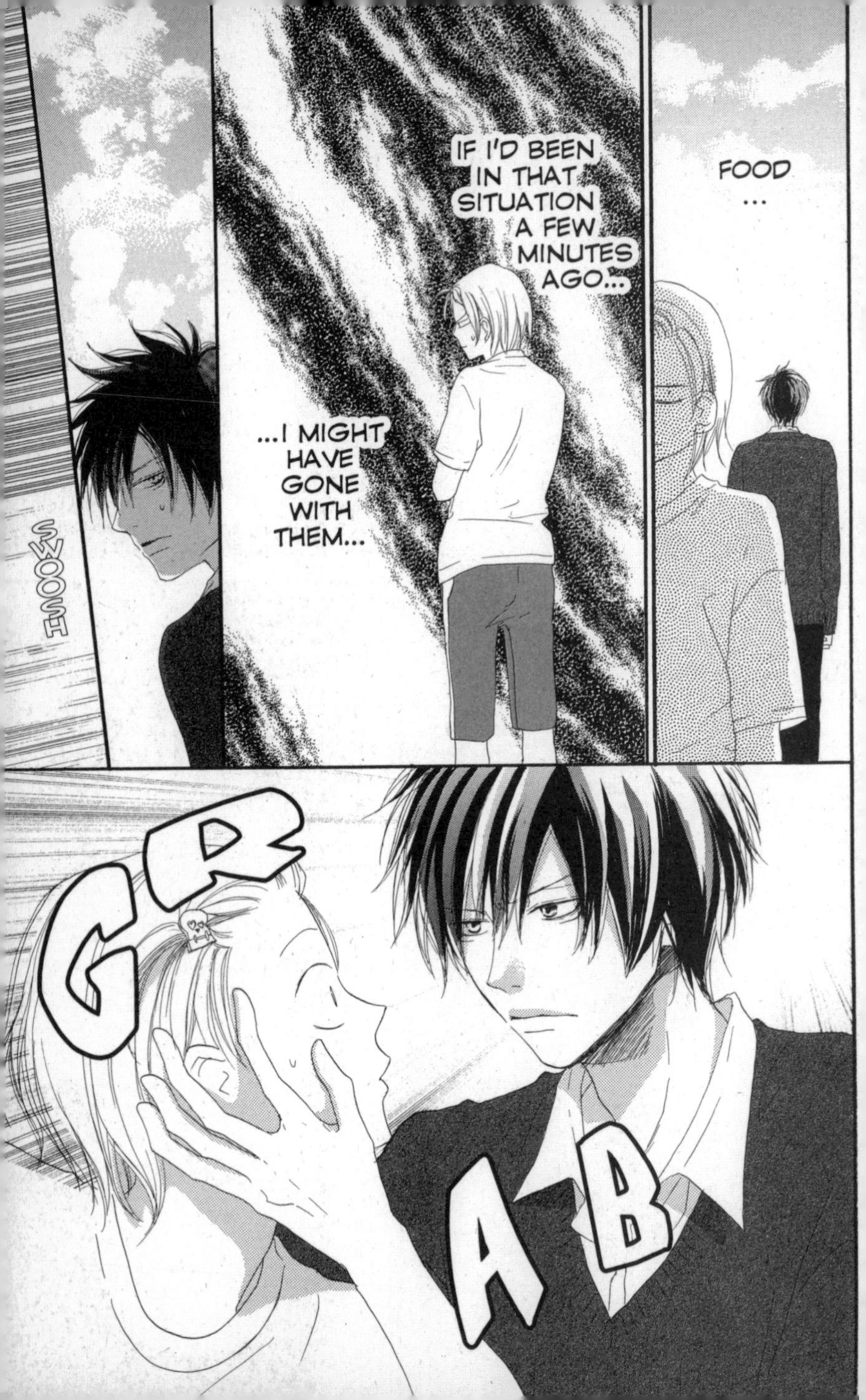
FOOD ...
IF I'D BEEN IN THAT SITUATION A FEW MINUTES AGO...
...I MIGHT HAVE GONE WITH THEM...
SWOOSH
GRAB

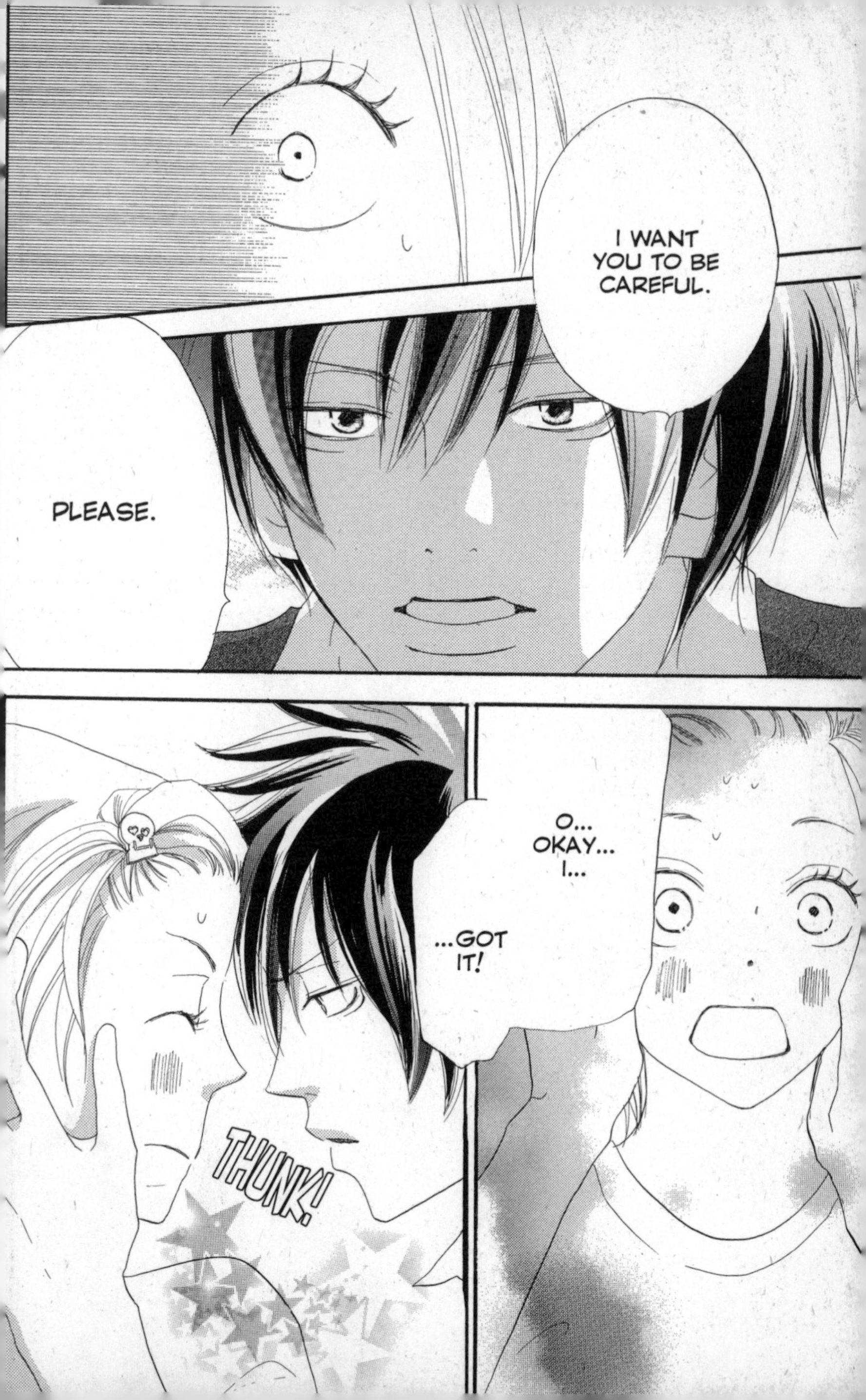
I WANT YOU TO BE CAREFUL.
PLEASE.
O... OKAY... I...
...GOT IT!
THUNK!

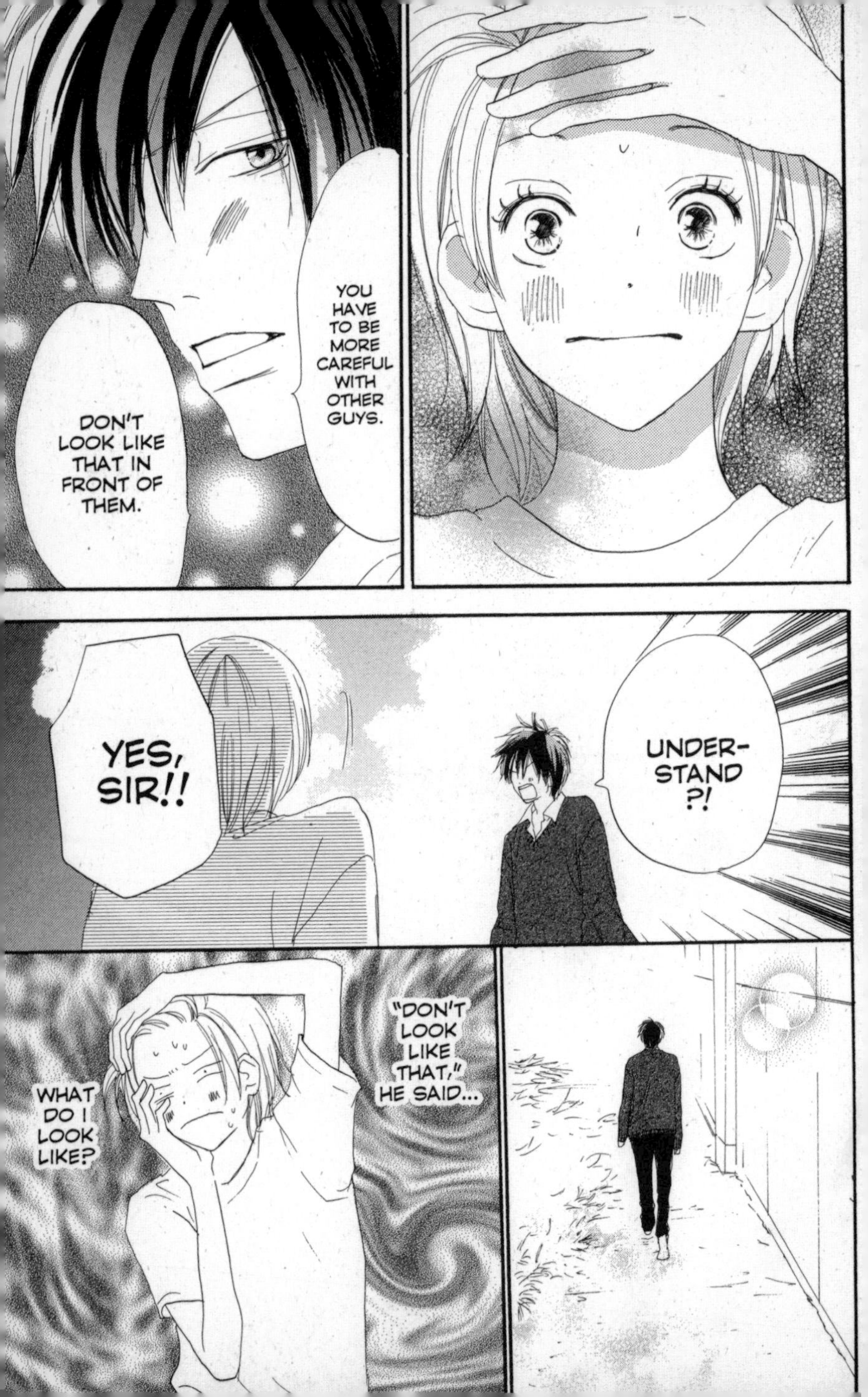
YOU HAVE TO BE MORE CAREFUL WITH OTHER GUYS.
DON'T LOOK LIKE THAT IN FRONT OF THEM.
UNDER-STAND?!
YES, SIR!!
"DON'T LOOK LIKE THAT," HE SAID...
WHAT DO I LOOK LIKE?

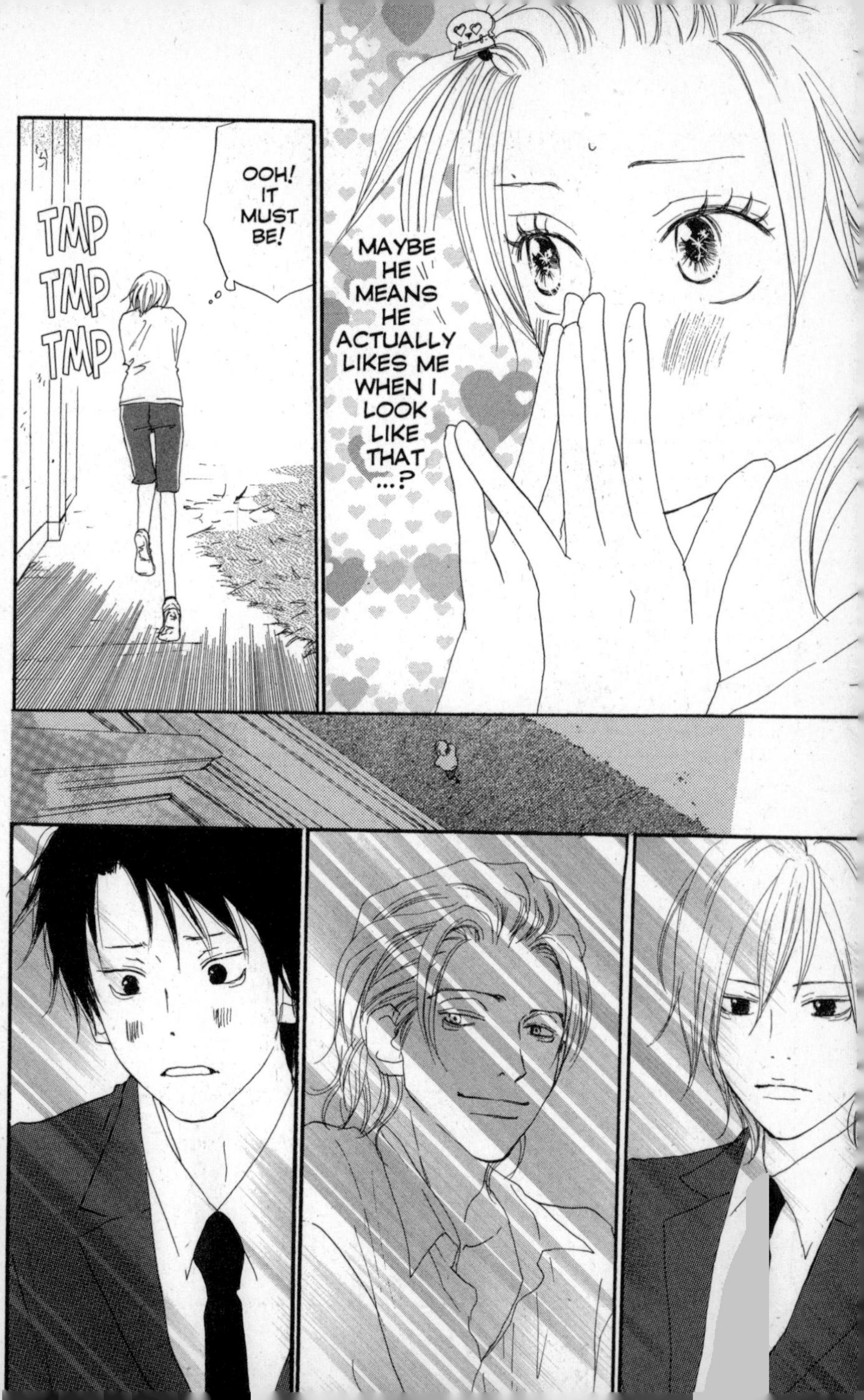
MAYBE HE MEANS HE ACTUALLY LIKES ME WHEN I LOOK LIKE THAT ...?
OOH! IT MUST BE!
TMP TMP TMP

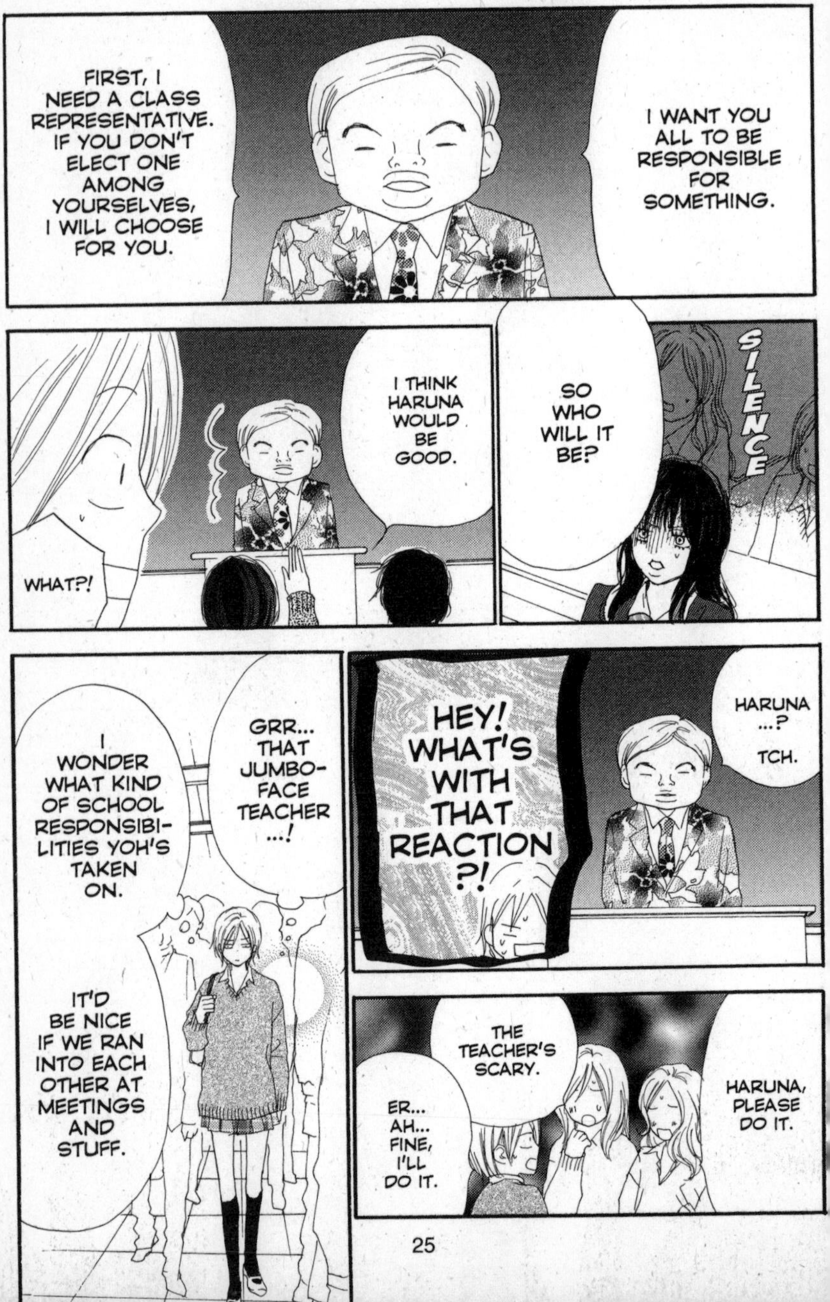
I WANT YOU ALL TO BE RESPONSIBLE FOR SOMETHING.
FIRST, I NEED A CLASS REPRESENTATIVE. IF YOU DON'T ELECT ONE AMONG YOURSELVES, I WILL CHOOSE FOR YOU.
SILENCE
SO WHO WILL IT BE?
I THINK HARUNA WOULD BE GOOD.
WHAT?!
HARUNA ...?
TCH.
HEY! WHAT'S WITH THAT REACTION ?!
HARUNA, PLEASE DO IT.
THE TEACHER'S SCARY.
ER... AH... FINE, I'LL DO IT.
GRR... THAT JUMBO-FACE TEACHER ...!
I WONDER WHAT KIND OF SCHOOL RESPONSIBILITIES YOH'S TAKEN ON.
IT'D BE NICE IF WE RAN INTO EACH OTHER AT MEETINGS AND STUFF.

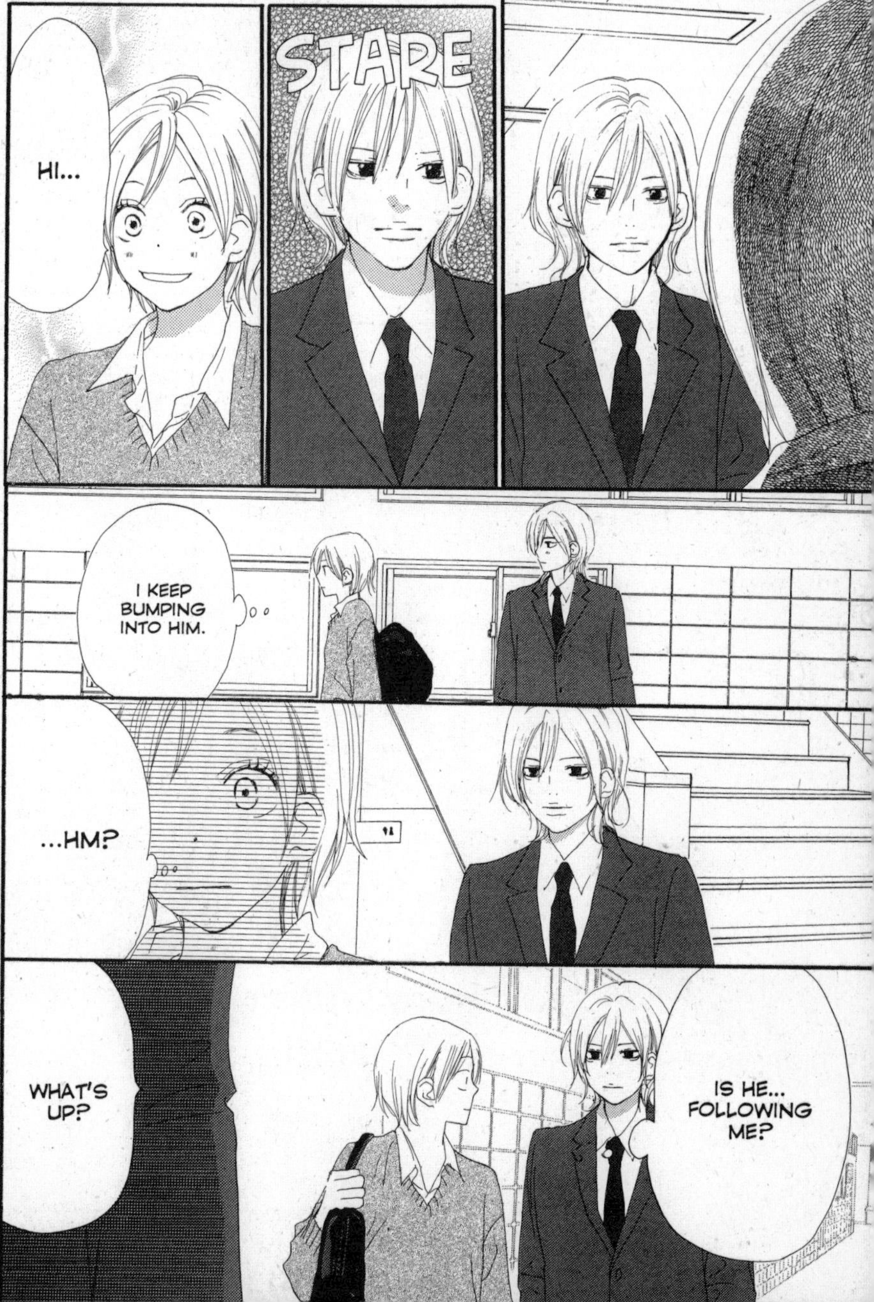
STARE
HI...
I KEEP BUMPING INTO HIM.
...HM?
IS HE... FOLLOWING ME?
WHAT'S UP?

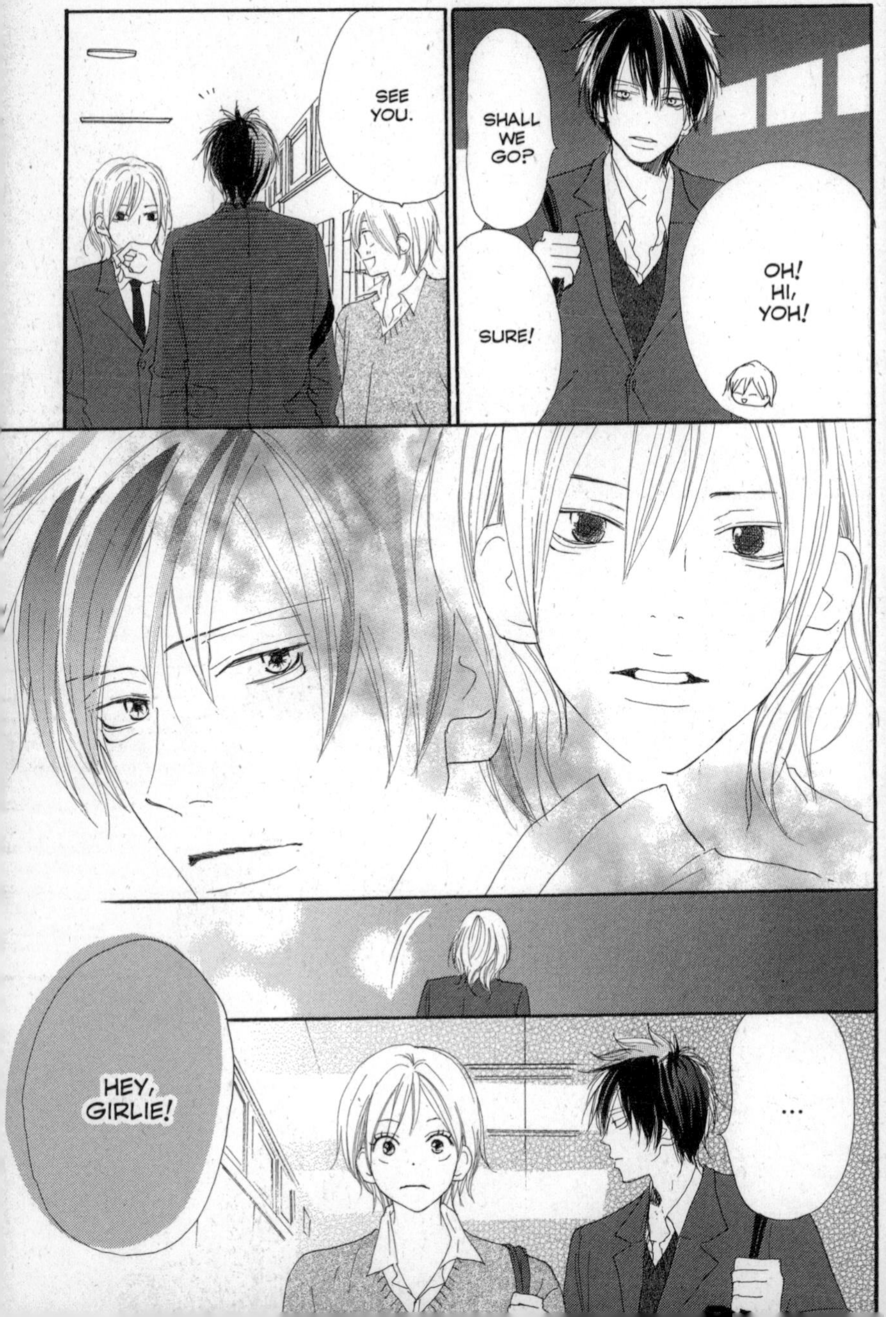
OH! HI, YOH!
SHALL WE GO?
SURE!
SEE YOU.
...
HEY, GIRLIE!

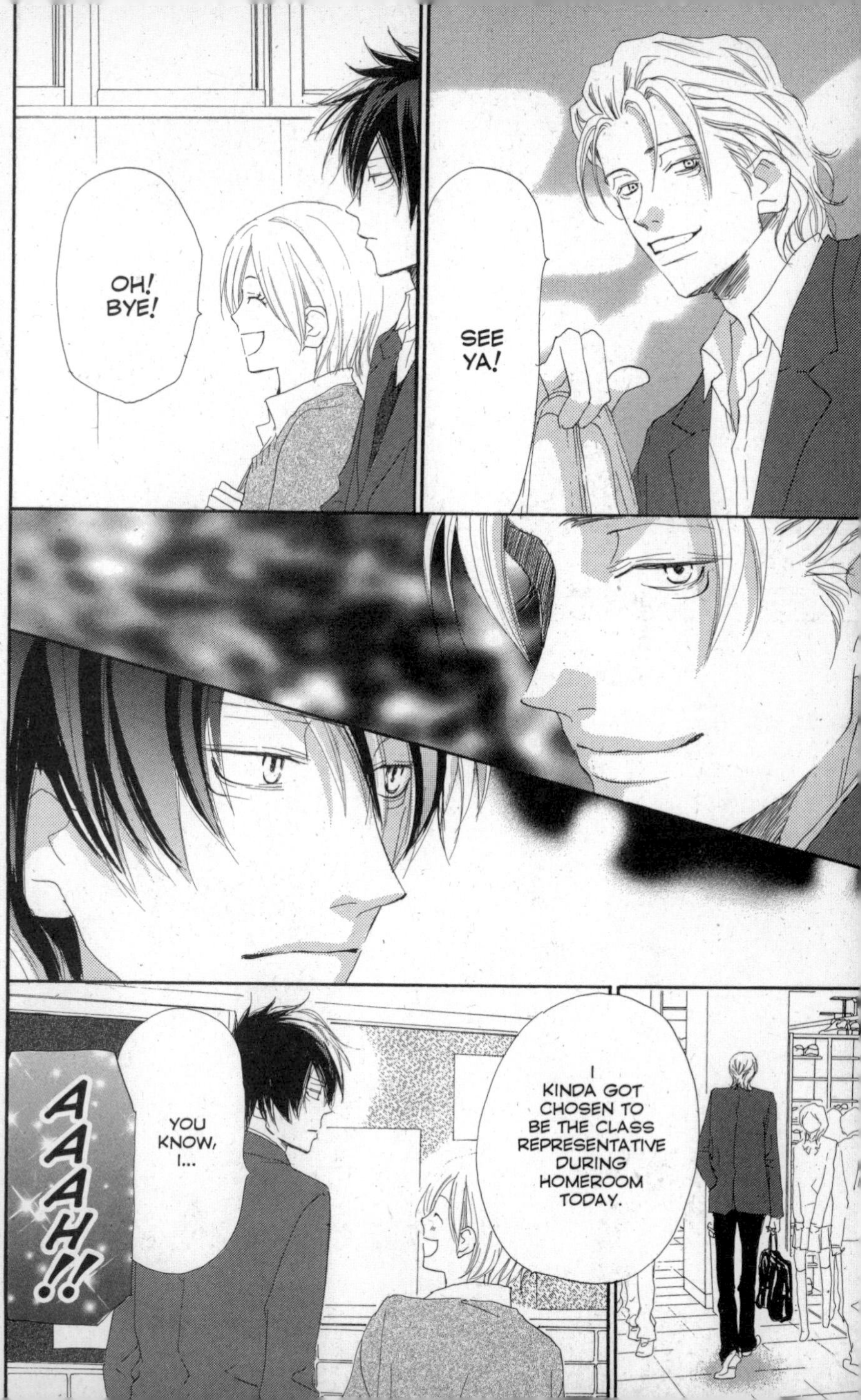
SEE YA!
OH! BYE!
I KINDA GOT CHOSEN TO BE THE CLASS REPRESENTATIVE DURING HOMEROOM TODAY.
YOU KNOW, I...
AAAAH!!

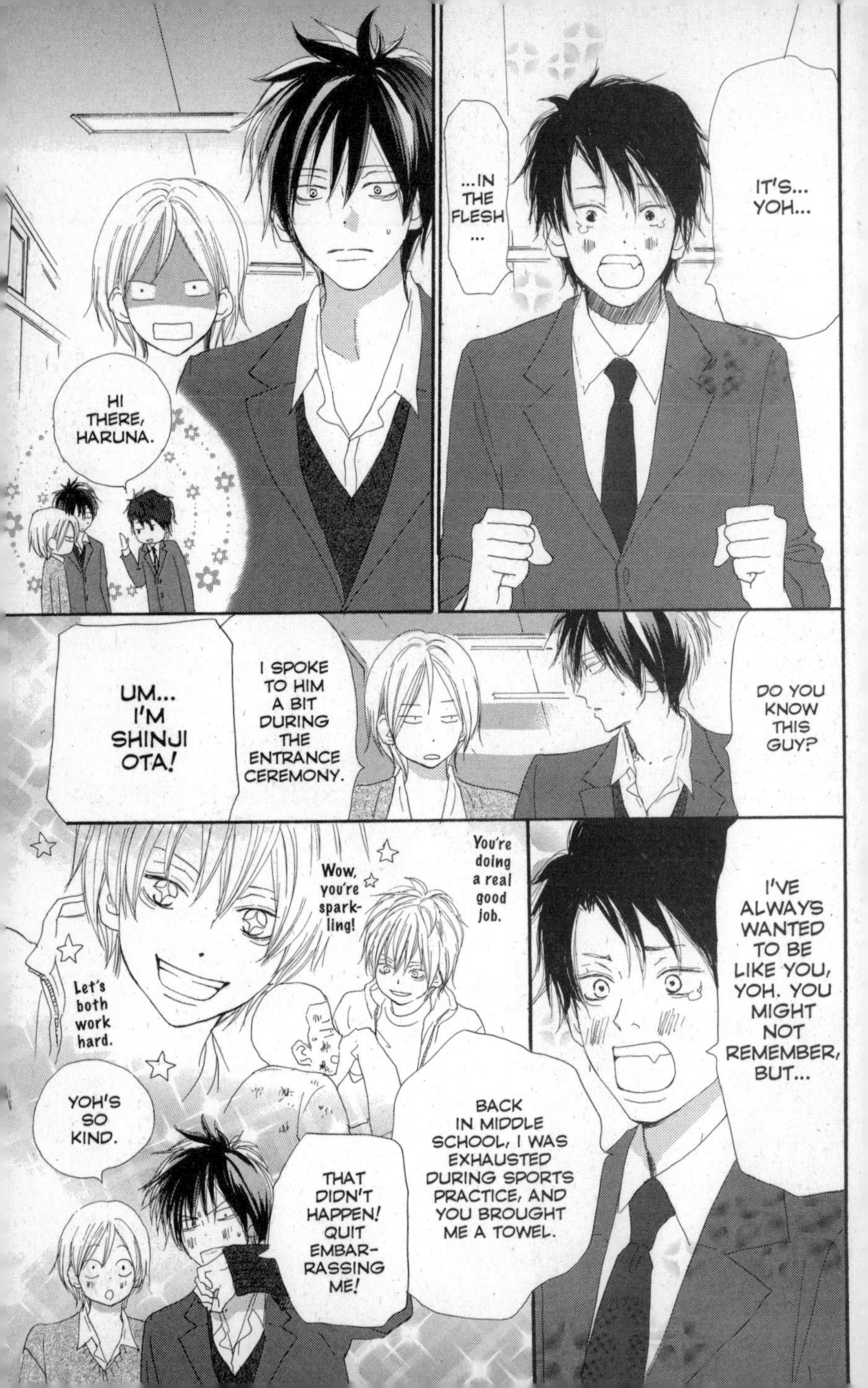
IT'S... YOH...
...IN THE FLESH ...
HI THERE, HARUNA.
DO YOU KNOW THIS GUY?
I SPOKE TO HIM A BIT DURING THE ENTRANCE CEREMONY.
UM... I'M SHINJI OTA!
I'VE ALWAYS WANTED TO BE LIKE YOU, YOH. YOU MIGHT NOT REMEMBER, BUT...
BACK IN MIDDLE SCHOOL, I WAS EXHAUSTED DURING SPORTS PRACTICE, AND YOU BROUGHT ME A TOWEL.
You're doing a real good job.
Wow, you're spark-ling!
Let's both work hard.
YOH'S SO KIND.
THAT DIDN'T HAPPEN! QUIT EMBAR-RASSING ME!

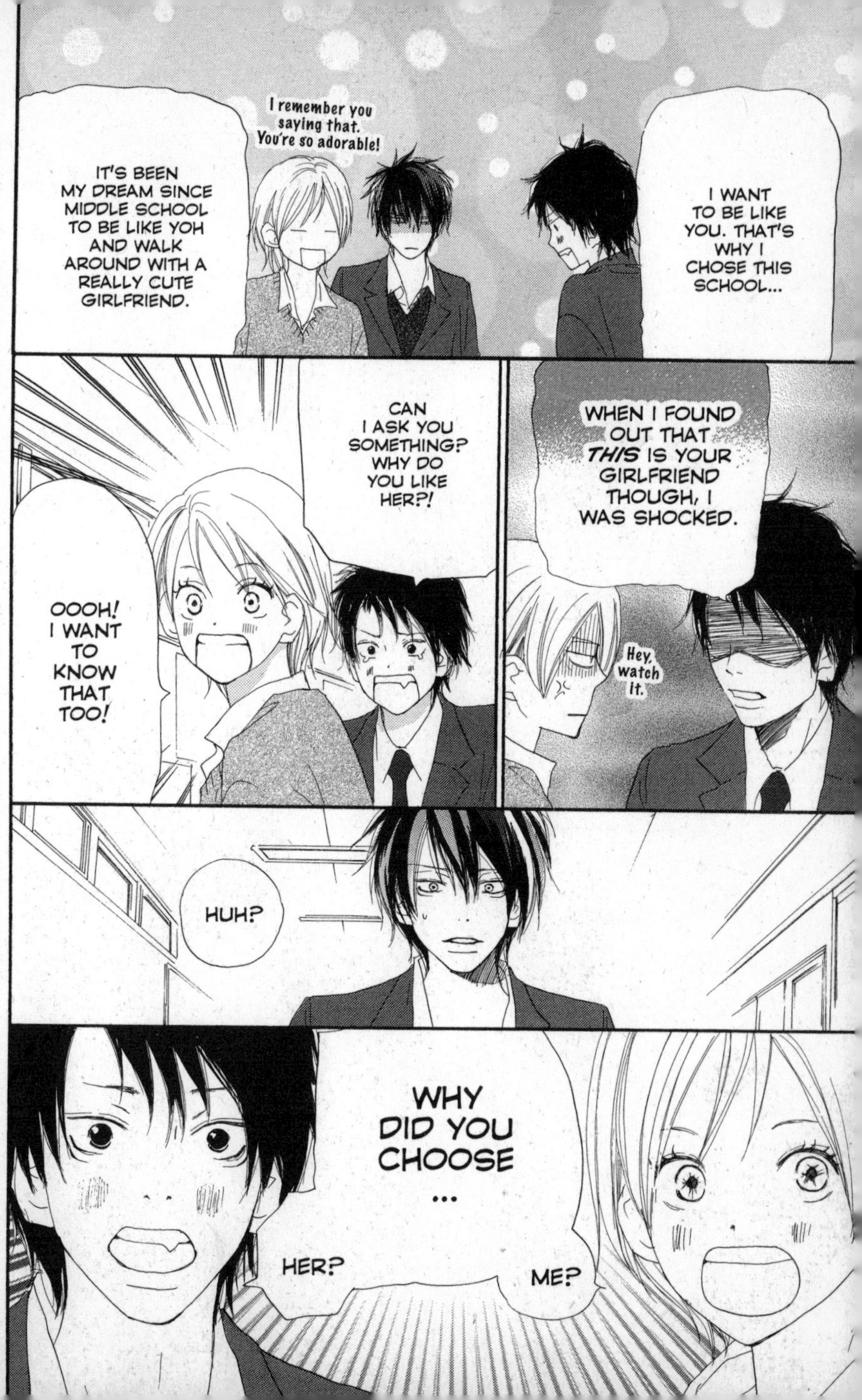
I WANT TO BE LIKE YOU. THAT'S WHY I CHOSE THIS SCHOOL...
I remember you saying that. You're so adorable!
IT'S BEEN MY DREAM SINCE MIDDLE SCHOOL TO BE LIKE YOH AND WALK AROUND WITH A REALLY CUTE GIRLFRIEND.
WHEN I FOUND OUT THAT *THIS* IS YOUR GIRLFRIEND THOUGH, I WAS SHOCKED.
Hey, watch it.
CAN I ASK YOU SOMETHING? WHY DO YOU LIKE HER?!
OOOH! I WANT TO KNOW THAT TOO!
HUH?
WHY DID YOU CHOOSE ...
ME?
HER?

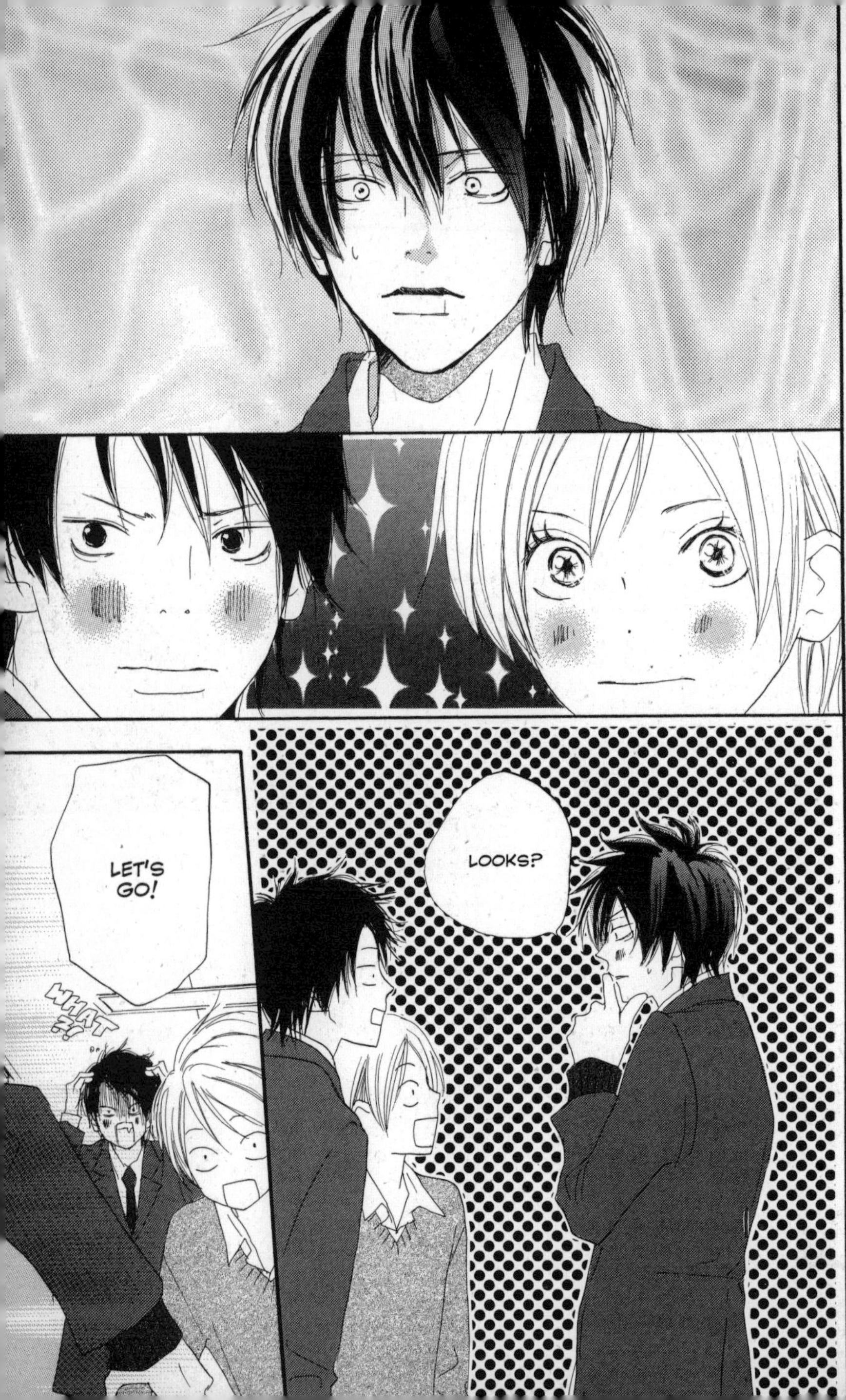
LOOKS?
LET'S GO!
WHAT?!

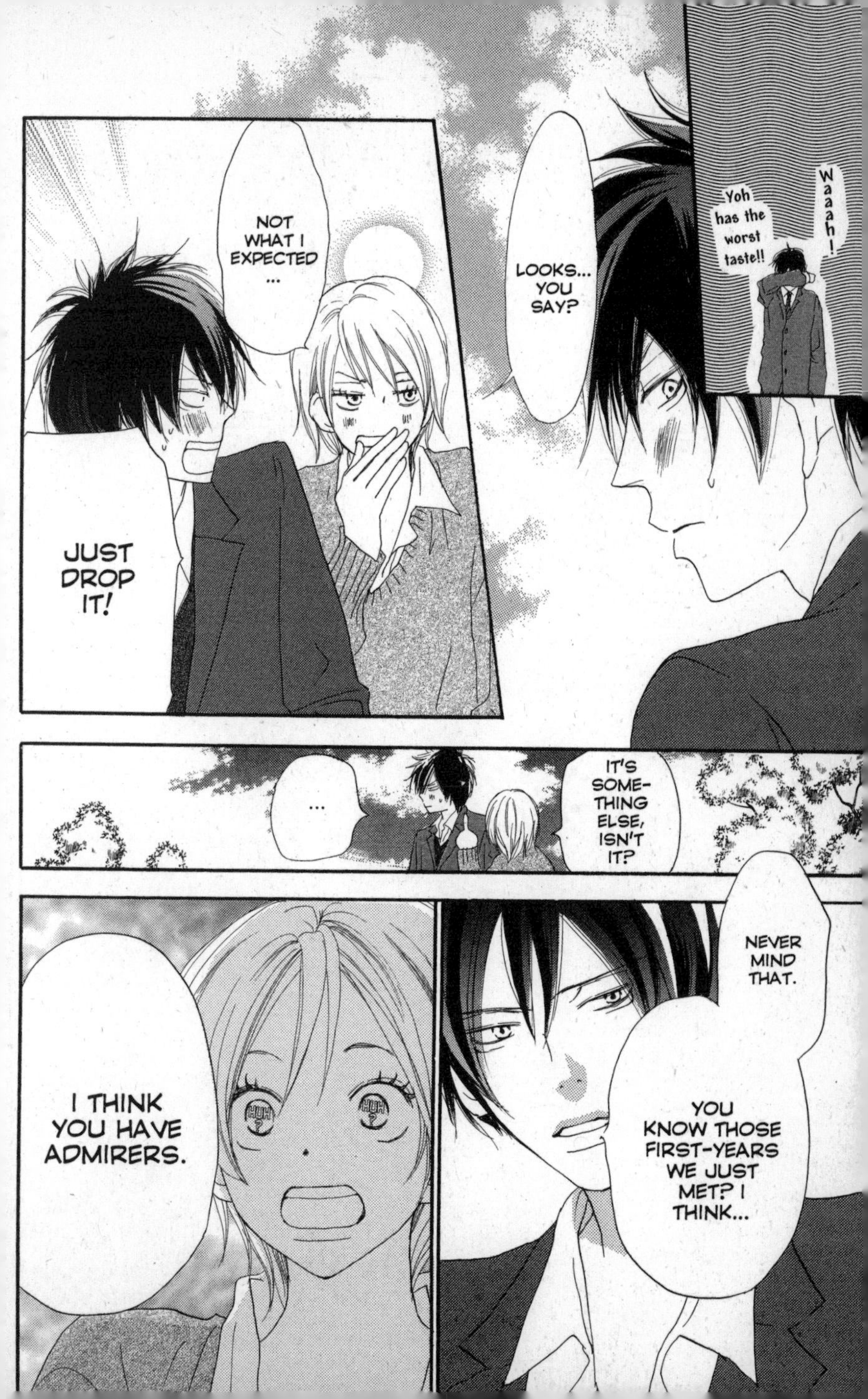
Waaaah!
Yoh has the worst taste!!
LOOKS... YOU SAY?
NOT WHAT I EXPECTED...
JUST DROP IT!
IT'S SOME-THING ELSE, ISN'T IT?
...
NEVER MIND THAT.
YOU KNOW THOSE FIRST-YEARS WE JUST MET? I THINK...
I THINK YOU HAVE ADMIRERS.
HUH?

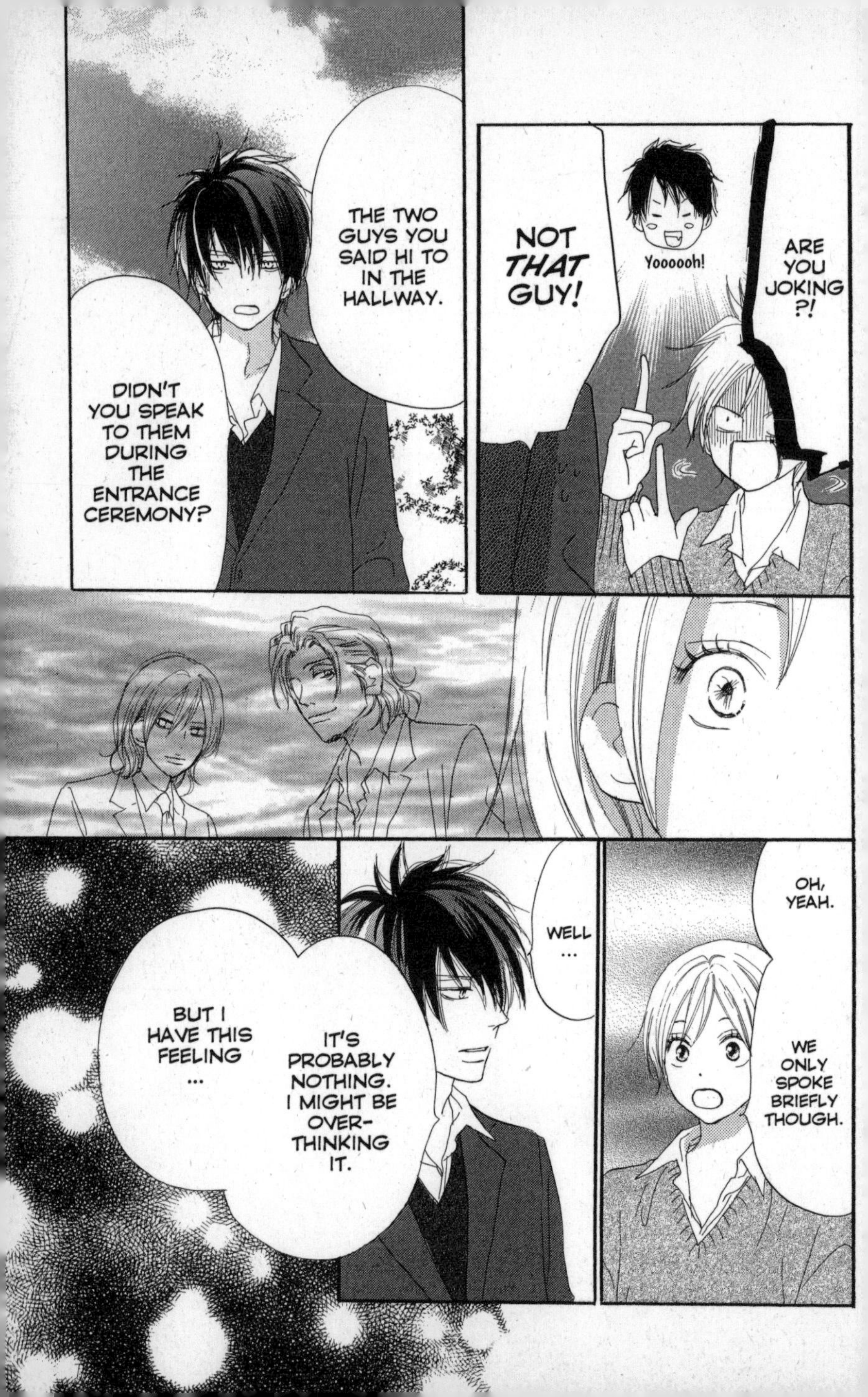
ARE YOU JOKING ?!
Yoooooh!
NOT THAT GUY!
THE TWO GUYS YOU SAID HI TO IN THE HALLWAY.
DIDN'T YOU SPEAK TO THEM DURING THE ENTRANCE CEREMONY?
OH, YEAH.
WE ONLY SPOKE BRIEFLY THOUGH.
WELL ...
IT'S PROBABLY NOTHING. I MIGHT BE OVER-THINKING IT.
BUT I HAVE THIS FEELING ...

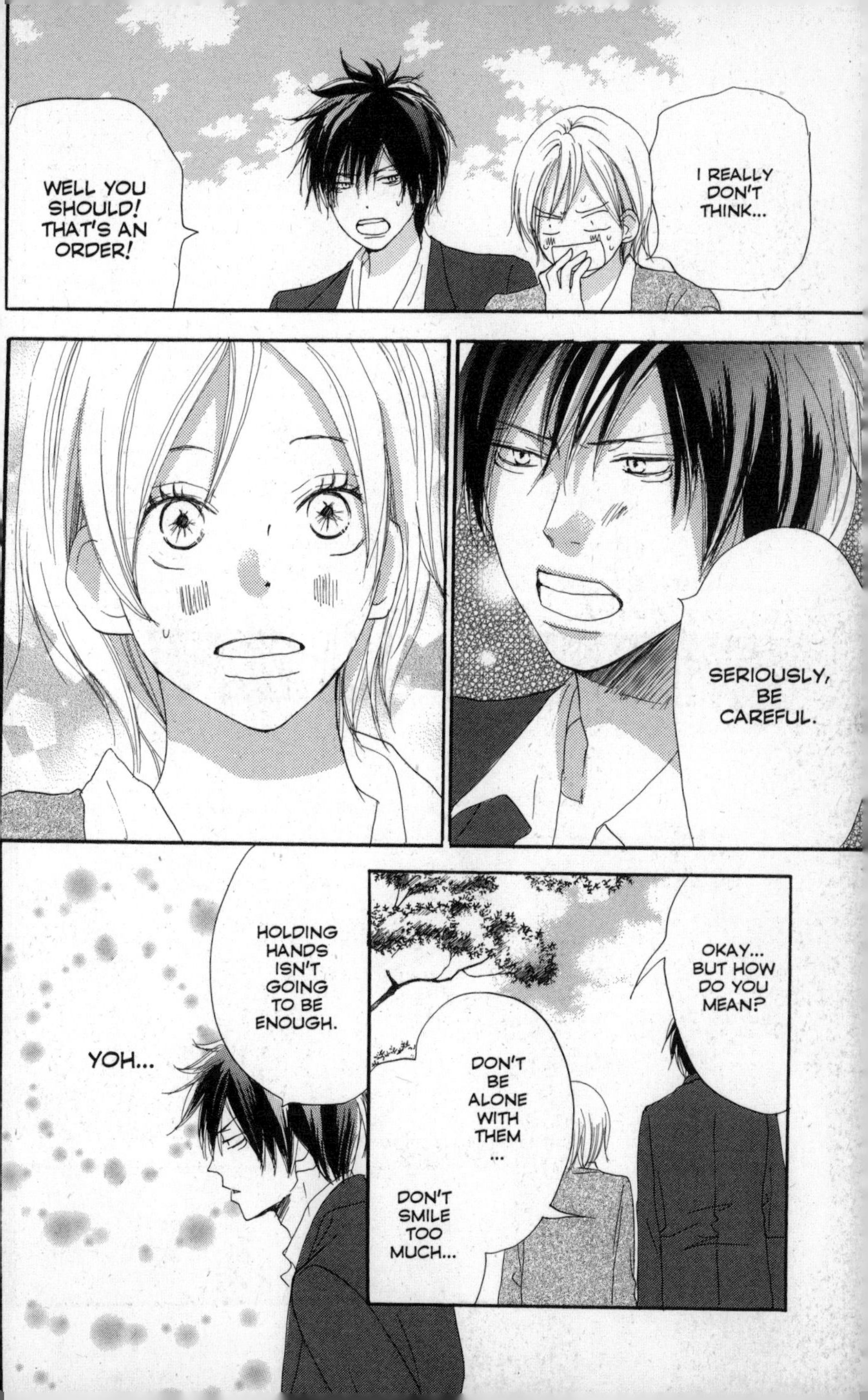
I REALLY DON'T THINK...
WELL YOU SHOULD! THAT'S AN ORDER!
SERIOUSLY, BE CAREFUL.
OKAY... BUT HOW DO YOU MEAN?
DON'T BE ALONE WITH THEM ...
DON'T SMILE TOO MUCH...
HOLDING HANDS ISN'T GOING TO BE ENOUGH.
YOH...

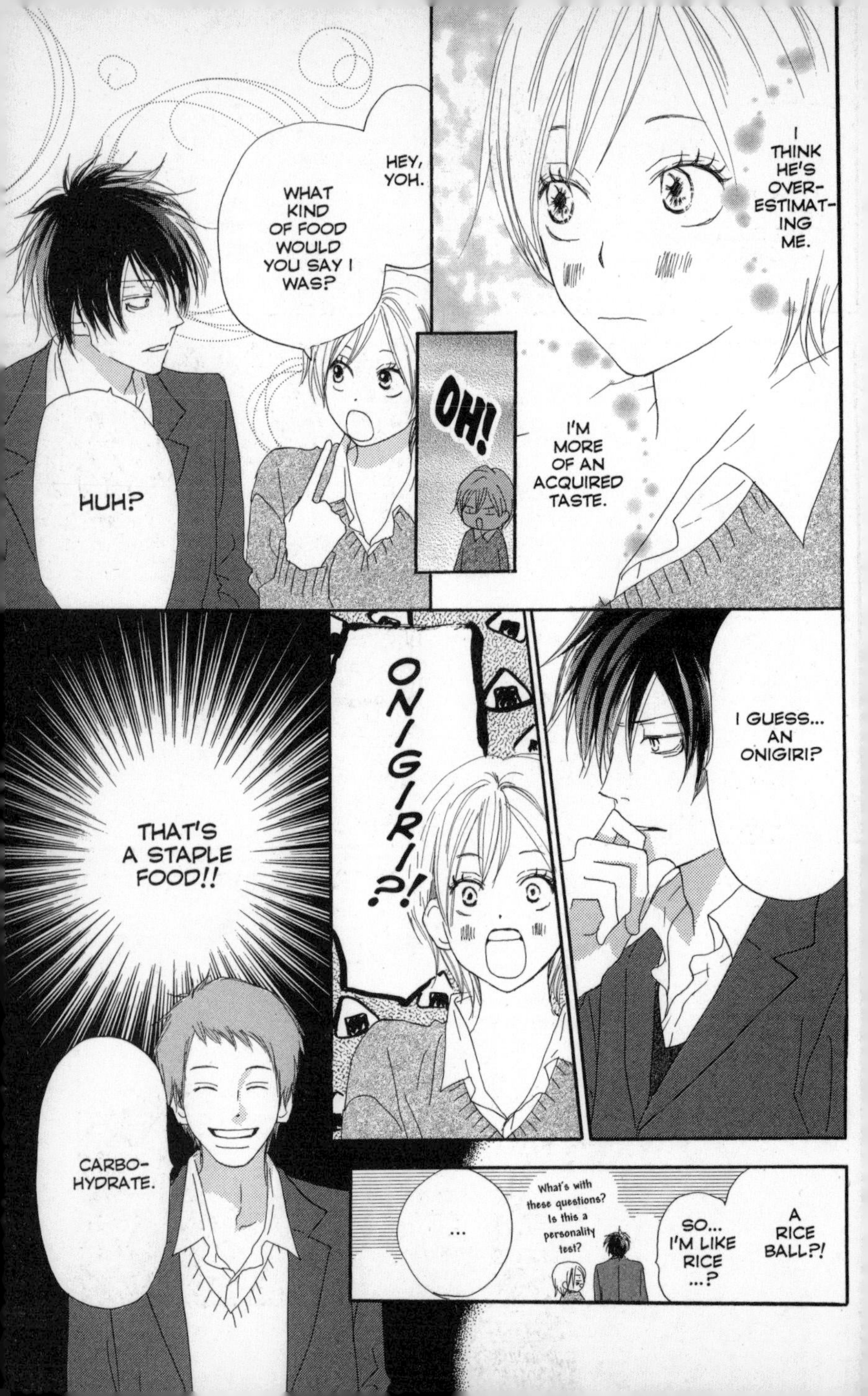
I THINK HE'S OVER-ESTIMATING ME.
I'M MORE OF AN ACQUIRED TASTE.
OH!
HEY, YOH.
WHAT KIND OF FOOD WOULD YOU SAY I WAS?
HUH?
I GUESS... AN ONIGIRI?
ONIGIRI?!
A RICE BALL?!
SO... I'M LIKE RICE ...?
What's with these questions? Is this a personality test?
...
THAT'S A STAPLE FOOD!!
CARBO-HYDRATE.

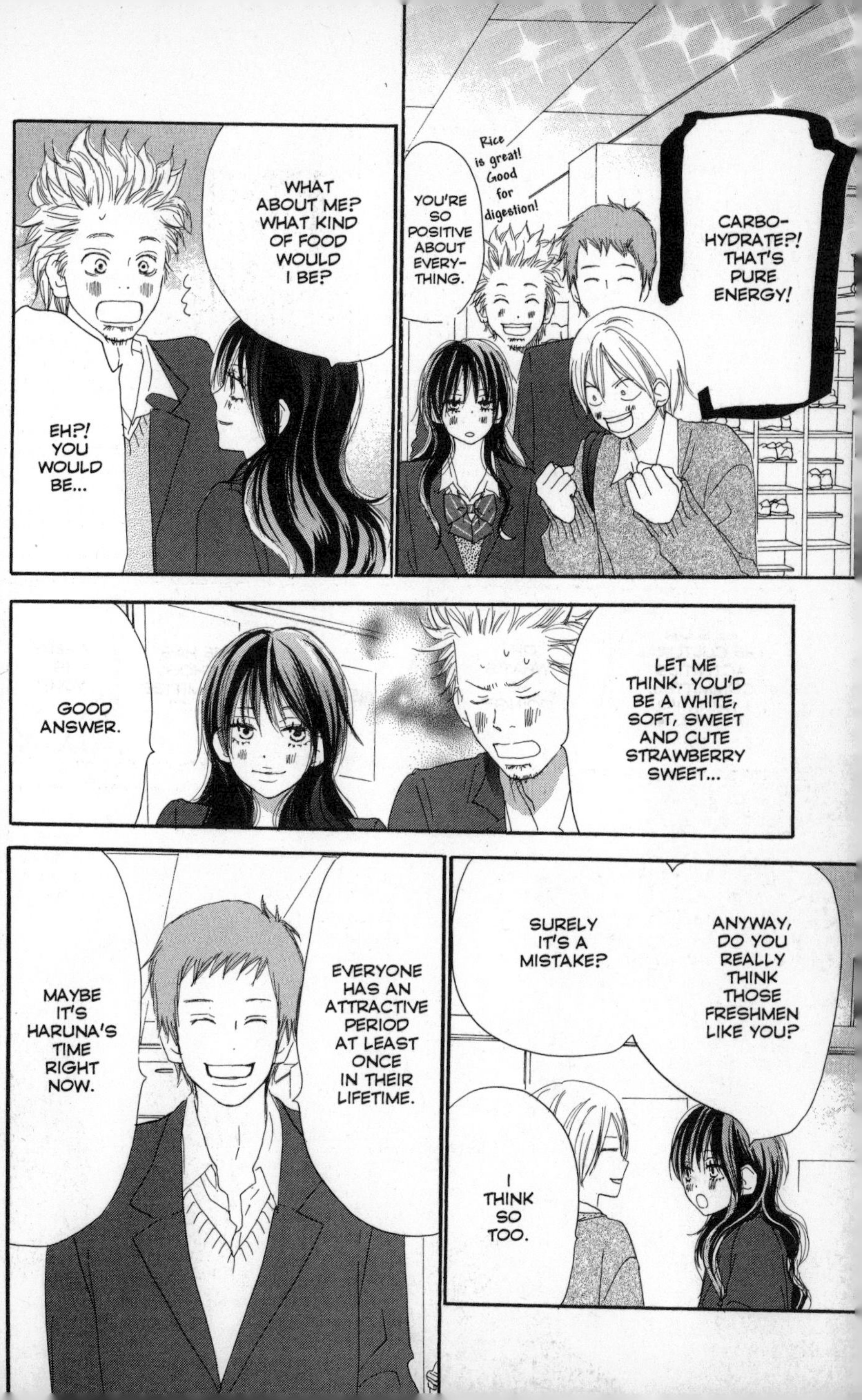
CARBO-HYDRATE?! THAT'S PURE ENERGY!
Rice is great! Good for digestion!
YOU'RE SO POSITIVE ABOUT EVERY-THING.
WHAT ABOUT ME? WHAT KIND OF FOOD WOULD I BE?
EH?! YOU WOULD BE...
LET ME THINK. YOU'D BE A WHITE, SOFT, SWEET AND CUTE STRAWBERRY SWEET...
GOOD ANSWER.
ANYWAY, DO YOU REALLY THINK THOSE FRESHMEN LIKE YOU?
SURELY IT'S A MISTAKE?
I THINK SO TOO.
EVERYONE HAS AN ATTRACTIVE PERIOD AT LEAST ONCE IN THEIR LIFETIME.
MAYBE IT'S HARUNA'S TIME RIGHT NOW.

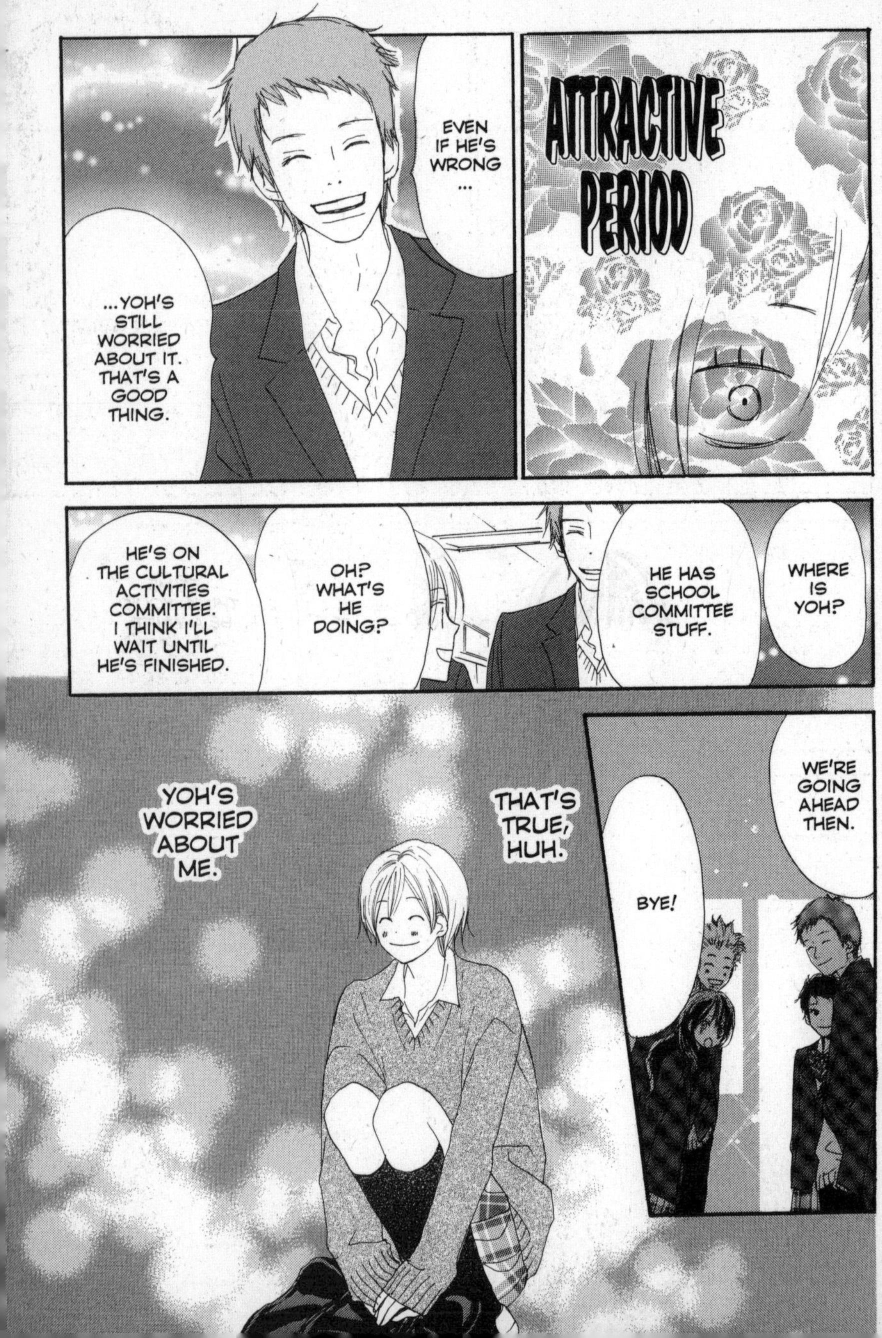
ATTRACTIVE PERIOD
EVEN IF HE'S WRONG ...
...YOH'S STILL WORRIED ABOUT IT. THAT'S A GOOD THING.
WHERE IS YOH?
HE HAS SCHOOL COMMITTEE STUFF.
OH? WHAT'S HE DOING?
HE'S ON THE CULTURAL ACTIVITIES COMMITTEE. I THINK I'LL WAIT UNTIL HE'S FINISHED.
WE'RE GOING AHEAD THEN.
BYE!
THAT'S TRUE, HUH.
YOH'S WORRIED ABOUT ME.

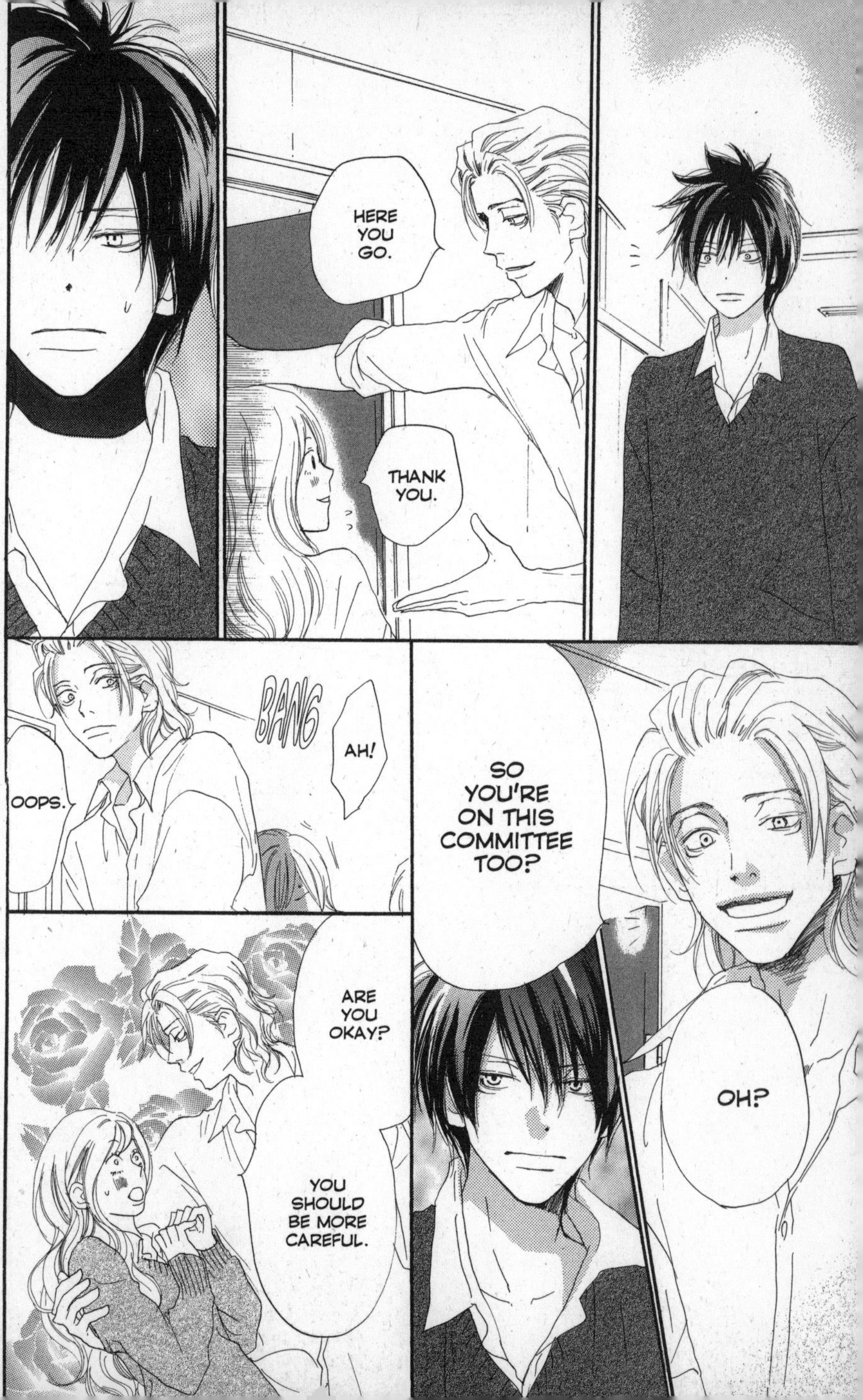
HERE YOU GO.
THANK YOU.
SO YOU'RE ON THIS COMMITTEE TOO?
OH?
BANG
AH!
OOPS.
ARE YOU OKAY?
YOU SHOULD BE MORE CAREFUL.

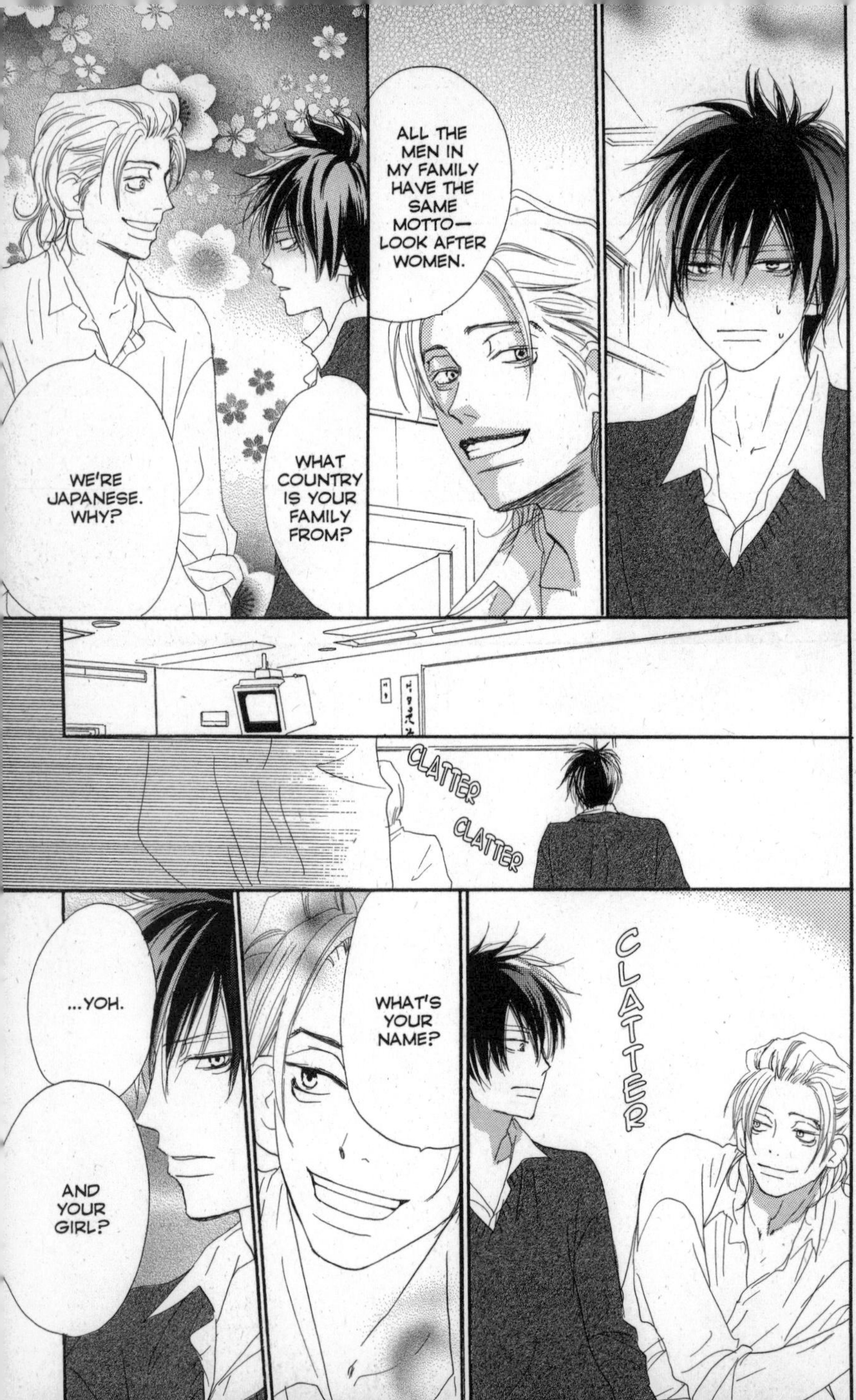
ALL THE MEN IN MY FAMILY HAVE THE SAME MOTTO—LOOK AFTER WOMEN.
WHAT COUNTRY IS YOUR FAMILY FROM?
WE'RE JAPANESE. WHY?
CLATTER
CLATTER
CLATTER
WHAT'S YOUR NAME?
...YOH.
AND YOUR GIRL?

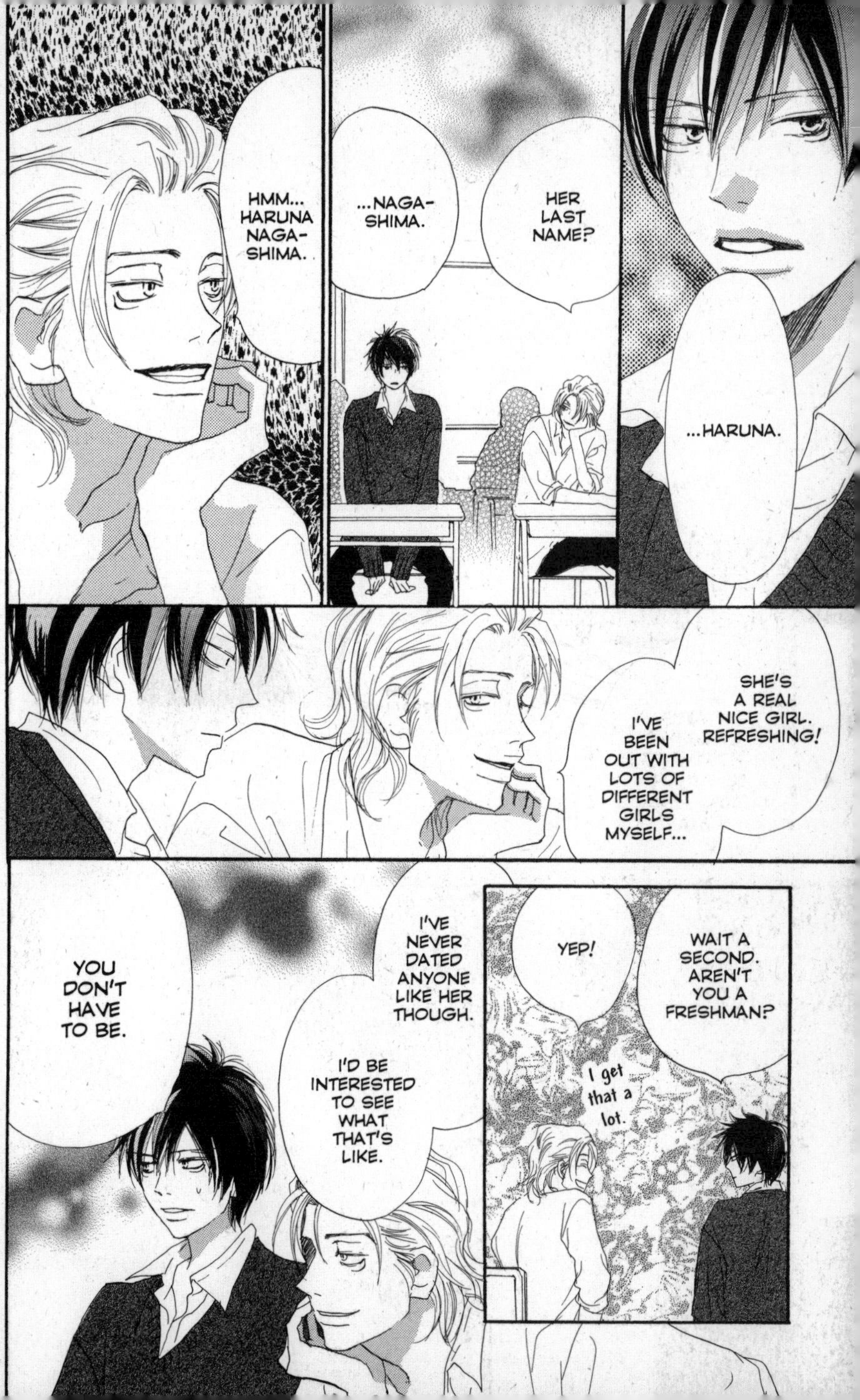
...HARUNA.
HER LAST NAME?
...NAGA-SHIMA.
HMM... HARUNA NAGA-SHIMA.
SHE'S A REAL NICE GIRL. REFRESHING!
I'VE BEEN OUT WITH LOTS OF DIFFERENT GIRLS MYSELF...
WAIT A SECOND. AREN'T YOU A FRESHMAN?
YEP!
I get that a lot.
I'VE NEVER DATED ANYONE LIKE HER THOUGH.
I'D BE INTERESTED TO SEE WHAT THAT'S LIKE.
YOU DON'T HAVE TO BE.

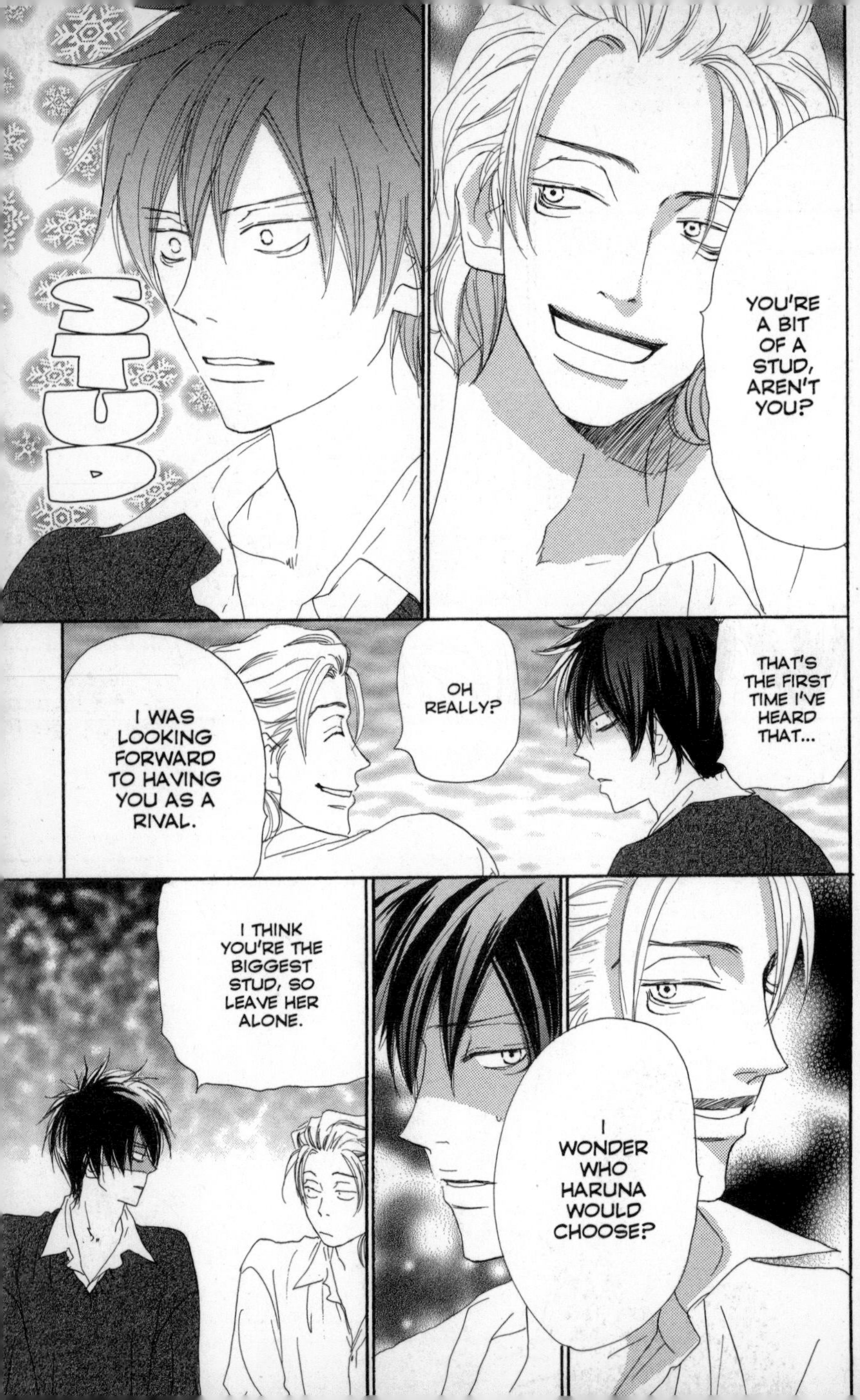
YOU'RE A BIT OF A STUD, AREN'T YOU?
STUD
THAT'S THE FIRST TIME I'VE HEARD THAT...
OH REALLY?
I WAS LOOKING FORWARD TO HAVING YOU AS A RIVAL.
I WONDER WHO HARUNA WOULD CHOOSE?
I THINK YOU'RE THE BIGGEST STUD, SO LEAVE HER ALONE.

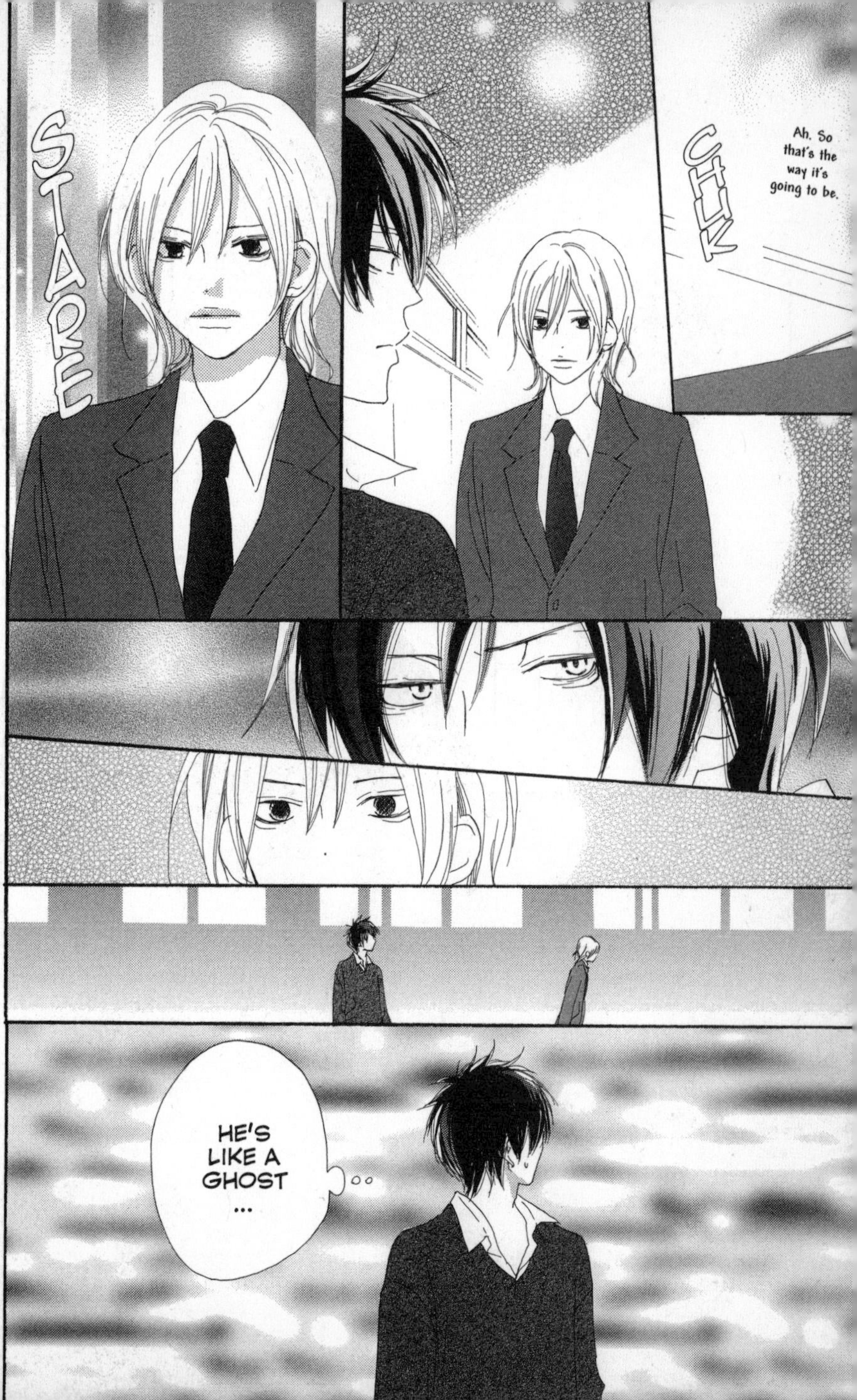
Ah. So that's the way it's going to be.
CHUK
STARE
HE'S LIKE A GHOST ...

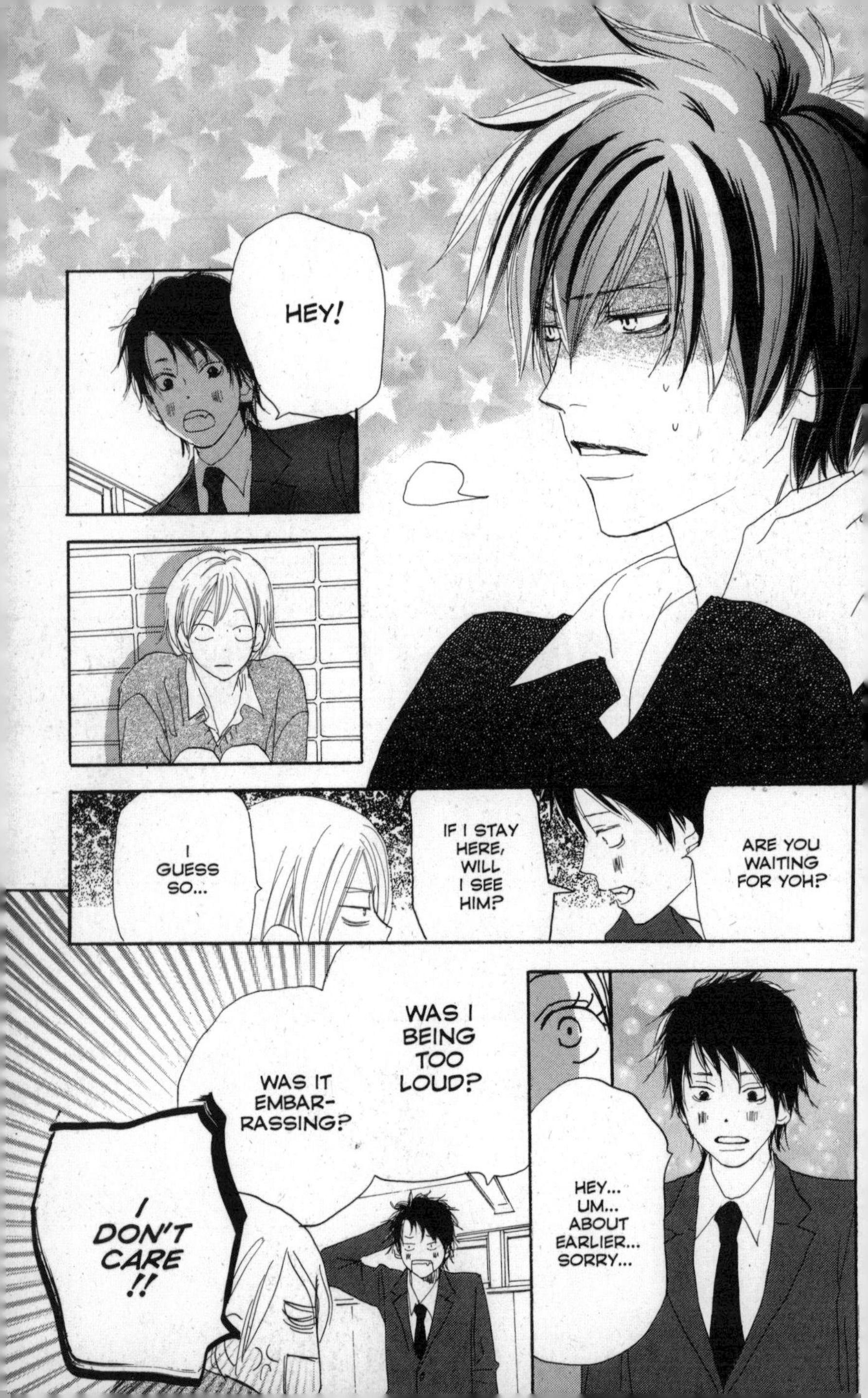
HEY!
ARE YOU WAITING FOR YOH?
IF I STAY HERE, WILL I SEE HIM?
I GUESS SO...
HEY... UM... ABOUT EARLIER... SORRY...
WAS I BEING TOO LOUD?
WAS IT EMBAR-RASSING?
I DON'T CARE!!

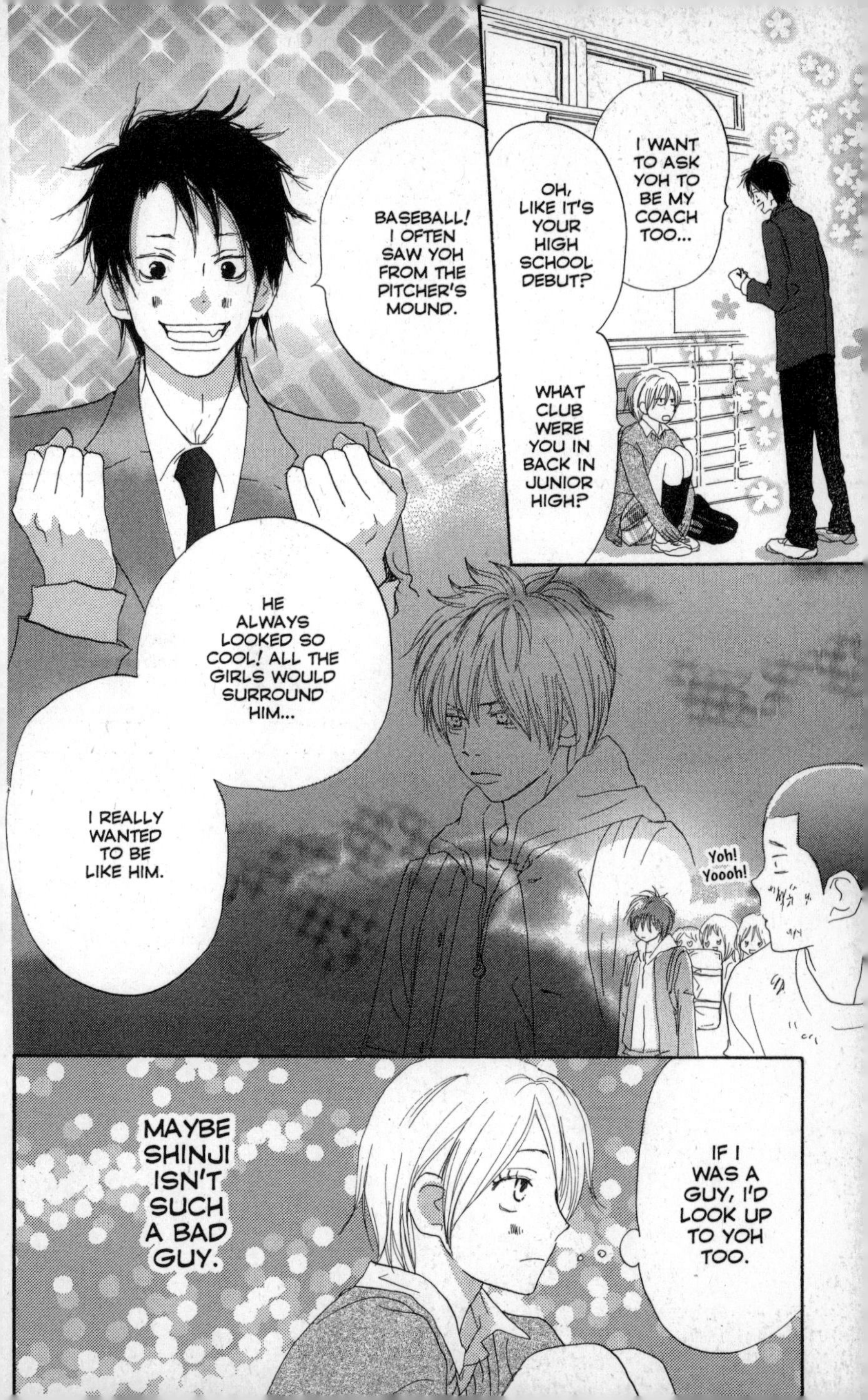
I WANT TO ASK YOH TO BE MY COACH TOO...
OH, LIKE IT'S YOUR HIGH SCHOOL DEBUT?
WHAT CLUB WERE YOU IN BACK IN JUNIOR HIGH?
BASEBALL! I OFTEN SAW YOH FROM THE PITCHER'S MOUND.
HE ALWAYS LOOKED SO COOL! ALL THE GIRLS WOULD SURROUND HIM...
Yoh! Yoooh!
I REALLY WANTED TO BE LIKE HIM.
IF I WAS A GUY, I'D LOOK UP TO YOH TOO.
MAYBE SHINJI ISN'T SUCH A BAD GUY.

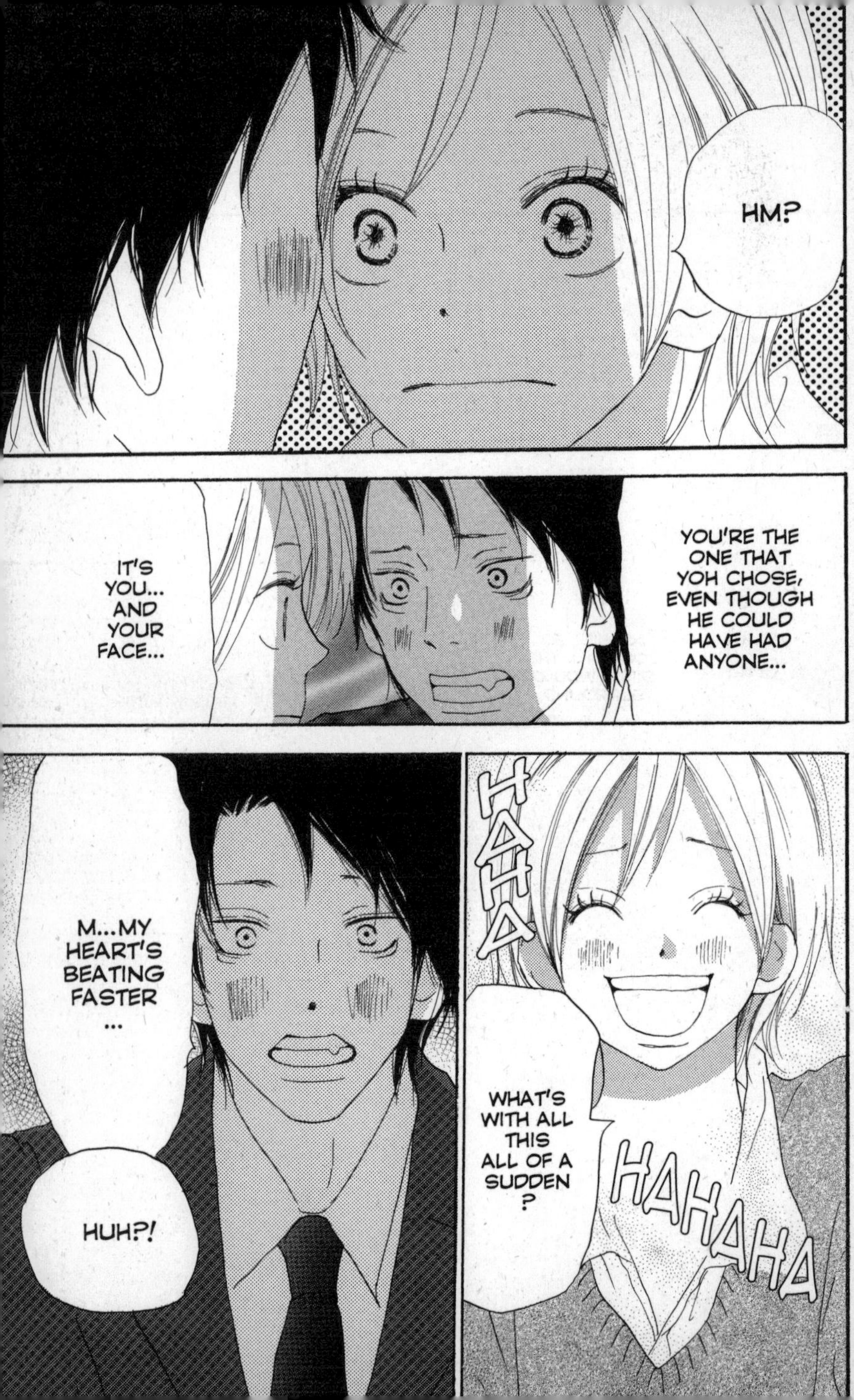
HM?
YOU'RE THE ONE THAT YOH CHOSE, EVEN THOUGH HE COULD HAVE HAD ANYONE...
IT'S YOU... AND YOUR FACE...
HAHAHA
WHAT'S WITH ALL THIS ALL OF A SUDDEN?
HAHAHA
M...MY HEART'S BEATING FASTER...
HUH?!

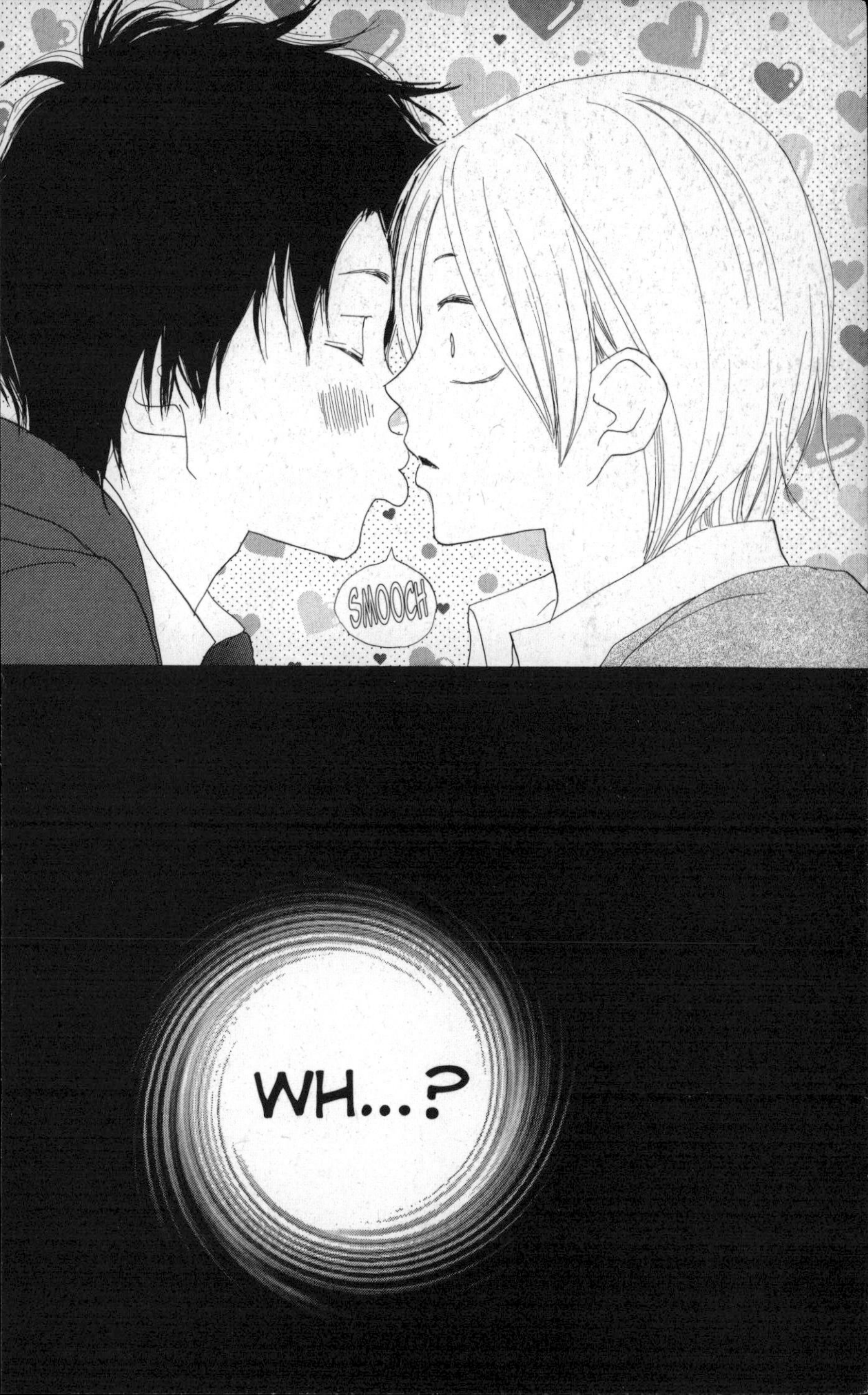
SMOOCH
WH...?

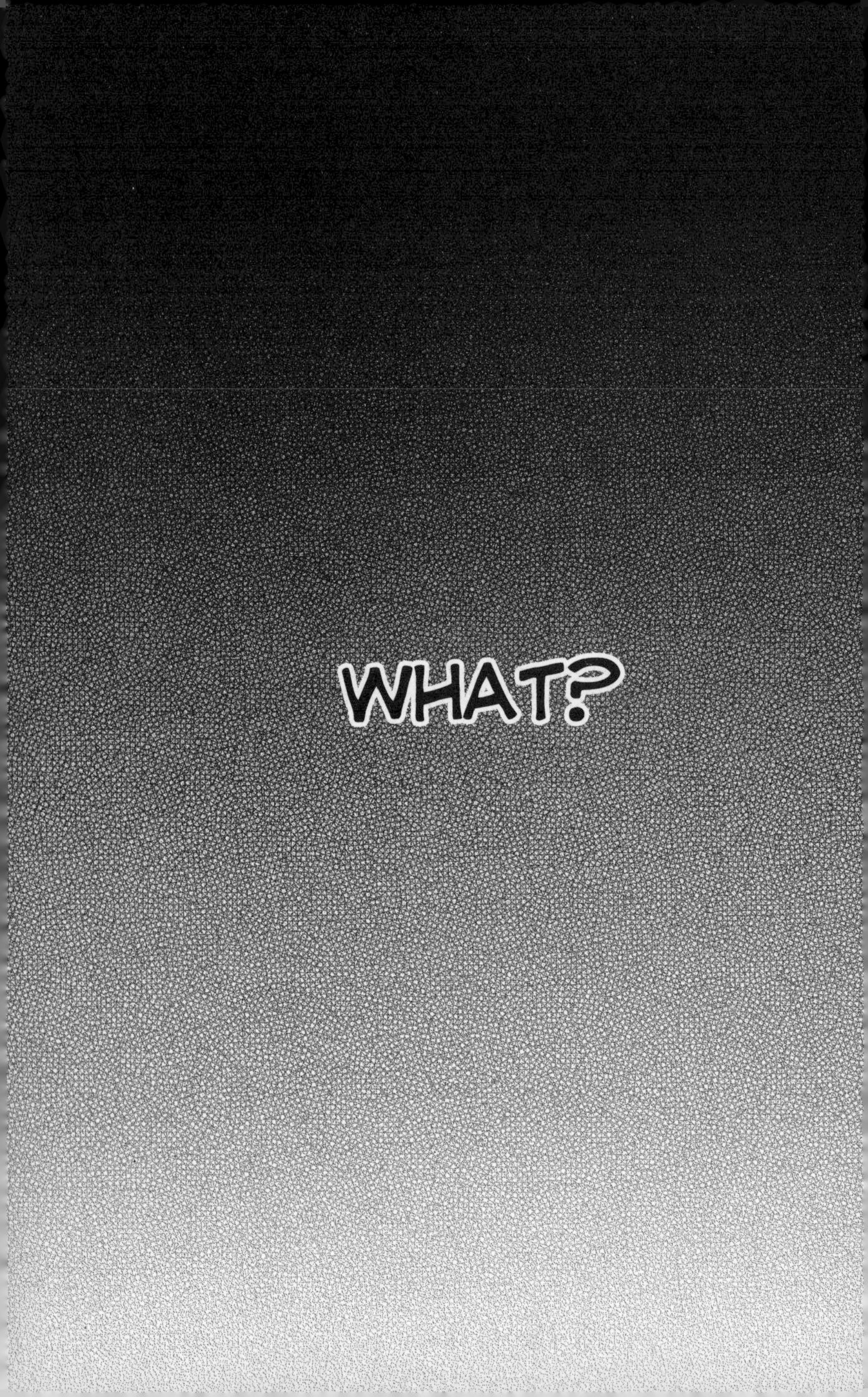
WHAT?

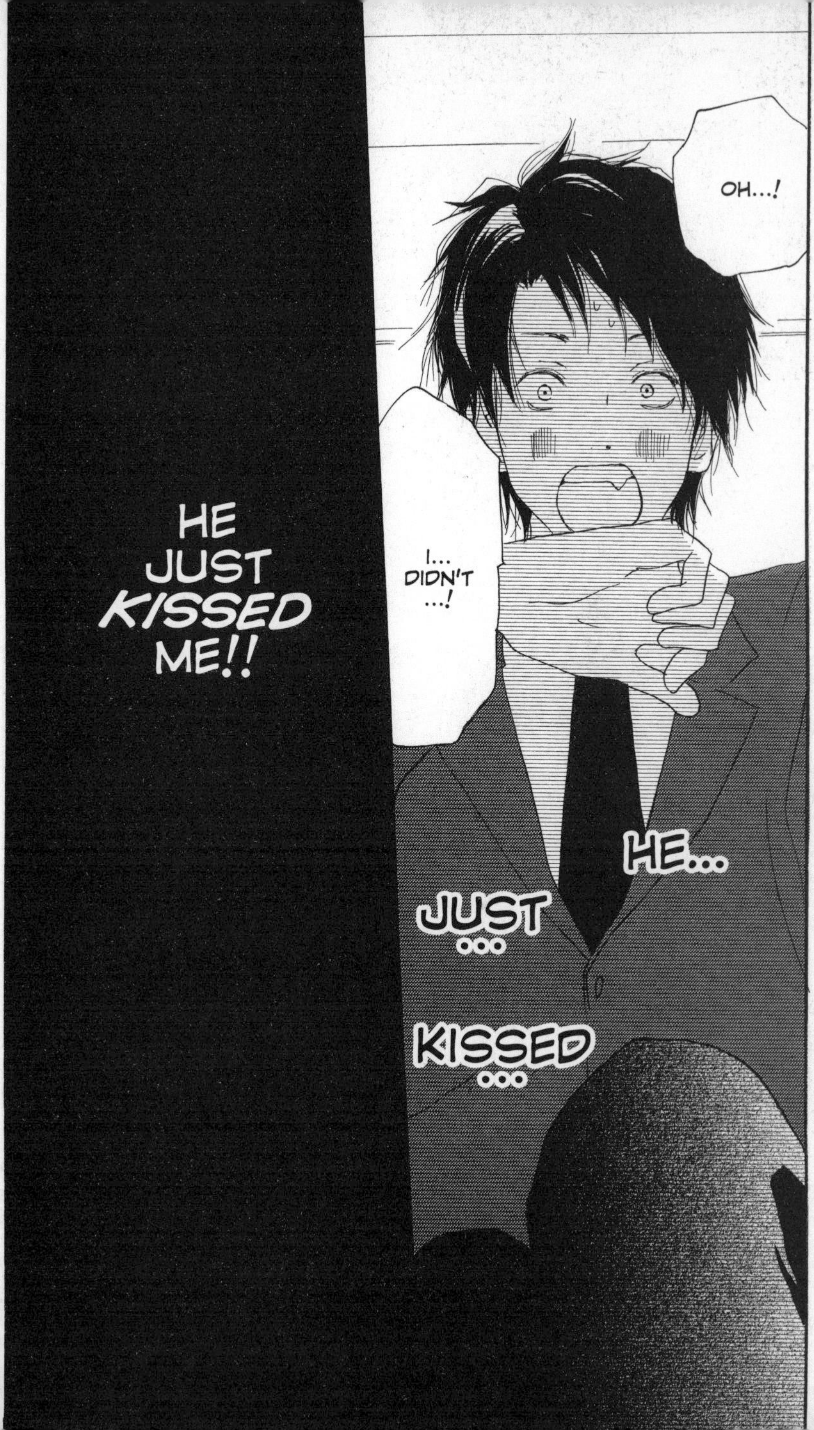
OH...!
I... DIDN'T ...!
HE...
JUST ...
KISSED ...
HE JUST KISSED ME!!

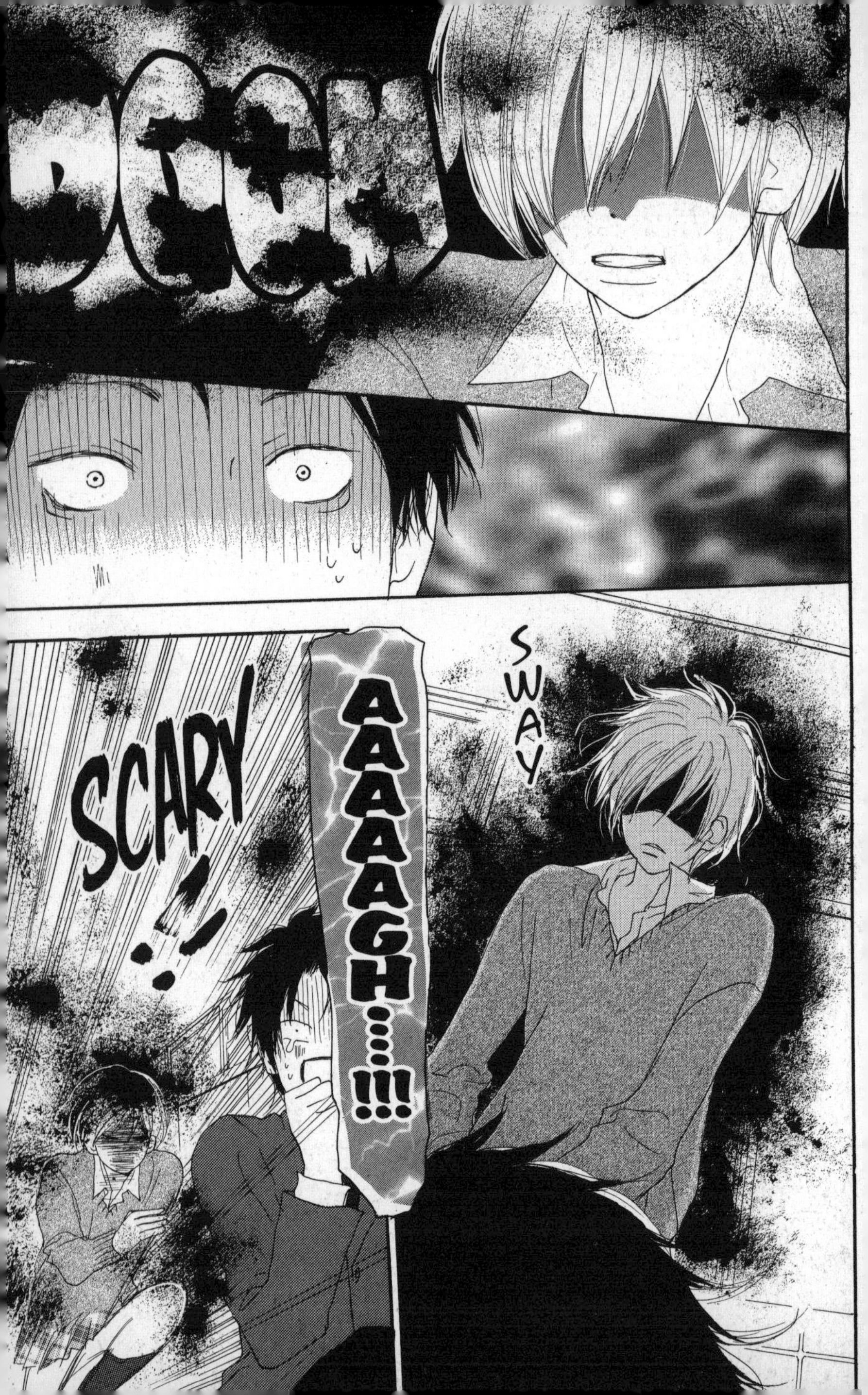
DOOOM
SWAY
AAAAAGH......!!!
SCARY!!!

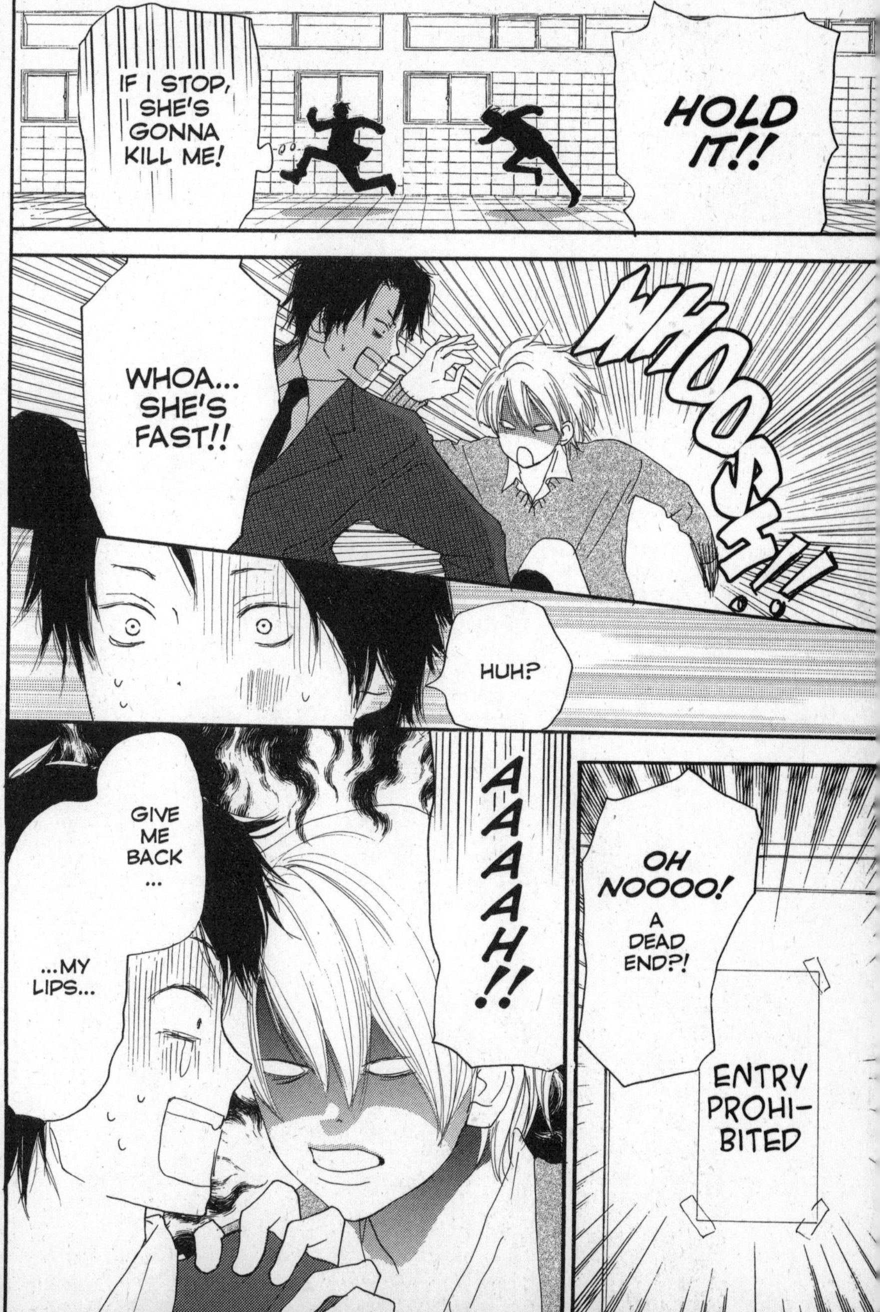
HOLD IT!!
IF I STOP, SHE'S GONNA KILL ME!
WHOOSH!!
WHOA... SHE'S FAST!!
HUH?
OH NOOOO!
A DEAD END?!
ENTRY PROHIBITED
AAAAAH!!
GIVE ME BACK ...
...MY LIPS...

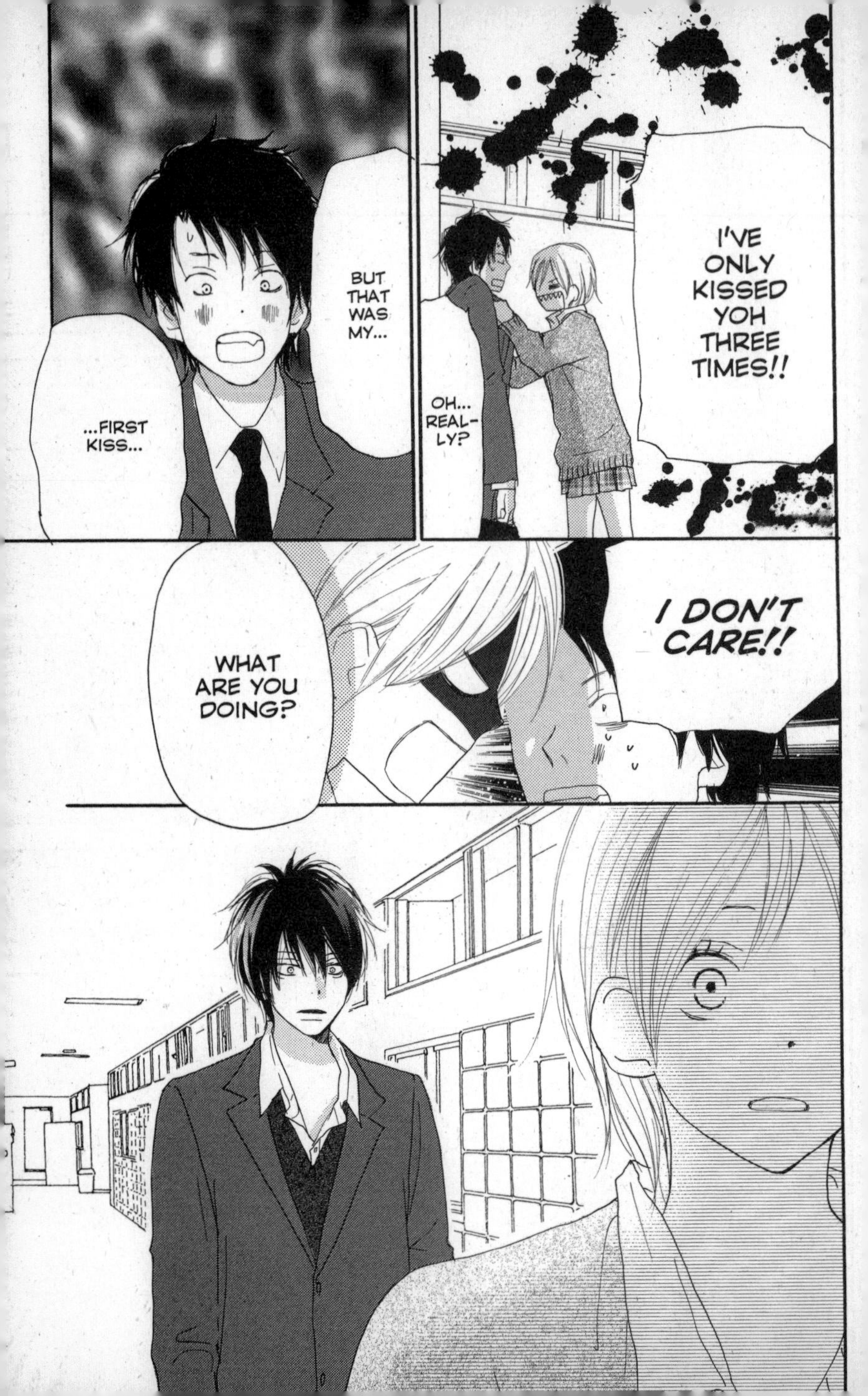
I'VE ONLY KISSED YOH THREE TIMES!!
OH... REAL-LY?
BUT THAT WAS MY...
...FIRST KISS...
I DON'T CARE!!
WHAT ARE YOU DOING?

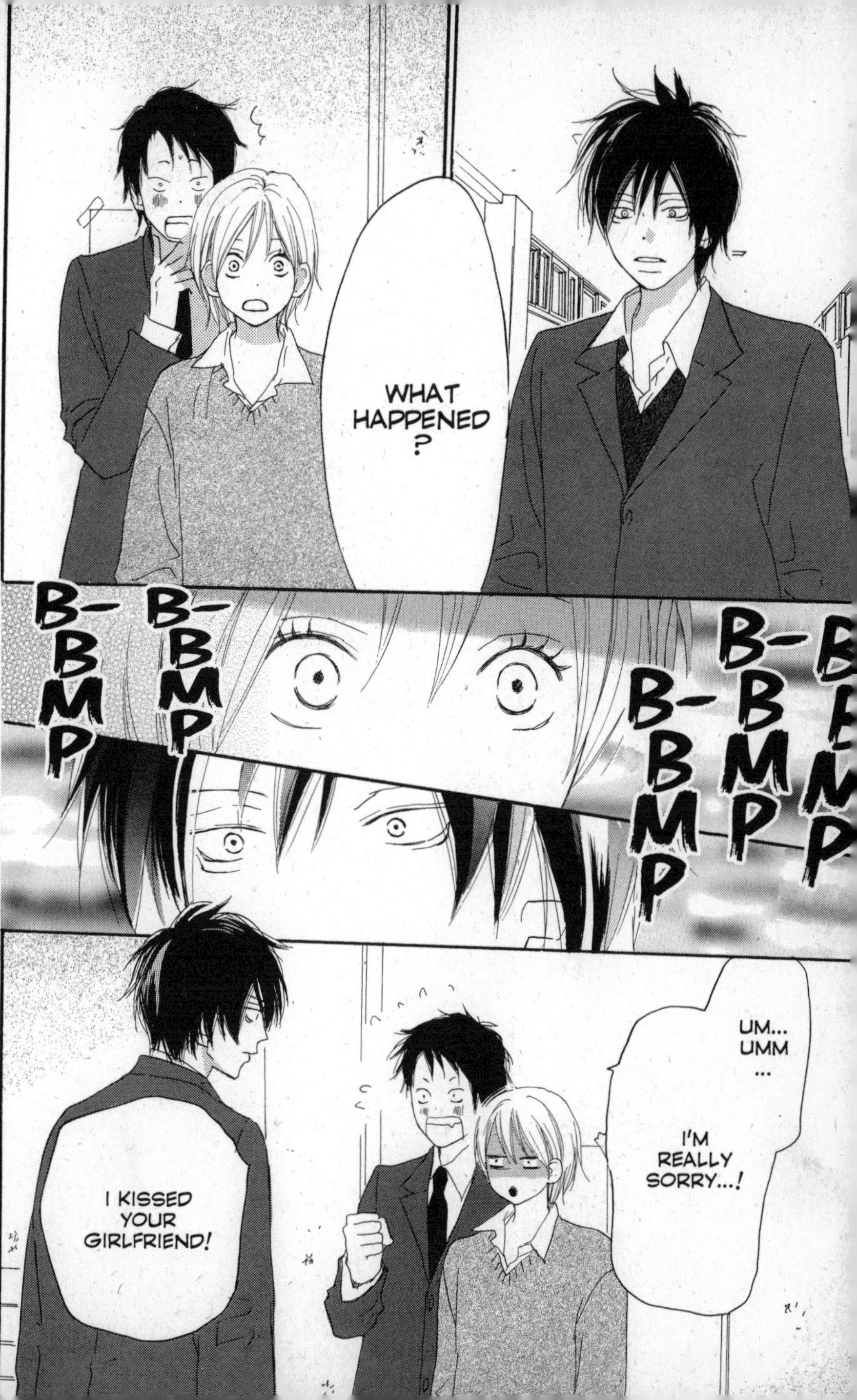
WHAT HAPPENED?
B-BMP B-BMP B-BMP B-BMP B-BMP B-BMP
UM... UMM...
I'M REALLY SORRY...!
I KISSED YOUR GIRLFRIEND!

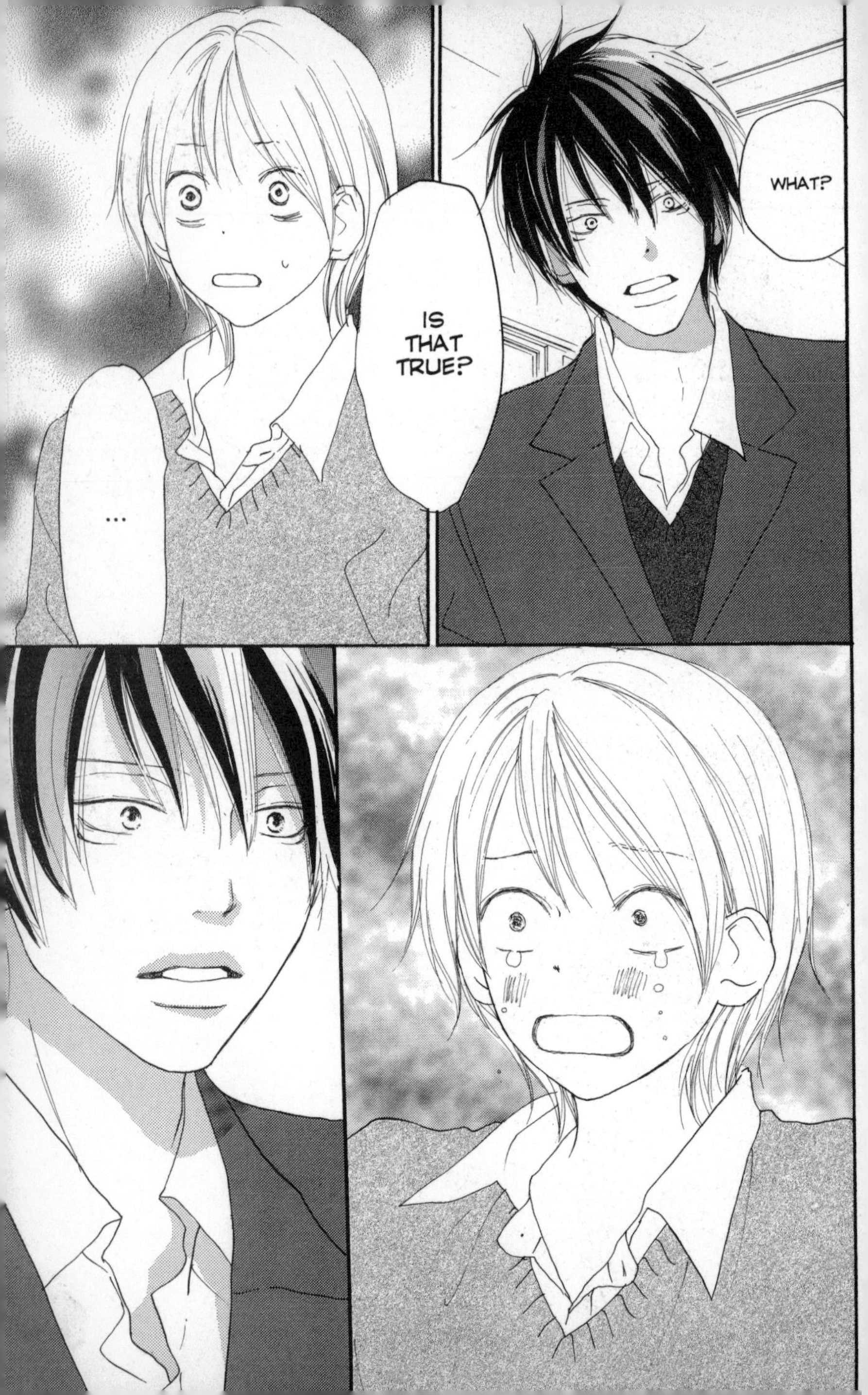
WHAT?
IS THAT TRUE?
...

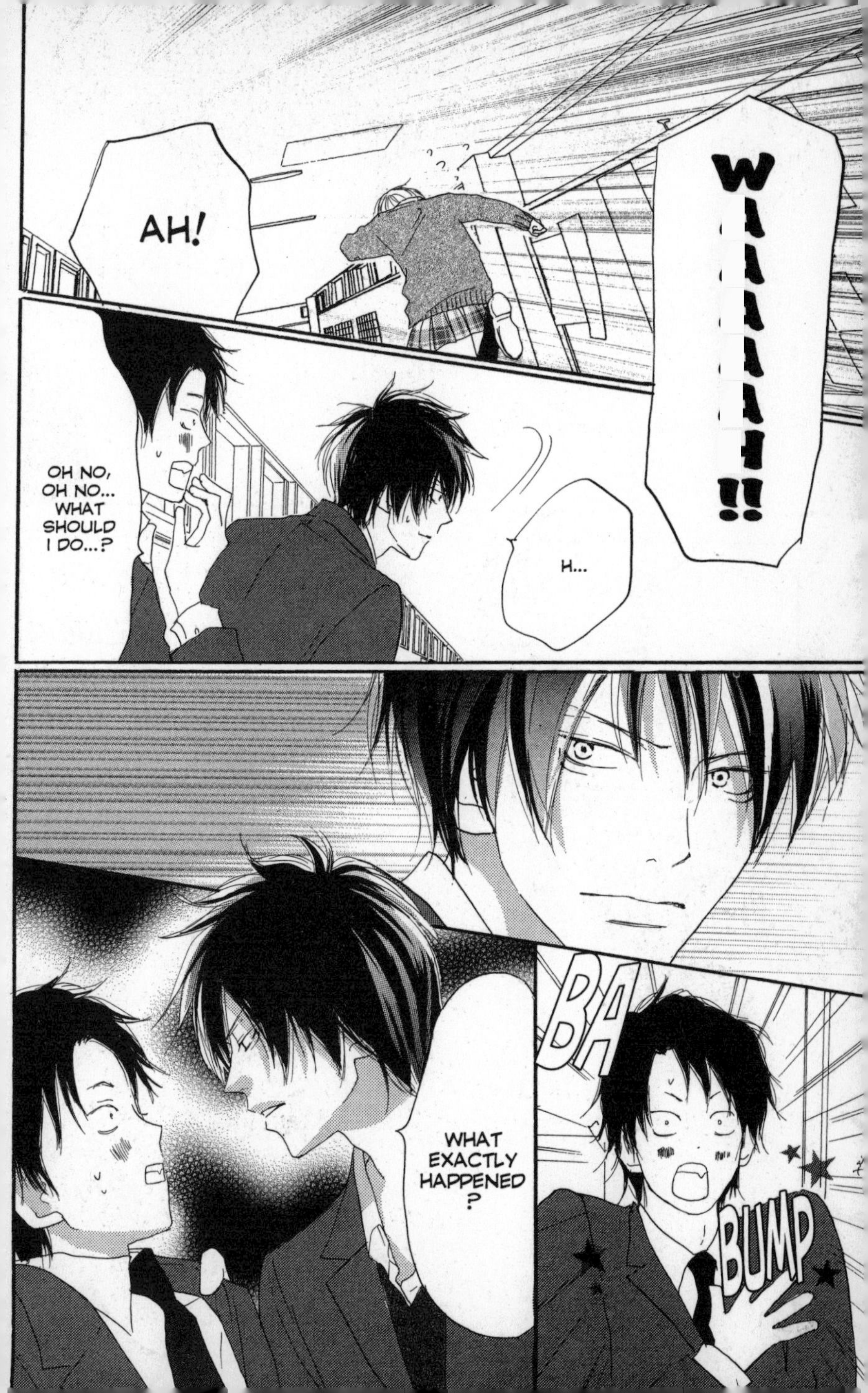
WAAAAAAH!!
AH!
H...
OH NO, OH NO... WHAT SHOULD I DO...?
BA
BUMP
WHAT EXACTLY HAPPENED?

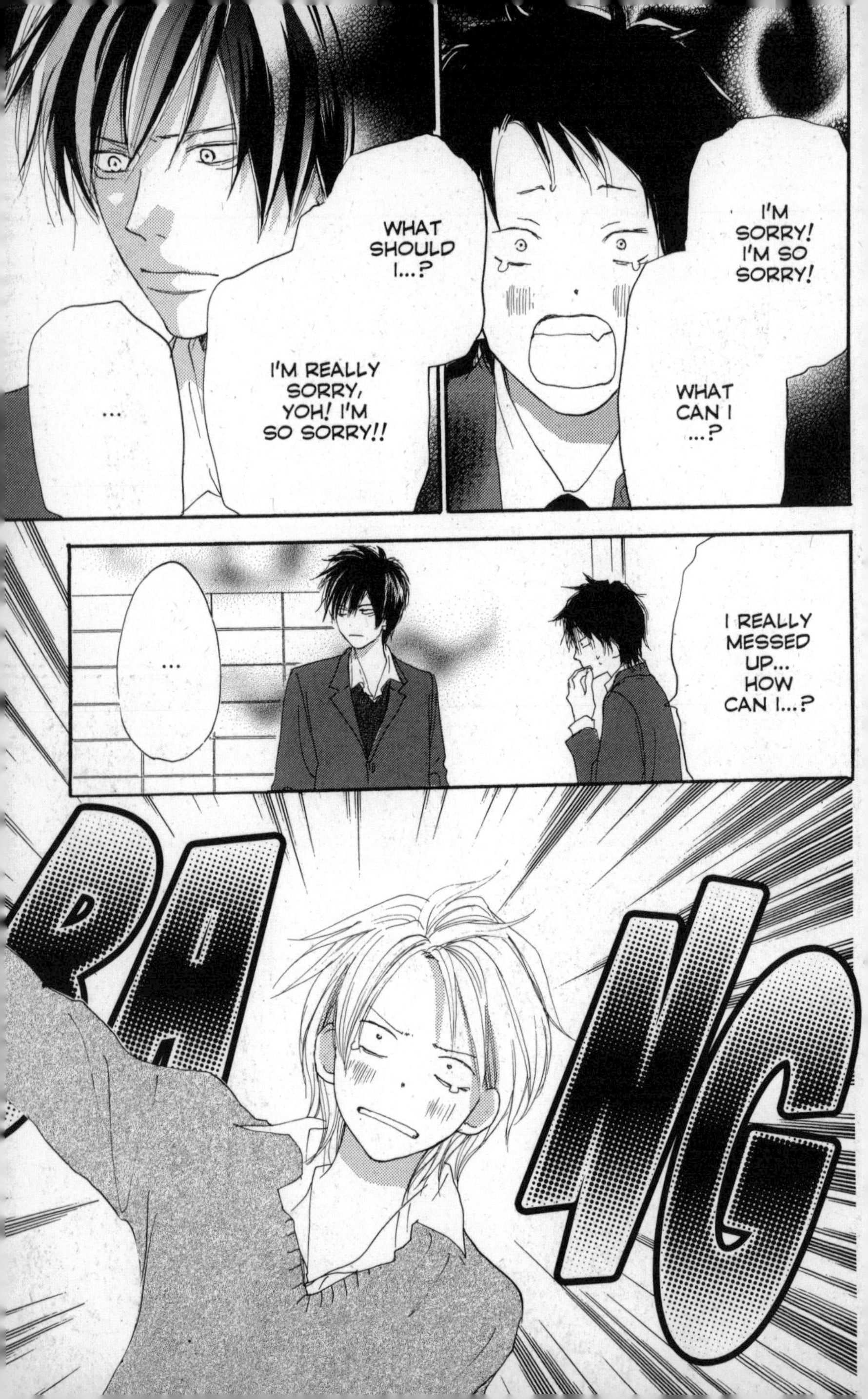
I'M SORRY! I'M SO SORRY!
WHAT SHOULD I...?
WHAT CAN I ...?
I'M REALLY SORRY, YOH! I'M SO SORRY!!
...
I REALLY MESSED UP... HOW CAN I...?
...
BANG

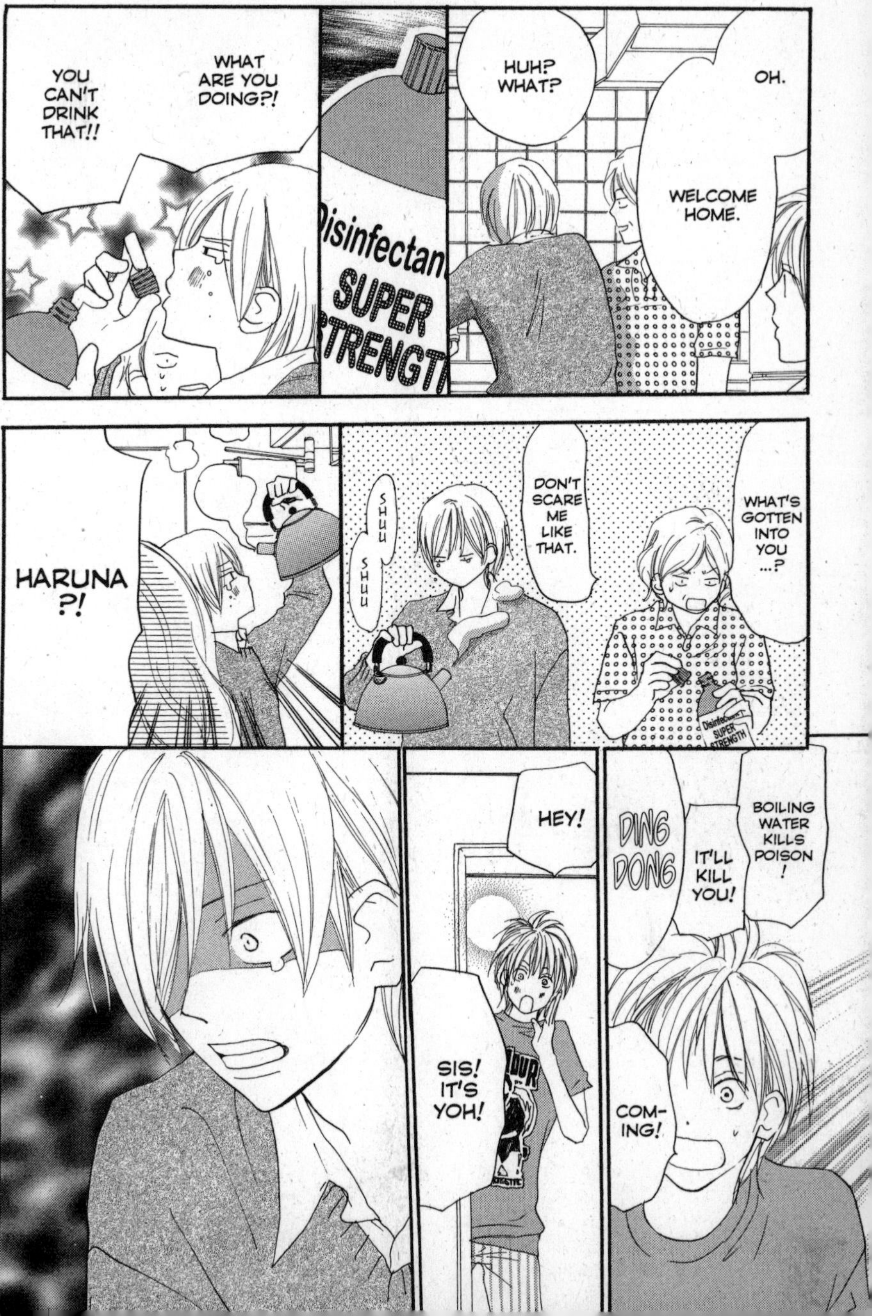
OH.
WELCOME HOME.
HUH? WHAT?
Disinfectant SUPER STRENGTH
WHAT ARE YOU DOING?!
YOU CAN'T DRINK THAT!!
WHAT'S GOTTEN INTO YOU ...?
DON'T SCARE ME LIKE THAT.
SHUU SHUU
HARUNA ?!
BOILING WATER KILLS POISON!
IT'LL KILL YOU!
DING DONG
COM-ING!
HEY!
SIS! IT'S YOH!

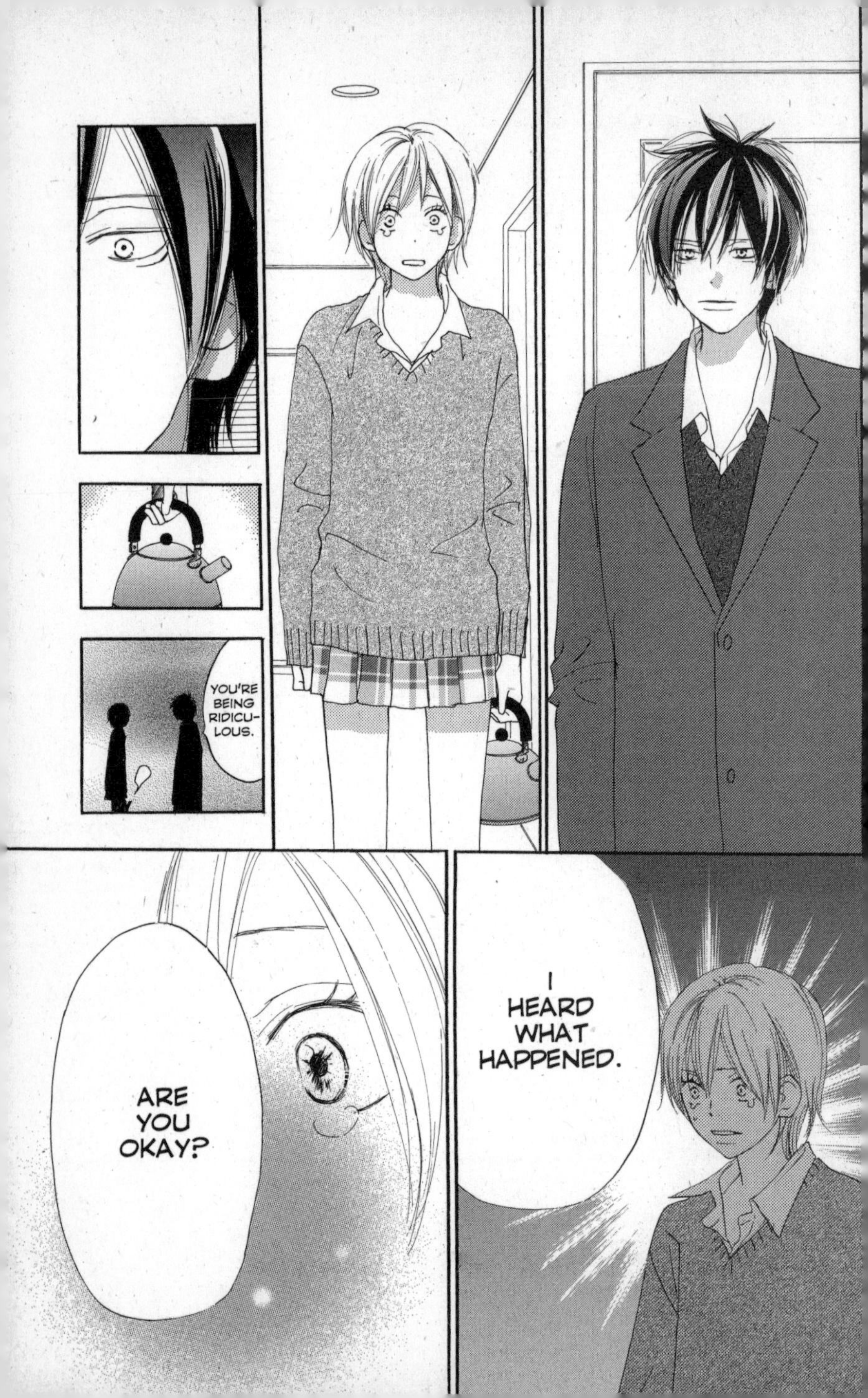
YOU'RE BEING RIDICU-LOUS.
I HEARD WHAT HAPPENED.
ARE YOU OKAY?

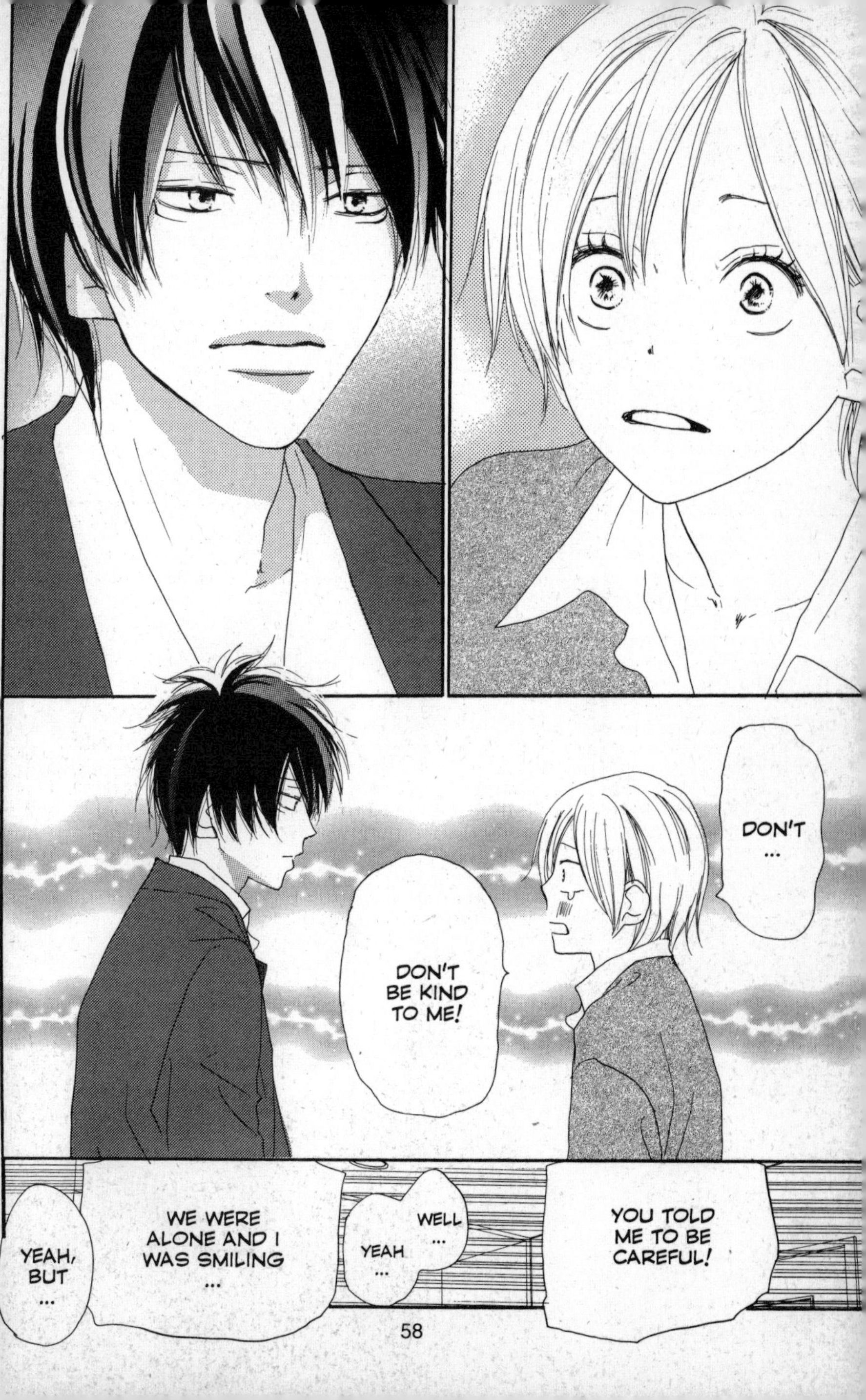
DON'T ...
DON'T BE KIND TO ME!
YOU TOLD ME TO BE CAREFUL!
WELL ...
YEAH ...
WE WERE ALONE AND I WAS SMILING ...
YEAH, BUT ...

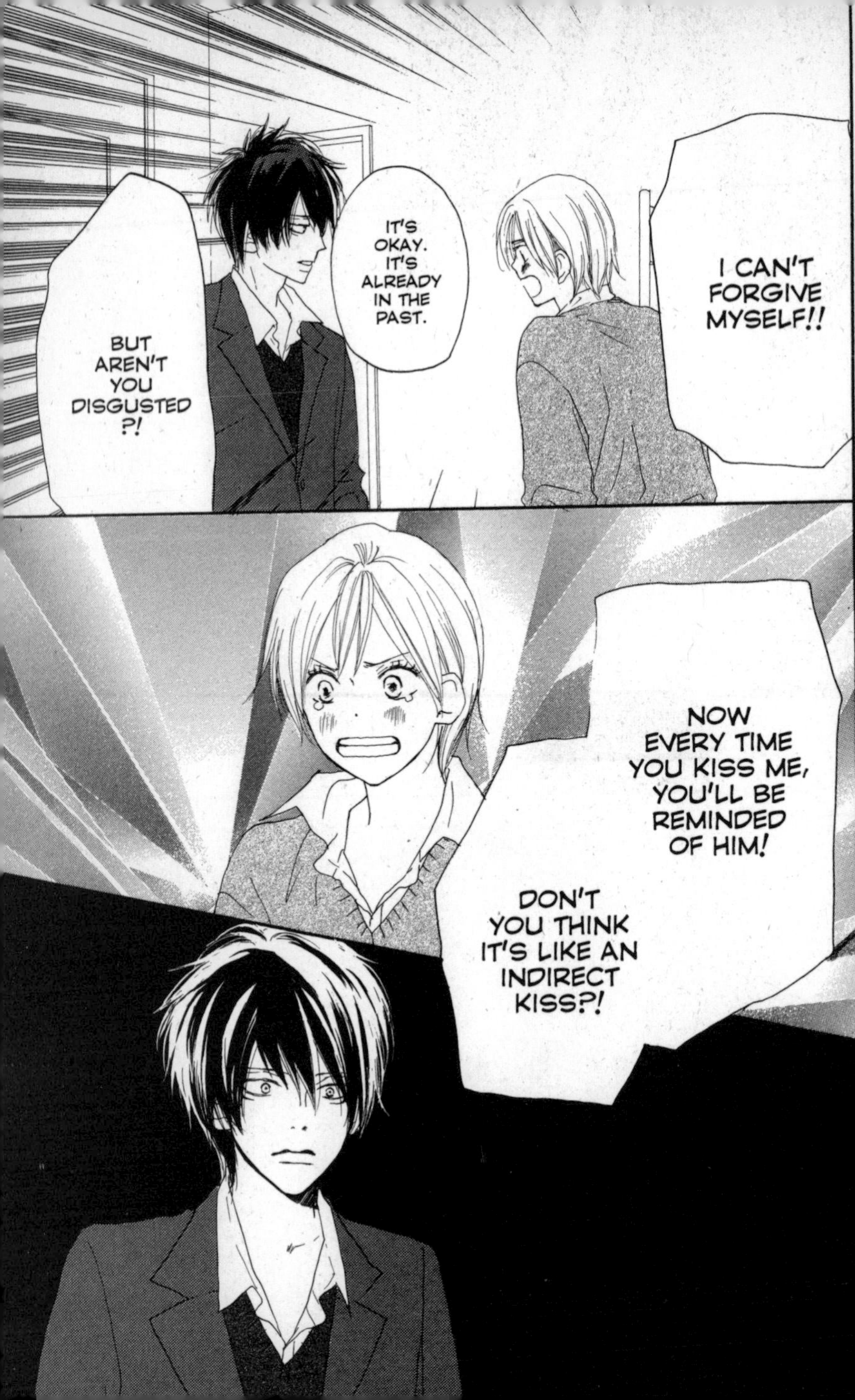
I CAN'T FORGIVE MYSELF!!
IT'S OKAY. IT'S ALREADY IN THE PAST.
BUT AREN'T YOU DISGUSTED?!
NOW EVERY TIME YOU KISS ME, YOU'LL BE REMINDED OF HIM!
DON'T YOU THINK IT'S LIKE AN INDIRECT KISS?!

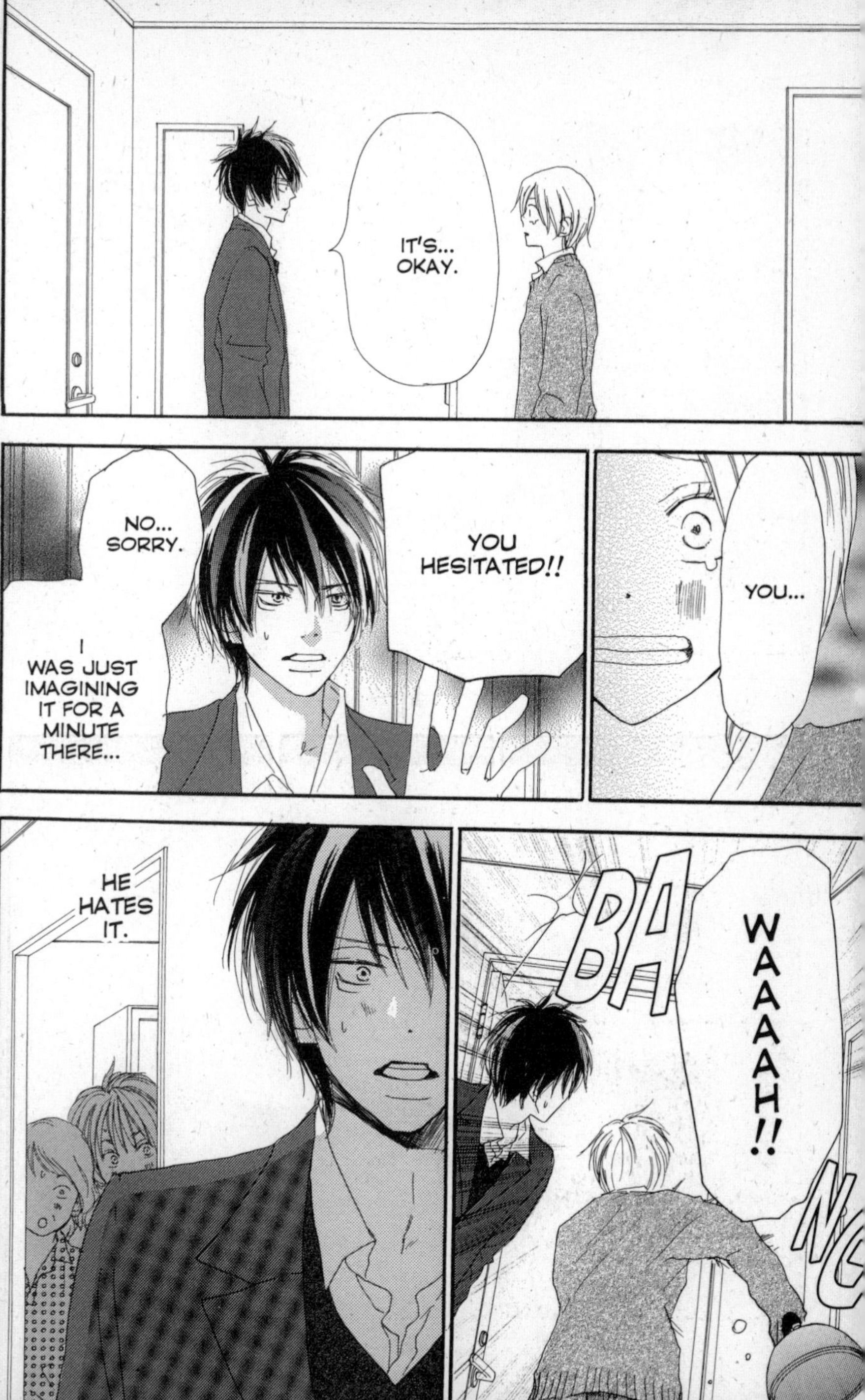
IT'S... OKAY.
YOU...
YOU HESITATED!!
NO... SORRY.
I WAS JUST IMAGINING IT FOR A MINUTE THERE...
WAAAAAH!!
BA
N
HE HATES IT.

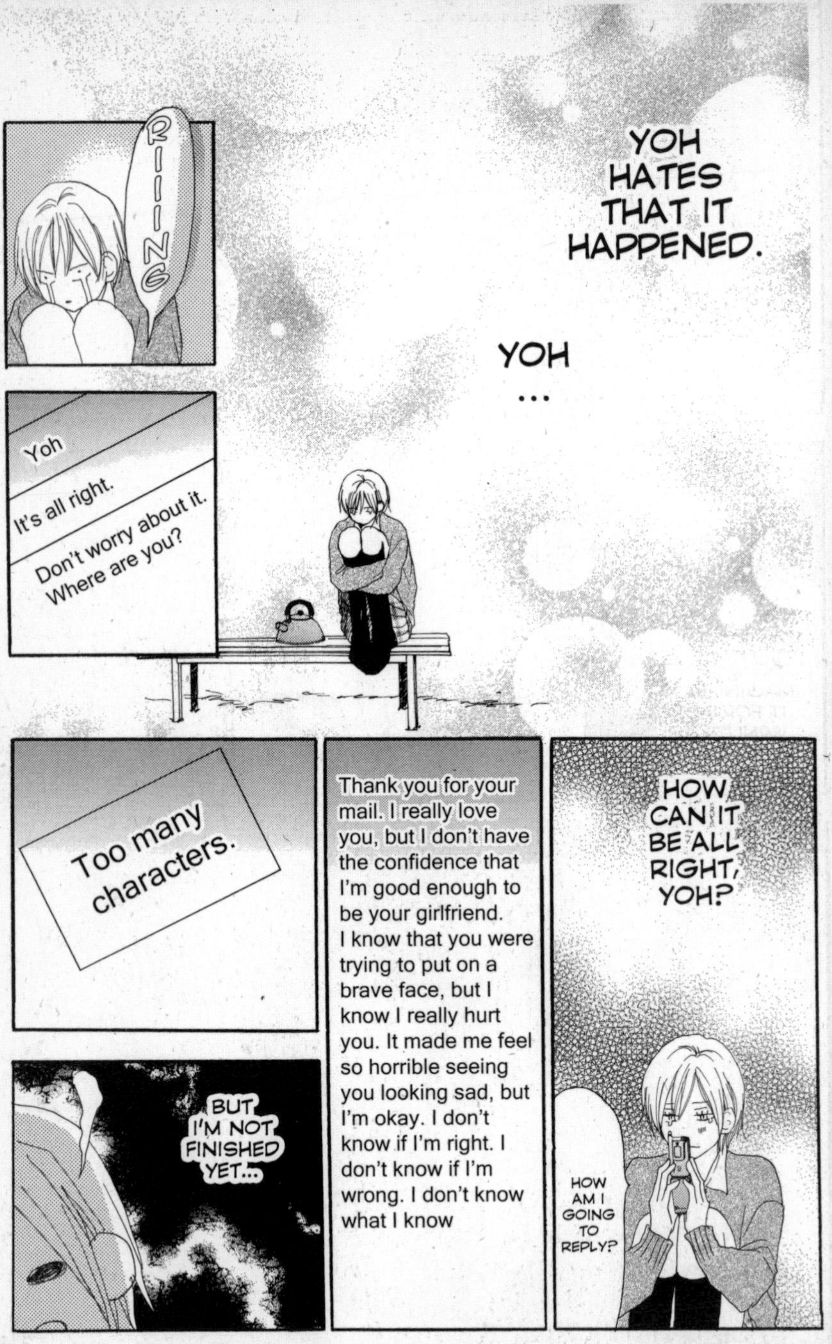
YOH HATES THAT IT HAPPENED.
YOH ...
RIIIING
Yoh
It's all right.
Don't worry about it. Where are you?
HOW CAN IT BE ALL RIGHT, YOH?
HOW AM I GOING TO REPLY?
Thank you for your mail. I really love you, but I don't have the confidence that I'm good enough to be your girlfriend. I know that you were trying to put on a brave face, but I know I really hurt you. It made me feel so horrible seeing you looking sad, but I'm okay. I don't know if I'm right. I don't know if I'm wrong. I don't know what I know
Too many characters.
BUT I'M NOT FINISHED YET...

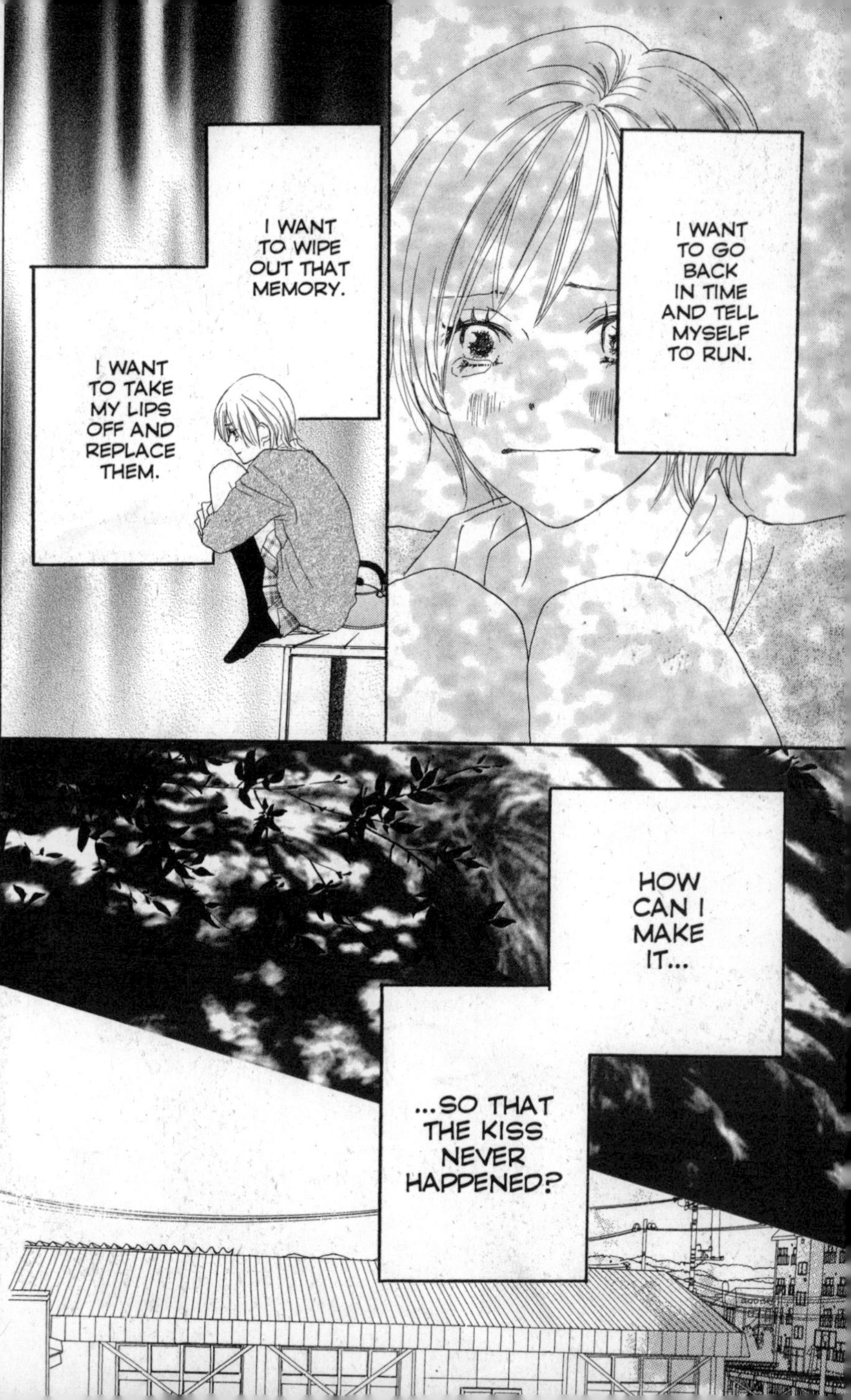
I WANT TO GO BACK IN TIME AND TELL MYSELF TO RUN.
I WANT TO WIPE OUT THAT MEMORY.
I WANT TO TAKE MY LIPS OFF AND REPLACE THEM.
HOW CAN I MAKE IT...
...SO THAT THE KISS NEVER HAPPENED?

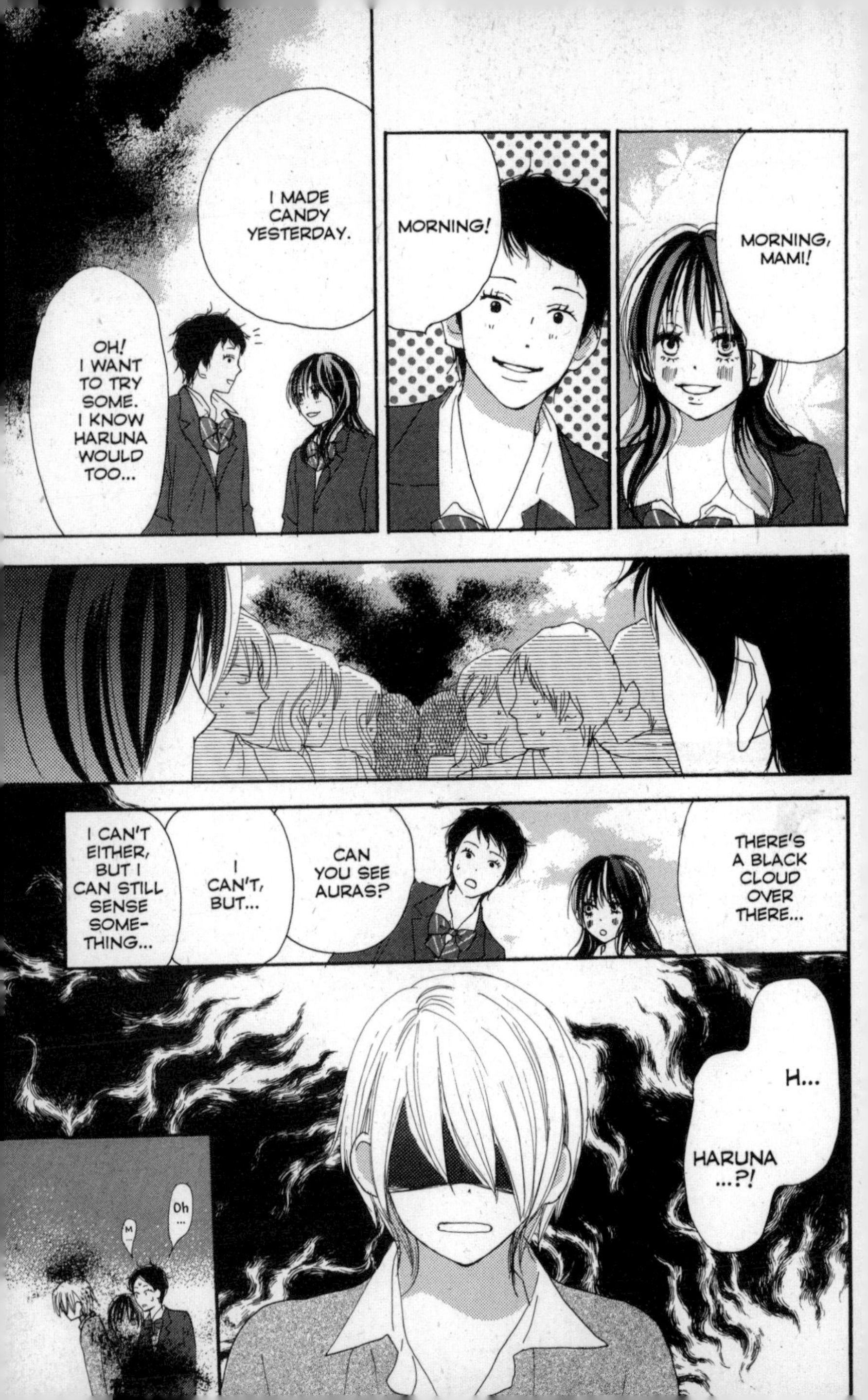
MORNING, MAMI!
MORNING!
I MADE CANDY YESTERDAY.
OH! I WANT TO TRY SOME. I KNOW HARUNA WOULD TOO...
THERE'S A BLACK CLOUD OVER THERE...
CAN YOU SEE AURAS?
I CAN'T, BUT...
I CAN'T EITHER, BUT I CAN STILL SENSE SOME-THING...
H...
HARUNA ...?!
Oh ...
M ...

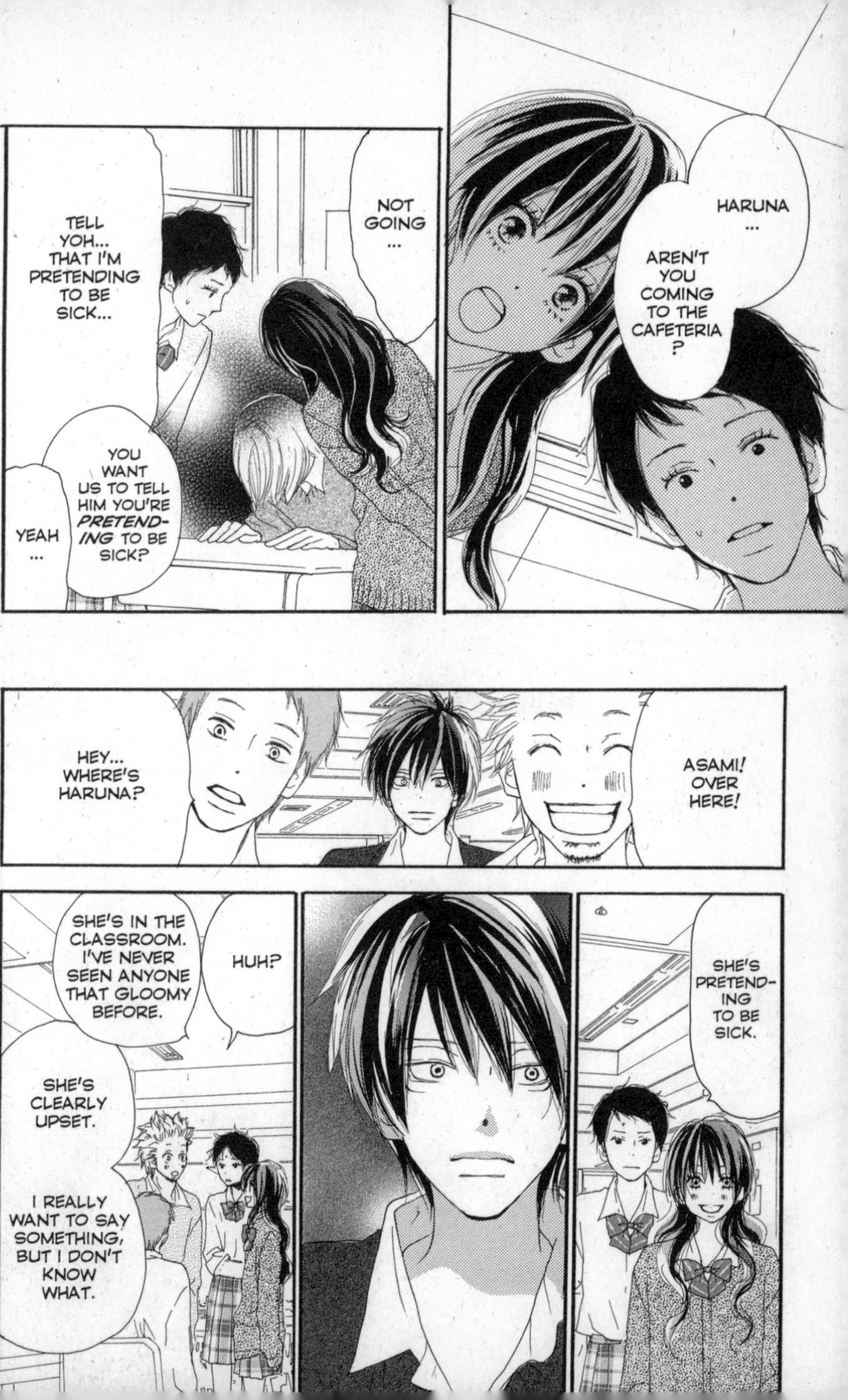
HARUNA ...
AREN'T YOU COMING TO THE CAFETERIA ?
NOT GOING ...
TELL YOH... THAT I'M PRETENDING TO BE SICK...
YOU WANT US TO TELL HIM YOU'RE *PRETENDING* TO BE SICK?
YEAH ...
ASAMI! OVER HERE!
HEY... WHERE'S HARUNA?
SHE'S PRETENDING TO BE SICK.
HUH?
SHE'S IN THE CLASSROOM. I'VE NEVER SEEN ANYONE THAT GLOOMY BEFORE.
SHE'S CLEARLY UPSET.
I REALLY WANT TO SAY SOMETHING, BUT I DON'T KNOW WHAT.

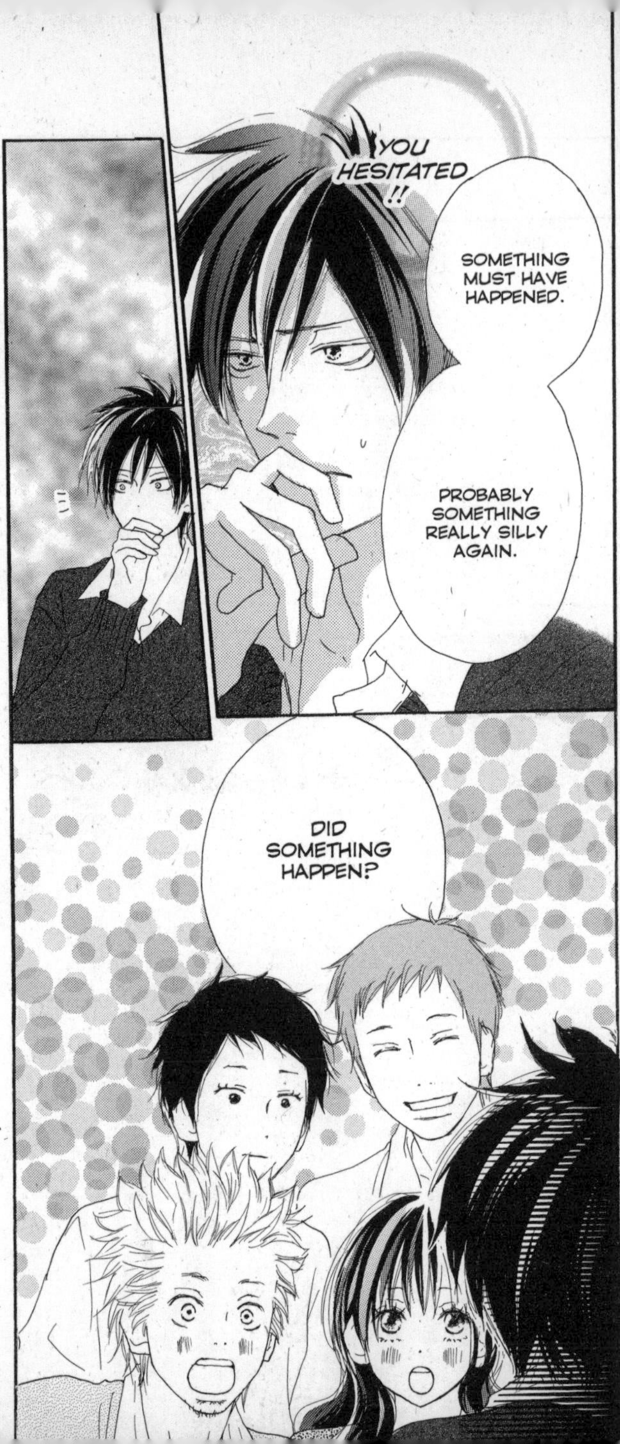
YOU HESITATED!!
SOMETHING MUST HAVE HAPPENED.
PROBABLY SOMETHING REALLY SILLY AGAIN.
DID SOMETHING HAPPEN?

1

Hi, everyone! It's Kazune! We're already at our eighth volume! Thank you for your support, everyone!

I know everyone wants one, but I really want a Nintendo Wii. I really want to play Zelda on the Wii. I know my sister and mother are going to roll their eyes when they read this...Sorry...I'll be a good adult. I promise...

I'm sorry that all I talk about is my family, but... I bought my niece some clothes recently. I chose them all myself.

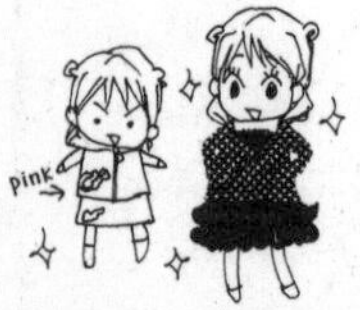
pink

I think that sisters often have different tastes.

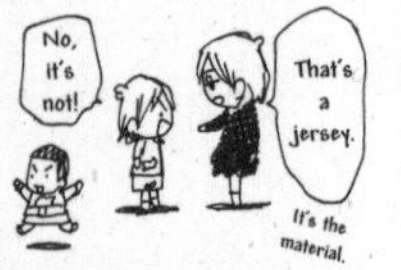
No, it's not!
That's a jersey.
It's the material.

I'm nothing like my sister either. She doesn't draw manga or play games...

Sorry you have such a weird sister.

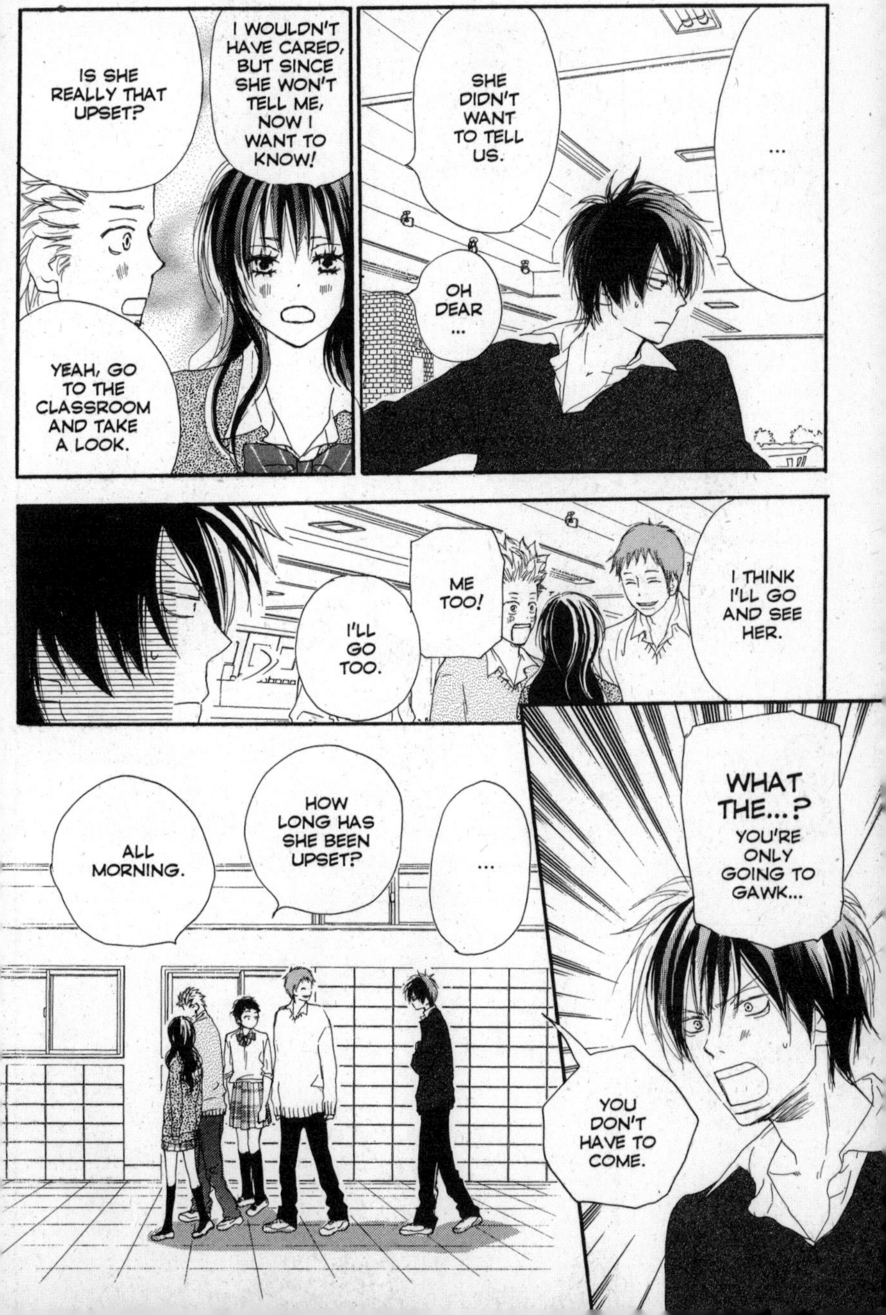
...
SHE DIDN'T WANT TO TELL US.
OH DEAR ...
I WOULDN'T HAVE CARED, BUT SINCE SHE WON'T TELL ME, NOW I WANT TO KNOW!
IS SHE REALLY THAT UPSET?
YEAH, GO TO THE CLASSROOM AND TAKE A LOOK.
I THINK I'LL GO AND SEE HER.
ME TOO!
I'LL GO TOO.
WHAT THE...? YOU'RE ONLY GOING TO GAWK...
YOU DON'T HAVE TO COME.
...
HOW LONG HAS SHE BEEN UPSET?
ALL MORNING.

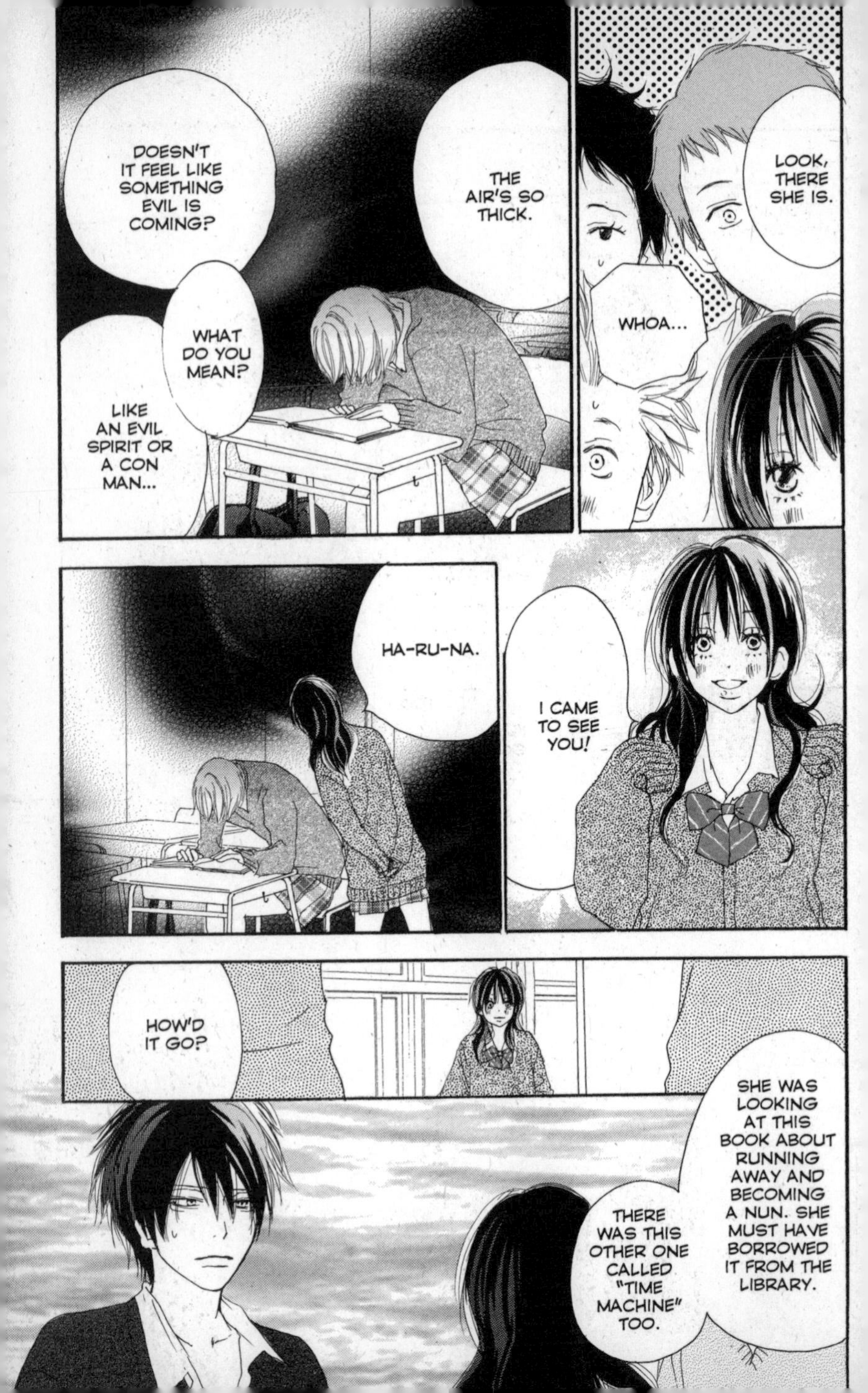
LOOK, THERE SHE IS.
WHOA...
THE AIR'S SO THICK.
DOESN'T IT FEEL LIKE SOMETHING EVIL IS COMING?
WHAT DO YOU MEAN?
LIKE AN EVIL SPIRIT OR A CON MAN...
I CAME TO SEE YOU!
HA-RU-NA.
HOW'D IT GO?
SHE WAS LOOKING AT THIS BOOK ABOUT RUNNING AWAY AND BECOMING A NUN. SHE MUST HAVE BORROWED IT FROM THE LIBRARY.
THERE WAS THIS OTHER ONE CALLED "TIME MACHINE" TOO.

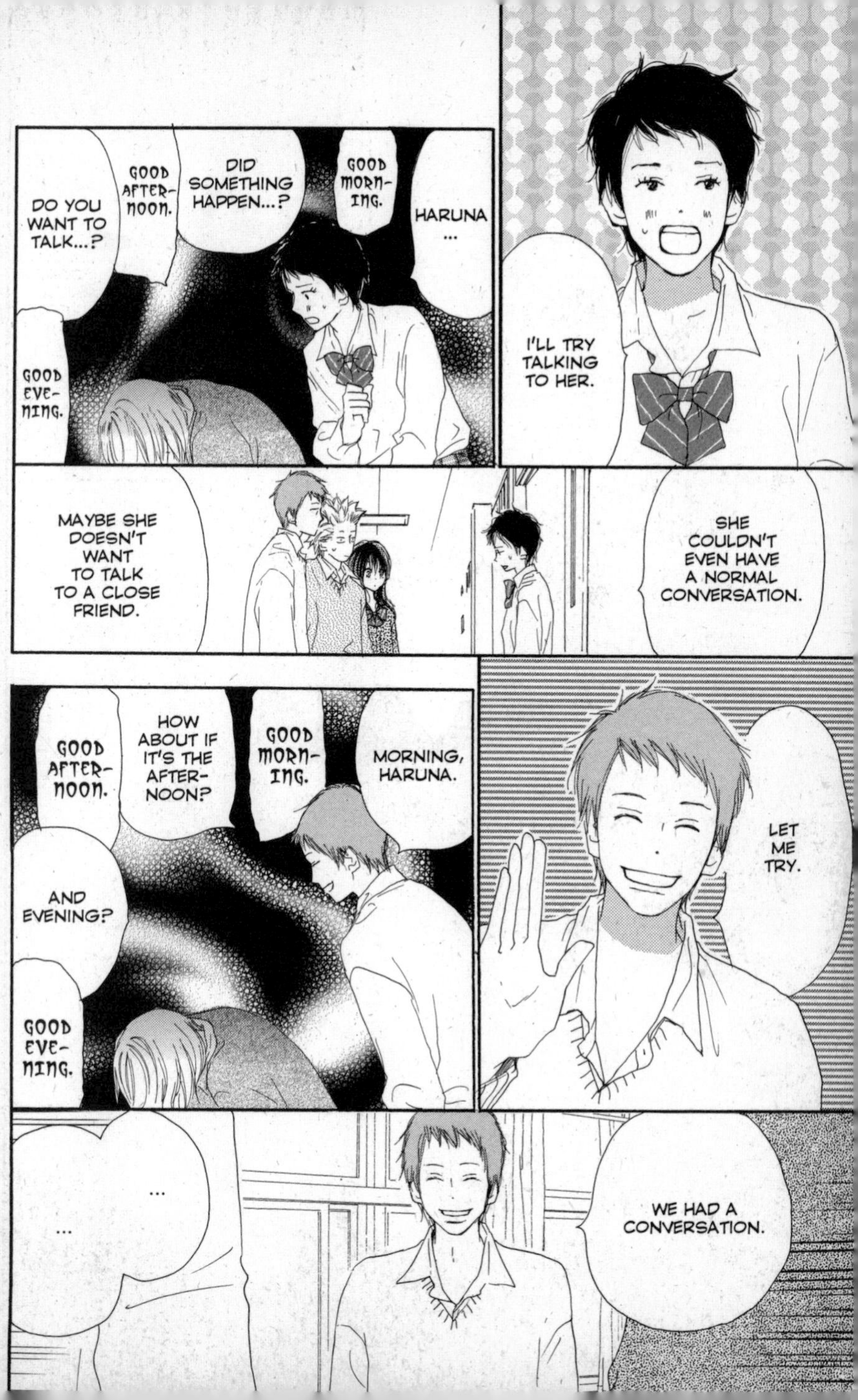

I'LL TRY TALKING TO HER.
HARUNA ...
GOOD MORN-ING.
DID SOMETHING HAPPEN...?
GOOD AFTER-NOON.
DO YOU WANT TO TALK...?
GOOD EVE-NING.
SHE COULDN'T EVEN HAVE A NORMAL CONVERSATION.
MAYBE SHE DOESN'T WANT TO TALK TO A CLOSE FRIEND.
LET ME TRY.
MORNING, HARUNA.
GOOD MORN-ING.
HOW ABOUT IF IT'S THE AFTER-NOON?
GOOD AFTER-NOON.
AND EVENING?
GOOD EVE-NING.
WE HAD A CONVERSATION.
...
...

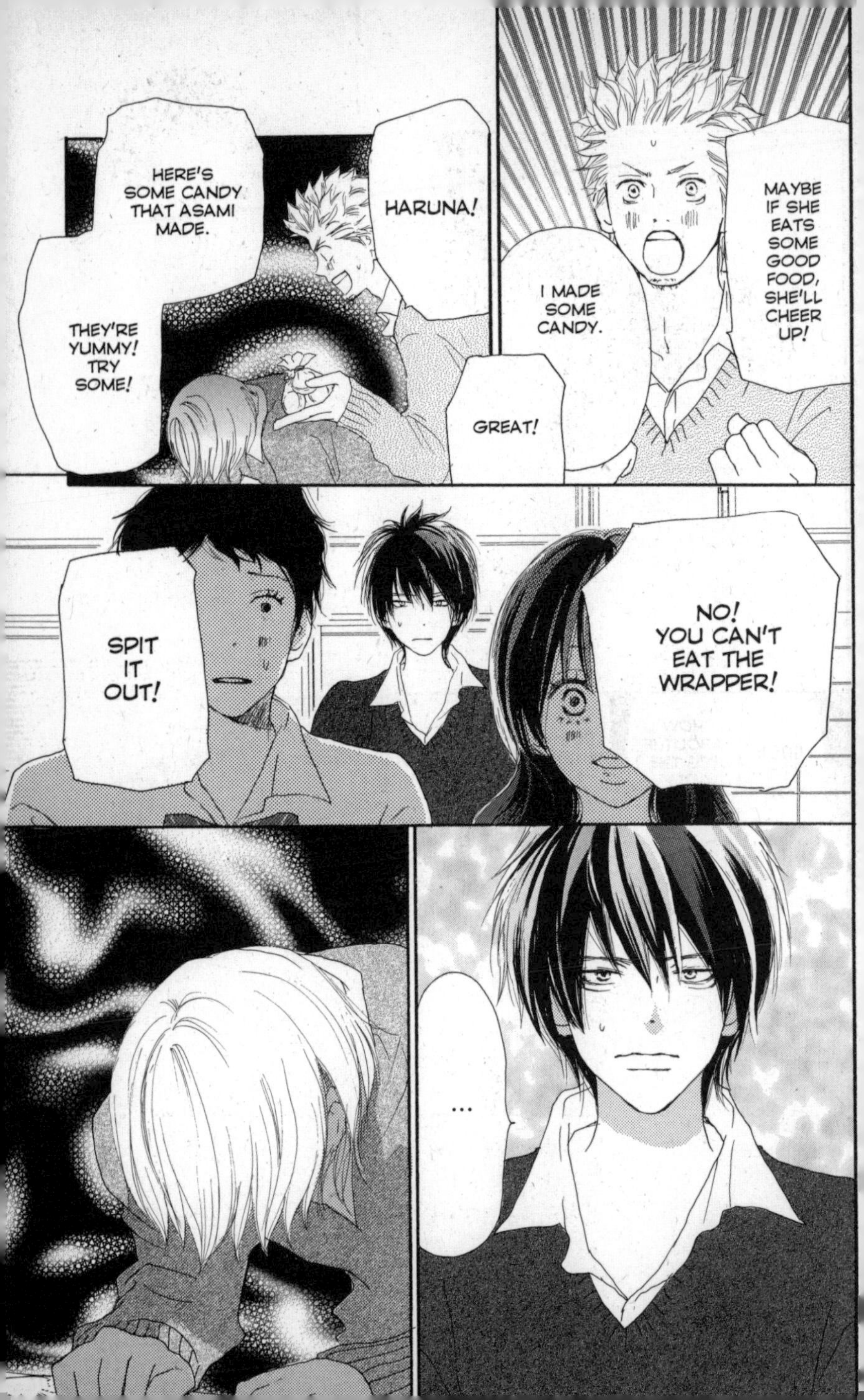
MAYBE IF SHE EATS SOME GOOD FOOD, SHE'LL CHEER UP!
I MADE SOME CANDY.
GREAT!
HARUNA!
HERE'S SOME CANDY THAT ASAMI MADE.
THEY'RE YUMMY! TRY SOME!
NO! YOU CAN'T EAT THE WRAPPER!
SPIT IT OUT!
...

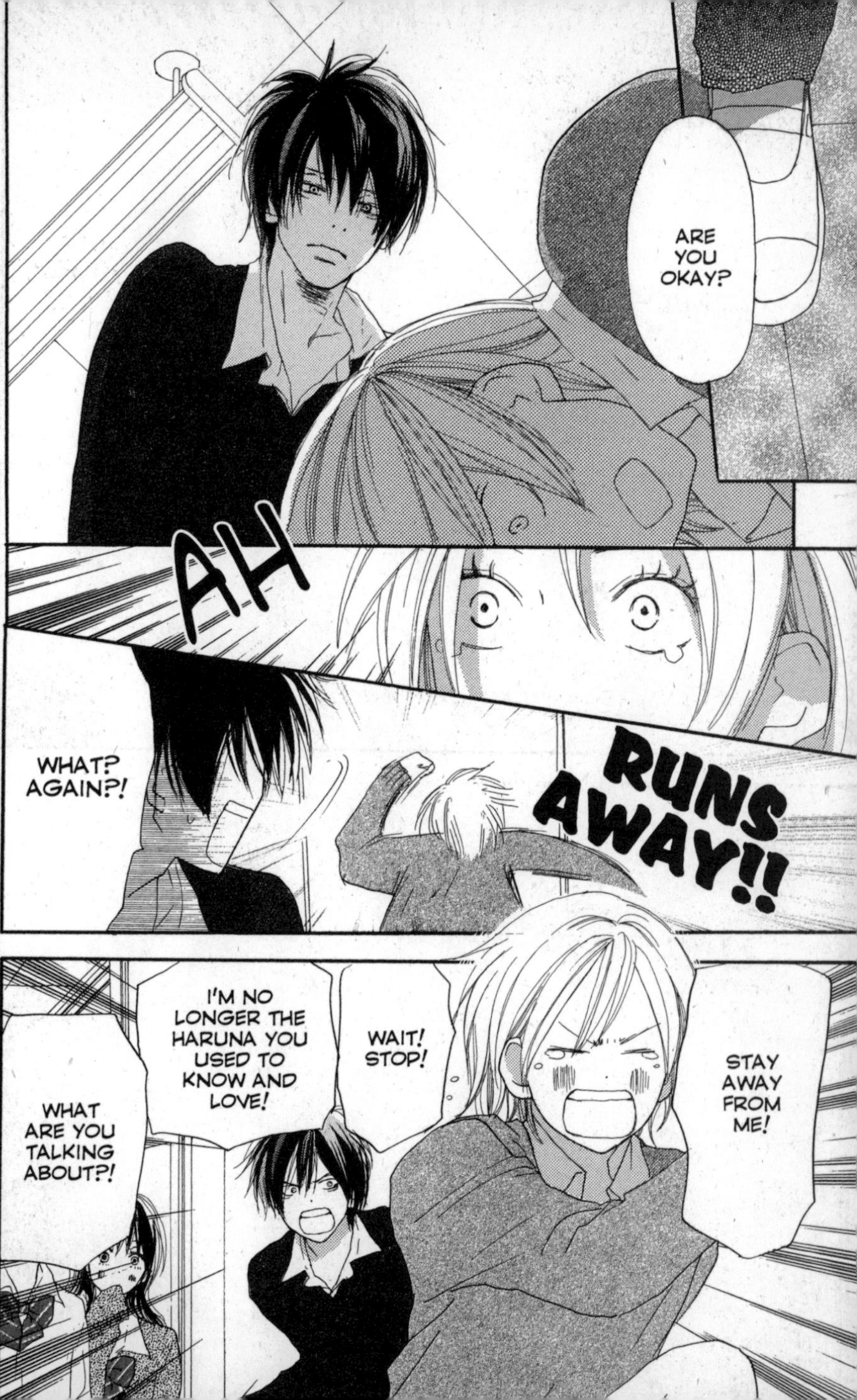
ARE YOU OKAY?
AH
RUNS AWAY!!
WHAT? AGAIN?!
STAY AWAY FROM ME!
WAIT! STOP!
I'M NO LONGER THE HARUNA YOU USED TO KNOW AND LOVE!
WHAT ARE YOU TALKING ABOUT?!

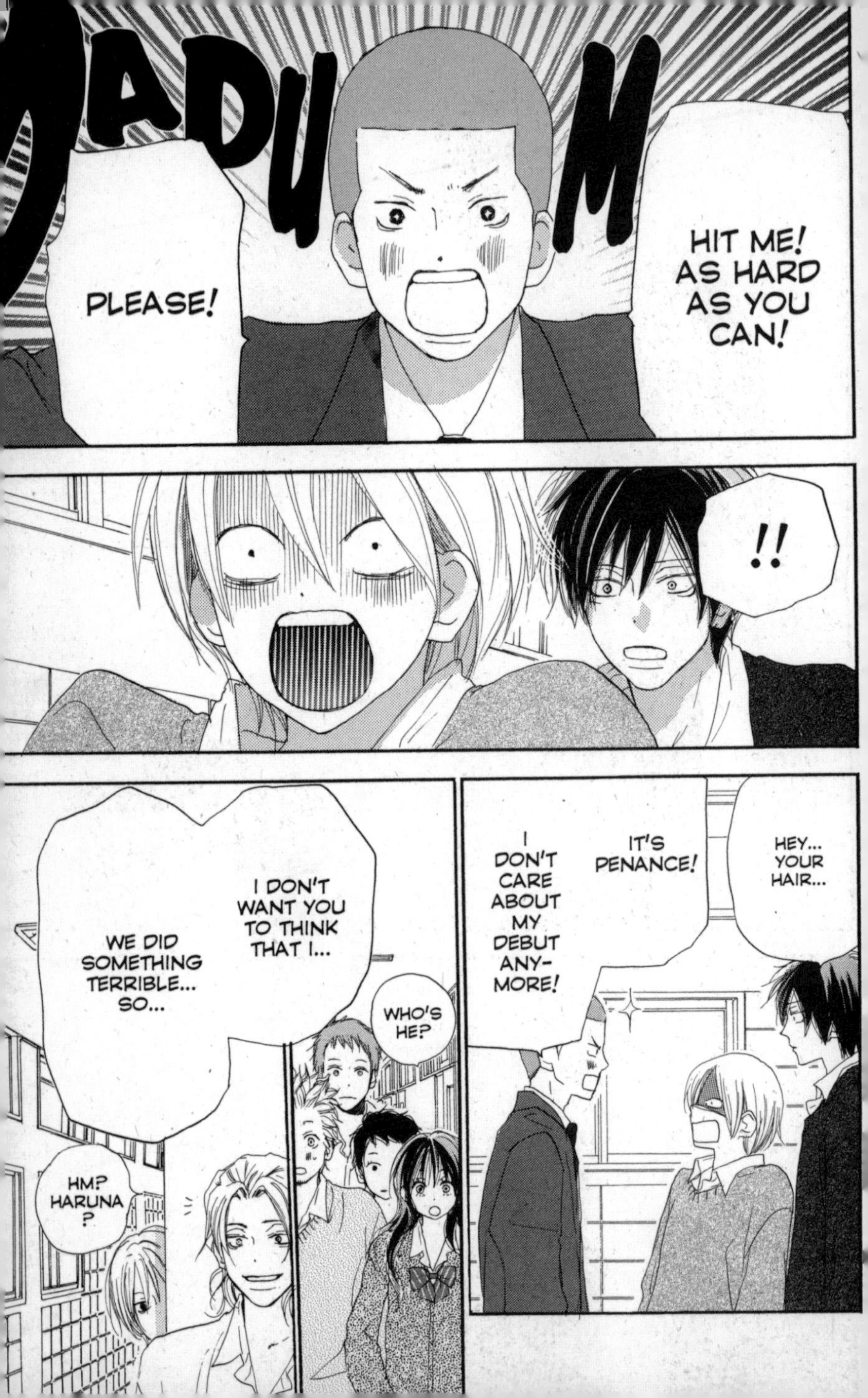
ADUM
HIT ME! AS HARD AS YOU CAN!
PLEASE!
!!
HEY... YOUR HAIR...
IT'S PENANCE!
I DON'T CARE ABOUT MY DEBUT ANY-MORE!
I DON'T WANT YOU TO THINK THAT I...
WE DID SOMETHING TERRIBLE... SO...
WHO'S HE?
HM? HARUNA?

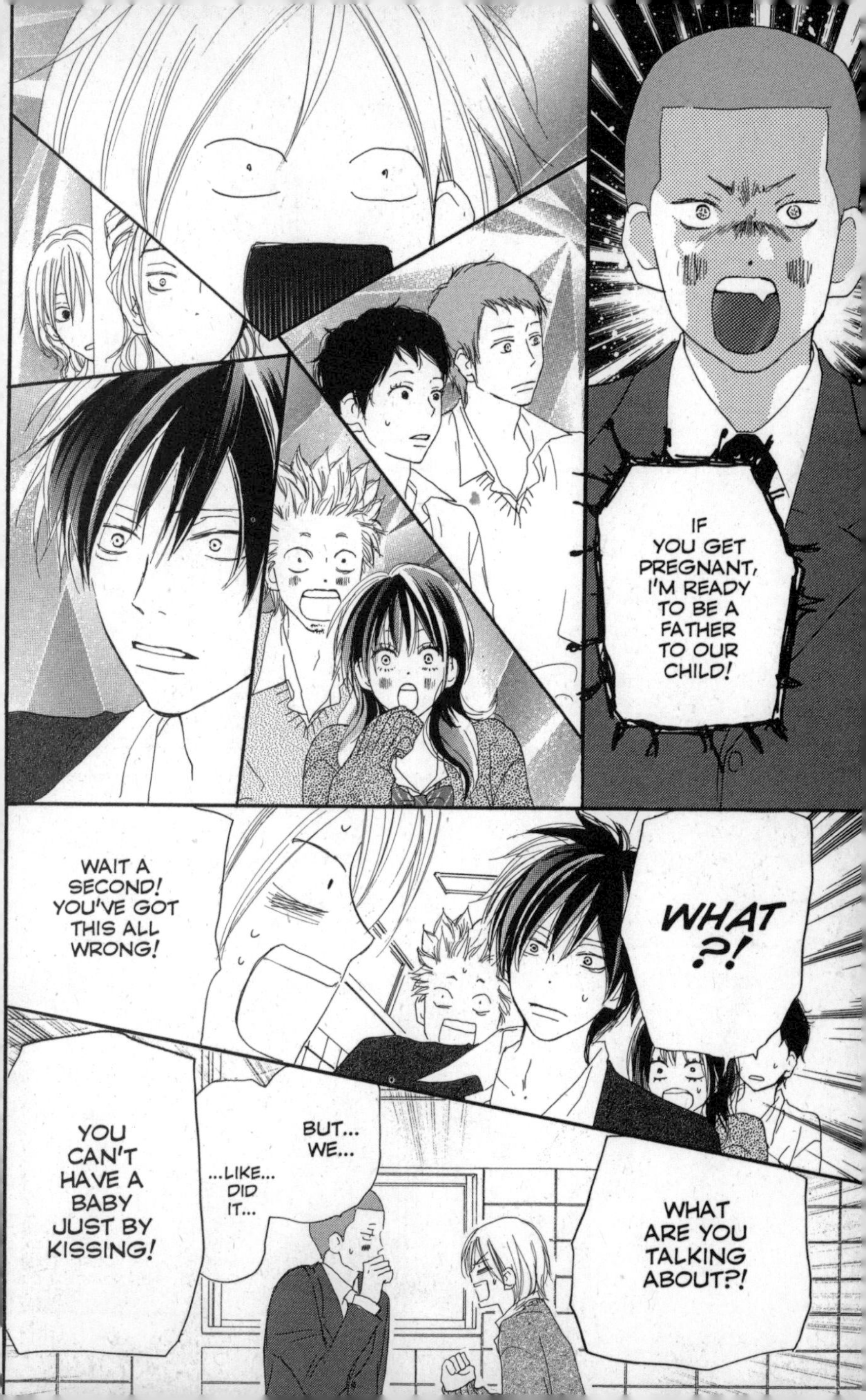
IF YOU GET PREGNANT, I'M READY TO BE A FATHER TO OUR CHILD!
WHAT?!
WAIT A SECOND! YOU'VE GOT THIS ALL WRONG!
WHAT ARE YOU TALKING ABOUT?!
BUT... WE...
...LIKE... DID IT...
YOU CAN'T HAVE A BABY JUST BY KISSING!

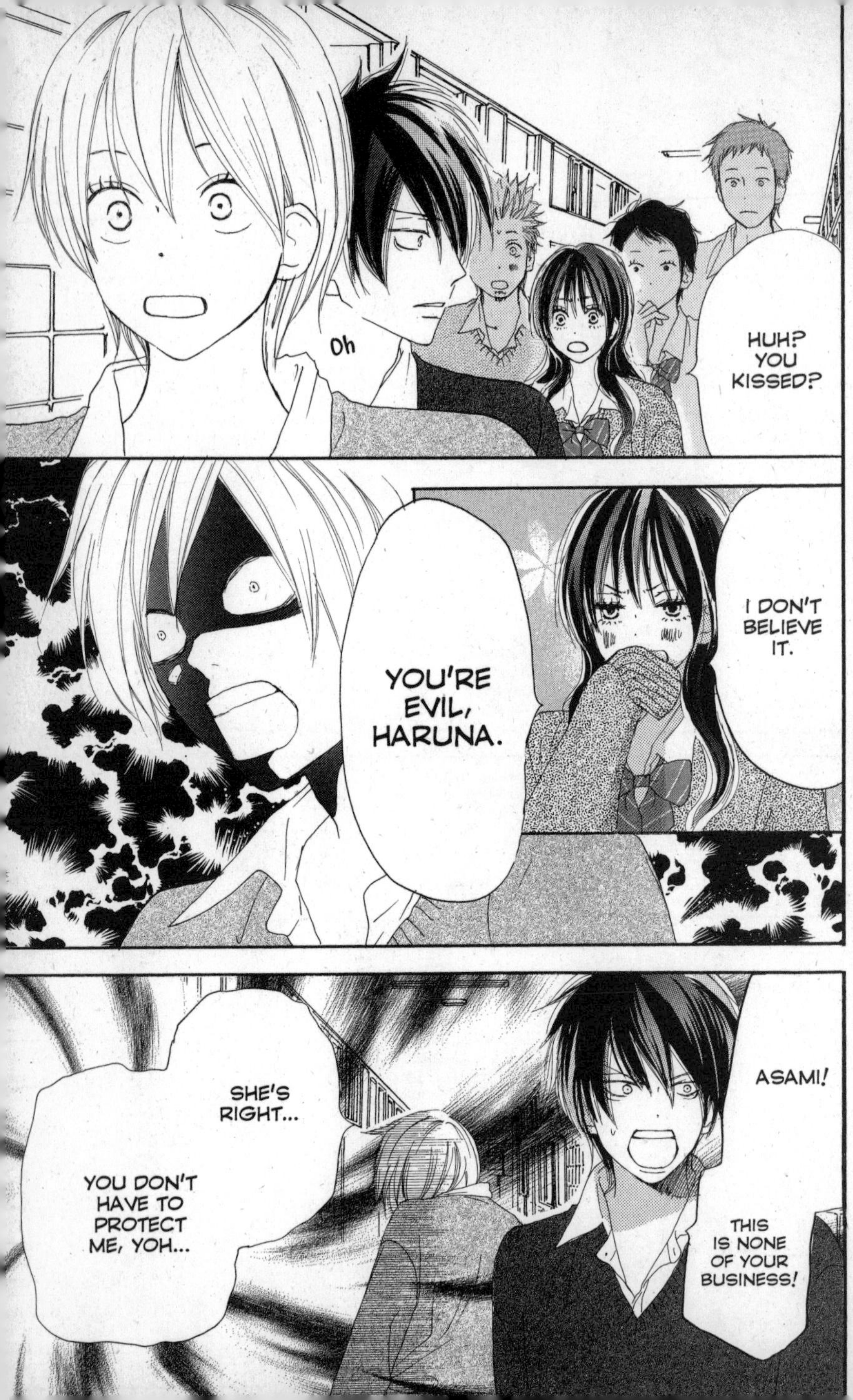
HUH? YOU KISSED?
Oh
I DON'T BELIEVE IT.
YOU'RE EVIL, HARUNA.
ASAMI!
THIS IS NONE OF YOUR BUSINESS!
SHE'S RIGHT...
YOU DON'T HAVE TO PROTECT ME, YOH...

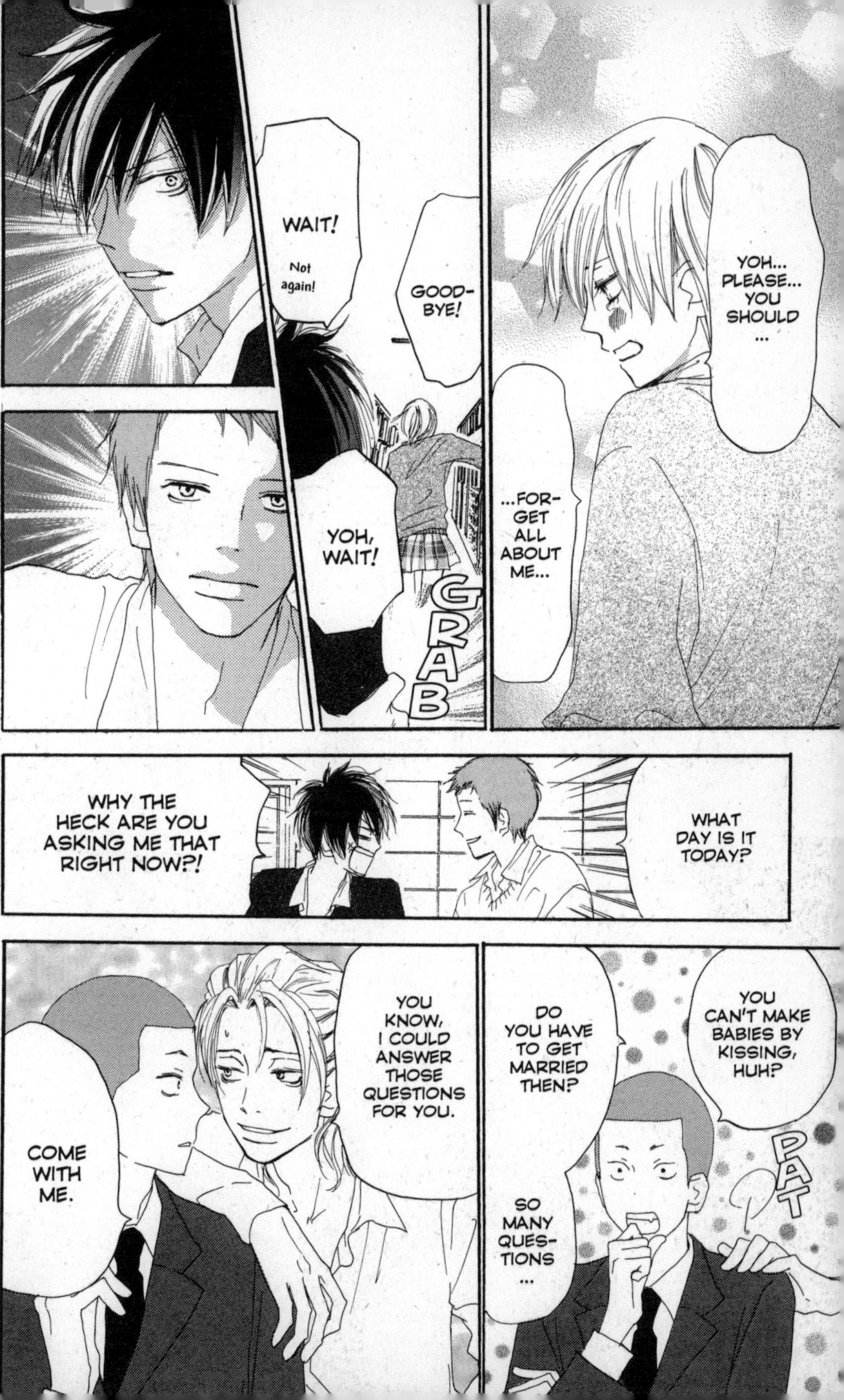
YOH... PLEASE... YOU SHOULD ...
...FOR-GET ALL ABOUT ME...
GOOD-BYE!
WAIT!
Not again!
YOH, WAIT!
GRAB
WHAT DAY IS IT TODAY?
WHY THE HECK ARE YOU ASKING ME THAT RIGHT NOW?!
YOU CAN'T MAKE BABIES BY KISSING, HUH?
DO YOU HAVE TO GET MARRIED THEN?
PAT
SO MANY QUES-TIONS ...
YOU KNOW, I COULD ANSWER THOSE QUESTIONS FOR YOU.
COME WITH ME.

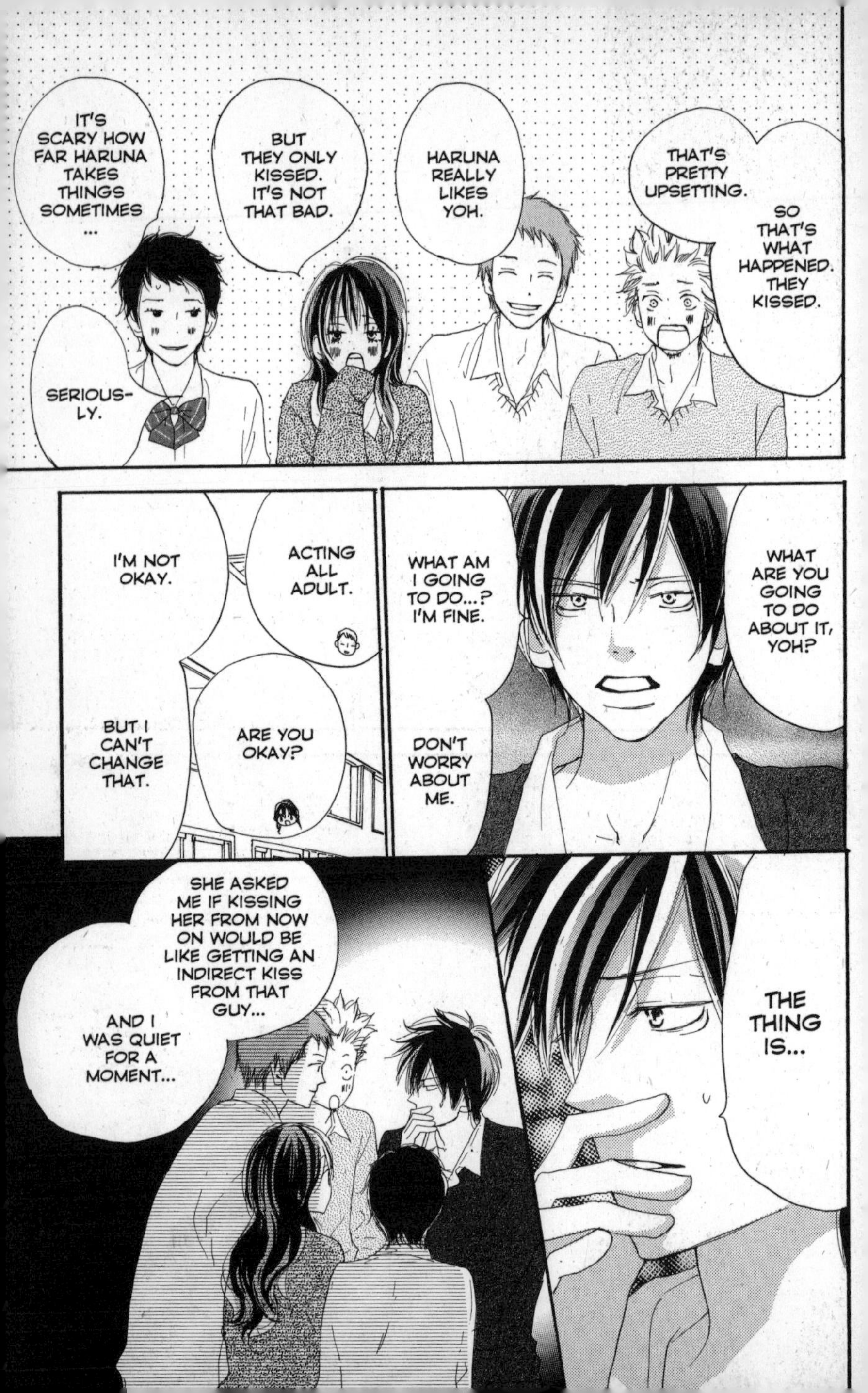
THAT'S PRETTY UPSETTING.
SO THAT'S WHAT HAPPENED. THEY KISSED.
HARUNA REALLY LIKES YOH.
BUT THEY ONLY KISSED. IT'S NOT THAT BAD.
IT'S SCARY HOW FAR HARUNA TAKES THINGS SOMETIMES...
SERIOUS-LY.
WHAT ARE YOU GOING TO DO ABOUT IT, YOH?
WHAT AM I GOING TO DO...? I'M FINE.
DON'T WORRY ABOUT ME.
ACTING ALL ADULT.
I'M NOT OKAY.
ARE YOU OKAY?
BUT I CAN'T CHANGE THAT.
THE THING IS...
SHE ASKED ME IF KISSING HER FROM NOW ON WOULD BE LIKE GETTING AN INDIRECT KISS FROM THAT GUY...
AND I WAS QUIET FOR A MOMENT...

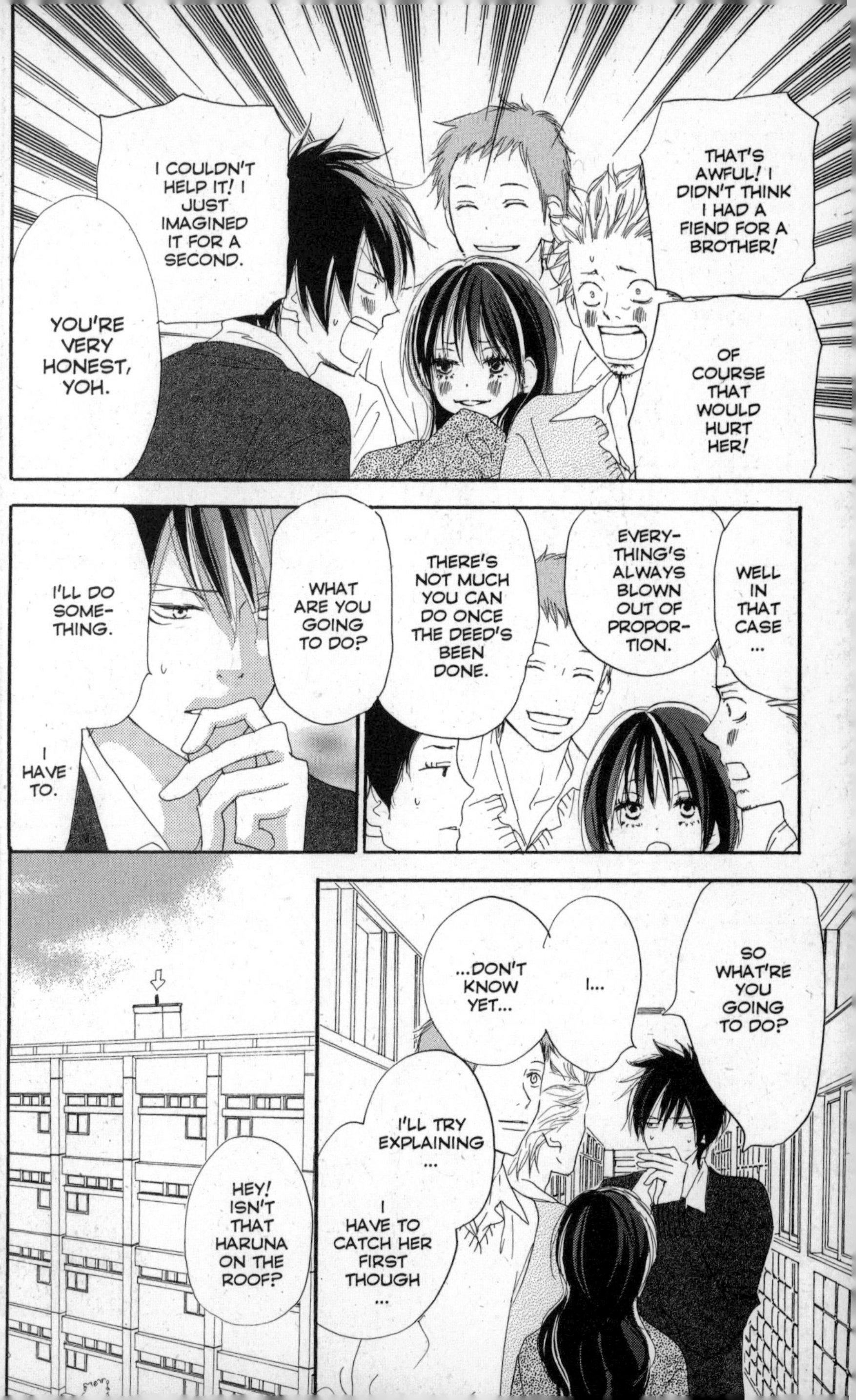
THAT'S AWFUL! I DIDN'T THINK I HAD A FIEND FOR A BROTHER!
OF COURSE THAT WOULD HURT HER!
I COULDN'T HELP IT! I JUST IMAGINED IT FOR A SECOND.
YOU'RE VERY HONEST, YOH.
WELL IN THAT CASE ...
EVERY-THING'S ALWAYS BLOWN OUT OF PROPOR-TION.
THERE'S NOT MUCH YOU CAN DO ONCE THE DEED'S BEEN DONE.
WHAT ARE YOU GOING TO DO?
I'LL DO SOME-THING.
I HAVE TO.
SO WHAT'RE YOU GOING TO DO?
I...
...DON'T KNOW YET...
I'LL TRY EXPLAINING ...
I HAVE TO CATCH HER FIRST THOUGH ...
HEY! ISN'T THAT HARUNA ON THE ROOF?

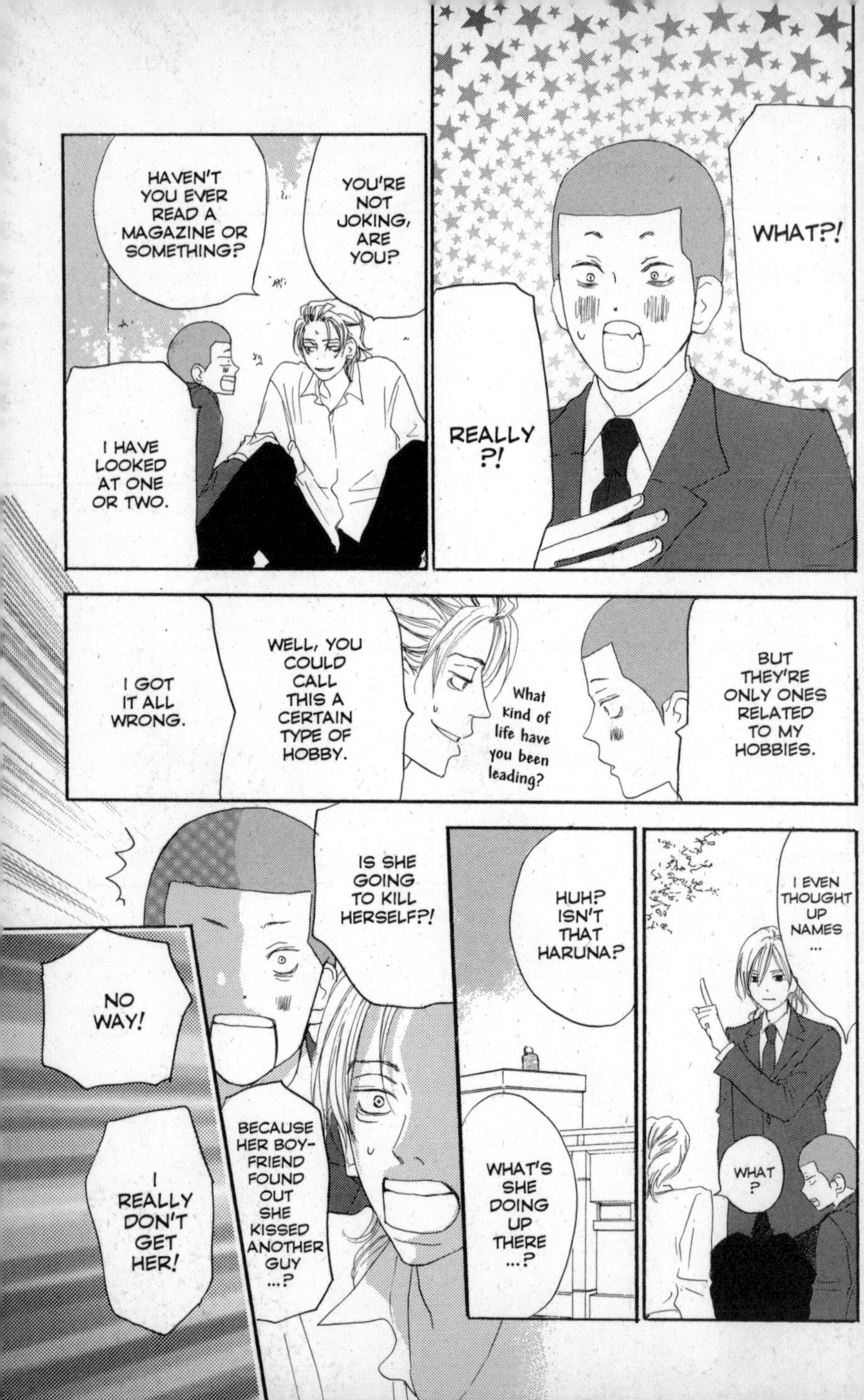
WHAT?!
REALLY ?!
YOU'RE NOT JOKING, ARE YOU?
HAVEN'T YOU EVER READ A MAGAZINE OR SOMETHING?
I HAVE LOOKED AT ONE OR TWO.
BUT THEY'RE ONLY ONES RELATED TO MY HOBBIES.
What kind of life have you been leading?
WELL, YOU COULD CALL THIS A CERTAIN TYPE OF HOBBY.
I GOT IT ALL WRONG.
I EVEN THOUGHT UP NAMES ...
WHAT ?
HUH? ISN'T THAT HARUNA?
WHAT'S SHE DOING UP THERE ...?
IS SHE GOING TO KILL HERSELF?!
NO WAY!
BECAUSE HER BOY-FRIEND FOUND OUT SHE KISSED ANOTHER GUY ...?
I REALLY DON'T GET HER!

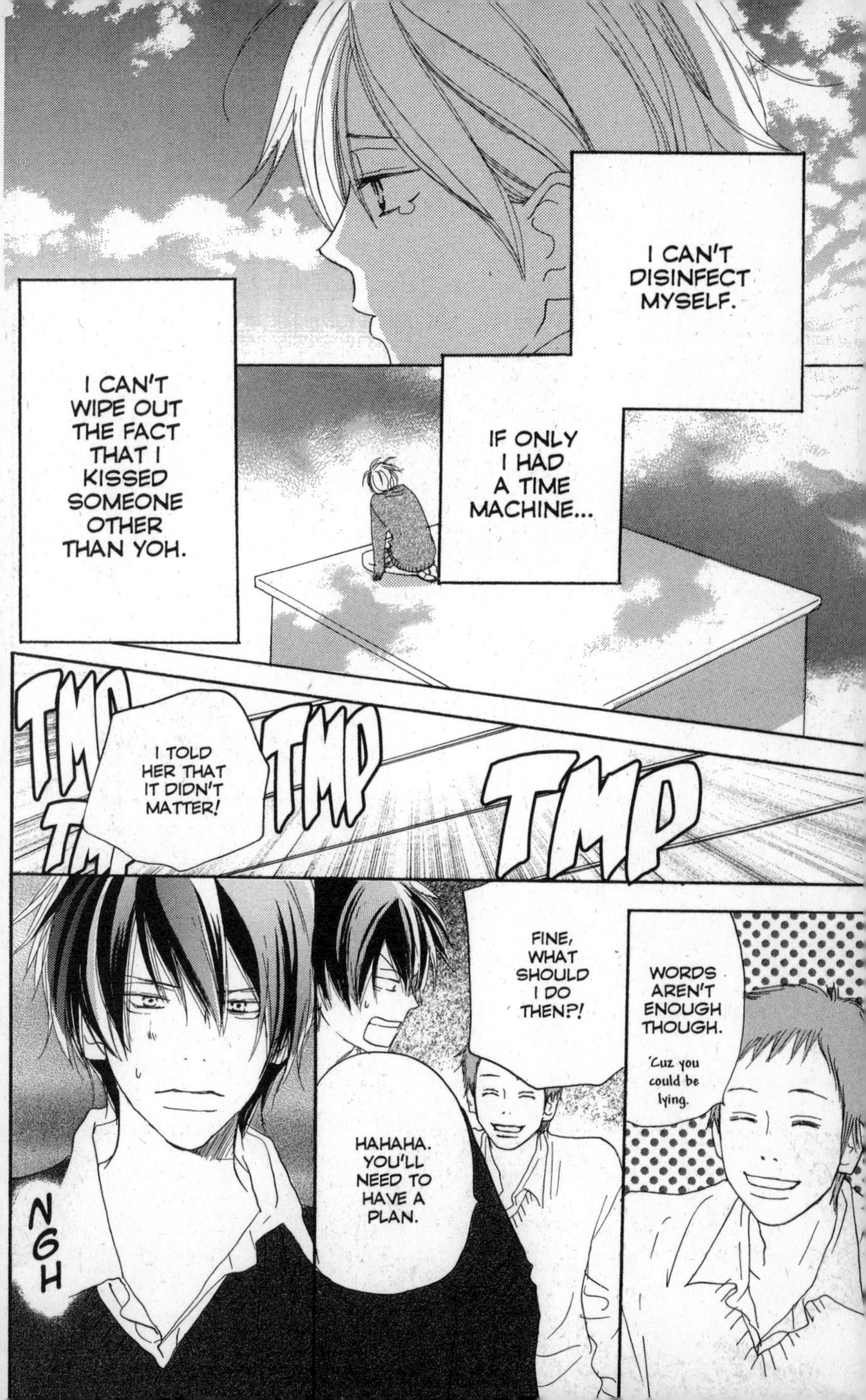
I CAN'T DISINFECT MYSELF.
IF ONLY I HAD A TIME MACHINE...
I CAN'T WIPE OUT THE FACT THAT I KISSED SOMEONE OTHER THAN YOH.
TMP
TMP
TMP
TMP
I TOLD HER THAT IT DIDN'T MATTER!
WORDS AREN'T ENOUGH THOUGH.
'Cuz you could be lying.
FINE, WHAT SHOULD I DO THEN?!
HAHAHA. YOU'LL NEED TO HAVE A PLAN.
NGH

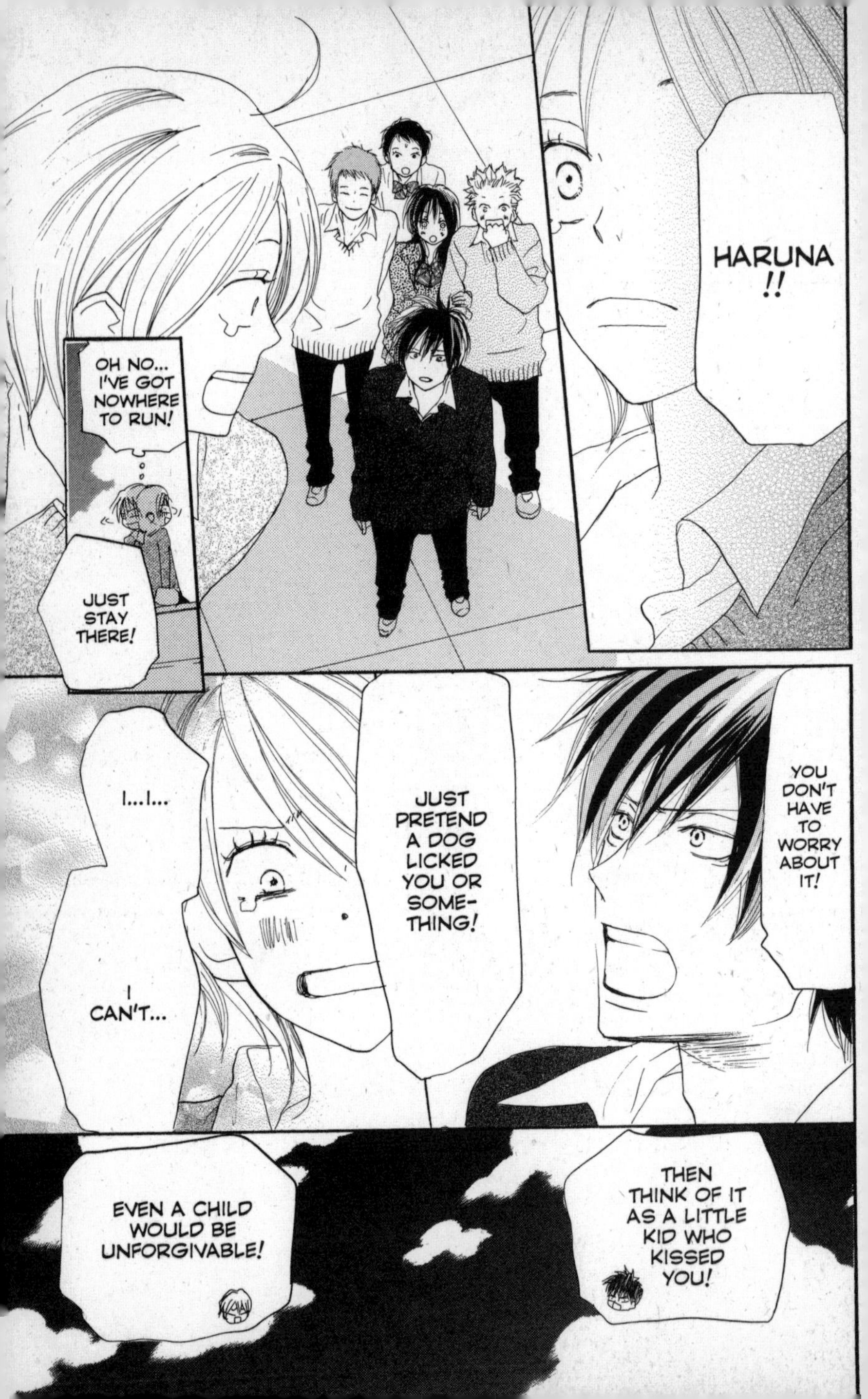
HARUNA!!
OH NO... I'VE GOT NOWHERE TO RUN!
JUST STAY THERE!
YOU DON'T HAVE TO WORRY ABOUT IT!
JUST PRETEND A DOG LICKED YOU OR SOME-THING!
I...I...
I CAN'T...
THEN THINK OF IT AS A LITTLE KID WHO KISSED YOU!
EVEN A CHILD WOULD BE UNFORGIVABLE!

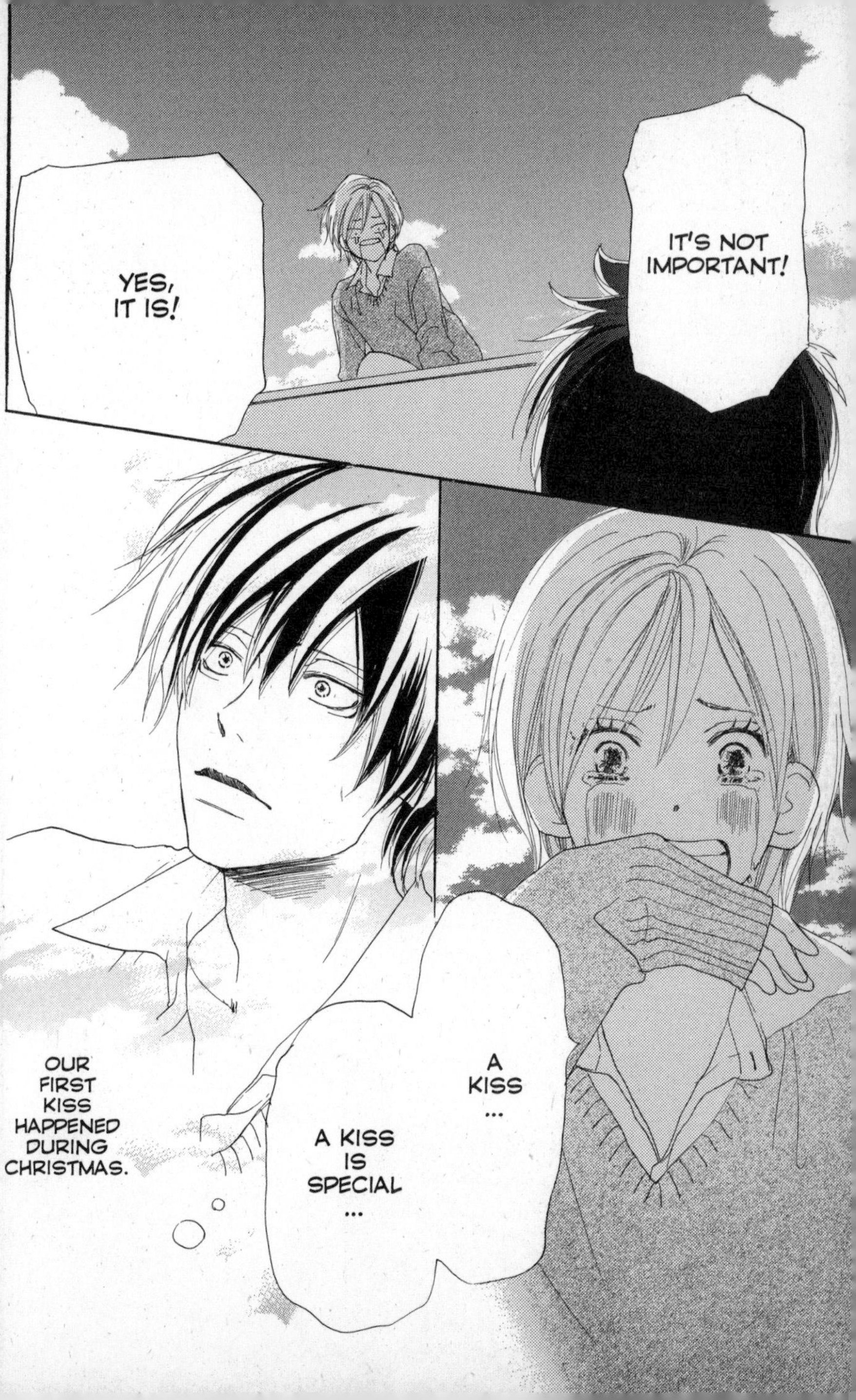
IT'S NOT IMPORTANT!
YES, IT IS!
A KISS ...
A KISS IS SPECIAL ...
OUR FIRST KISS HAPPENED DURING CHRISTMAS.

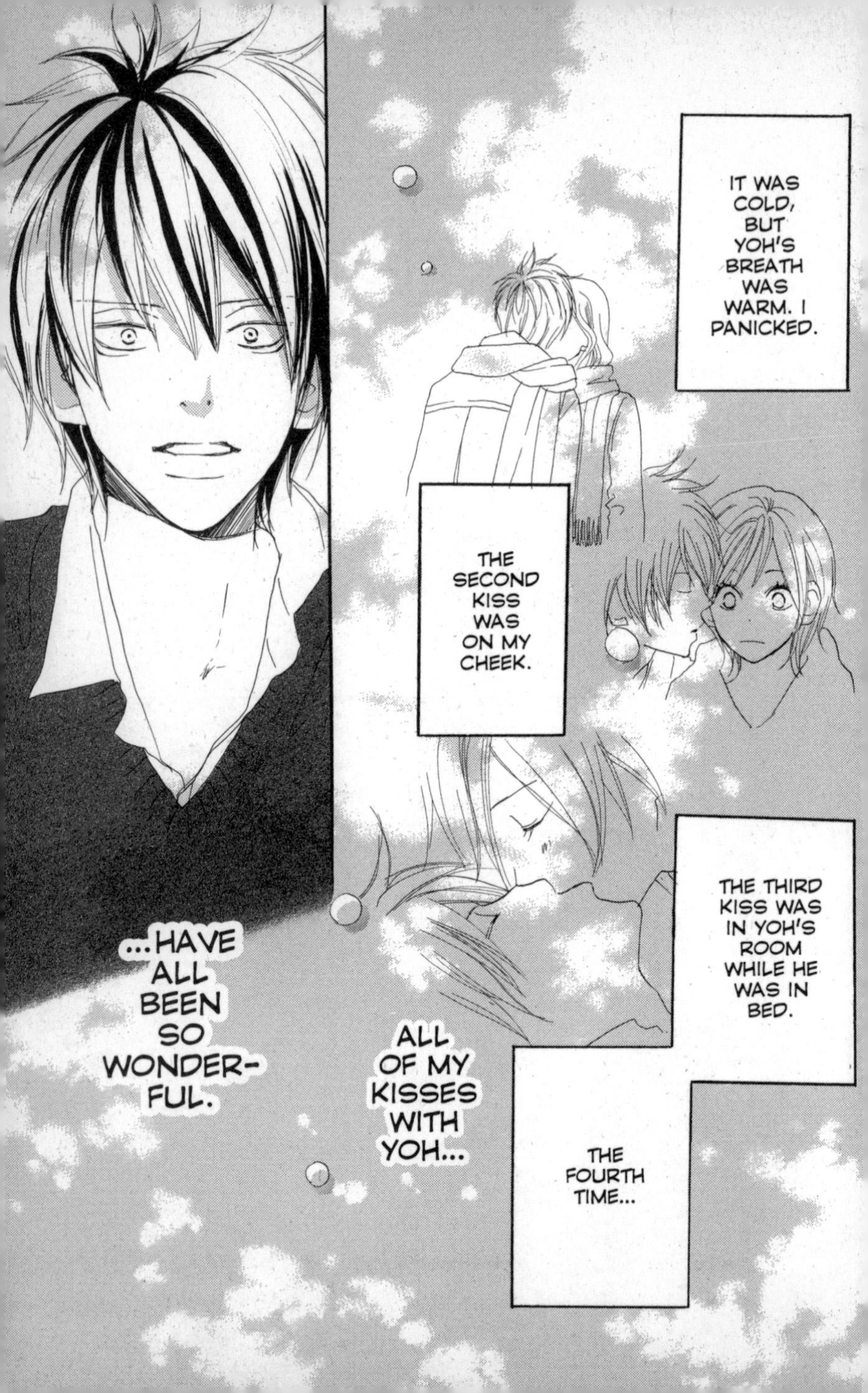
IT WAS COLD, BUT YOH'S BREATH WAS WARM. I PANICKED.
THE SECOND KISS WAS ON MY CHEEK.
THE THIRD KISS WAS IN YOH'S ROOM WHILE HE WAS IN BED.
THE FOURTH TIME...
ALL OF MY KISSES WITH YOH...
...HAVE ALL BEEN SO WONDER-FUL.

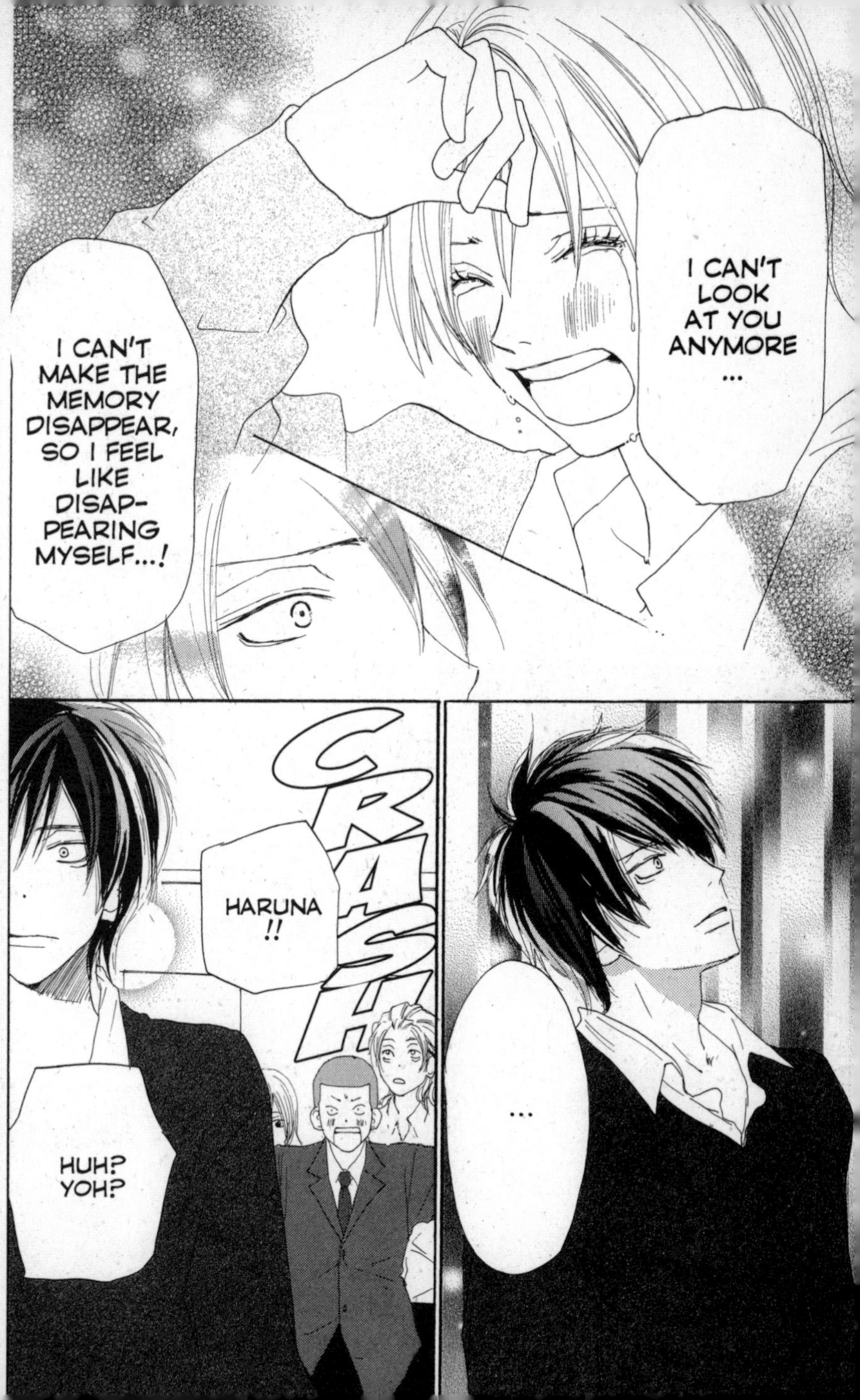
I CAN'T LOOK AT YOU ANYMORE ...
I CAN'T MAKE THE MEMORY DISAPPEAR, SO I FEEL LIKE DISAP-PEARING MYSELF...!
...
CRASH
HARUNA !!
HUH? YOH?

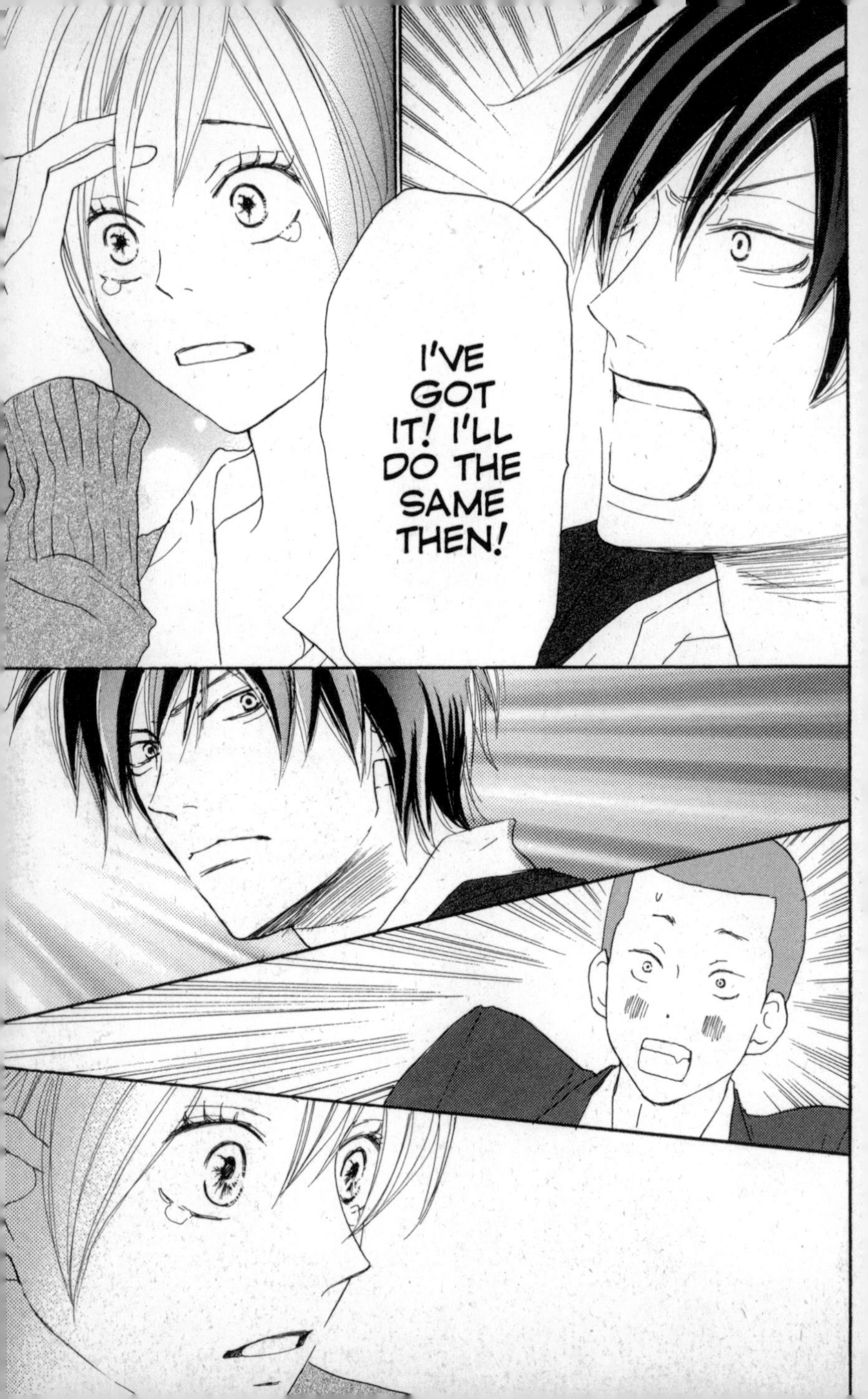
I'VE GOT IT! I'LL DO THE SAME THEN!

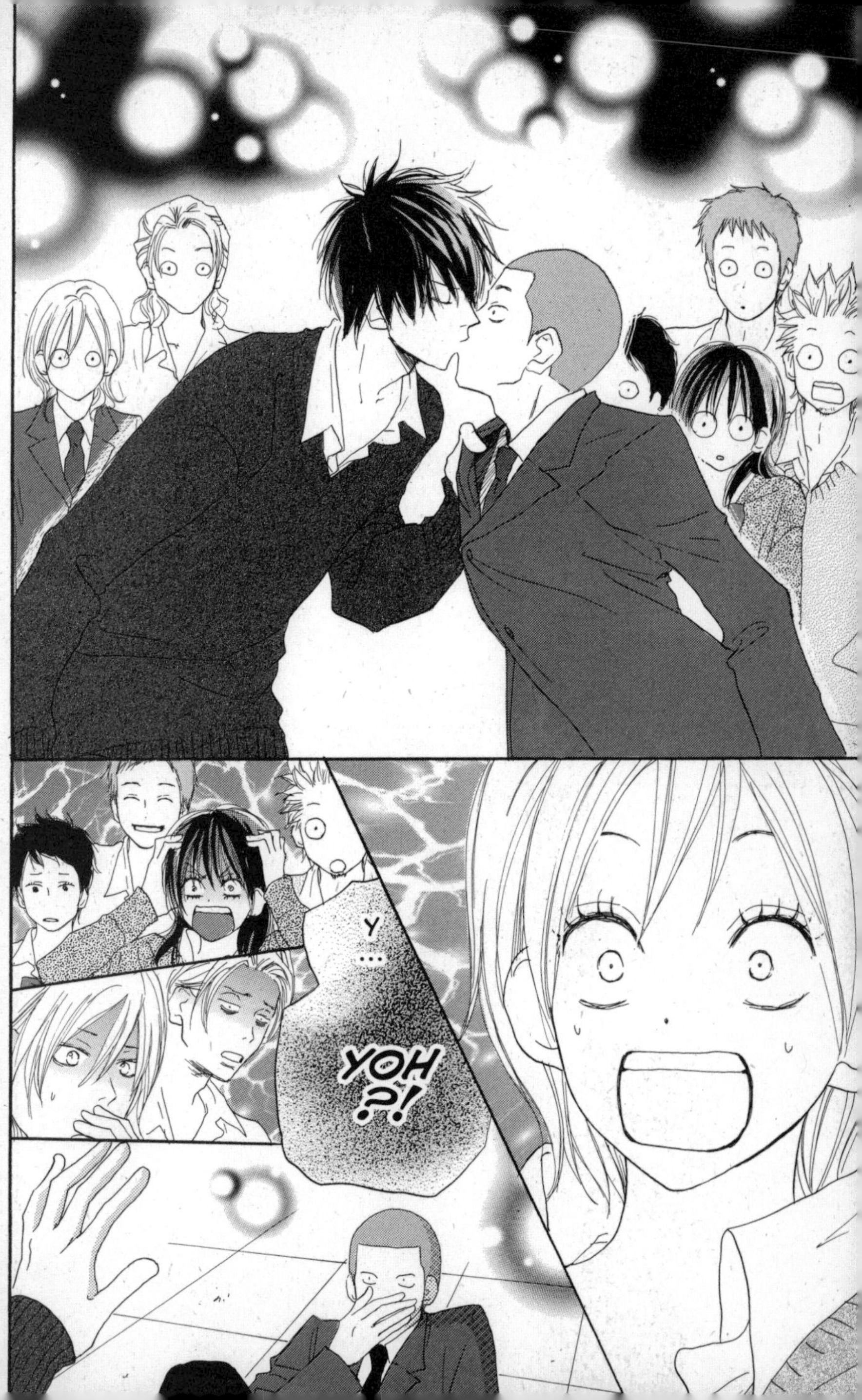
Y
...
YOH ?!

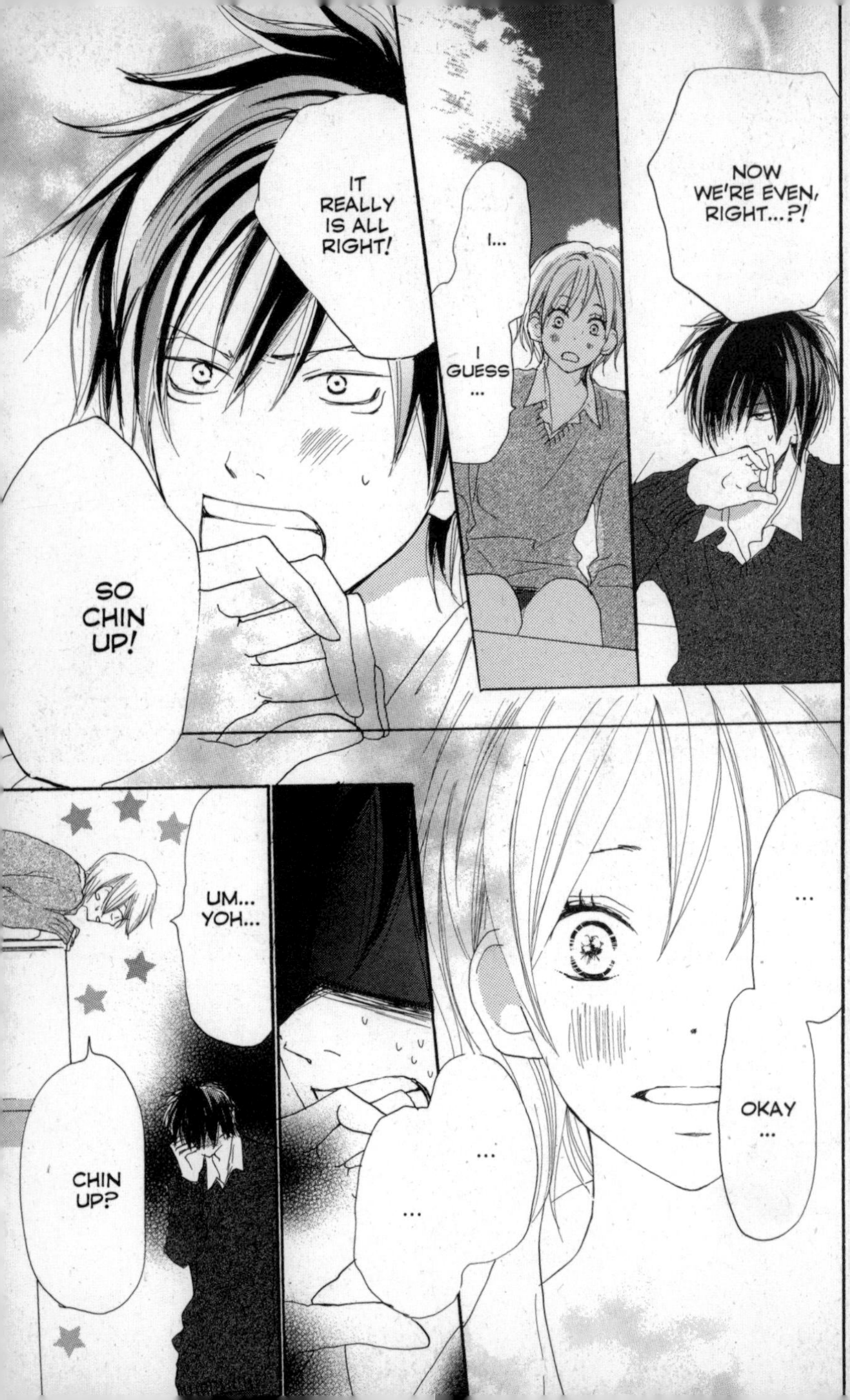
NOW WE'RE EVEN, RIGHT...?!
I...
I GUESS...
IT REALLY IS ALL RIGHT!
SO CHIN UP!
...
OKAY...
...
...
UM... YOH...
CHIN UP?

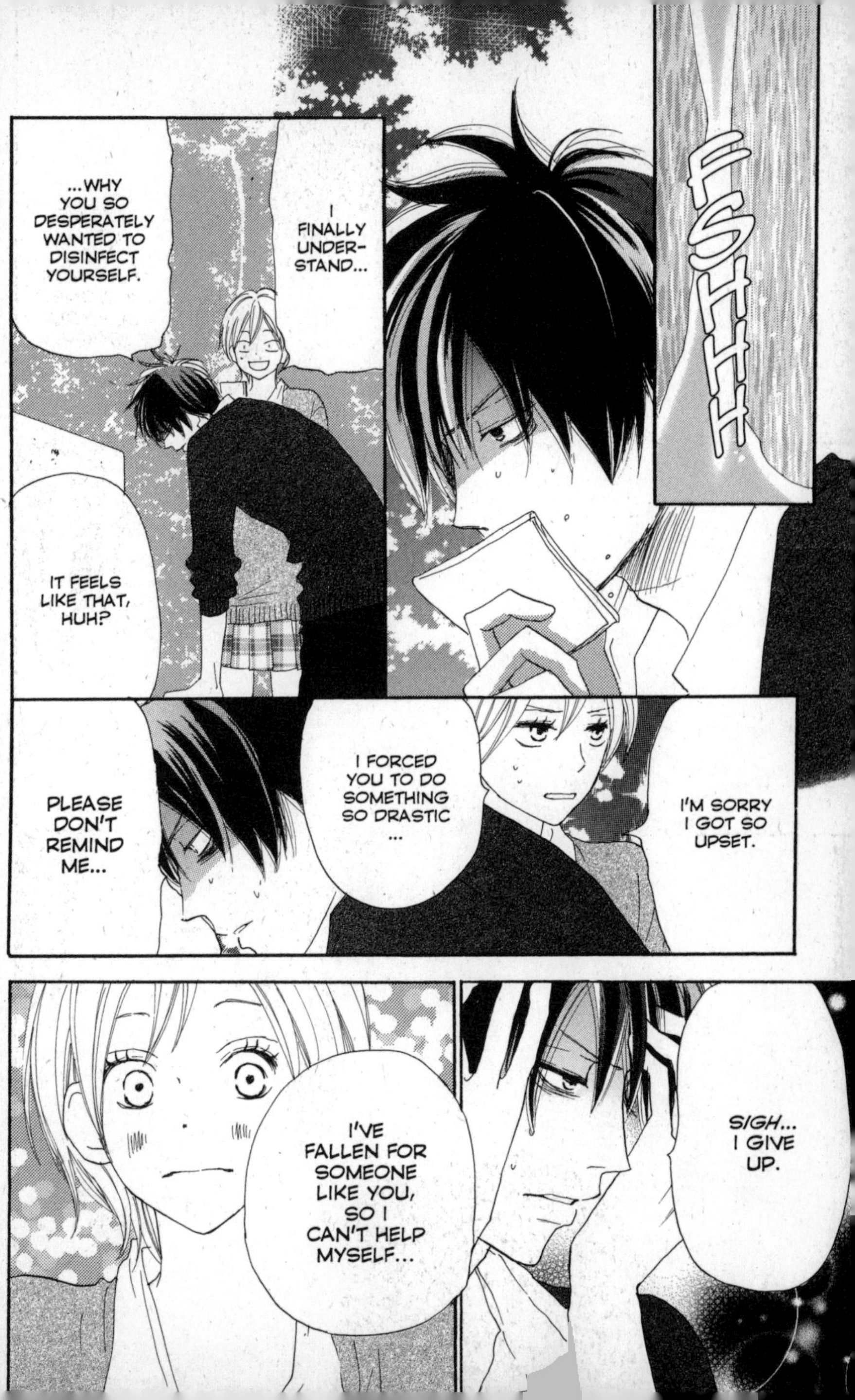
FSHHHH
I FINALLY UNDER-STAND...
...WHY YOU SO DESPERATELY WANTED TO DISINFECT YOURSELF.
IT FEELS LIKE THAT, HUH?
I'M SORRY I GOT SO UPSET.
I FORCED YOU TO DO SOMETHING SO DRASTIC ...
PLEASE DON'T REMIND ME...
SIGH... I GIVE UP.
I'VE FALLEN FOR SOMEONE LIKE YOU, SO I CAN'T HELP MYSELF...

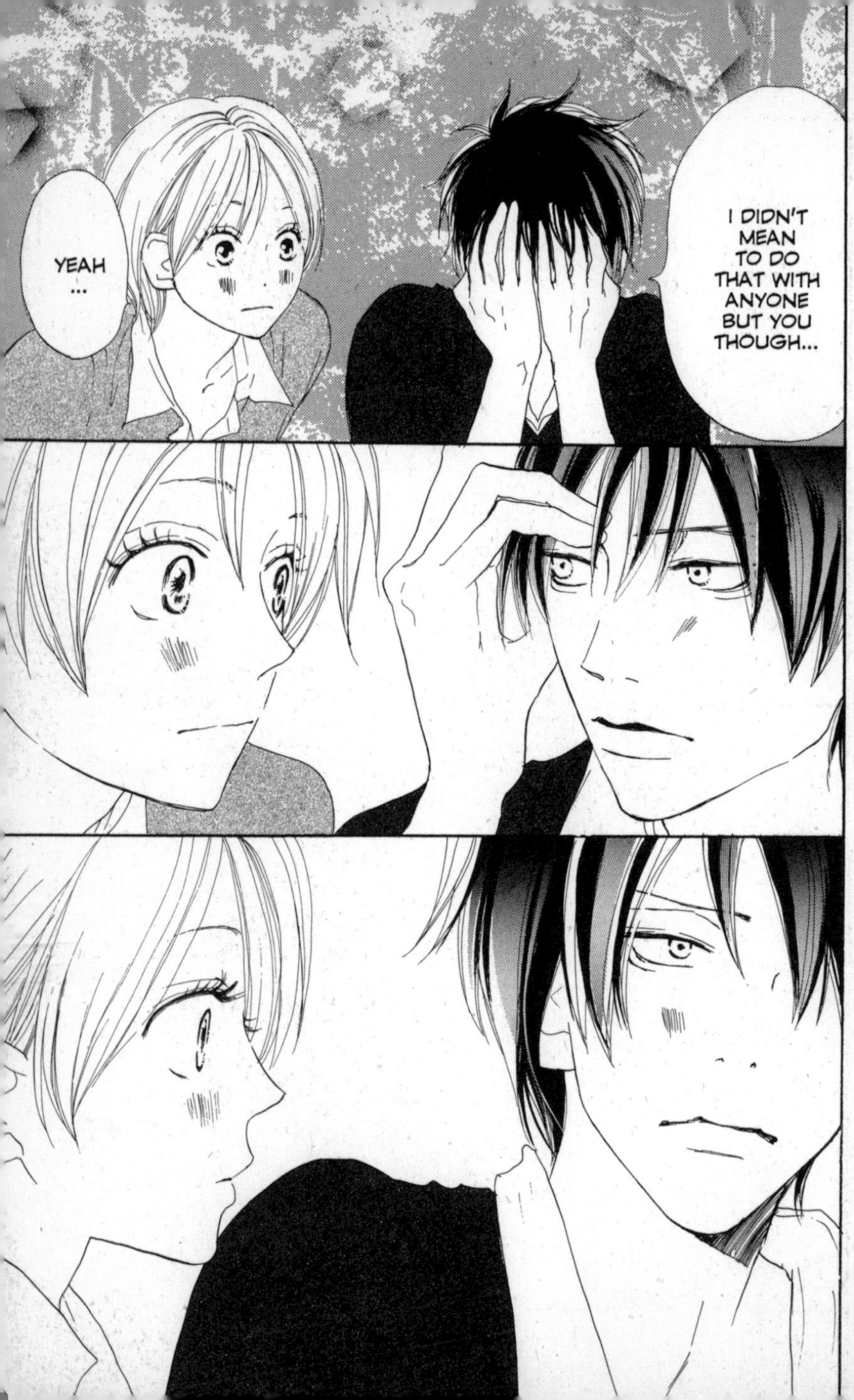
I DIDN'T MEAN TO DO THAT WITH ANYONE BUT YOU THOUGH...
YEAH ...

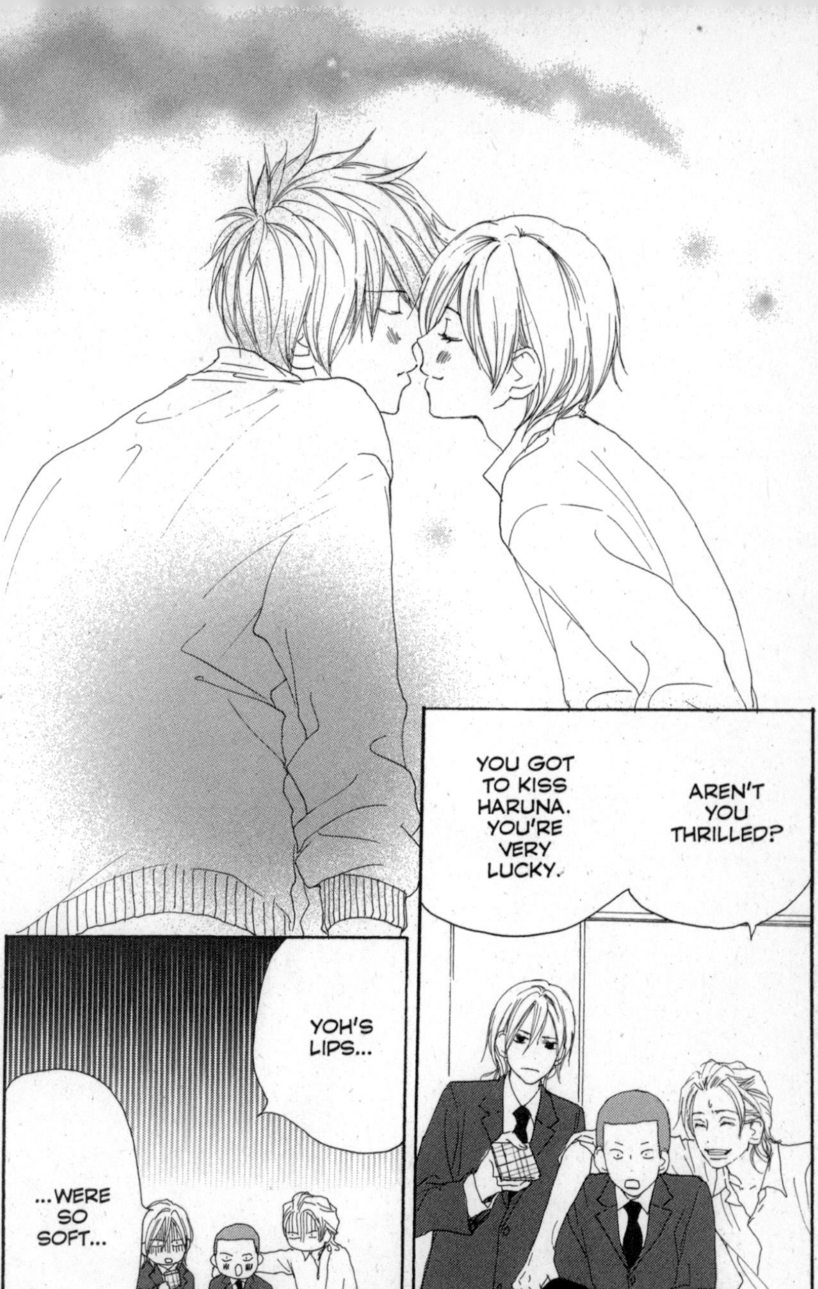
YOU GOT TO KISS HARUNA. YOU'RE VERY LUCKY.
AREN'T YOU THRILLED?
YOH'S LIPS...
...WERE SO SOFT...

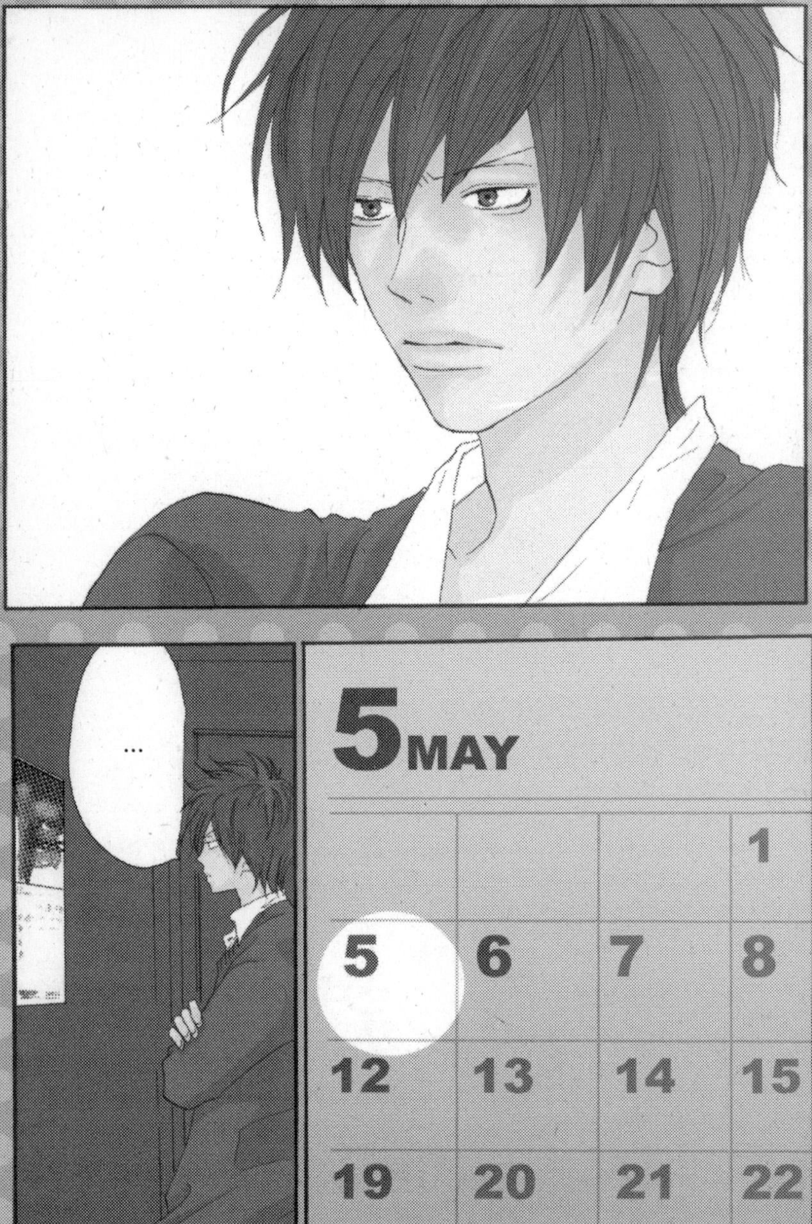
5 MAY
1
5 6 7 8
12 13 14 15
19 20 21 22
...

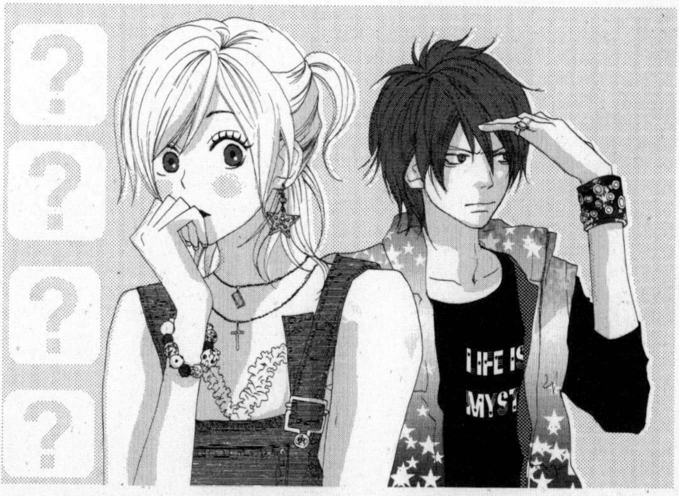
LIFE IS
MYST

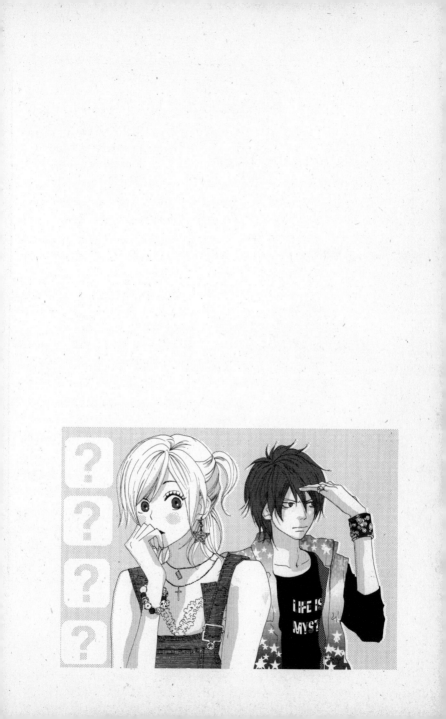

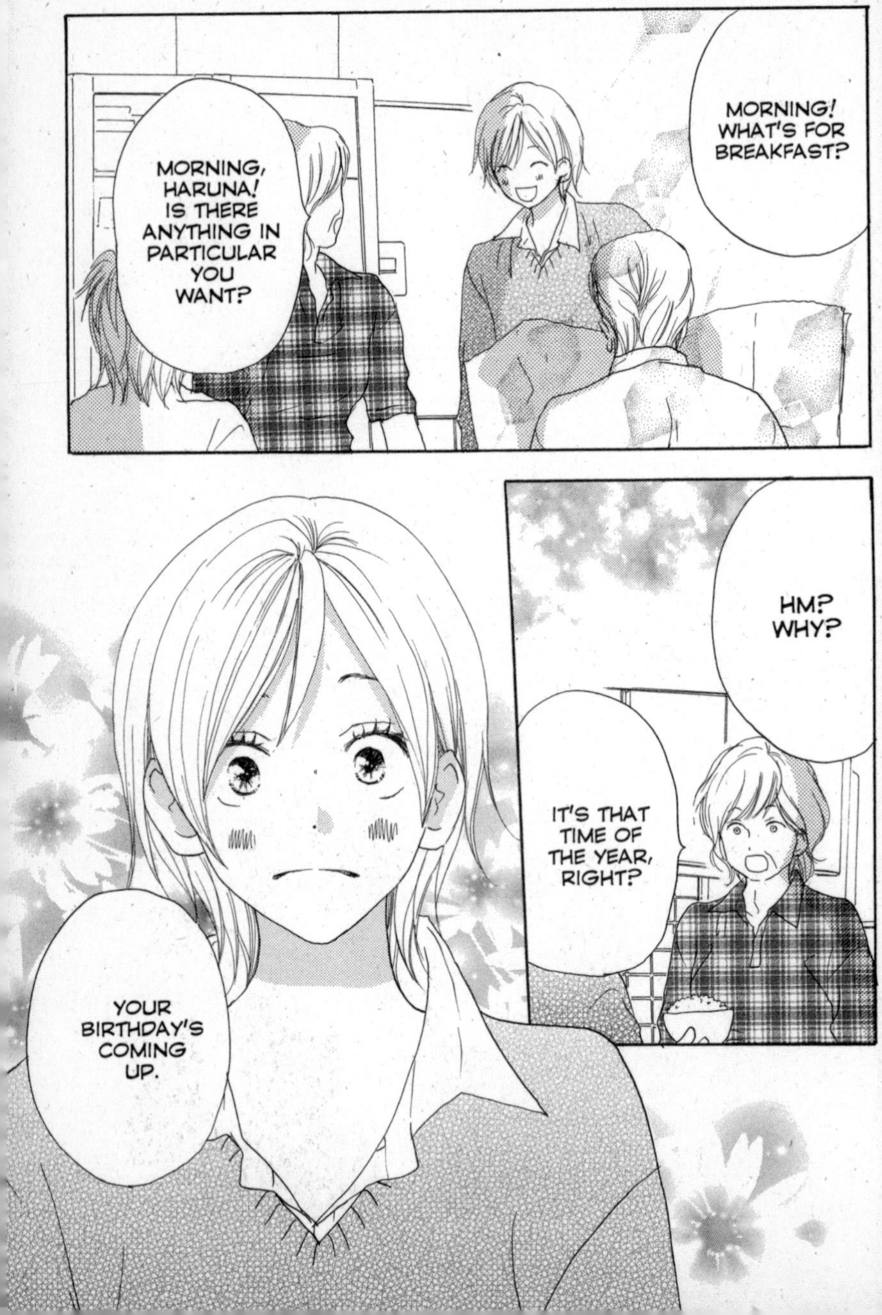
MORNING! WHAT'S FOR BREAKFAST?
MORNING, HARUNA! IS THERE ANYTHING IN PARTICULAR YOU WANT?
HM? WHY?
IT'S THAT TIME OF THE YEAR, RIGHT?
YOUR BIRTHDAY'S COMING UP.

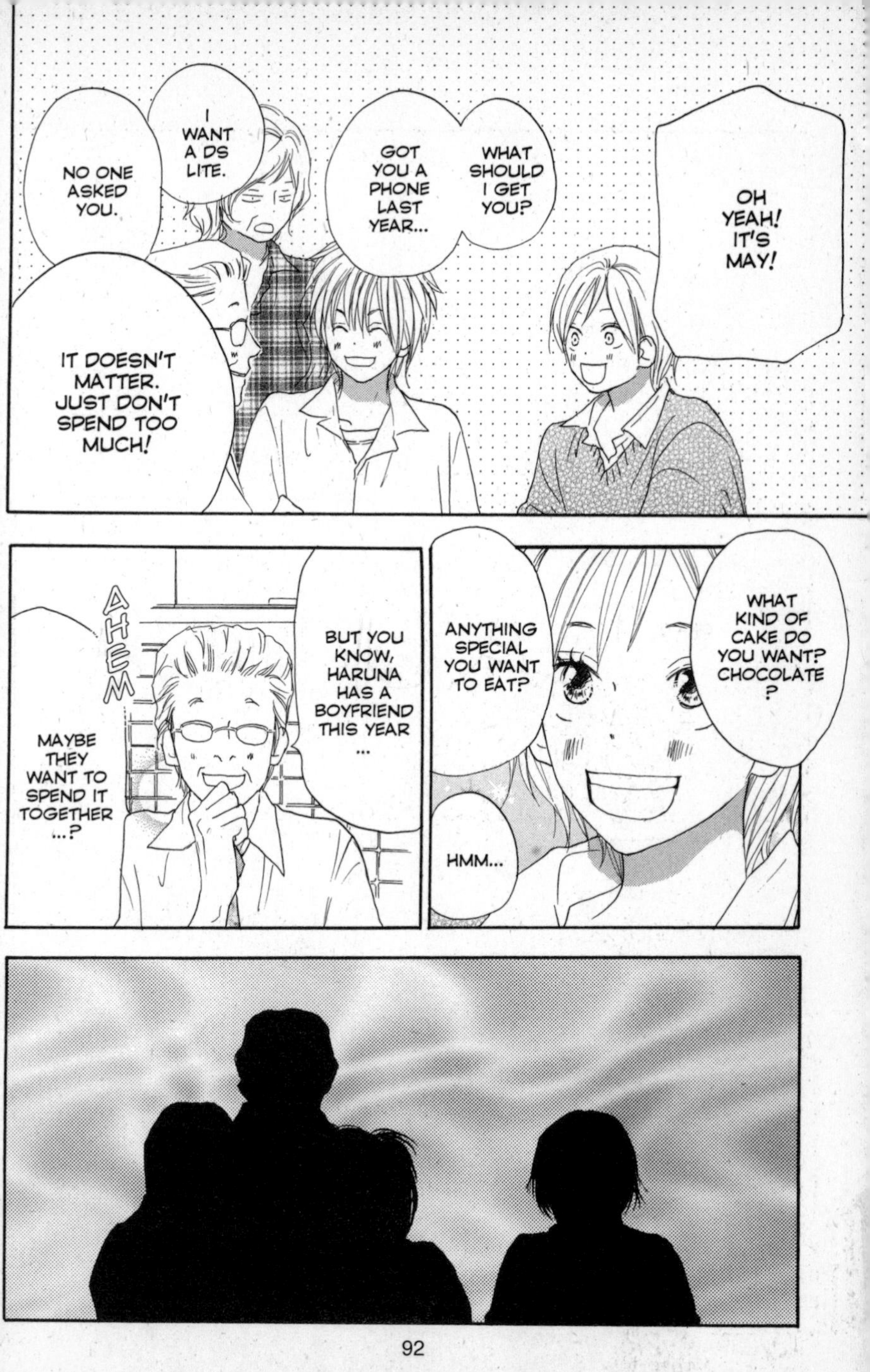
OH YEAH! IT'S MAY!
WHAT SHOULD I GET YOU?
GOT YOU A PHONE LAST YEAR...
I WANT A DS LITE.
NO ONE ASKED YOU.
IT DOESN'T MATTER. JUST DON'T SPEND TOO MUCH!
WHAT KIND OF CAKE DO YOU WANT? CHOCOLATE?
ANYTHING SPECIAL YOU WANT TO EAT?
HMM...
BUT YOU KNOW, HARUNA HAS A BOYFRIEND THIS YEAR...
AHEM
MAYBE THEY WANT TO SPEND IT TOGETHER...?

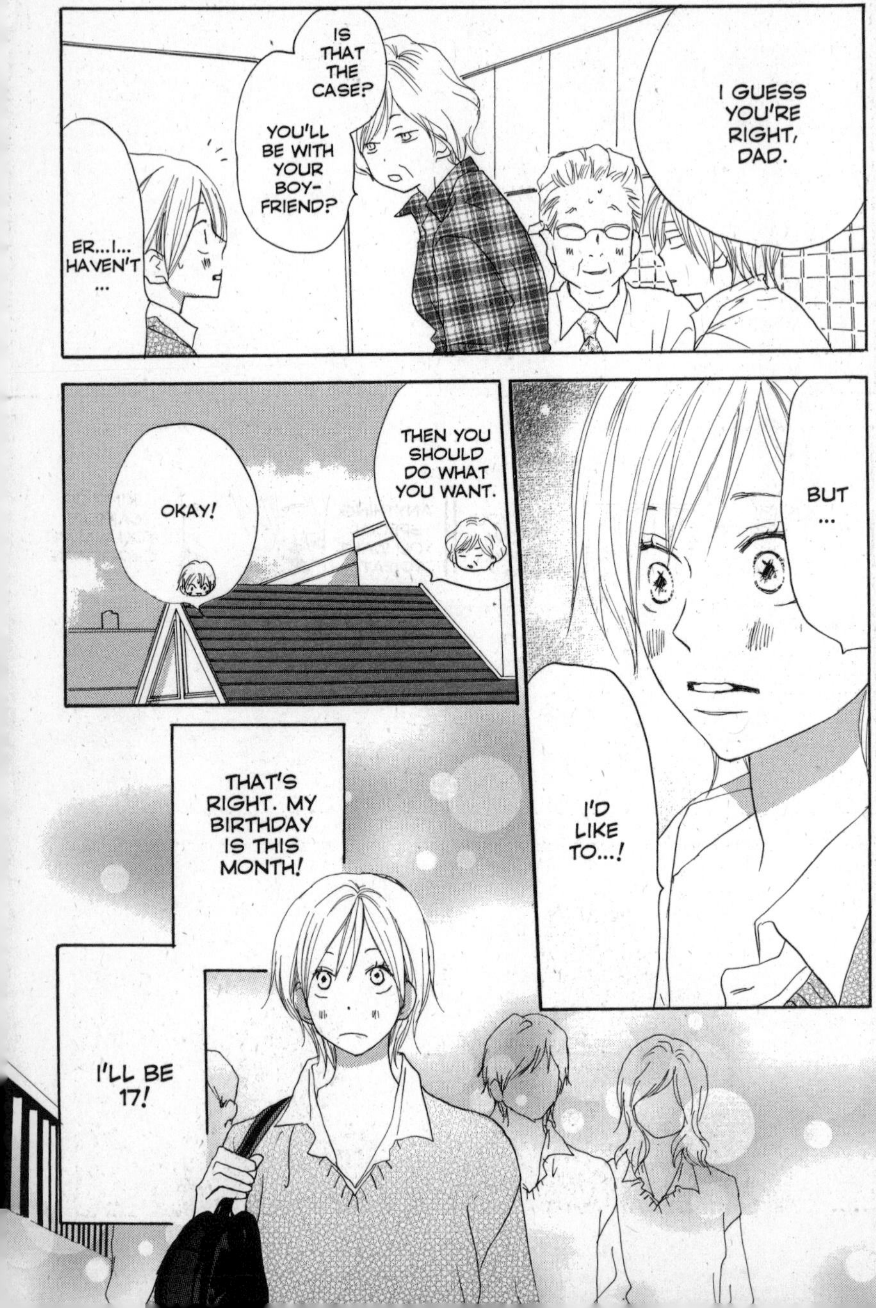
I GUESS YOU'RE RIGHT, DAD.
IS THAT THE CASE?
YOU'LL BE WITH YOUR BOY-FRIEND?
ER...I... HAVEN'T ...
BUT ...
I'D LIKE TO...!
THEN YOU SHOULD DO WHAT YOU WANT.
OKAY!
THAT'S RIGHT. MY BIRTHDAY IS THIS MONTH!
I'LL BE 17!

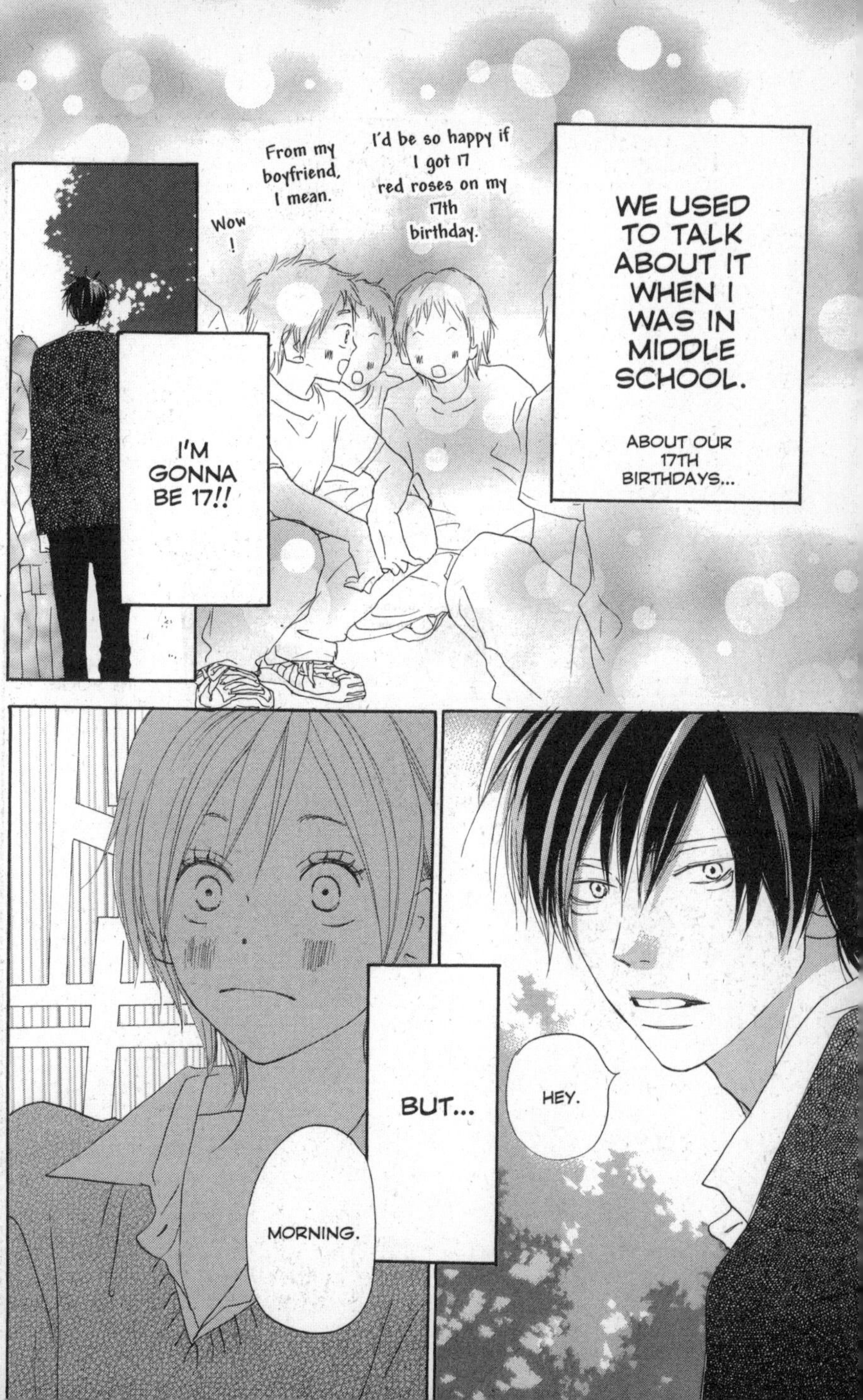
WE USED TO TALK ABOUT IT WHEN I WAS IN MIDDLE SCHOOL.
ABOUT OUR 17TH BIRTHDAYS...
I'd be so happy if I got 17 red roses on my 17th birthday.
From my boyfriend, I mean.
Wow!
I'M GONNA BE 17!!
HEY.
BUT...
MORNING.

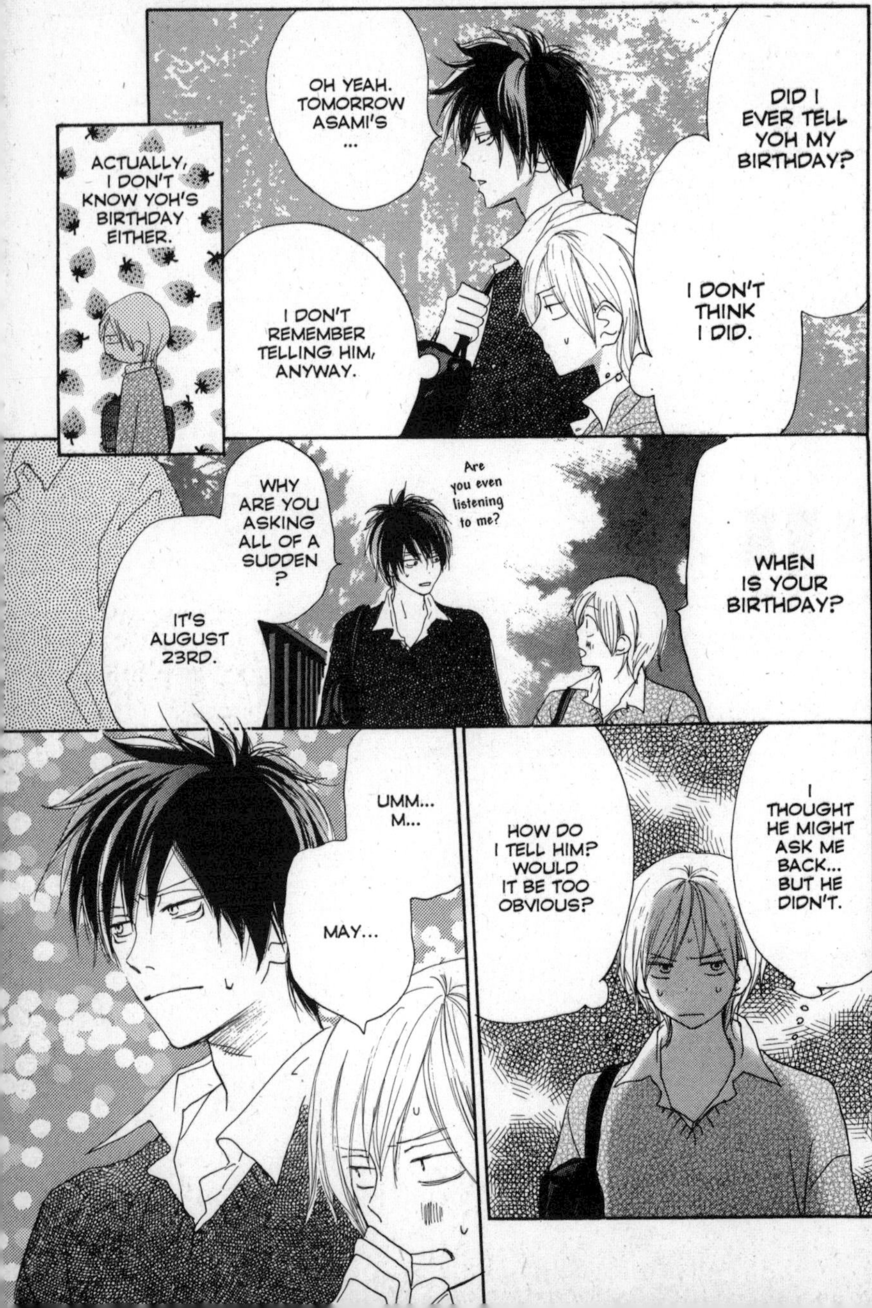
DID I EVER TELL YOH MY BIRTHDAY?
I DON'T THINK I DID.
OH YEAH. TOMORROW ASAMI'S ...
I DON'T REMEMBER TELLING HIM, ANYWAY.
ACTUALLY, I DON'T KNOW YOH'S BIRTHDAY EITHER.
WHEN IS YOUR BIRTHDAY?
Are you even listening to me?
WHY ARE YOU ASKING ALL OF A SUDDEN?
IT'S AUGUST 23RD.
I THOUGHT HE MIGHT ASK ME BACK... BUT HE DIDN'T.
HOW DO I TELL HIM? WOULD IT BE TOO OBVIOUS?
UMM... M...
MAY...

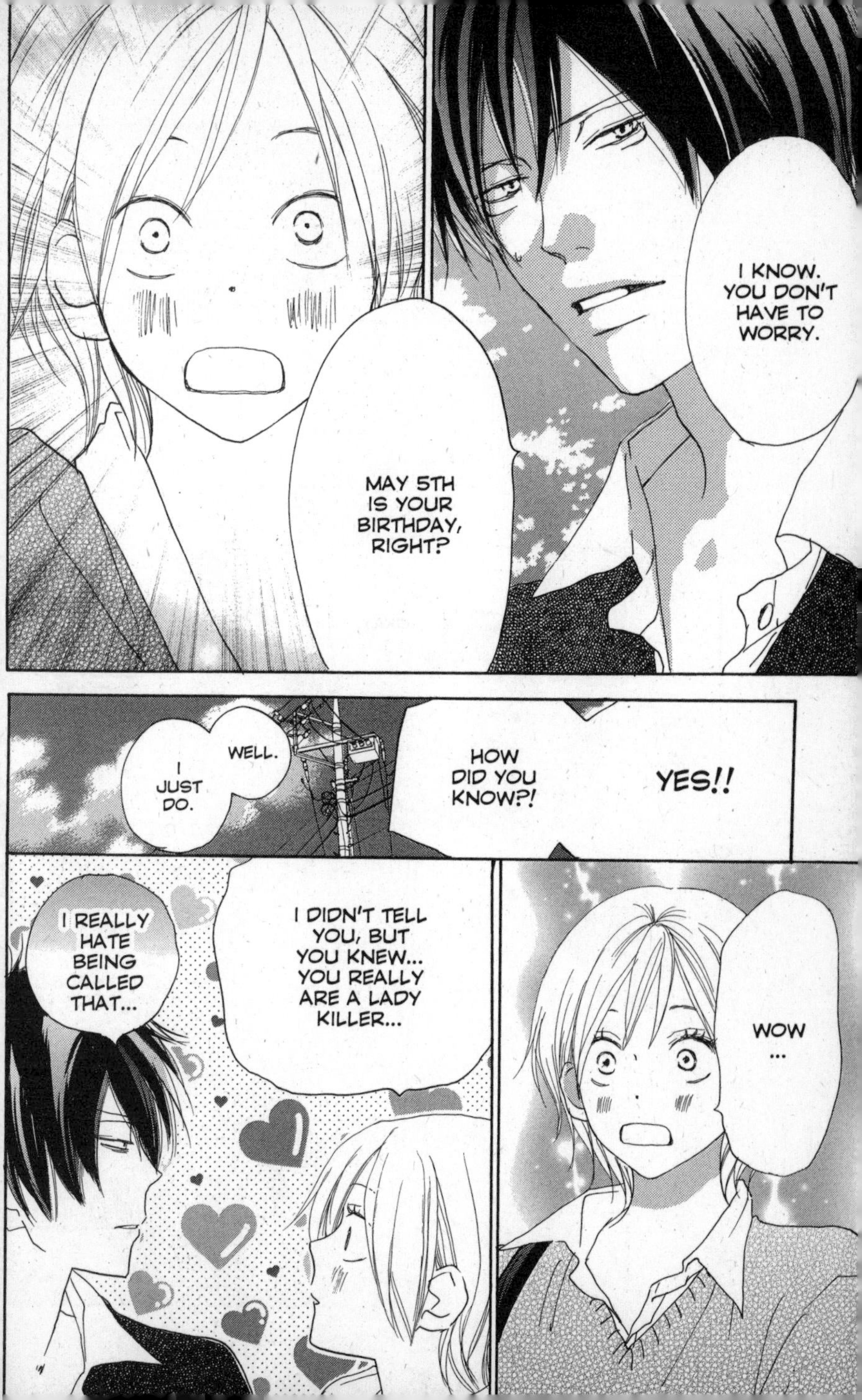
I KNOW. YOU DON'T HAVE TO WORRY.
MAY 5TH IS YOUR BIRTHDAY, RIGHT?
YES!!
HOW DID YOU KNOW?!
WELL.
I JUST DO.
WOW ...
I DIDN'T TELL YOU, BUT YOU KNEW... YOU REALLY ARE A LADY KILLER...
I REALLY HATE BEING CALLED THAT...

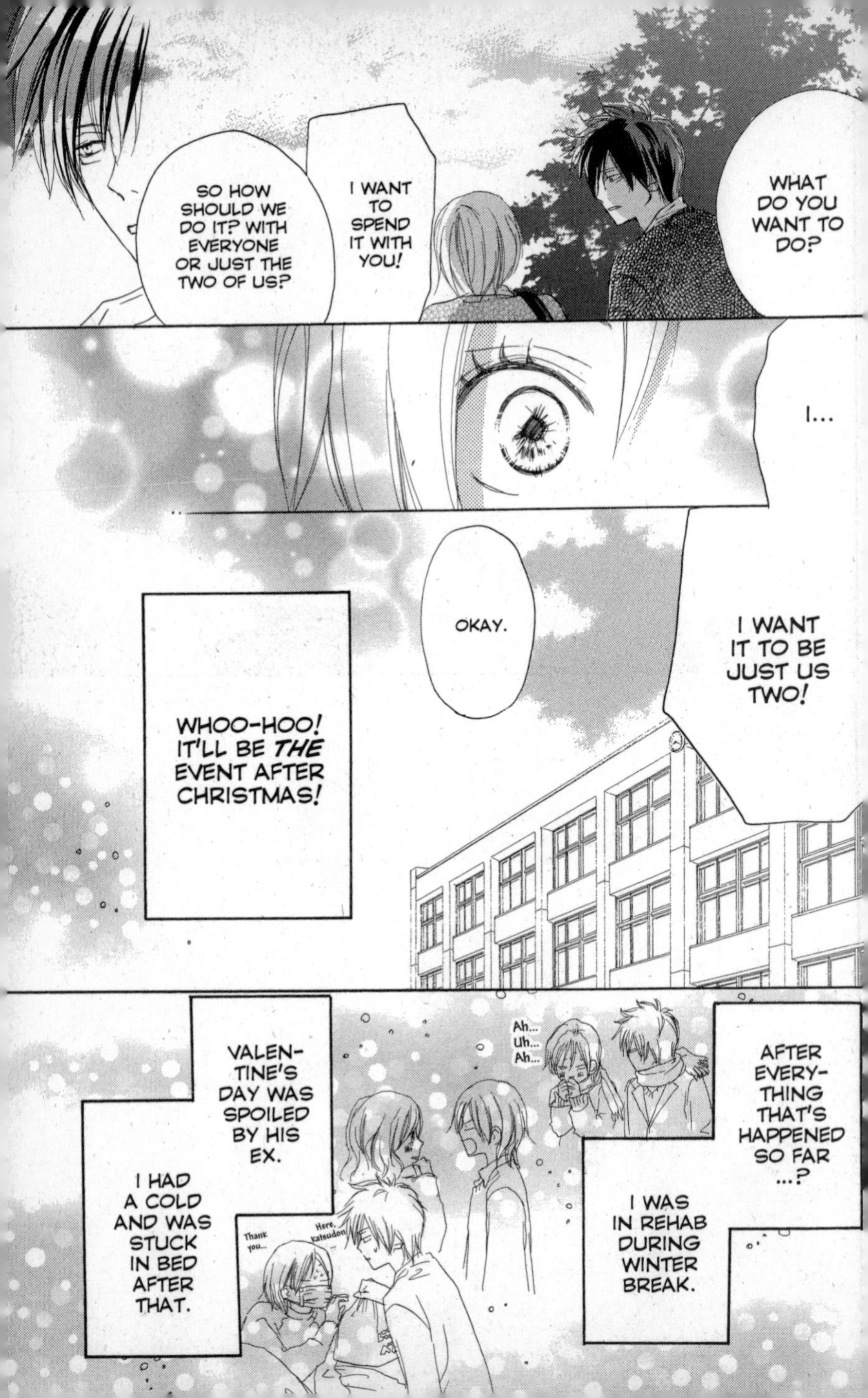
WHAT DO YOU WANT TO DO?
I WANT TO SPEND IT WITH YOU!
SO HOW SHOULD WE DO IT? WITH EVERYONE OR JUST THE TWO OF US?
I...
I WANT IT TO BE JUST US TWO!
OKAY.
WHOO-HOO! IT'LL BE *THE* EVENT AFTER CHRISTMAS!
AFTER EVERY-THING THAT'S HAPPENED SO FAR ...?
Ah... Uh... Ah...
I WAS IN REHAB DURING WINTER BREAK.
VALEN-TINE'S DAY WAS SPOILED BY HIS EX.
Here, Katsudon...
Thank you...
I HAD A COLD AND WAS STUCK IN BED AFTER THAT.

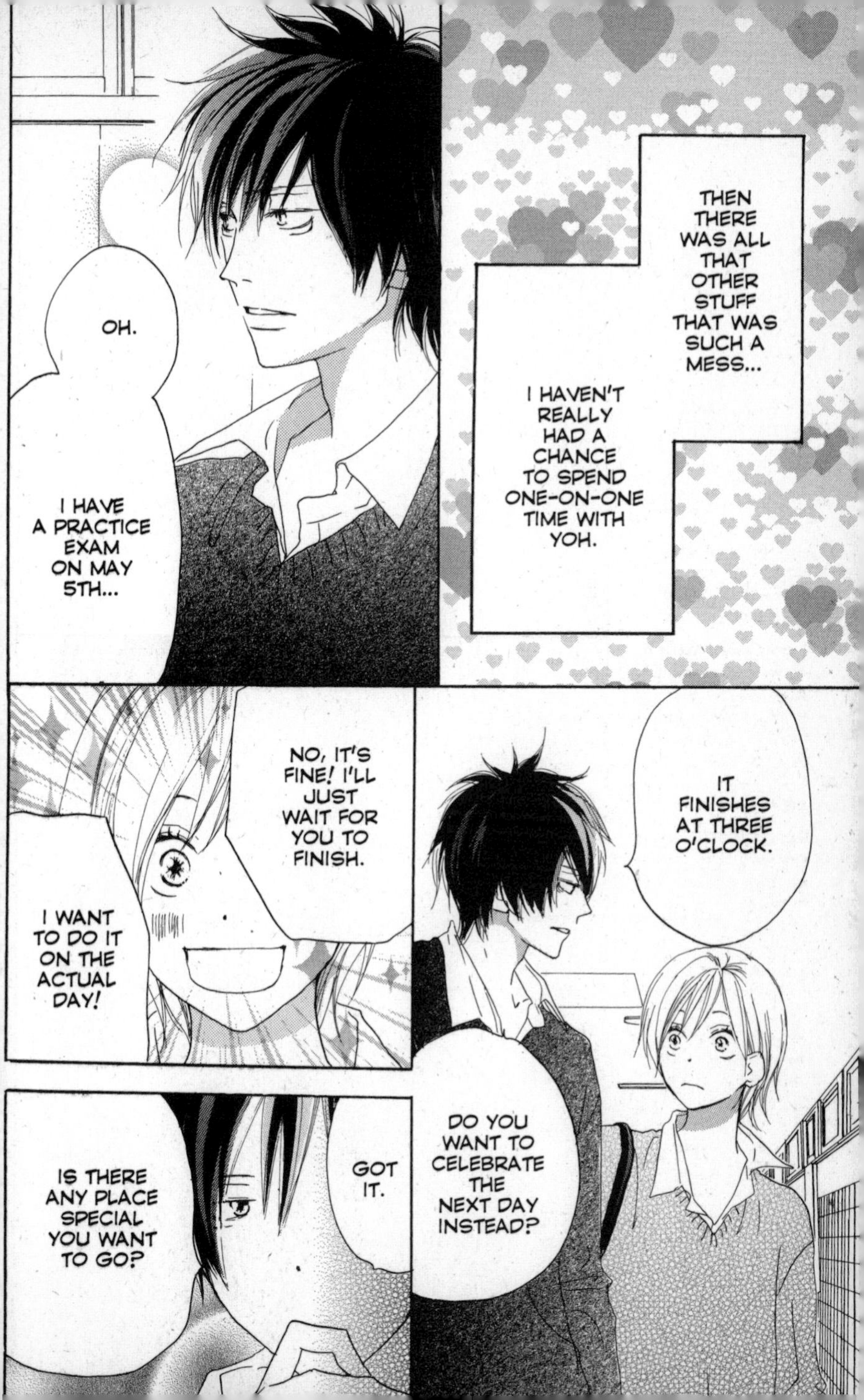
THEN THERE WAS ALL THAT OTHER STUFF THAT WAS SUCH A MESS...
I HAVEN'T REALLY HAD A CHANCE TO SPEND ONE-ON-ONE TIME WITH YOH.
OH.
I HAVE A PRACTICE EXAM ON MAY 5TH...
IT FINISHES AT THREE O'CLOCK.
DO YOU WANT TO CELEBRATE THE NEXT DAY INSTEAD?
NO, IT'S FINE! I'LL JUST WAIT FOR YOU TO FINISH.
I WANT TO DO IT ON THE ACTUAL DAY!
GOT IT.
IS THERE ANY PLACE SPECIAL YOU WANT TO GO?

2

I don't have a Wii, so I've been playing Zelda on the GameCube. I keep falling and dying. But it's fun.

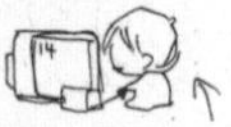

I'm not that good at it, but I'm working on getting better. Ah, it's so fun!

I don't have that much time to play, so I'll probably only get to play Zelda this year. It's a shame since games are really fun...

I would really like it if manga gave people the same kind of happy feeling. I always have these super high aspirations. They're too high though, and I always get defeated instead.

But it does feel like when I look up, there isn't a single cloud...so I'm able to escape reality.

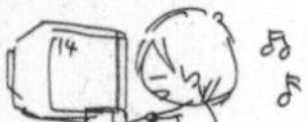
Not good!

My 14-inch TV only has the white and yellow ports for this thing.

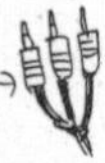

So I sit huddled in the corner of my room playing the game... It's kind of sad.

Calm down! I want to play! On a big screen! (Cries)

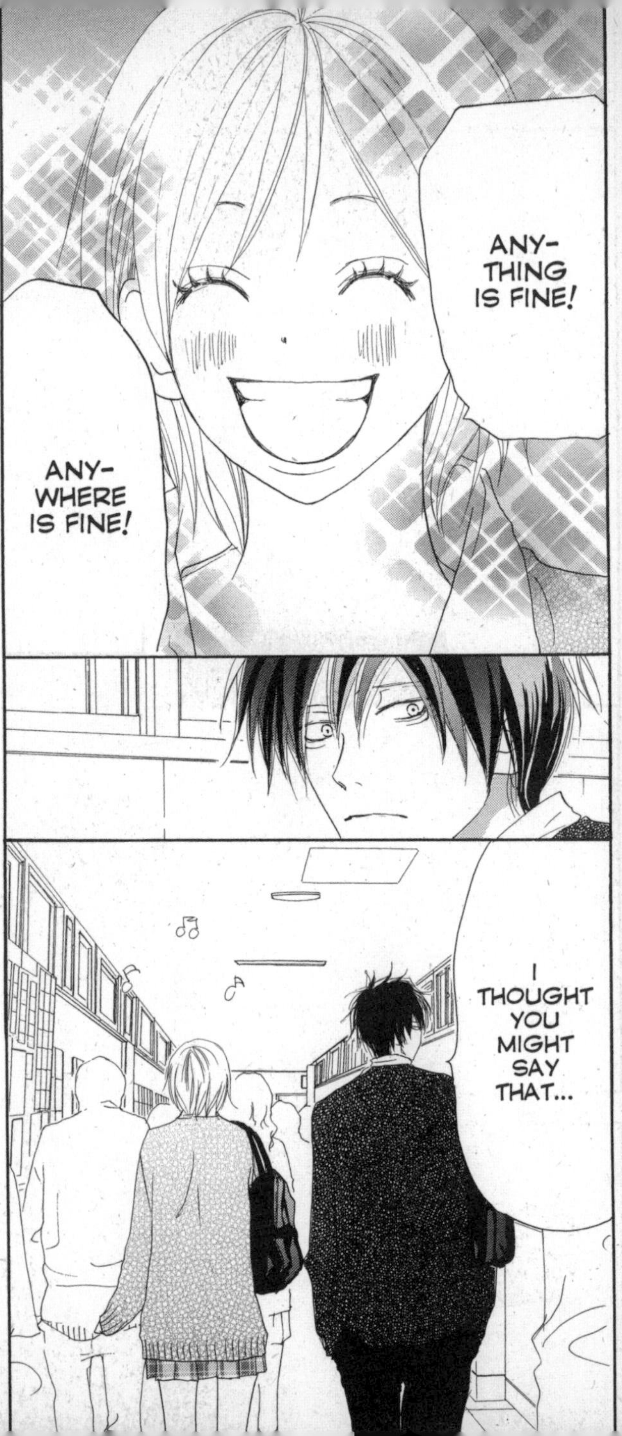
ANY-THING IS FINE!
ANY-WHERE IS FINE!
I THOUGHT YOU MIGHT SAY THAT...

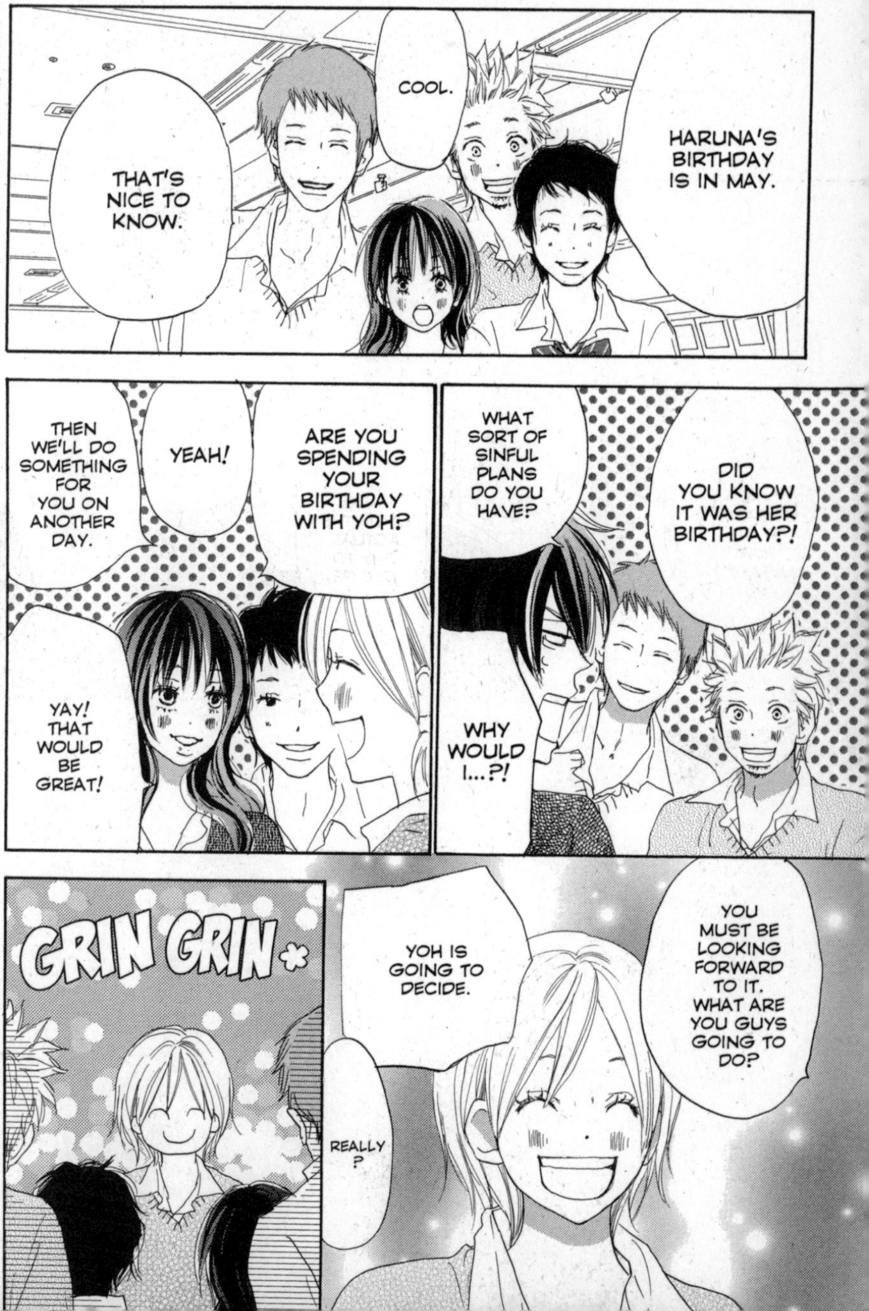
HARUNA'S BIRTHDAY IS IN MAY.
COOL.
THAT'S NICE TO KNOW.
DID YOU KNOW IT WAS HER BIRTHDAY?!
WHAT SORT OF SINFUL PLANS DO YOU HAVE?
WHY WOULD I...?!
ARE YOU SPENDING YOUR BIRTHDAY WITH YOH?
YEAH!
THEN WE'LL DO SOMETHING FOR YOU ON ANOTHER DAY.
YAY! THAT WOULD BE GREAT!
YOU MUST BE LOOKING FORWARD TO IT. WHAT ARE YOU GUYS GOING TO DO?
YOH IS GOING TO DECIDE.
REALLY ?
GRIN GRIN

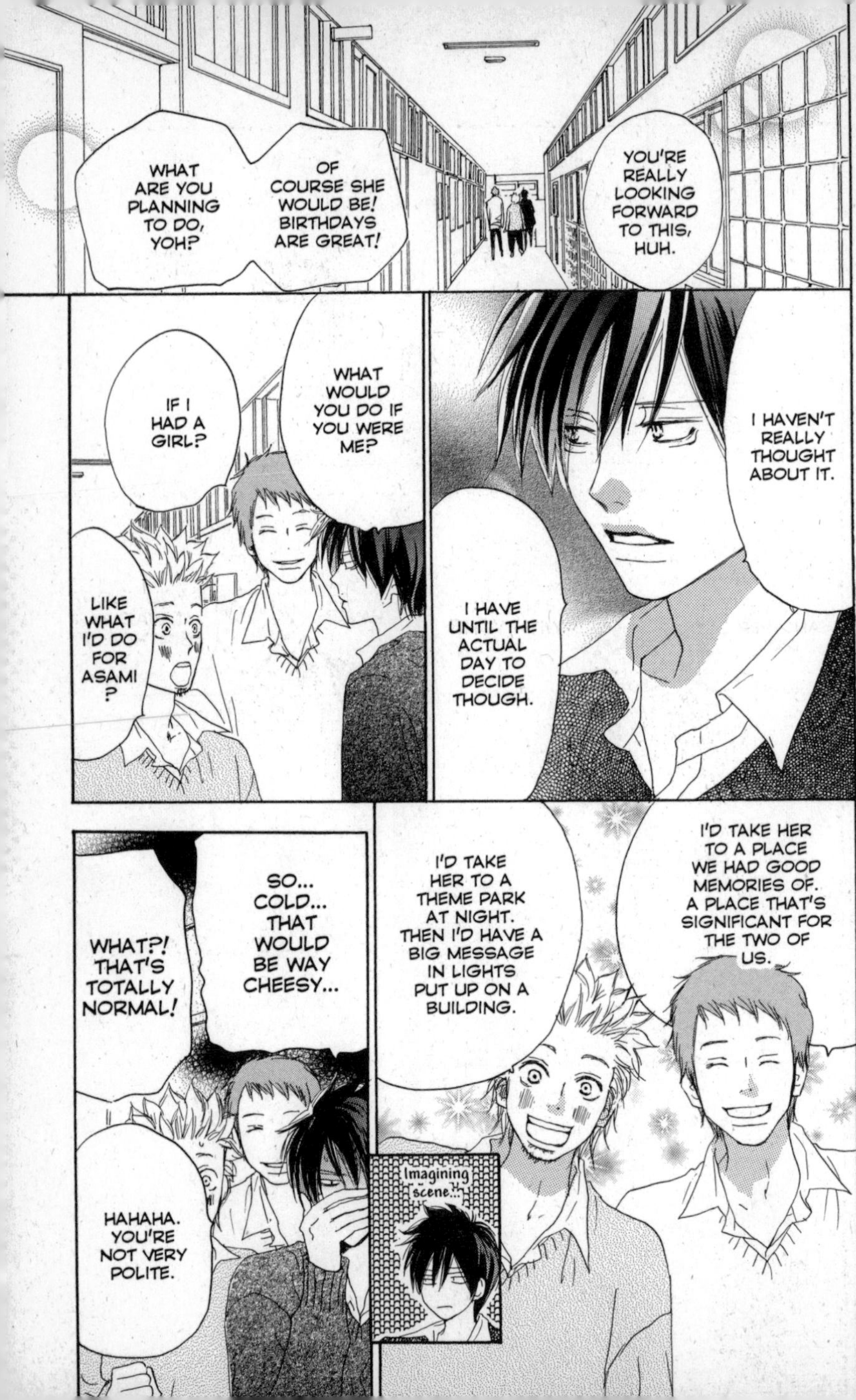
YOU'RE REALLY LOOKING FORWARD TO THIS, HUH.
OF COURSE SHE WOULD BE! BIRTHDAYS ARE GREAT!
WHAT ARE YOU PLANNING TO DO, YOH?
I HAVEN'T REALLY THOUGHT ABOUT IT.
I HAVE UNTIL THE ACTUAL DAY TO DECIDE THOUGH.
WHAT WOULD YOU DO IF YOU WERE ME?
IF I HAD A GIRL?
LIKE WHAT I'D DO FOR ASAMI?
I'D TAKE HER TO A PLACE WE HAD GOOD MEMORIES OF. A PLACE THAT'S SIGNIFICANT FOR THE TWO OF US.
I'D TAKE HER TO A THEME PARK AT NIGHT. THEN I'D HAVE A BIG MESSAGE IN LIGHTS PUT UP ON A BUILDING.
Imagining scene...
SO... COLD... THAT WOULD BE WAY CHEESY...
WHAT?! THAT'S TOTALLY NORMAL!
HAHAHA. YOU'RE NOT VERY POLITE.

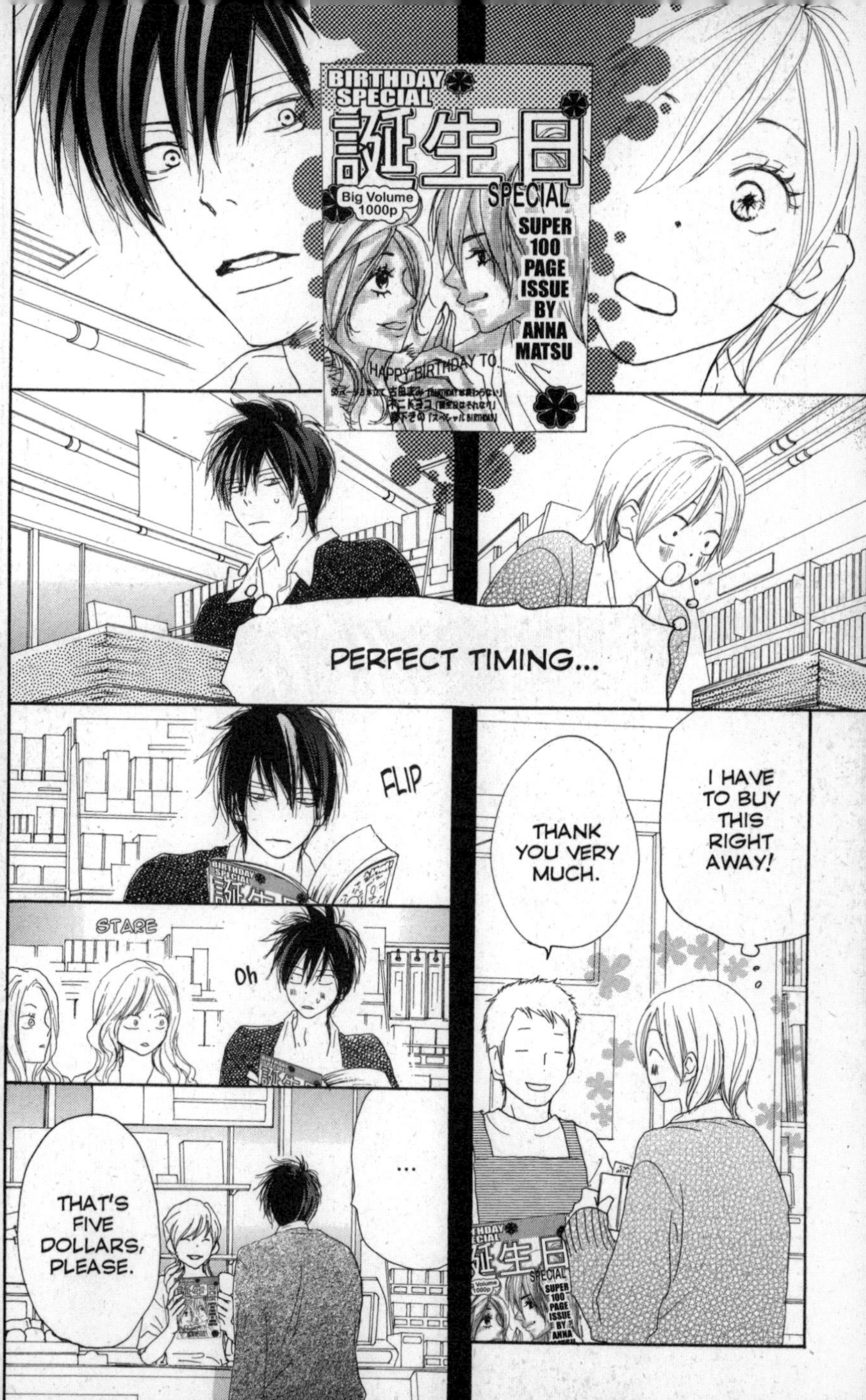
BIRTHDAY SPECIAL
誕生日
SPECIAL
Big Volume 1000p
SUPER 100 PAGE ISSUE BY ANNA MATSU
HAPPY BIRTHDAY TO......
PERFECT TIMING...
I HAVE TO BUY THIS RIGHT AWAY!
THANK YOU VERY MUCH.
FLIP
STARE
Oh
...
THAT'S FIVE DOLLARS, PLEASE.

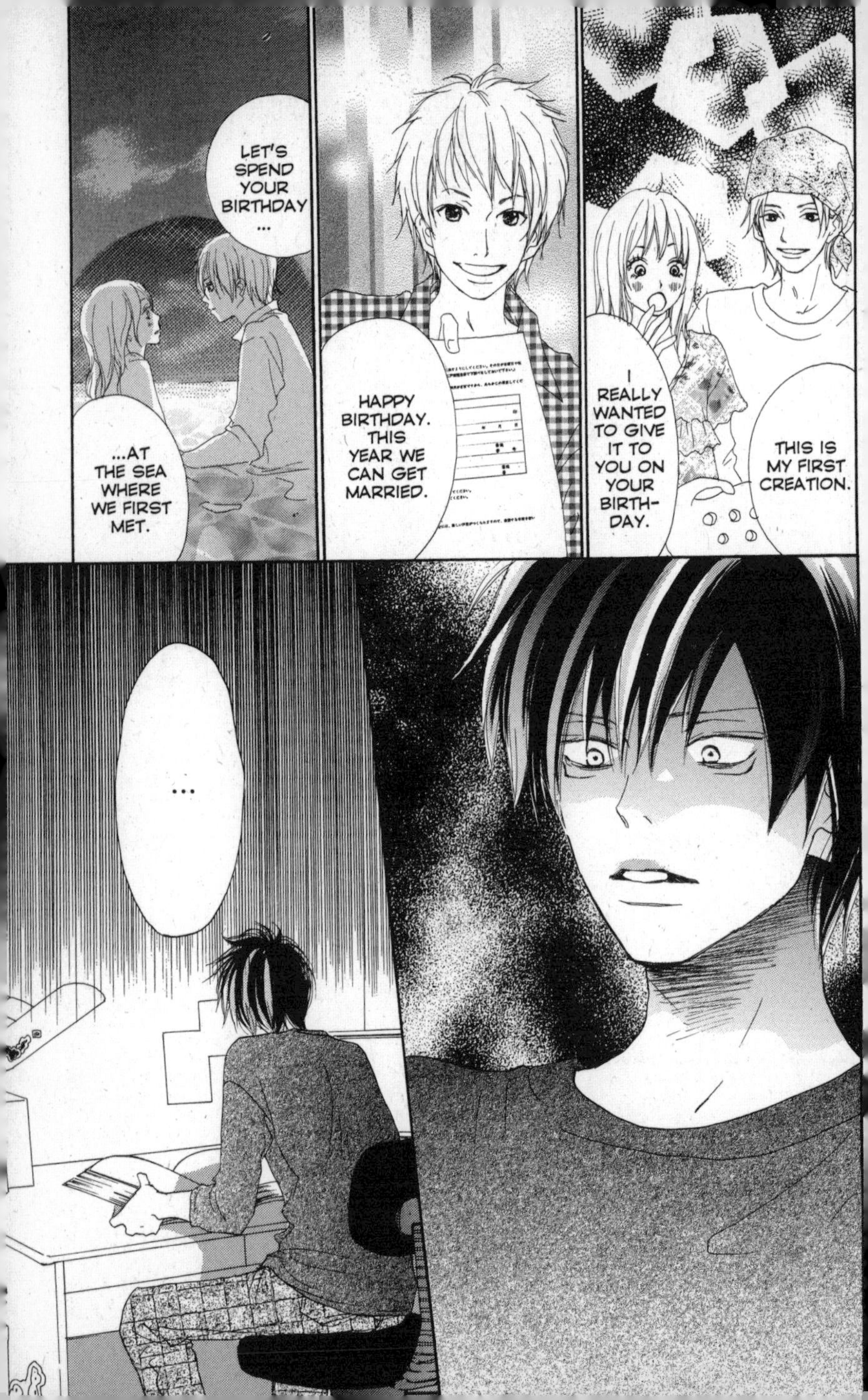
THIS IS MY FIRST CREATION.
I REALLY WANTED TO GIVE IT TO YOU ON YOUR BIRTH-DAY.
HAPPY BIRTHDAY. THIS YEAR WE CAN GET MARRIED.
LET'S SPEND YOUR BIRTHDAY ...
...AT THE SEA WHERE WE FIRST MET.
...

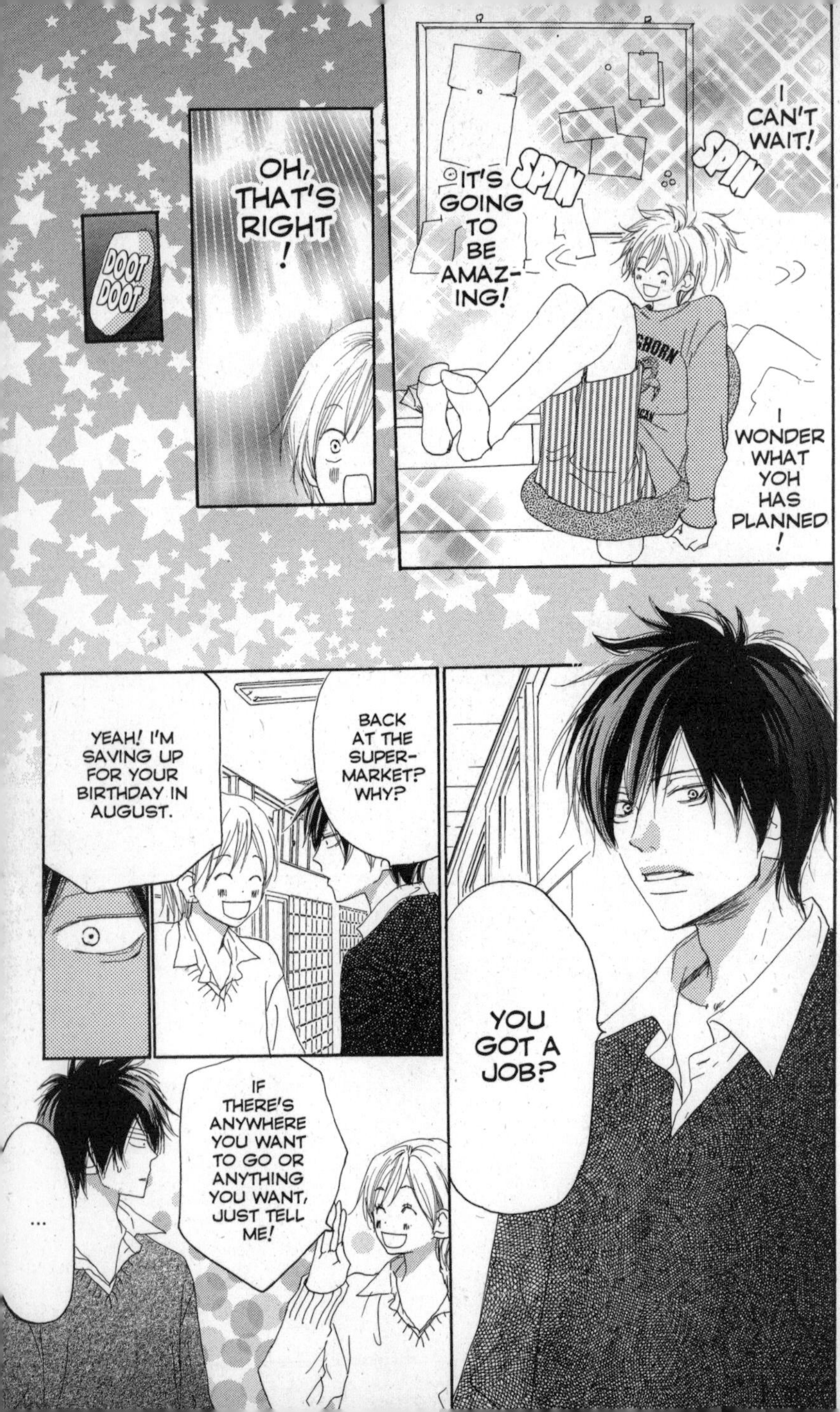
I CAN'T WAIT!
SPIN
SPIN
IT'S GOING TO BE AMAZING!
I WONDER WHAT YOH HAS PLANNED!
OH, THAT'S RIGHT!
DOOT DOOT
YOU GOT A JOB?
BACK AT THE SUPER-MARKET? WHY?
YEAH! I'M SAVING UP FOR YOUR BIRTHDAY IN AUGUST.
IF THERE'S ANYWHERE YOU WANT TO GO OR ANYTHING YOU WANT, JUST TELL ME!
...

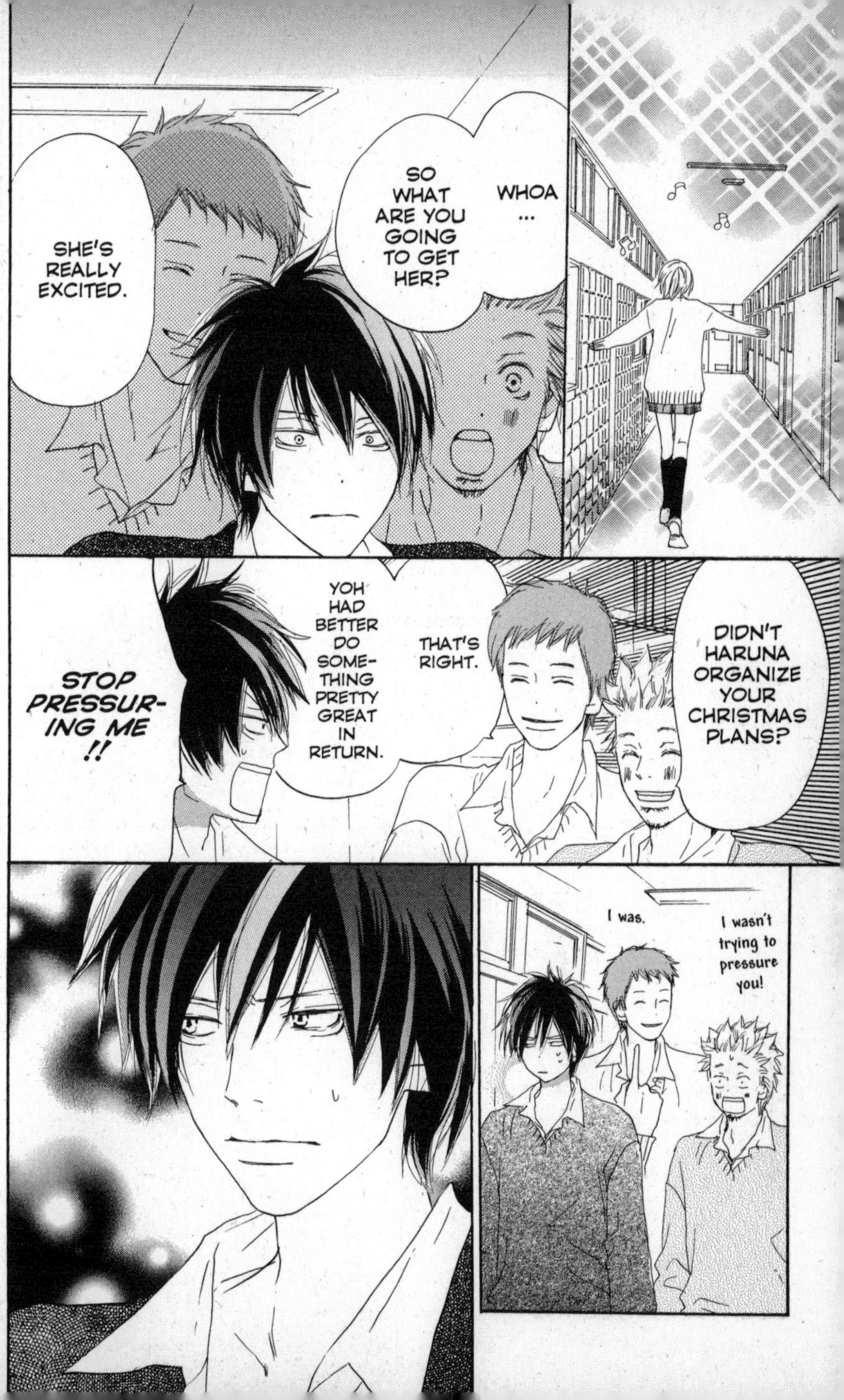
WHOA ...
SO WHAT ARE YOU GOING TO GET HER?
SHE'S REALLY EXCITED.
DIDN'T HARUNA ORGANIZE YOUR CHRISTMAS PLANS?
THAT'S RIGHT.
YOH HAD BETTER DO SOMETHING PRETTY GREAT IN RETURN.
STOP PRESSURING ME!!
I wasn't trying to pressure you!
I was.

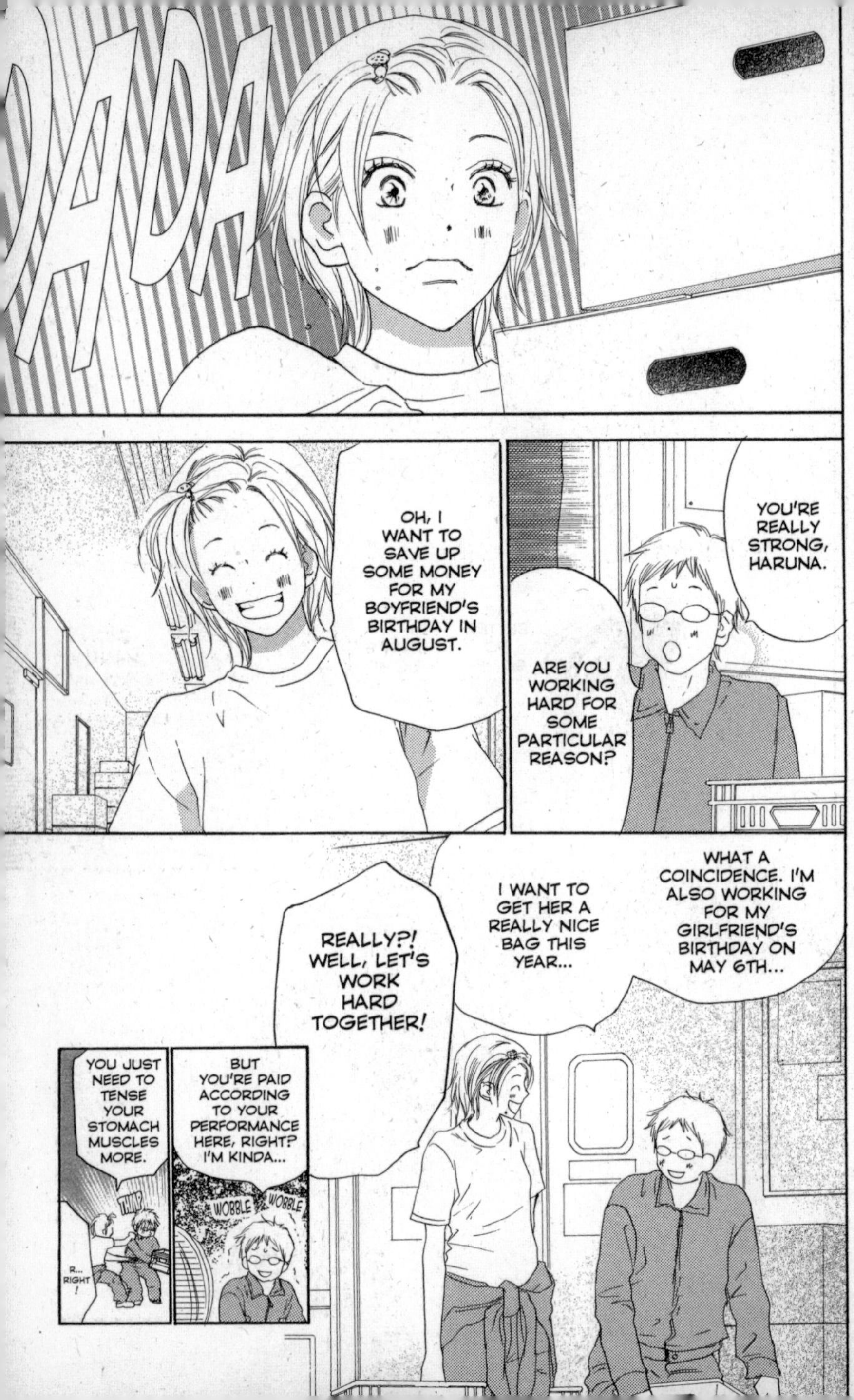
DADA
YOU'RE REALLY STRONG, HARUNA.
ARE YOU WORKING HARD FOR SOME PARTICULAR REASON?
OH, I WANT TO SAVE UP SOME MONEY FOR MY BOYFRIEND'S BIRTHDAY IN AUGUST.
WHAT A COINCIDENCE. I'M ALSO WORKING FOR MY GIRLFRIEND'S BIRTHDAY ON MAY 6TH...
I WANT TO GET HER A REALLY NICE BAG THIS YEAR...
REALLY?! WELL, LET'S WORK HARD TOGETHER!
BUT YOU'RE PAID ACCORDING TO YOUR PERFORMANCE HERE, RIGHT? I'M KINDA...
WOBBLE
WOBBLE
YOU JUST NEED TO TENSE YOUR STOMACH MUSCLES MORE.
THAP
R... RIGHT!

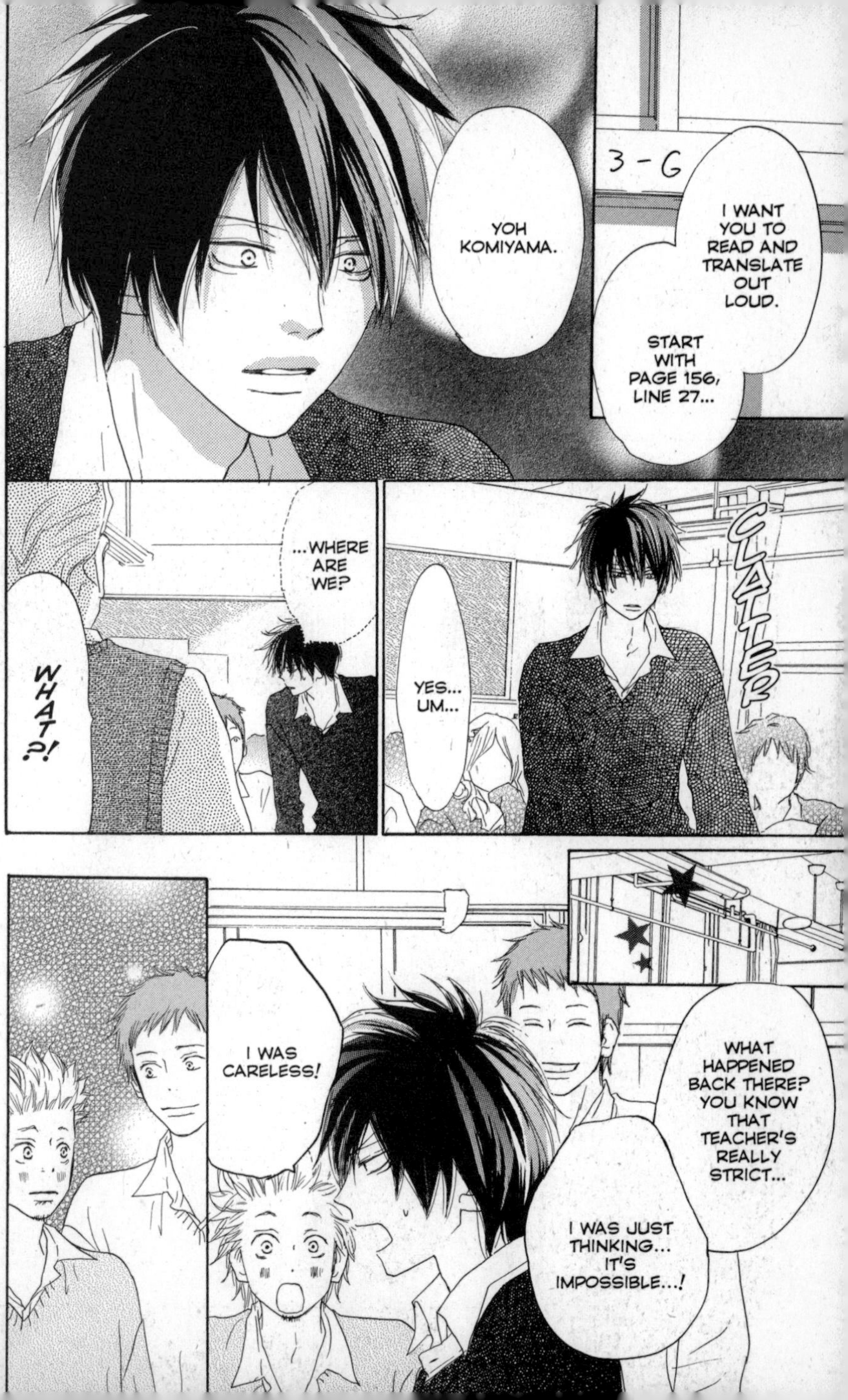
3-G
I WANT YOU TO READ AND TRANSLATE OUT LOUD.
START WITH PAGE 156, LINE 27...
YOH KOMIYAMA.
CLATTER
YES... UM...
...WHERE ARE WE?
WHAT?!
WHAT HAPPENED BACK THERE? YOU KNOW THAT TEACHER'S REALLY STRICT...
I WAS JUST THINKING... IT'S IMPOSSIBLE...!
I WAS CARELESS!

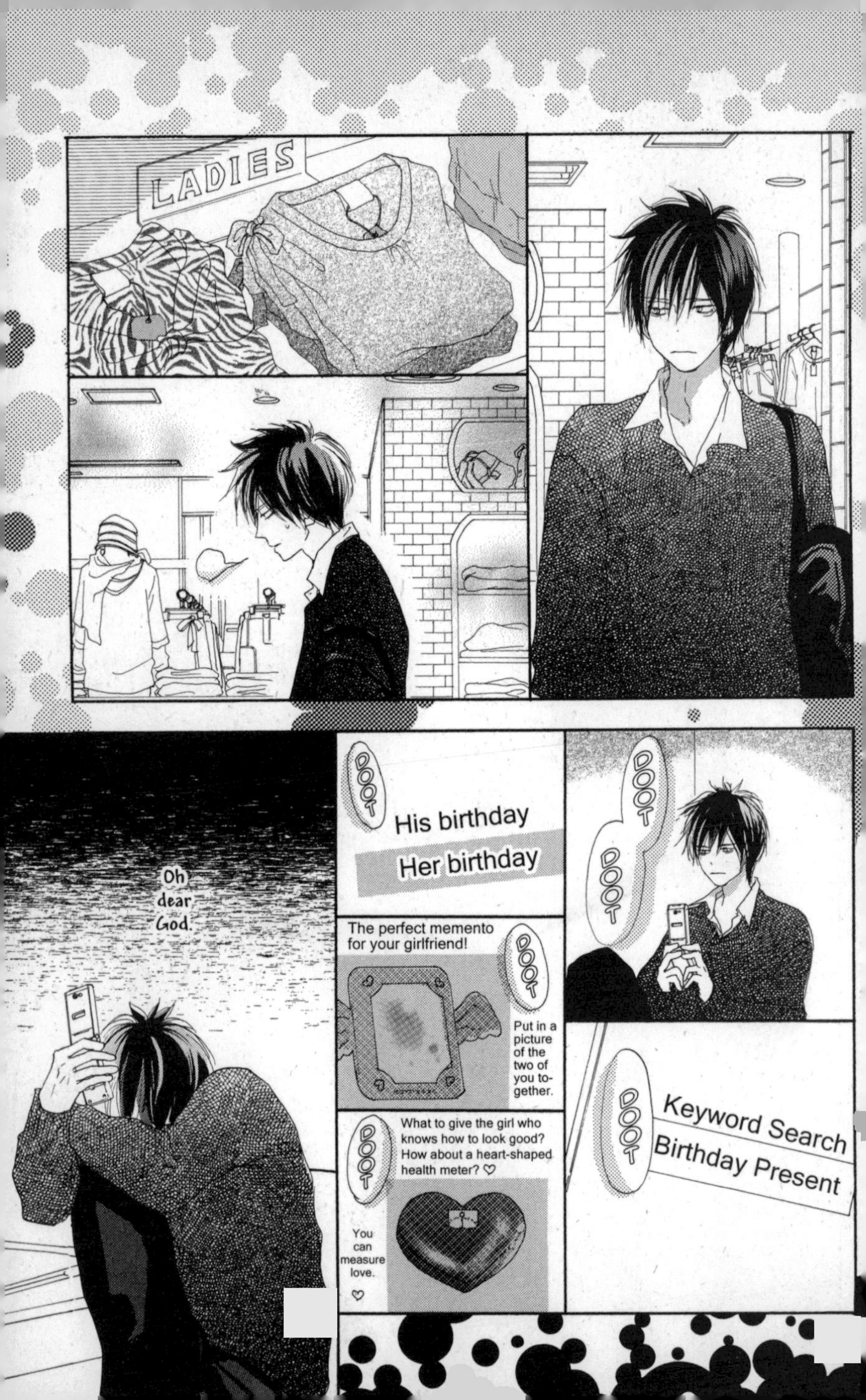
LADIES
DOOT
DOOT
DOOT
Keyword Search
Birthday Present
DOOT
His birthday
Her birthday
The perfect memento for your girlfriend!
DOOT
Put in a picture of the two of you to-gether.
What to give the girl who knows how to look good? How about a heart-shaped health meter? ♡
DOOT
You can measure love. ♡
Oh dear God.

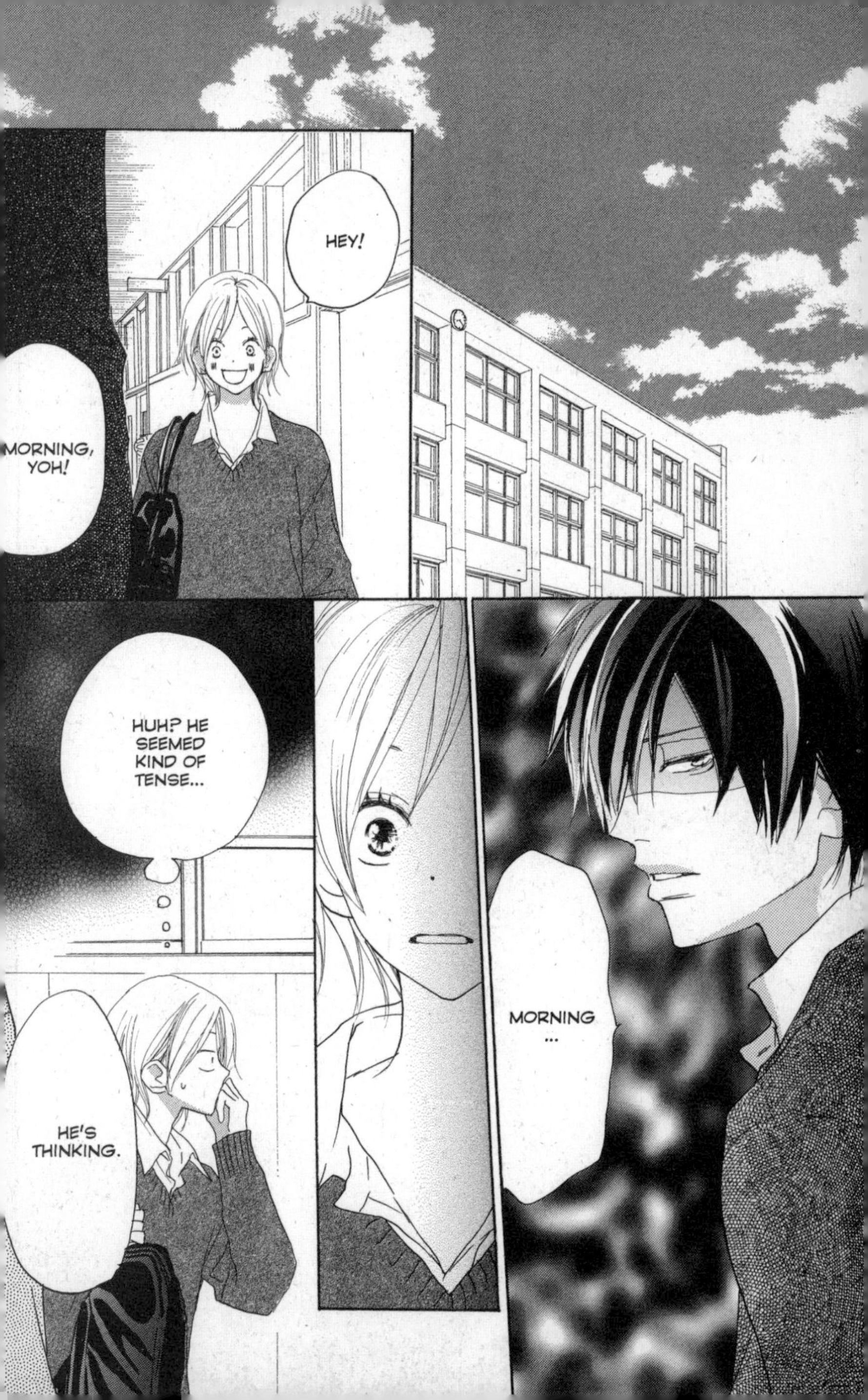
HEY!
MORNING, YOH!
MORNING ...
HUH? HE SEEMED KIND OF TENSE...
HE'S THINKING.

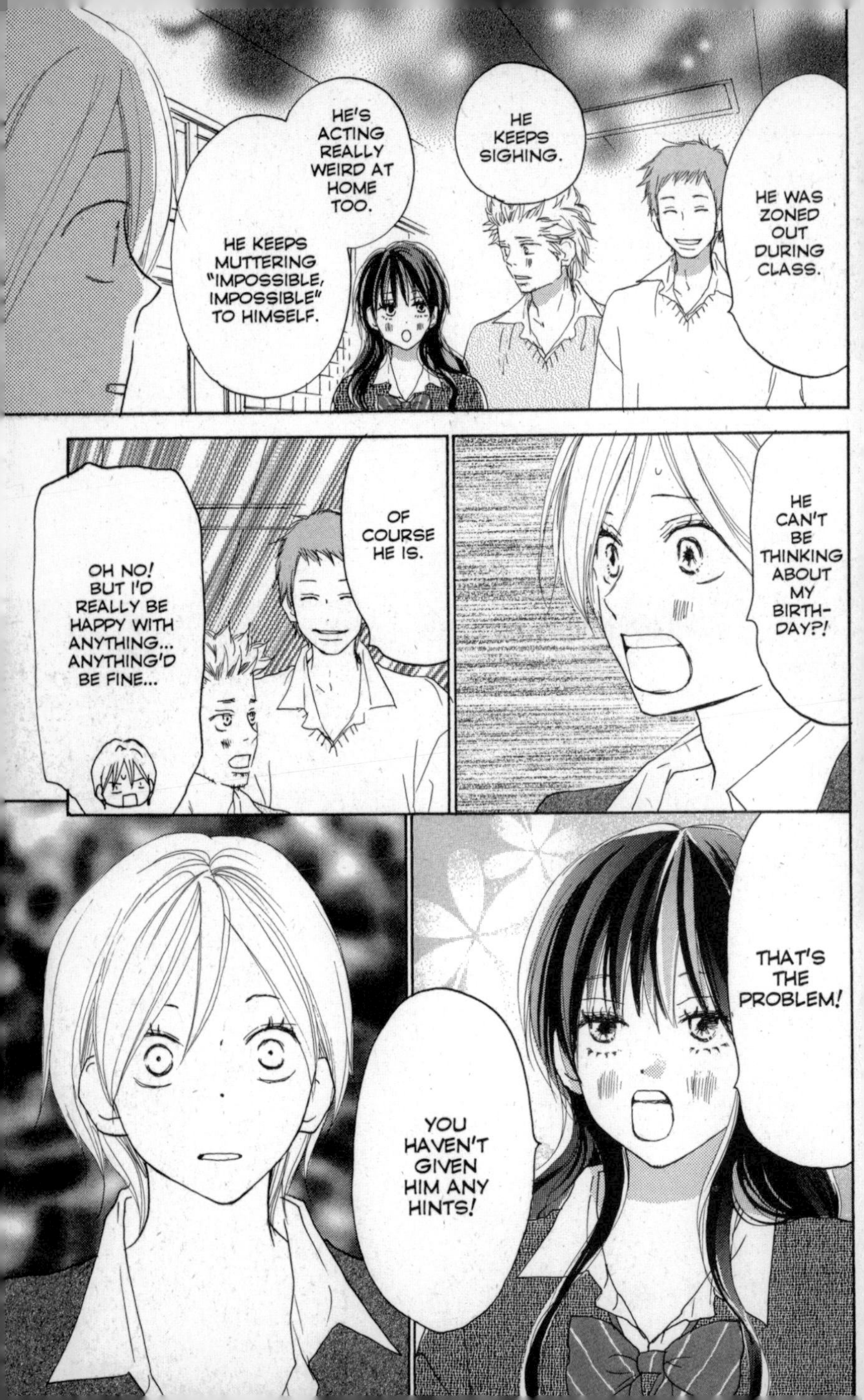
HE WAS ZONED OUT DURING CLASS.
HE KEEPS SIGHING.
HE'S ACTING REALLY WEIRD AT HOME TOO.
HE KEEPS MUTTERING "IMPOSSIBLE, IMPOSSIBLE" TO HIMSELF.
HE CAN'T BE THINKING ABOUT MY BIRTH-DAY?!
OF COURSE HE IS.
OH NO! BUT I'D REALLY BE HAPPY WITH ANYTHING... ANYTHING'D BE FINE...
THAT'S THE PROBLEM!
YOU HAVEN'T GIVEN HIM ANY HINTS!

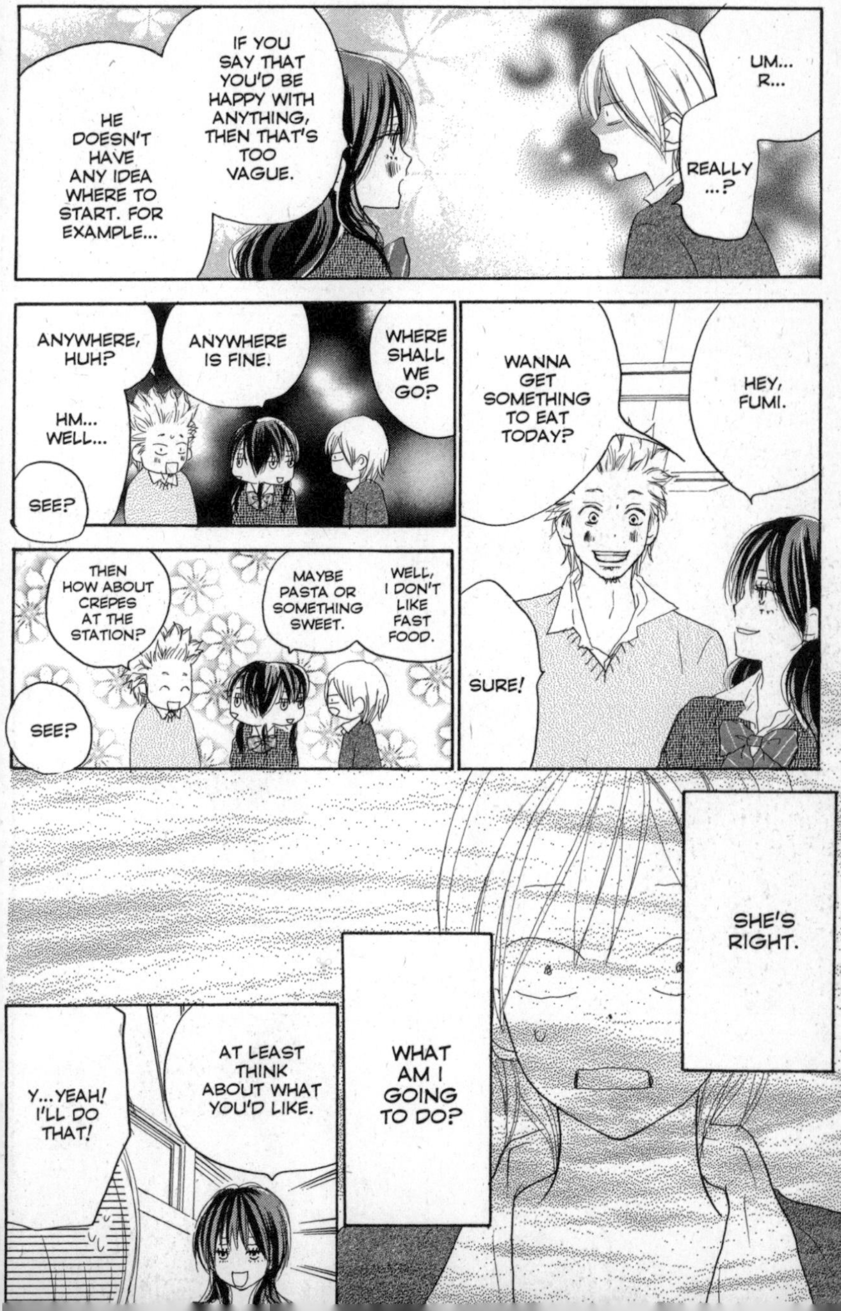
UM... R...
REALLY ...?
IF YOU SAY THAT YOU'D BE HAPPY WITH ANYTHING, THEN THAT'S TOO VAGUE.
HE DOESN'T HAVE ANY IDEA WHERE TO START. FOR EXAMPLE...
HEY, FUMI.
WANNA GET SOMETHING TO EAT TODAY?
SURE!
WHERE SHALL WE GO?
ANYWHERE IS FINE.
ANYWHERE, HUH?
HM... WELL...
SEE?
WELL, I DON'T LIKE FAST FOOD.
MAYBE PASTA OR SOMETHING SWEET.
THEN HOW ABOUT CREPES AT THE STATION?
SEE?
SHE'S RIGHT.
WHAT AM I GOING TO DO?
AT LEAST THINK ABOUT WHAT YOU'D LIKE.
Y...YEAH! I'LL DO THAT!

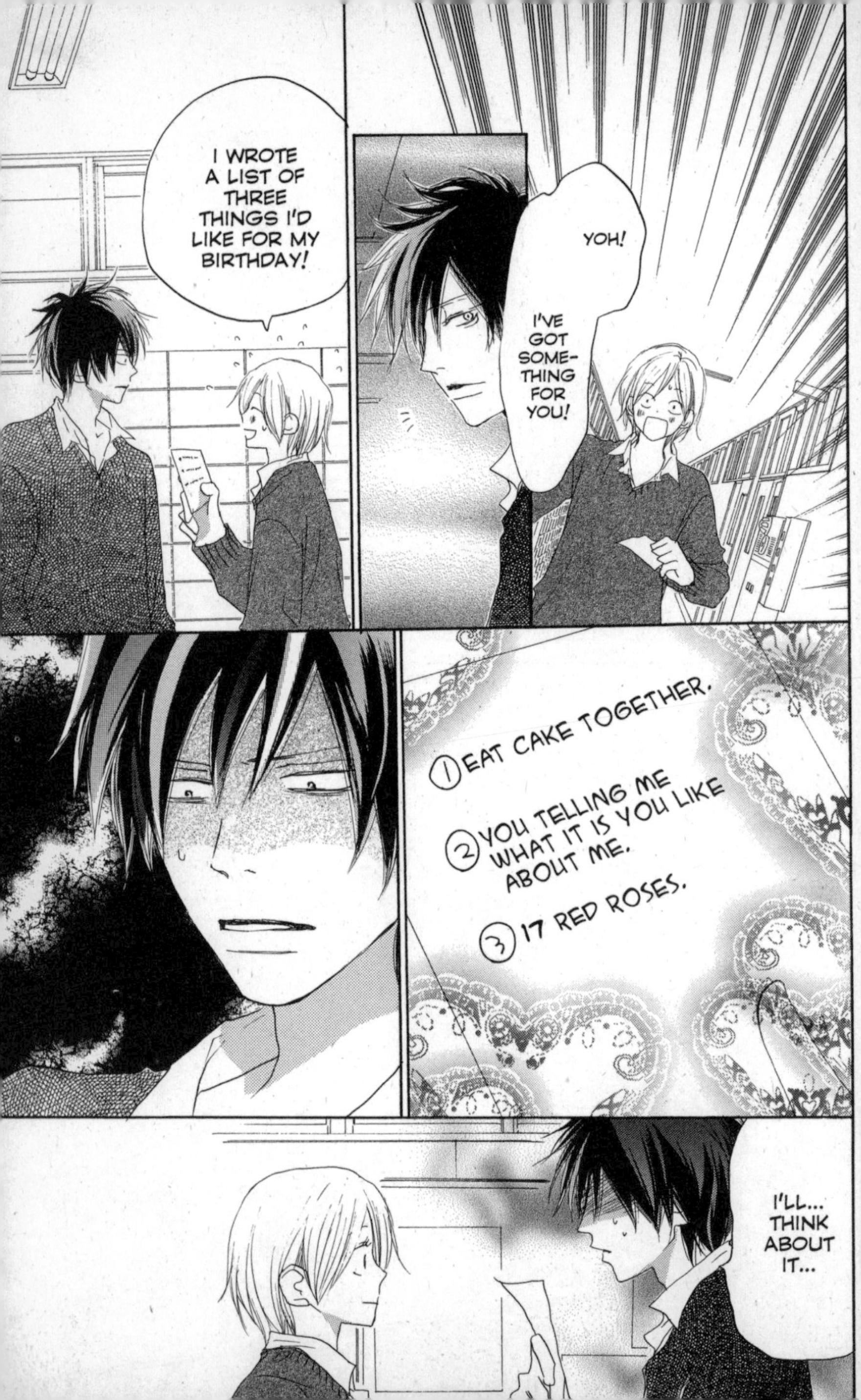
YOH!
I'VE GOT SOME-THING FOR YOU!
I WROTE A LIST OF THREE THINGS I'D LIKE FOR MY BIRTHDAY!
① EAT CAKE TOGETHER.
② YOU TELLING ME WHAT IT IS YOU LIKE ABOUT ME.
③ 17 RED ROSES.
I'LL... THINK ABOUT IT...

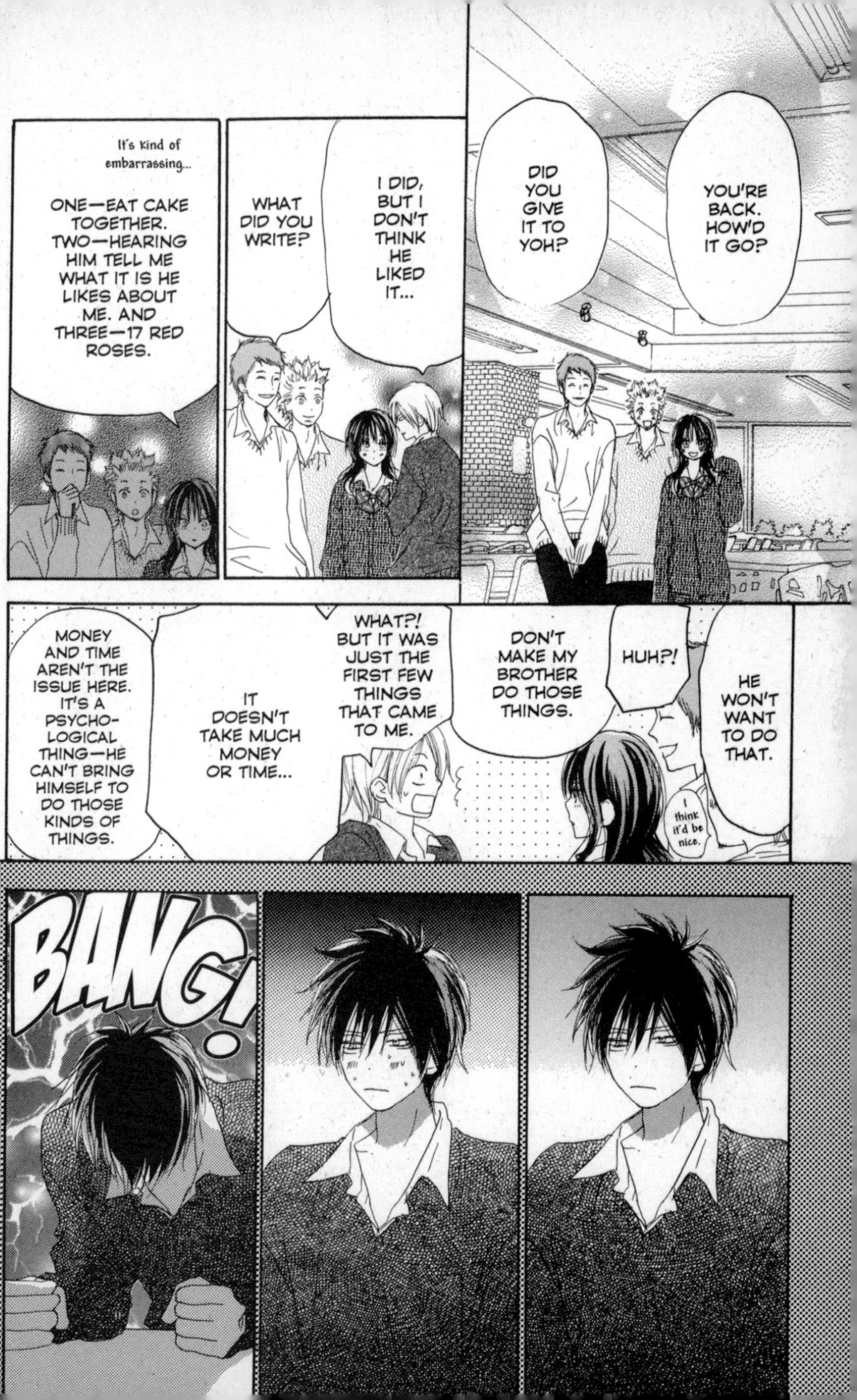
YOU'RE BACK. HOW'D IT GO?
DID YOU GIVE IT TO YOH?
I DID, BUT I DON'T THINK HE LIKED IT...
WHAT DID YOU WRITE?
It's kind of embarrassing...
ONE—EAT CAKE TOGETHER. TWO—HEARING HIM TELL ME WHAT IT IS HE LIKES ABOUT ME. AND THREE—17 RED ROSES.
HE WON'T WANT TO DO THAT.
HUH?!
I think it'd be nice.
DON'T MAKE MY BROTHER DO THOSE THINGS.
WHAT?! BUT IT WAS JUST THE FIRST FEW THINGS THAT CAME TO ME.
IT DOESN'T TAKE MUCH MONEY OR TIME...
MONEY AND TIME AREN'T THE ISSUE HERE. IT'S A PSYCHO-LOGICAL THING—HE CAN'T BRING HIMSELF TO DO THOSE KINDS OF THINGS.
BANG!

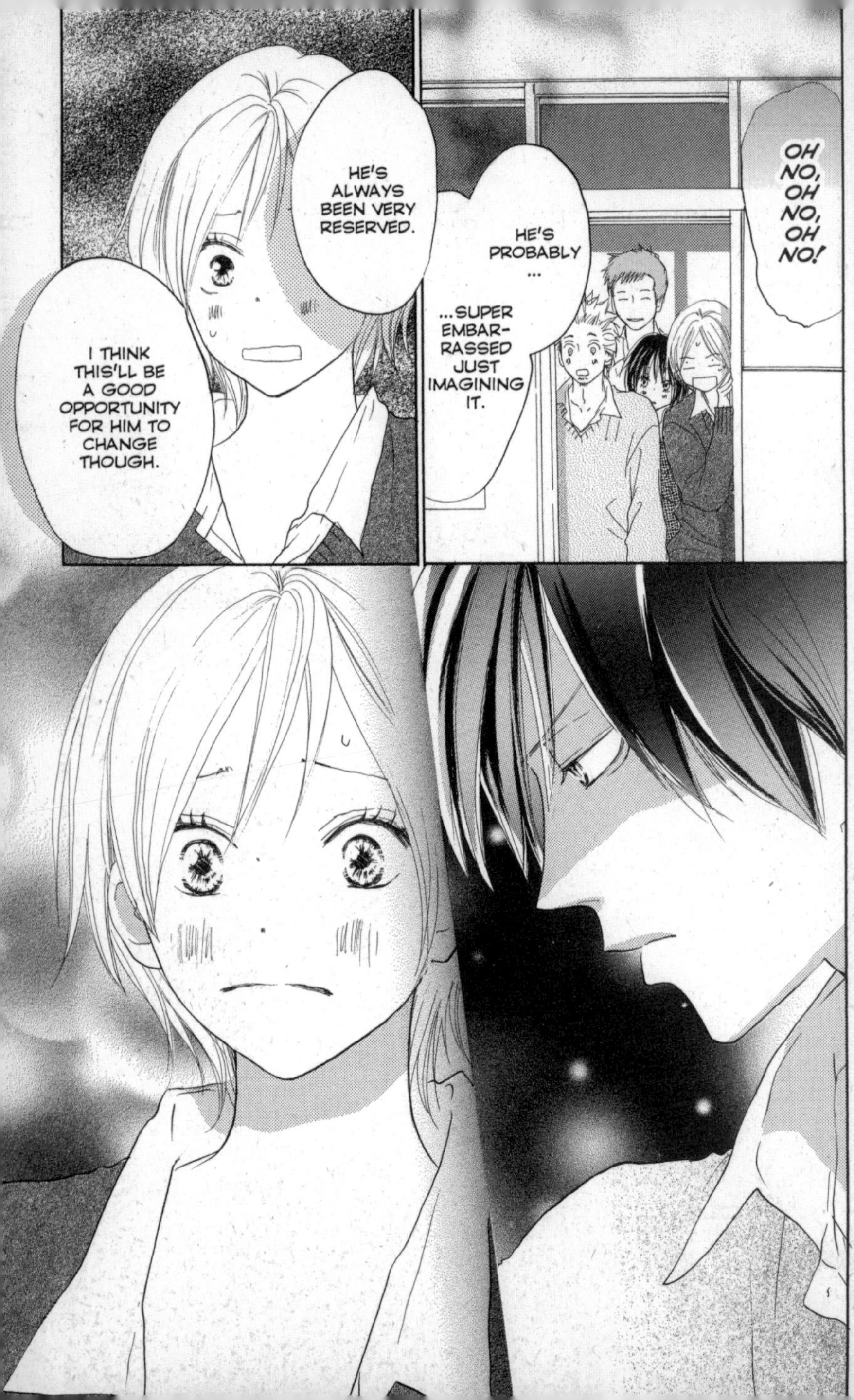
OH NO, OH NO, OH NO!
HE'S PROBABLY ...
...SUPER EMBARRASSED JUST IMAGINING IT.
HE'S ALWAYS BEEN VERY RESERVED.
I THINK THIS'LL BE A GOOD OPPORTUNITY FOR HIM TO CHANGE THOUGH.

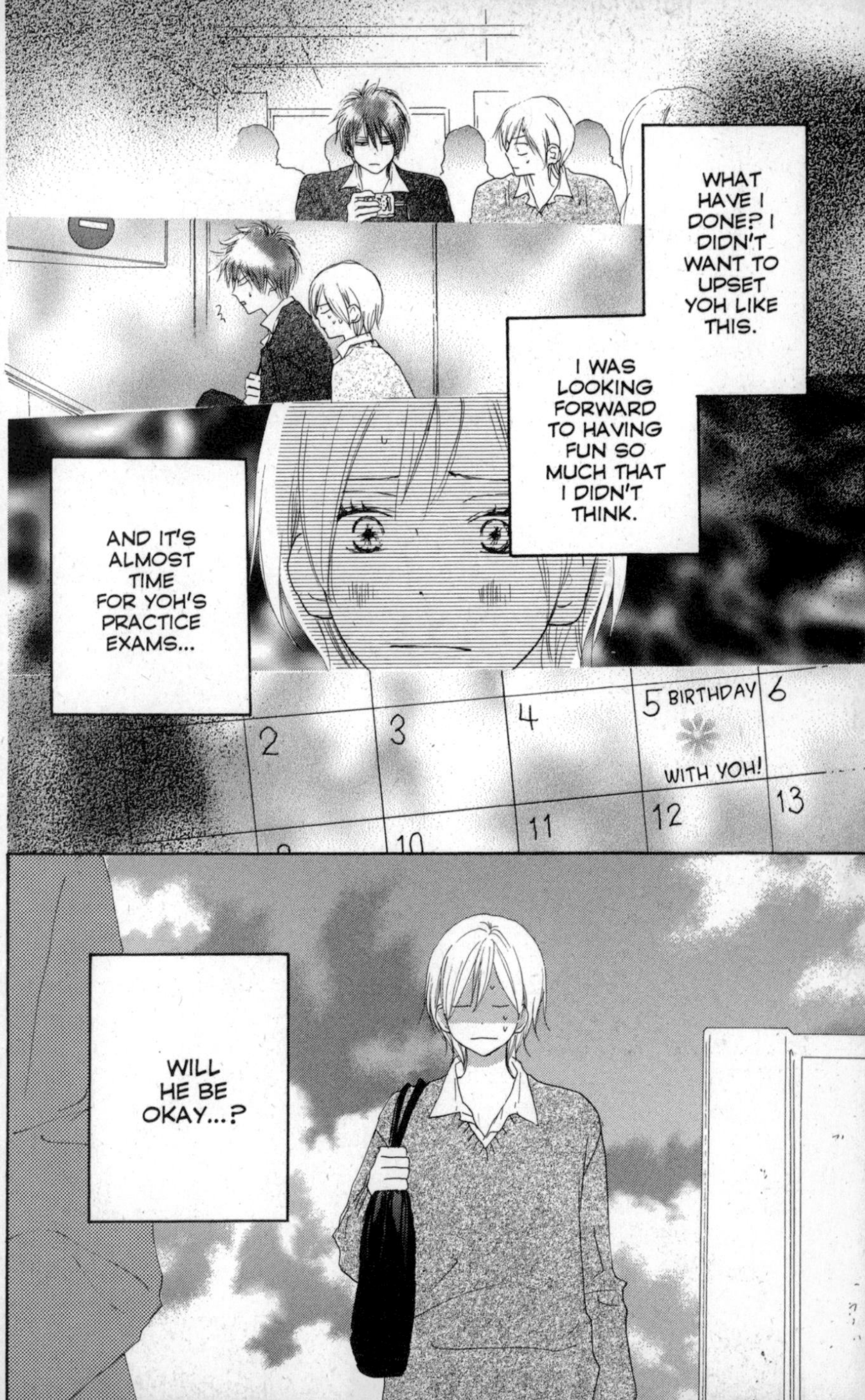
WHAT HAVE I DONE? I DIDN'T WANT TO UPSET YOH LIKE THIS.
I WAS LOOKING FORWARD TO HAVING FUN SO MUCH THAT I DIDN'T THINK.
AND IT'S ALMOST TIME FOR YOH'S PRACTICE EXAMS...
BIRTHDAY
WITH YOH!
WILL HE BE OKAY...?

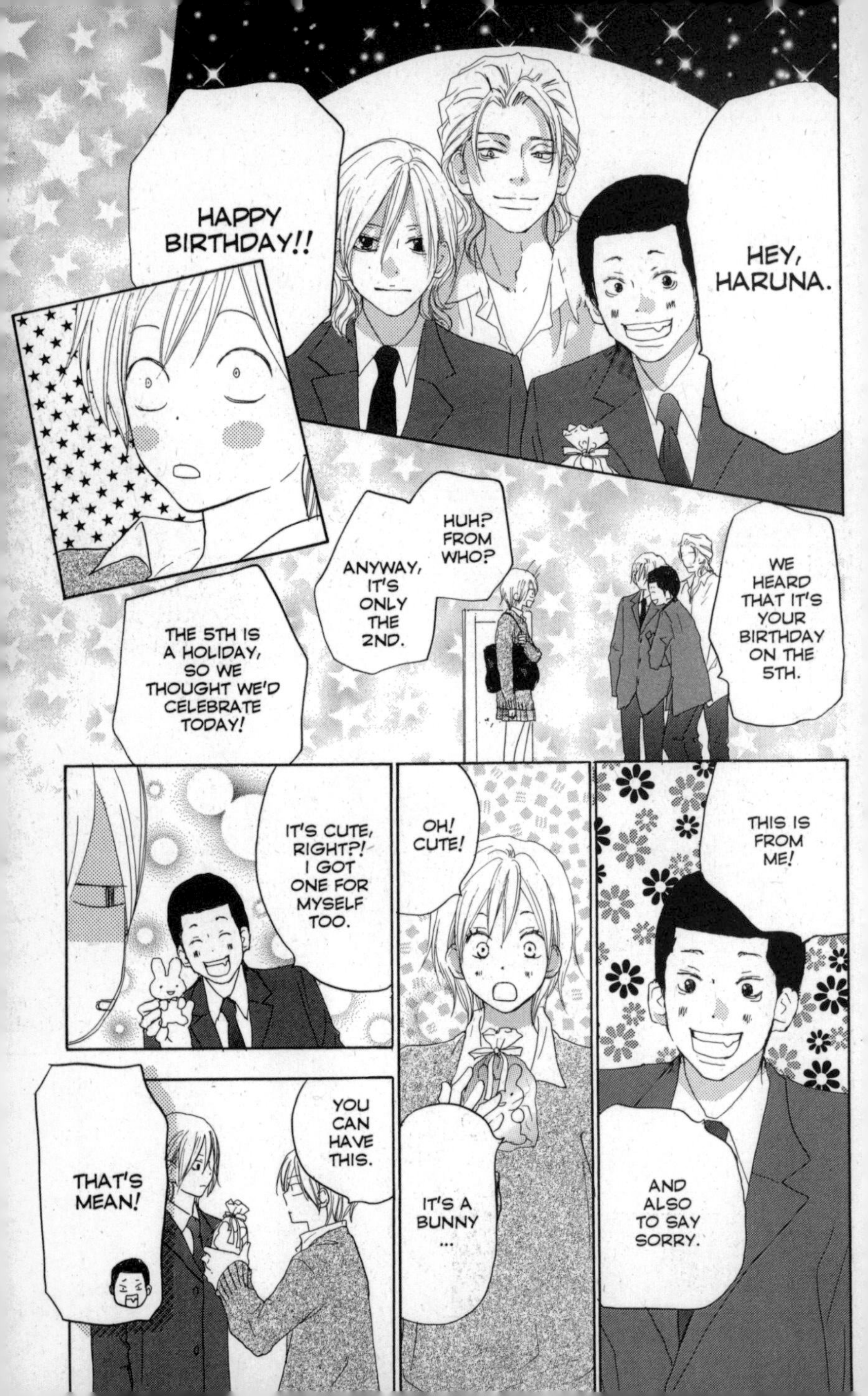
HEY, HARUNA.
HAPPY BIRTHDAY!!
WE HEARD THAT IT'S YOUR BIRTHDAY ON THE 5TH.
HUH? FROM WHO?
ANYWAY, IT'S ONLY THE 2ND.
THE 5TH IS A HOLIDAY, SO WE THOUGHT WE'D CELEBRATE TODAY!
THIS IS FROM ME!
AND ALSO TO SAY SORRY.
OH! CUTE!
IT'S A BUNNY ...
IT'S CUTE, RIGHT?! I GOT ONE FOR MYSELF TOO.
YOU CAN HAVE THIS.
THAT'S MEAN!

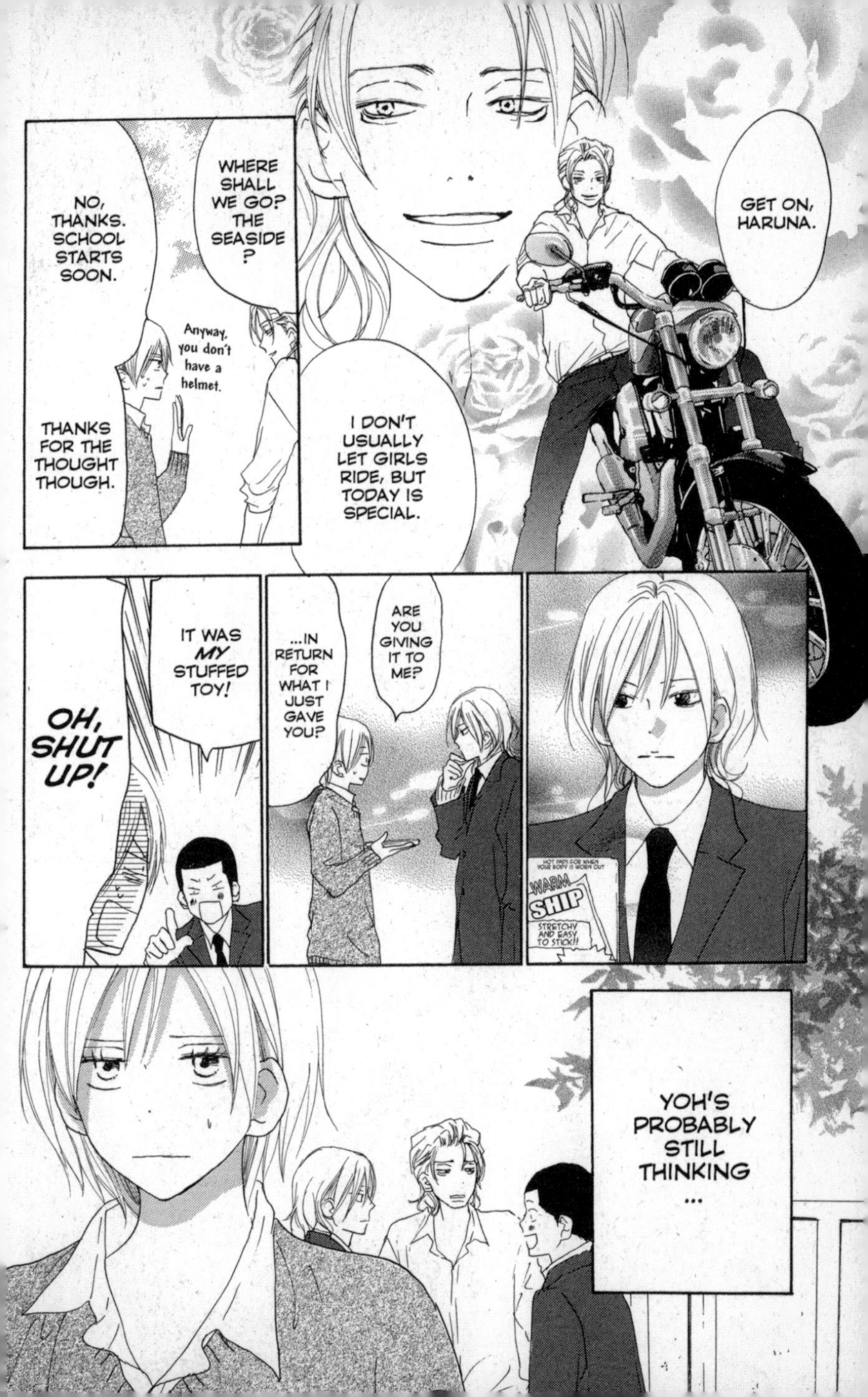
GET ON, HARUNA.
I DON'T USUALLY LET GIRLS RIDE, BUT TODAY IS SPECIAL.
WHERE SHALL WE GO? THE SEASIDE?
NO, THANKS. SCHOOL STARTS SOON.
Anyway, you don't have a helmet.
THANKS FOR THE THOUGHT THOUGH.
HOT PADS FOR WHEN YOUR BODY IS WORN OUT
WARM SHIP
STRETCHY AND EASY TO STICK!!
ARE YOU GIVING IT TO ME?
...IN RETURN FOR WHAT I JUST GAVE YOU?
IT WAS *MY* STUFFED TOY!
OH, SHUT UP!
YOH'S PROBABLY STILL THINKING ...

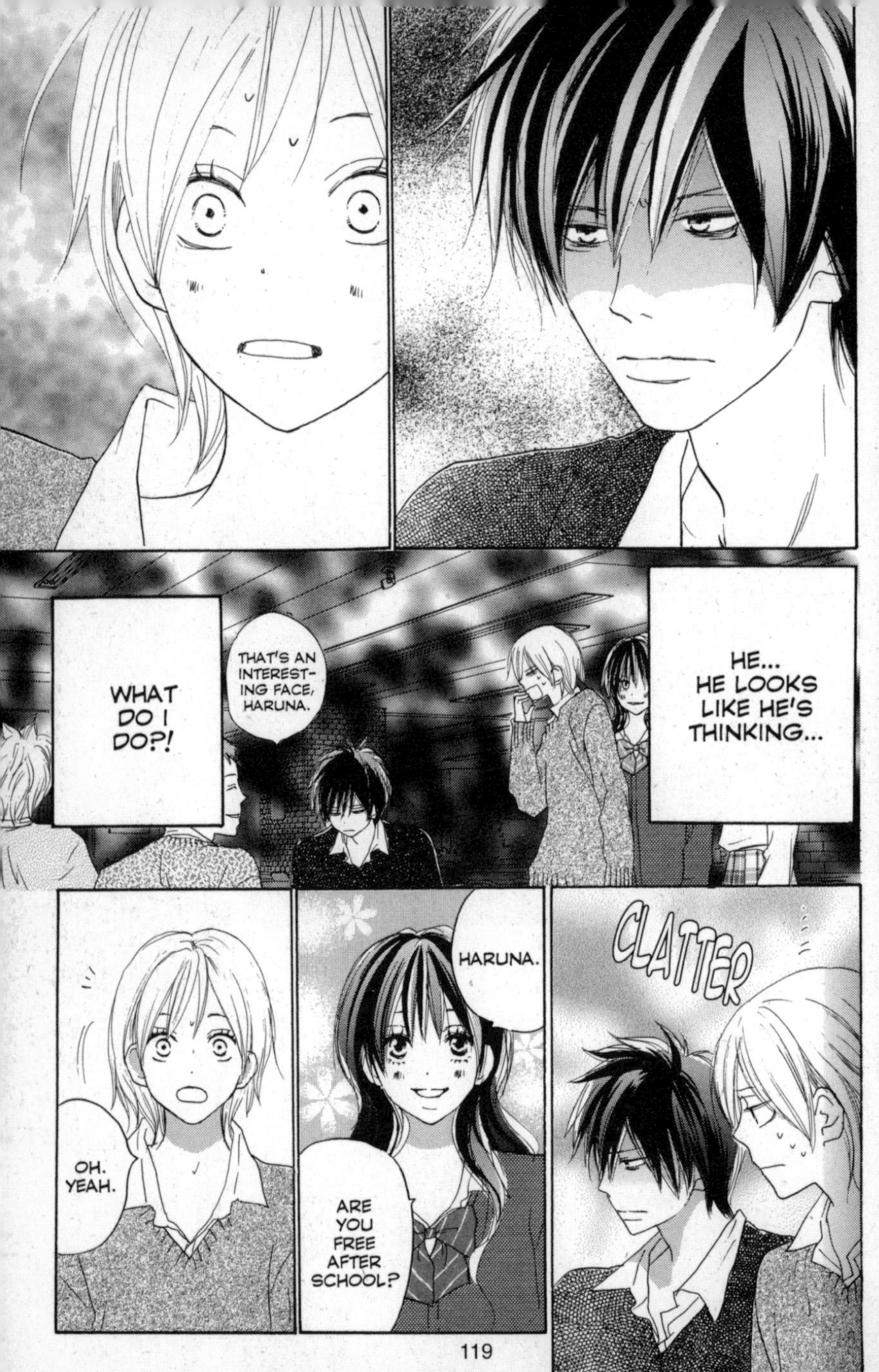
HE... HE LOOKS LIKE HE'S THINKING...
THAT'S AN INTERESTING FACE, HARUNA.
WHAT DO I DO?!
CLATTER
HARUNA.
ARE YOU FREE AFTER SCHOOL?
OH. YEAH.

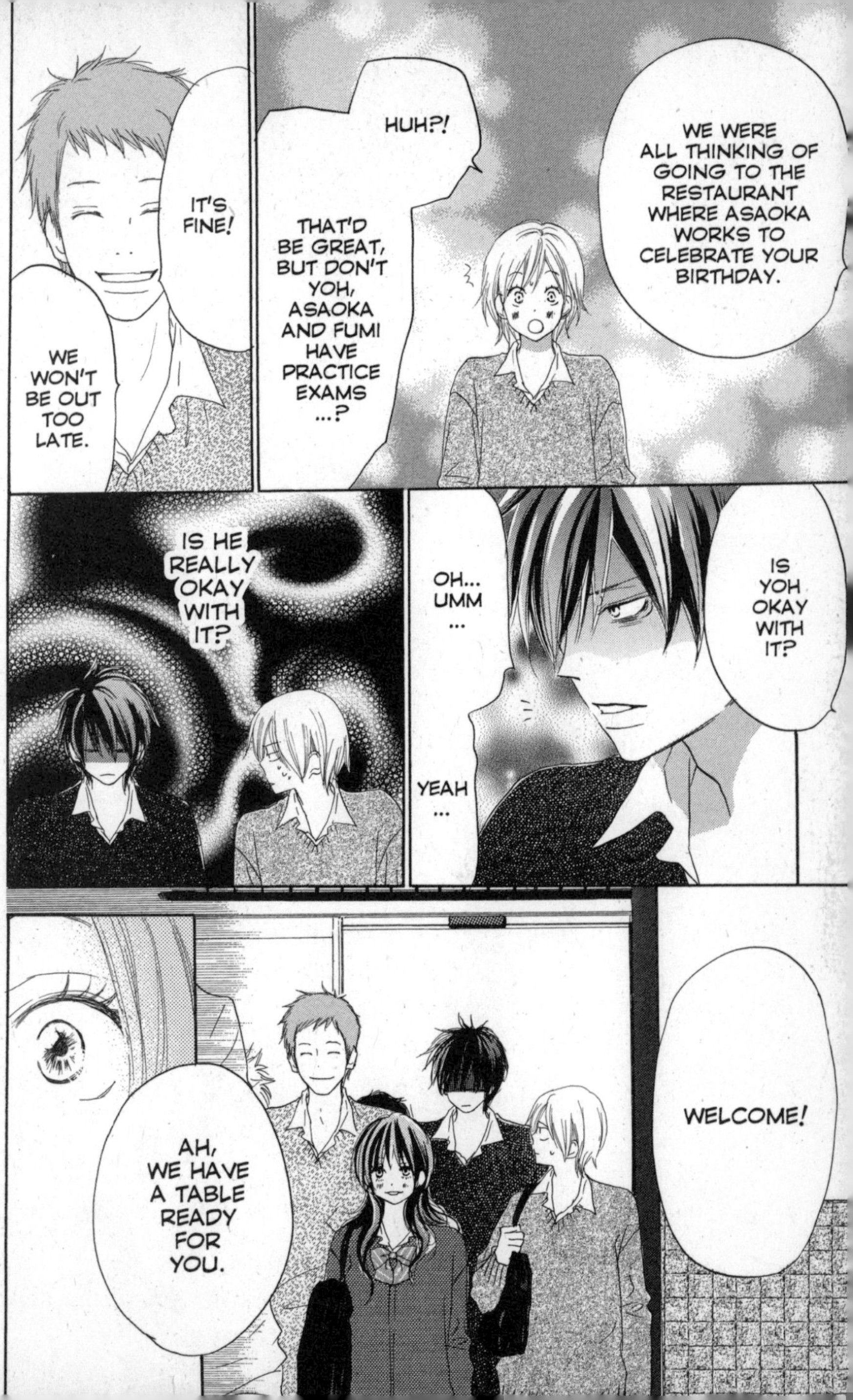
WE WERE ALL THINKING OF GOING TO THE RESTAURANT WHERE ASAOKA WORKS TO CELEBRATE YOUR BIRTHDAY.
HUH?!
THAT'D BE GREAT, BUT DON'T YOH, ASAOKA AND FUMI HAVE PRACTICE EXAMS ...?
IT'S FINE!
WE WON'T BE OUT TOO LATE.
IS YOH OKAY WITH IT?
OH... UMM ...
YEAH ...
IS HE REALLY OKAY WITH IT?
WELCOME!
AH, WE HAVE A TABLE READY FOR YOU.

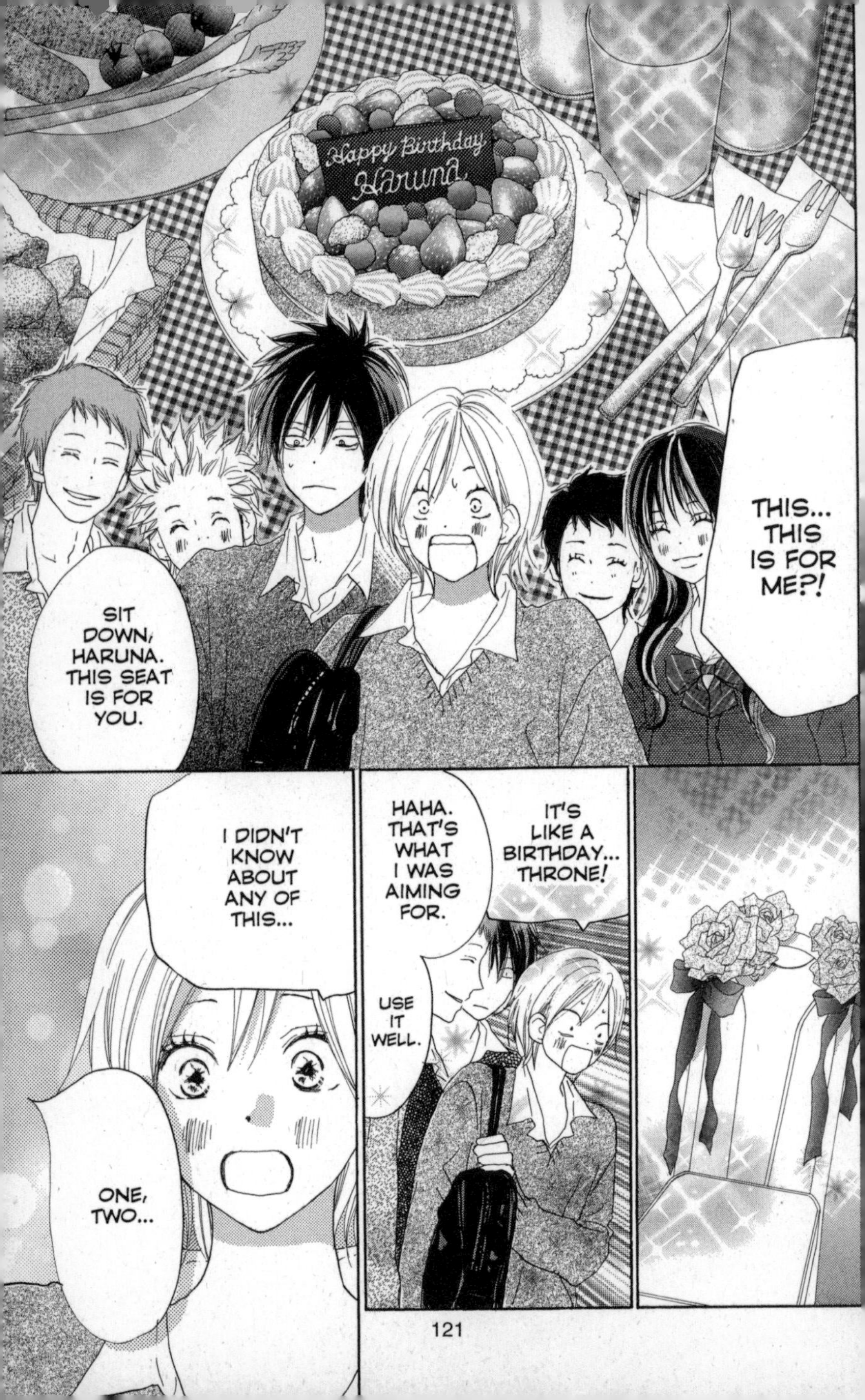
Happy Birthday Haruna
THIS... THIS IS FOR ME?!
SIT DOWN, HARUNA. THIS SEAT IS FOR YOU.
IT'S LIKE A BIRTHDAY... THRONE!
HAHA. THAT'S WHAT I WAS AIMING FOR.
USE IT WELL.
I DIDN'T KNOW ABOUT ANY OF THIS...
ONE, TWO...

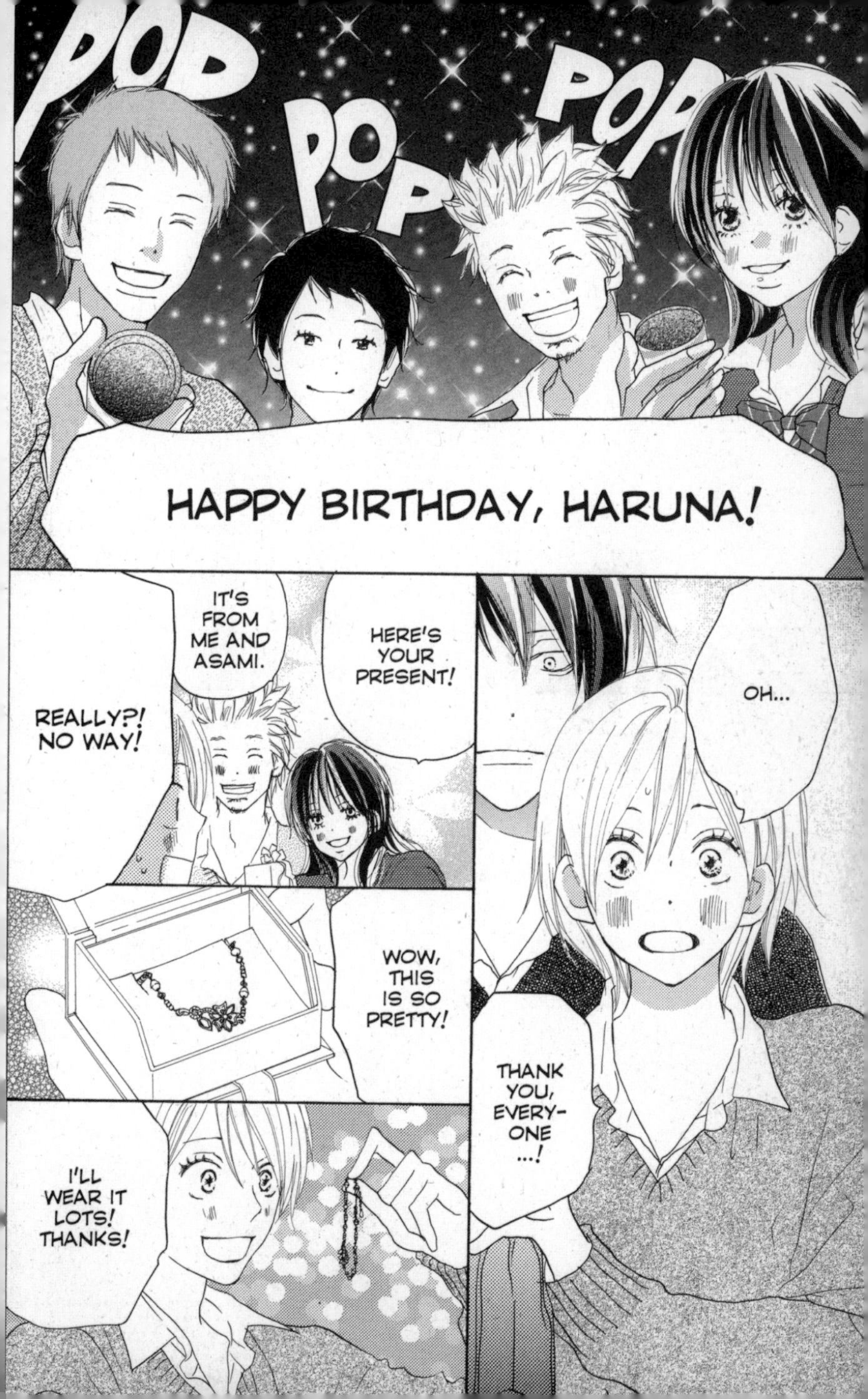
POP
POP
POP
HAPPY BIRTHDAY, HARUNA!
OH...
THANK YOU, EVERYONE ...!
HERE'S YOUR PRESENT!
IT'S FROM ME AND ASAMI.
REALLY?! NO WAY!
WOW, THIS IS SO PRETTY!
I'LL WEAR IT LOTS! THANKS!

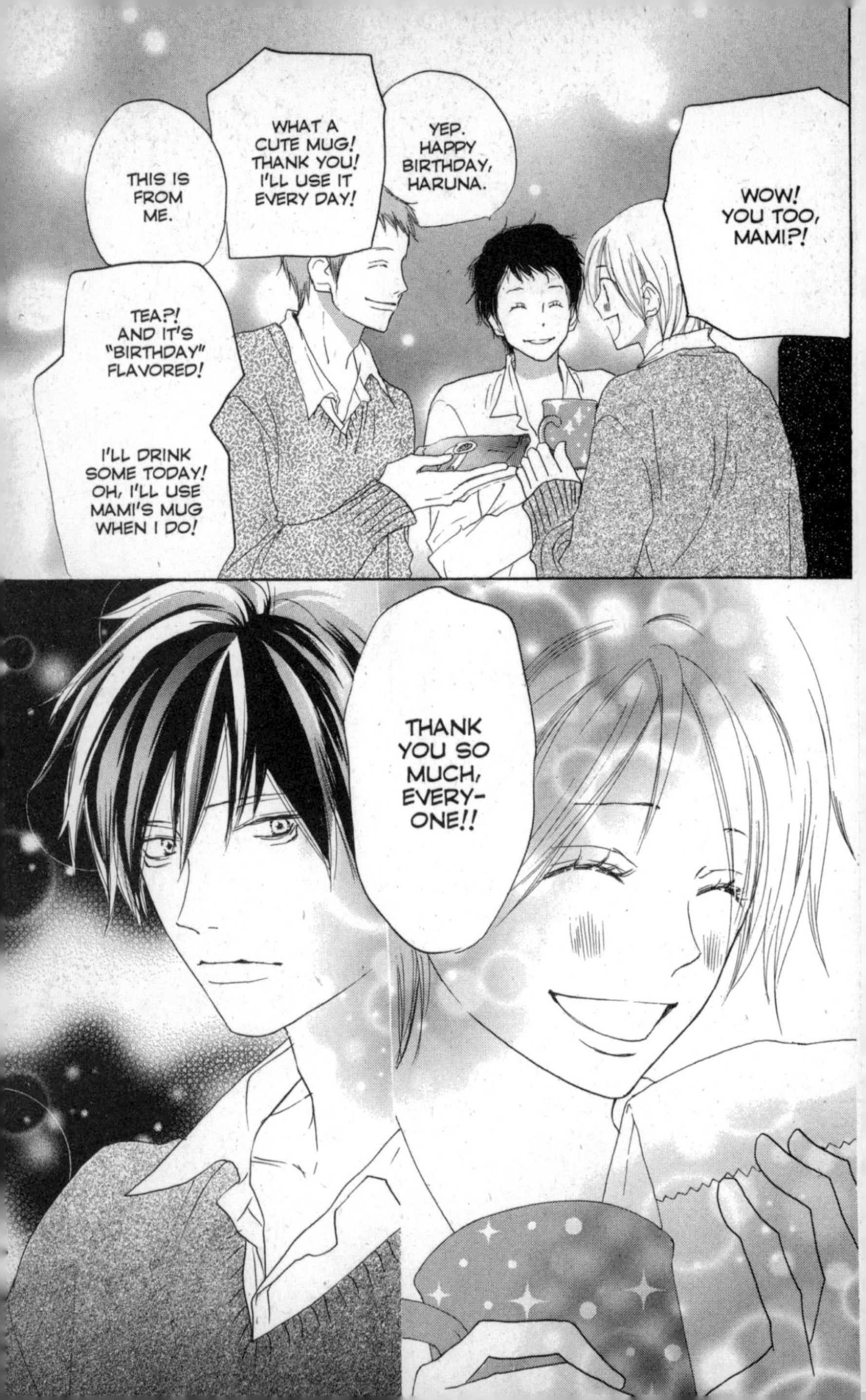
WOW! YOU TOO, MAMI?!
YEP. HAPPY BIRTHDAY, HARUNA.
WHAT A CUTE MUG! THANK YOU! I'LL USE IT EVERY DAY!
THIS IS FROM ME.
TEA?! AND IT'S "BIRTHDAY" FLAVORED!
I'LL DRINK SOME TODAY! OH, I'LL USE MAMI'S MUG WHEN I DO!
THANK YOU SO MUCH, EVERY-ONE!!

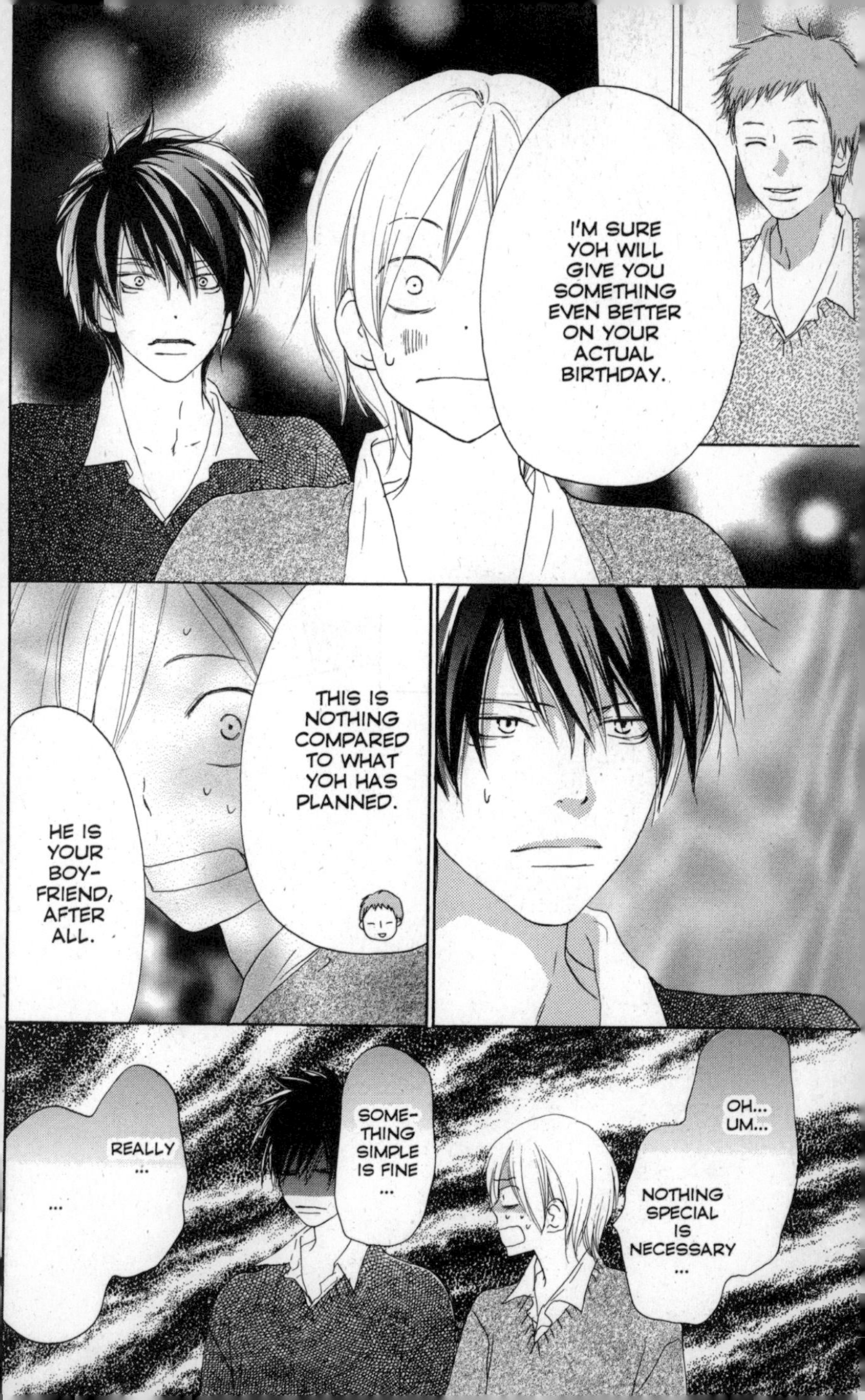
I'M SURE YOH WILL GIVE YOU SOMETHING EVEN BETTER ON YOUR ACTUAL BIRTHDAY.
THIS IS NOTHING COMPARED TO WHAT YOH HAS PLANNED.
HE IS YOUR BOY-FRIEND, AFTER ALL.
OH... UM...
NOTHING SPECIAL IS NECESSARY ...
SOME-THING SIMPLE IS FINE ...
REALLY ...
...

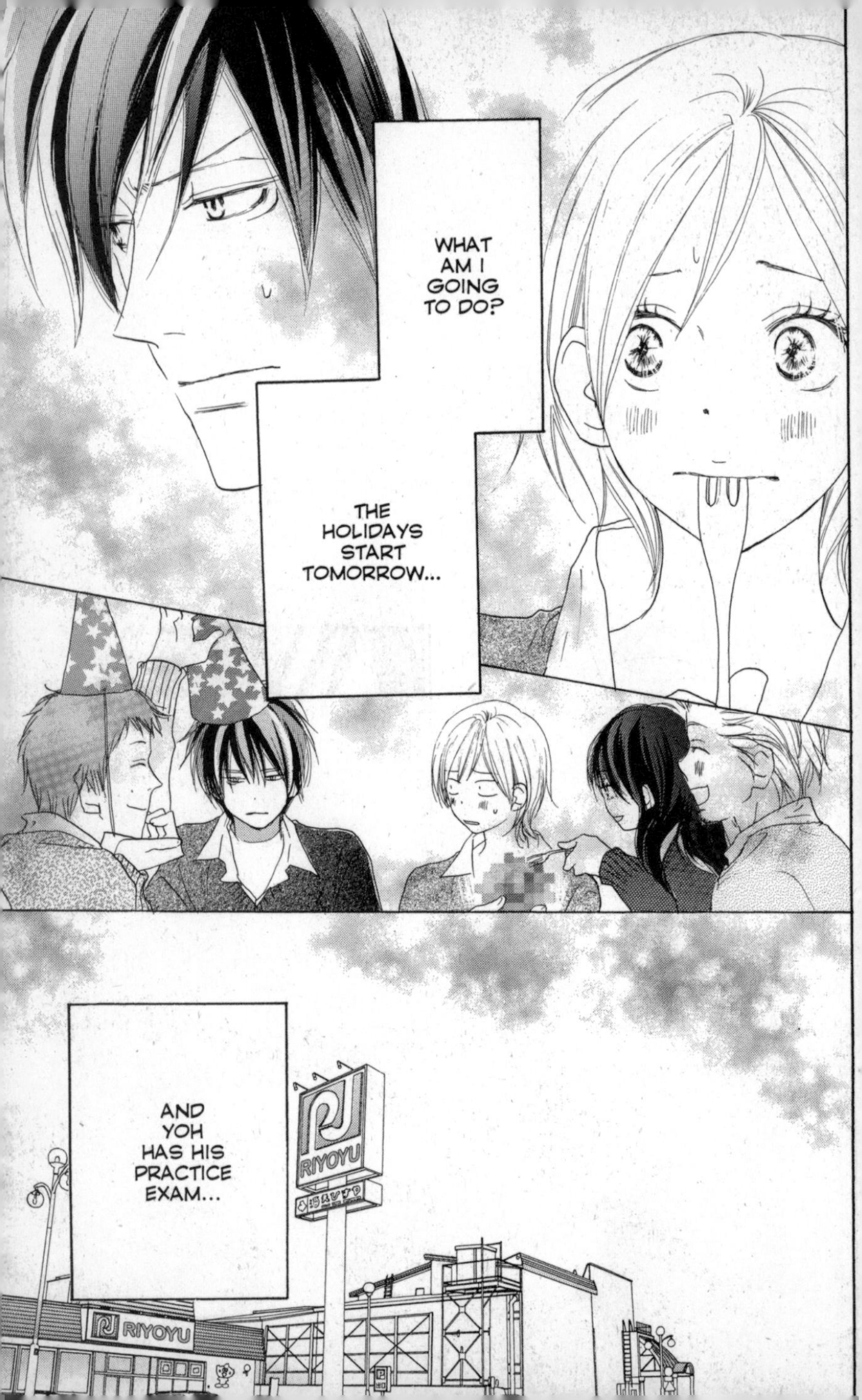
WHAT AM I GOING TO DO?
THE HOLIDAYS START TOMORROW...
AND YOH HAS HIS PRACTICE EXAM...
RIYOYU
RIYOYU

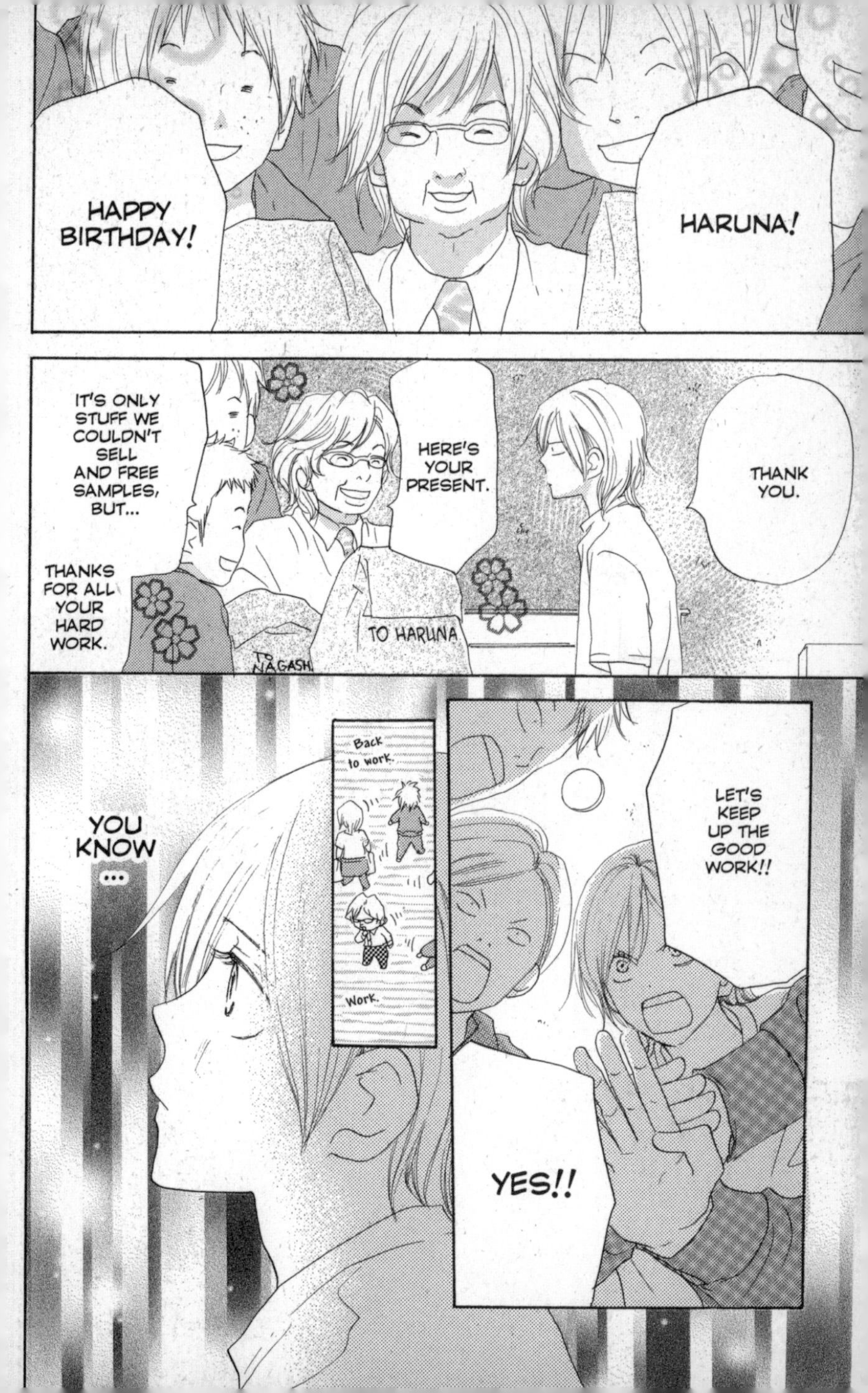
HARUNA!
HAPPY BIRTHDAY!
THANK YOU.
HERE'S YOUR PRESENT.
IT'S ONLY STUFF WE COULDN'T SELL AND FREE SAMPLES, BUT...
TO HARUNA
THANKS FOR ALL YOUR HARD WORK.
TO NAGASH
LET'S KEEP UP THE GOOD WORK!!
YES!!
Back to work.
Work.
YOU KNOW...

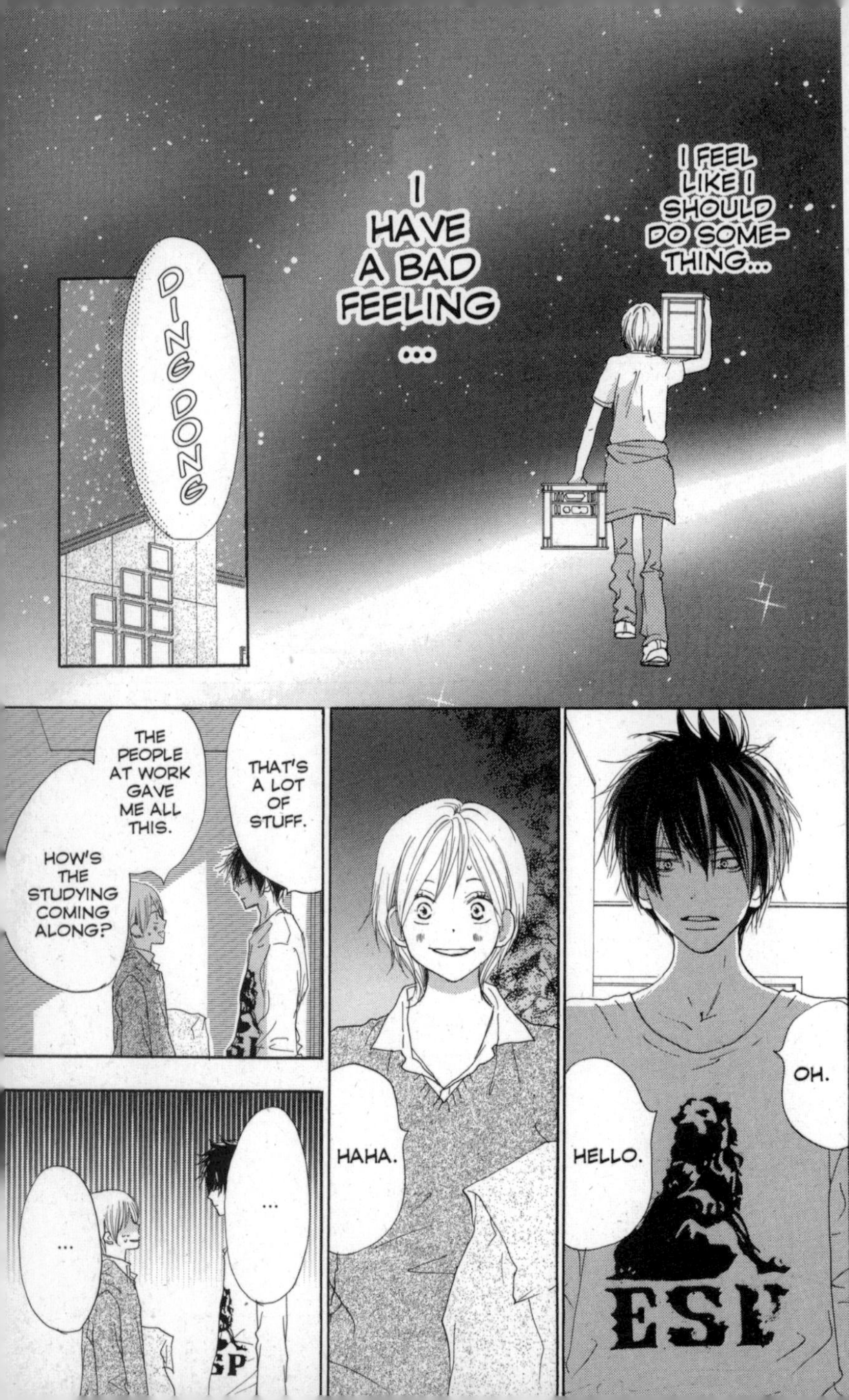
I FEEL LIKE I SHOULD DO SOME-THING...
I HAVE A BAD FEELING...
DING DONG
OH.
HELLO.
HAHA.
THAT'S A LOT OF STUFF.
THE PEOPLE AT WORK GAVE ME ALL THIS.
HOW'S THE STUDYING COMING ALONG?
...
...

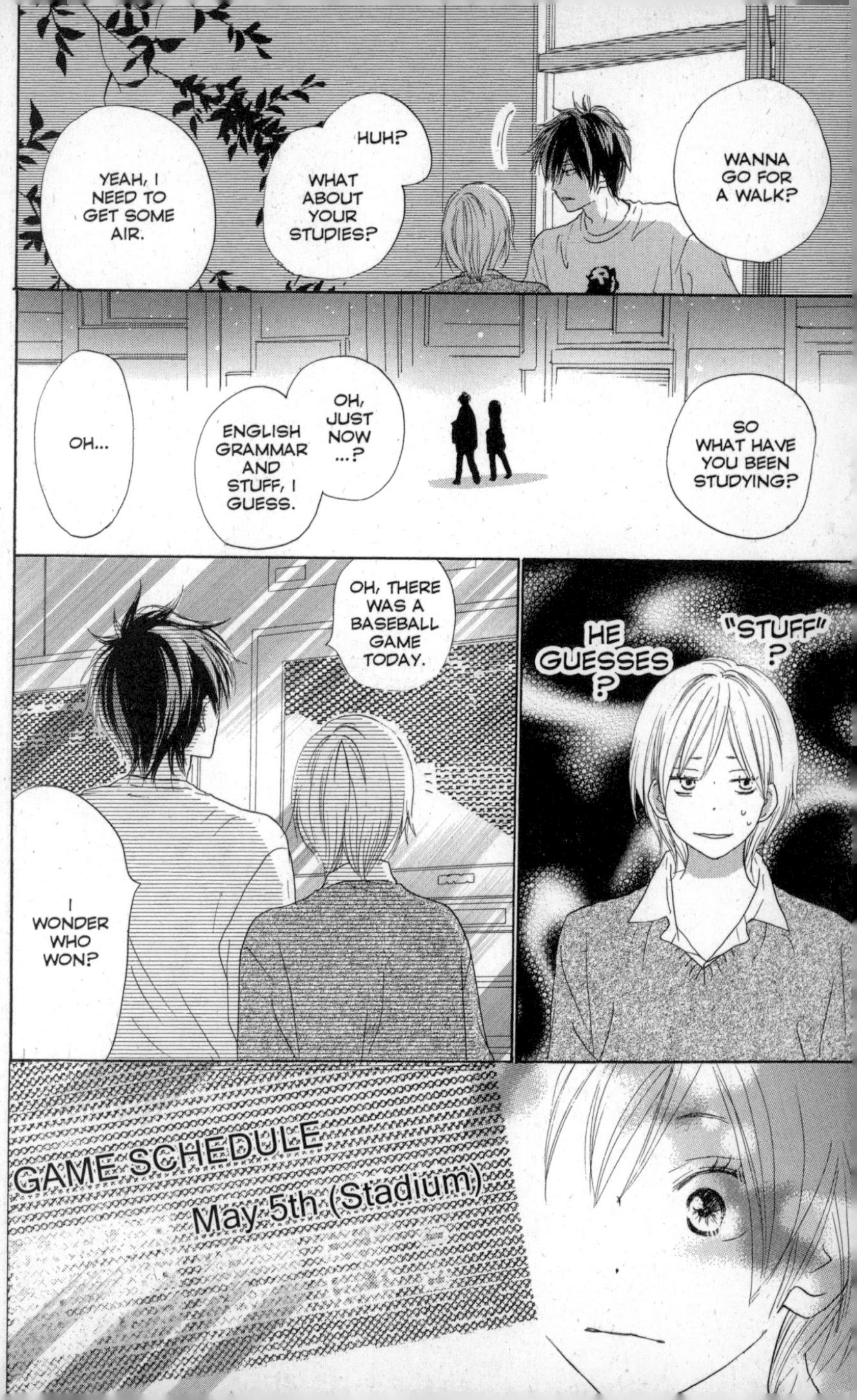
WANNA GO FOR A WALK?
HUH?
WHAT ABOUT YOUR STUDIES?
YEAH, I NEED TO GET SOME AIR.
SO WHAT HAVE YOU BEEN STUDYING?
OH, JUST NOW ...?
ENGLISH GRAMMAR AND STUFF, I GUESS.
OH...
"STUFF"?
HE GUESSES?
OH, THERE WAS A BASEBALL GAME TODAY.
I WONDER WHO WON?
GAME SCHEDULE
May 5th (Stadium)

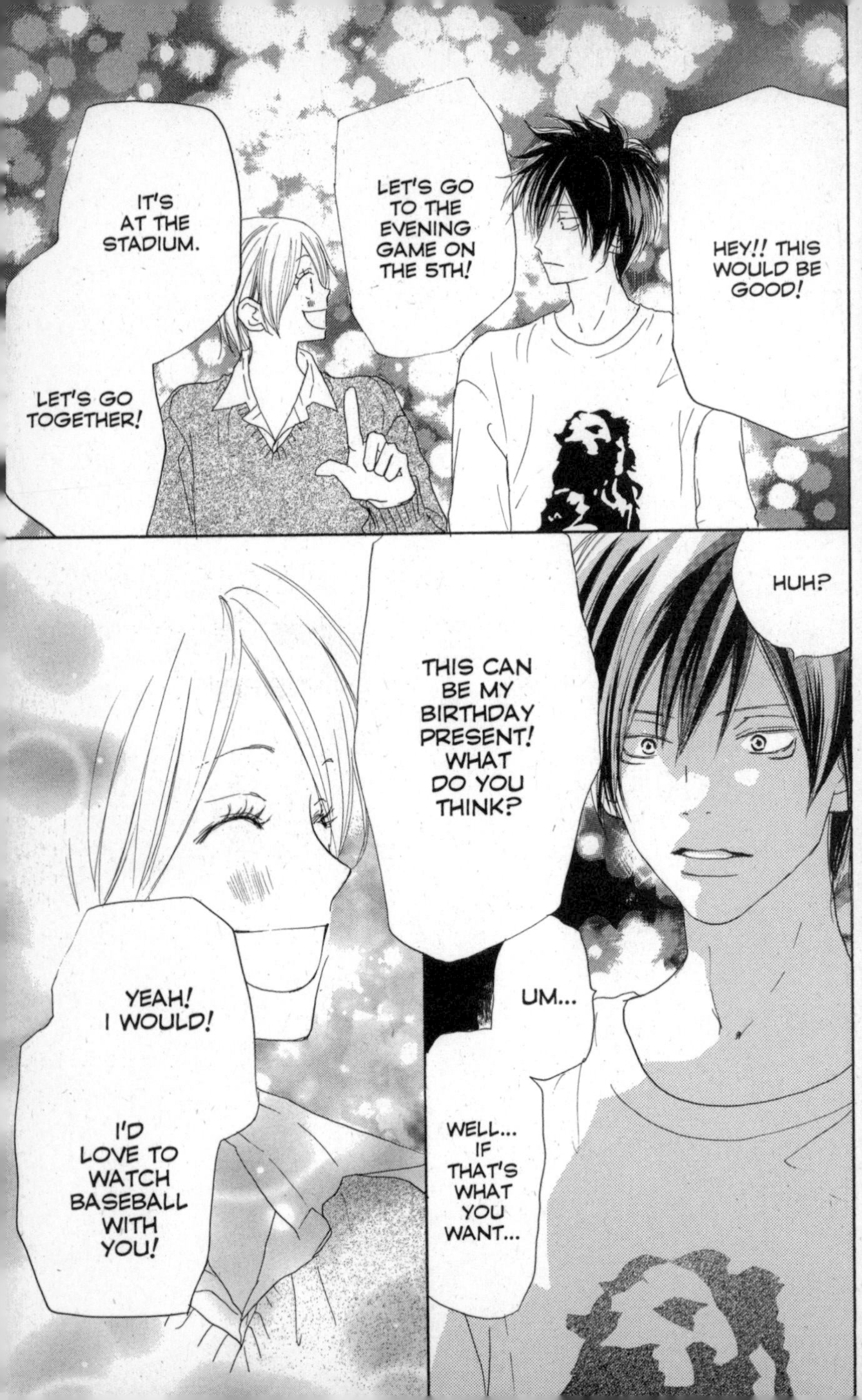
HEY!! THIS WOULD BE GOOD!
LET'S GO TO THE EVENING GAME ON THE 5TH!
IT'S AT THE STADIUM.
LET'S GO TOGETHER!
HUH?
THIS CAN BE MY BIRTHDAY PRESENT! WHAT DO YOU THINK?
UM...
WELL... IF THAT'S WHAT YOU WANT...
YEAH! I WOULD!
I'D LOVE TO WATCH BASEBALL WITH YOU!

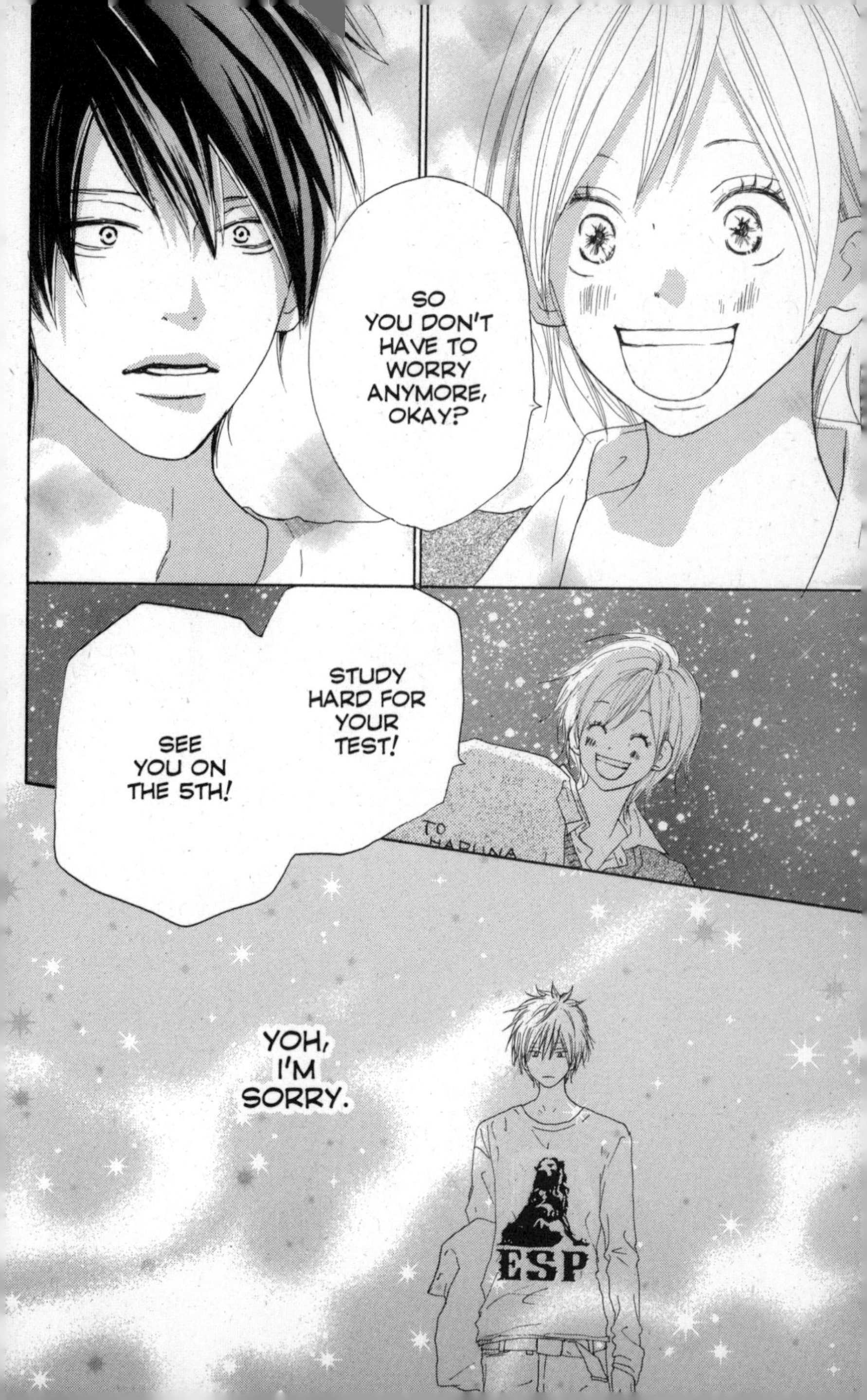
SO YOU DON'T HAVE TO WORRY ANYMORE, OKAY?
STUDY HARD FOR YOUR TEST!
SEE YOU ON THE 5TH!
YOH, I'M SORRY.
ESP

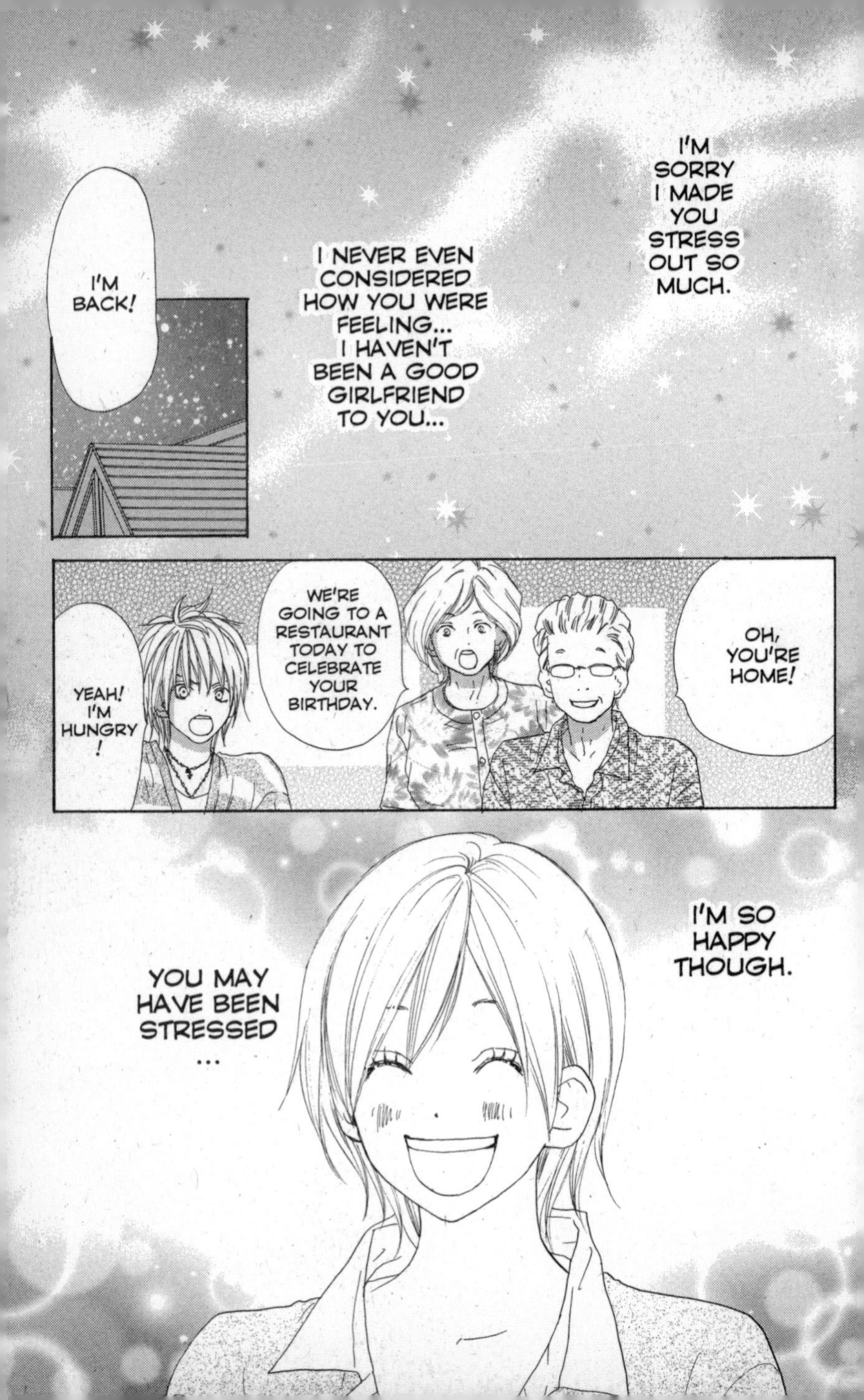
I'M SORRY I MADE YOU STRESS OUT SO MUCH.
I NEVER EVEN CONSIDERED HOW YOU WERE FEELING... I HAVEN'T BEEN A GOOD GIRLFRIEND TO YOU...
I'M BACK!
OH, YOU'RE HOME!
WE'RE GOING TO A RESTAURANT TODAY TO CELEBRATE YOUR BIRTHDAY.
YEAH! I'M HUNGRY!
I'M SO HAPPY THOUGH.
YOU MAY HAVE BEEN STRESSED...

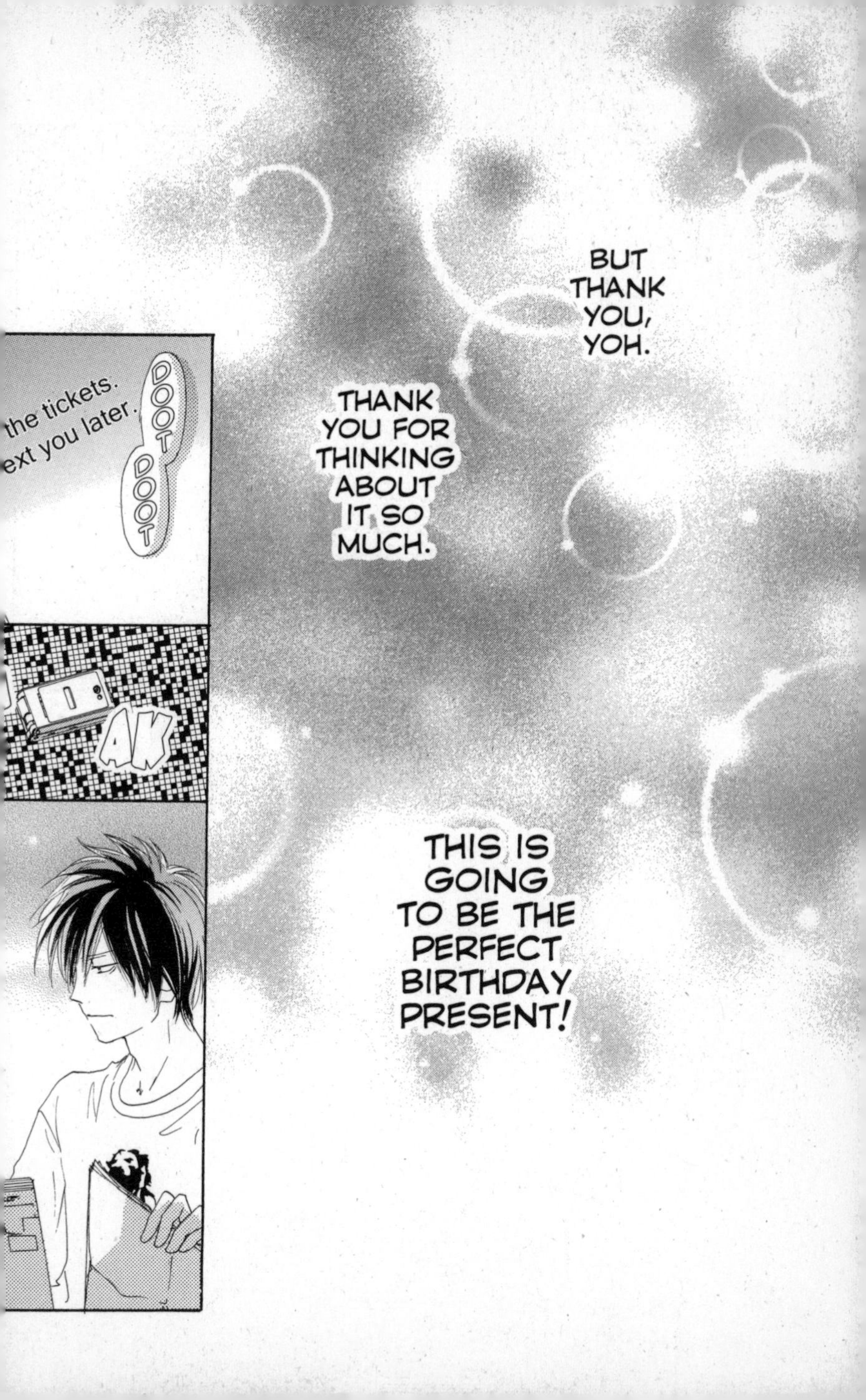
BUT THANK YOU, YOH.
THANK YOU FOR THINKING ABOUT IT SO MUCH.
THIS IS GOING TO BE THE PERFECT BIRTHDAY PRESENT!
the tickets.
ext you later.
DOOT DOOT
AK

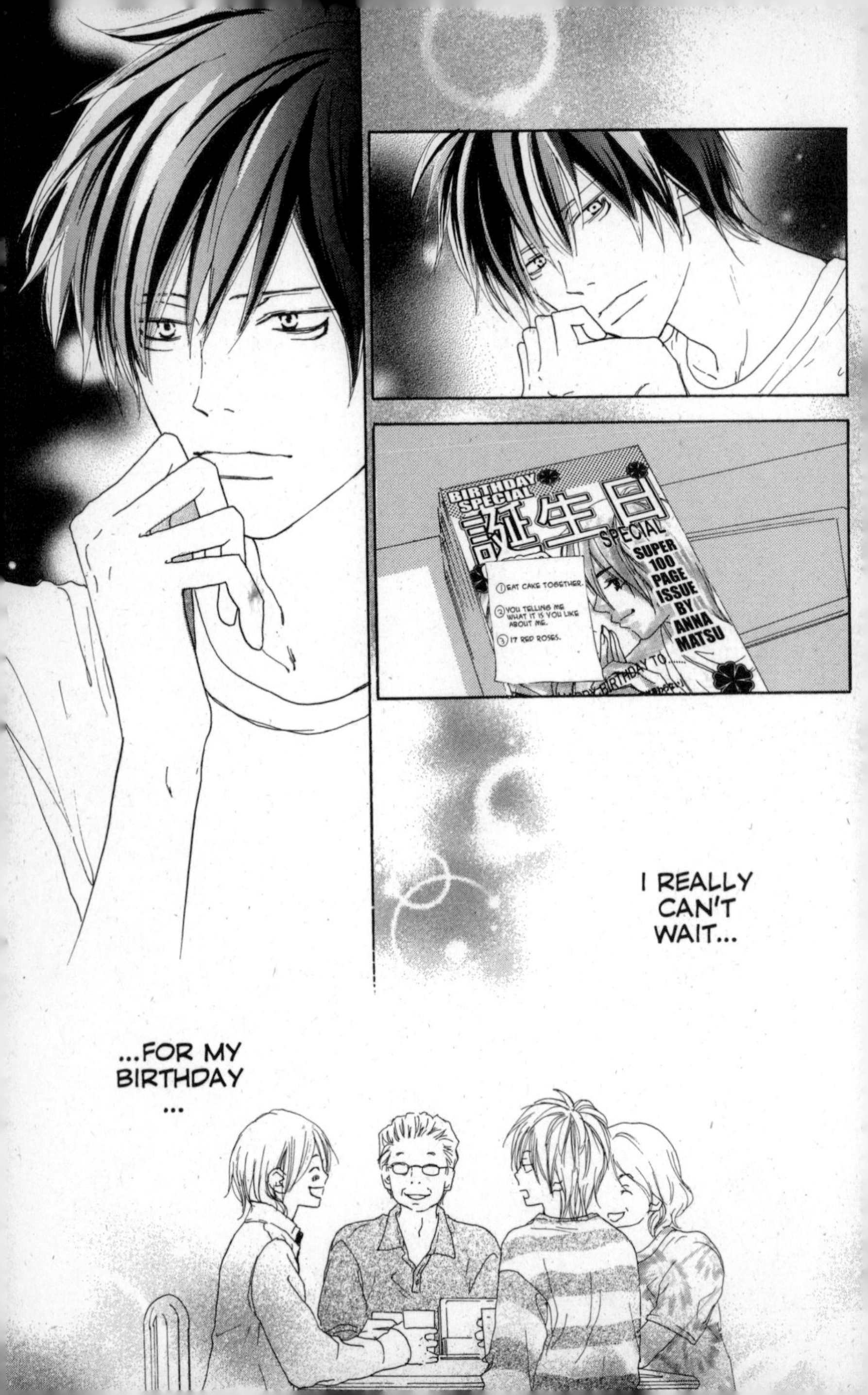
BIRTHDAY SPECIAL
誕生日
SPECIAL
SUPER 100 PAGE ISSUE BY ANNA MATSU
① EAT CAKE TOGETHER.
② YOU TELLING ME WHAT IT IS YOU LIKE ABOUT ME.
③ 17 RED ROSES.
BIRTHDAY TO......
I REALLY CAN'T WAIT...
...FOR MY BIRTHDAY
...

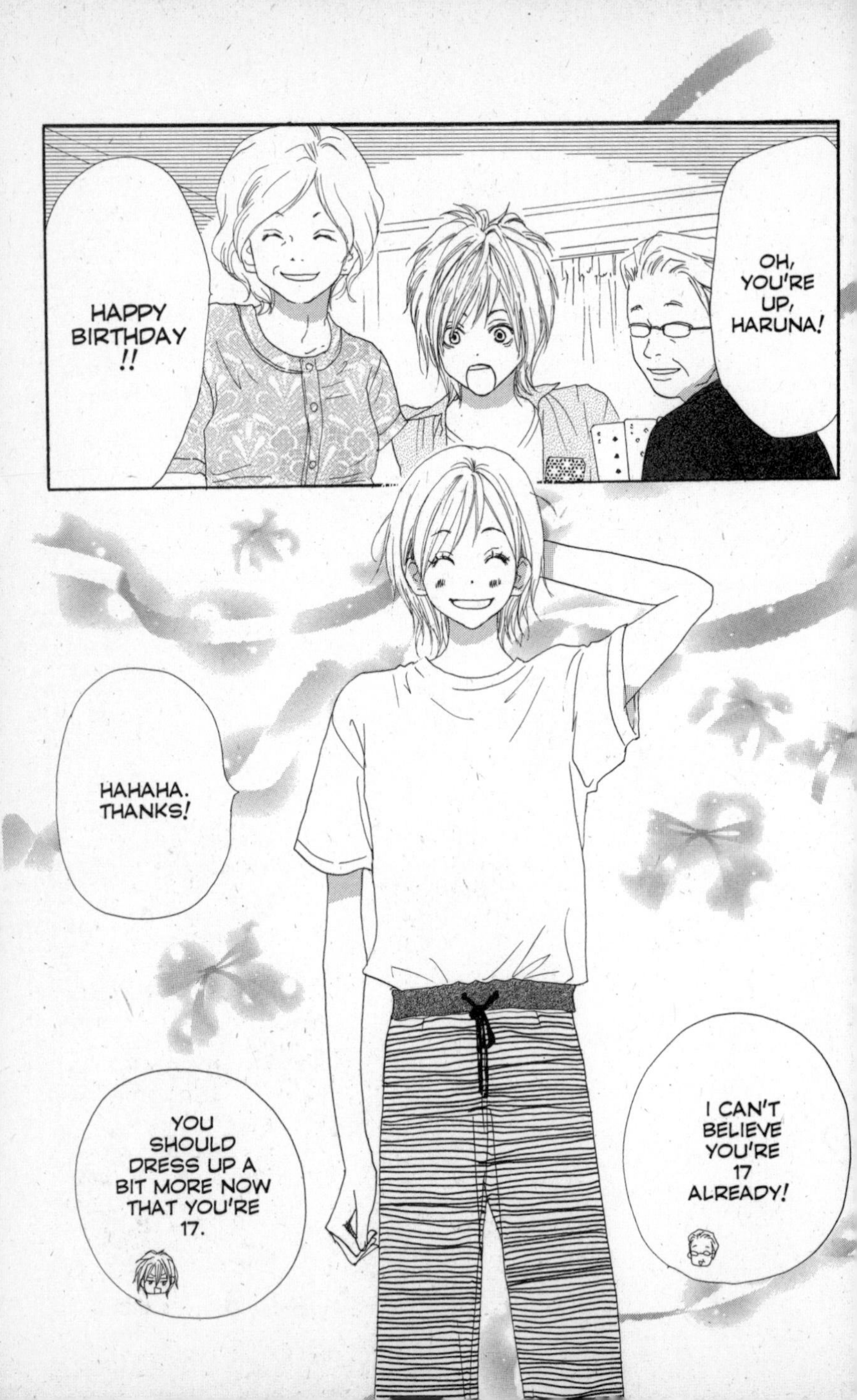
OH, YOU'RE UP, HARUNA!
HAPPY BIRTHDAY!!
HAHAHA. THANKS!
I CAN'T BELIEVE YOU'RE 17 ALREADY!
YOU SHOULD DRESS UP A BIT MORE NOW THAT YOU'RE 17.

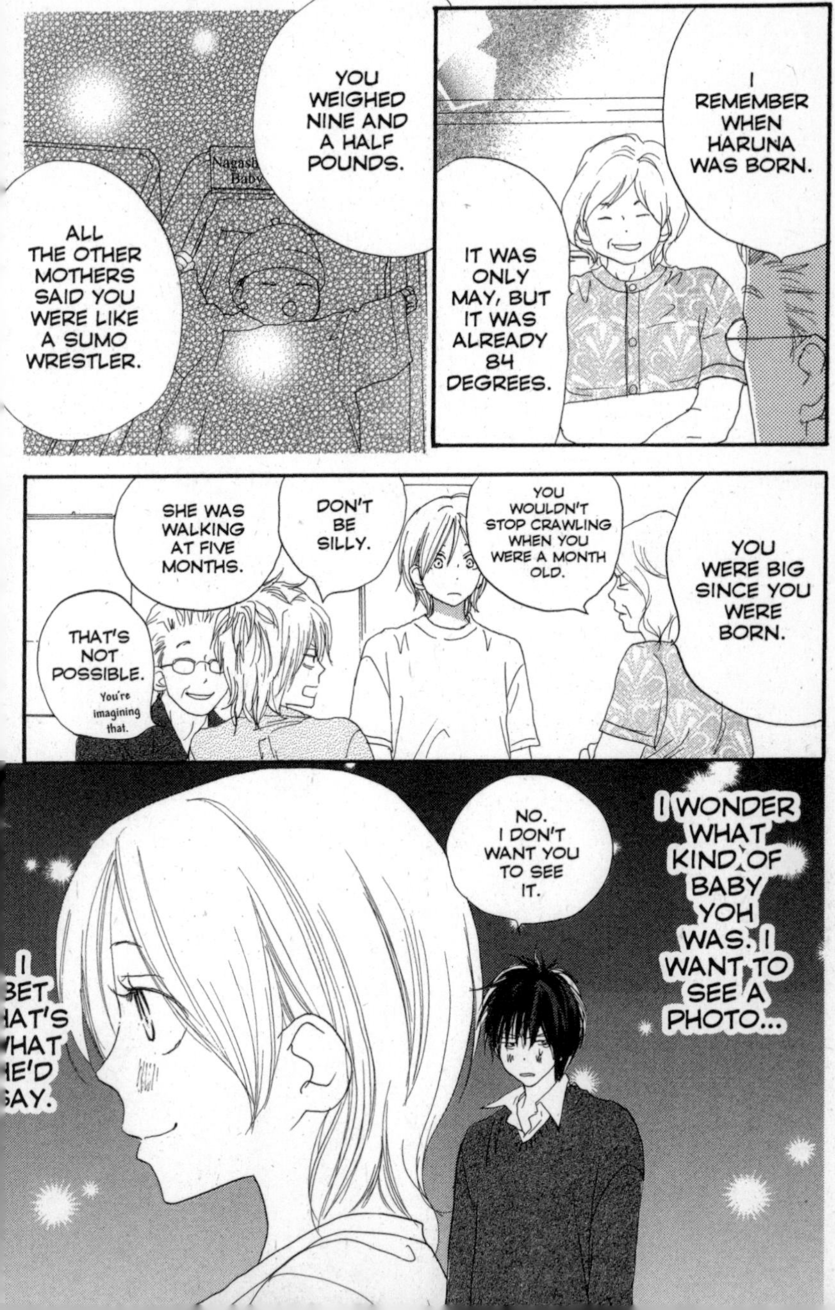

I REMEMBER WHEN HARUNA WAS BORN.
IT WAS ONLY MAY, BUT IT WAS ALREADY 84 DEGREES.
YOU WEIGHED NINE AND A HALF POUNDS.
ALL THE OTHER MOTHERS SAID YOU WERE LIKE A SUMO WRESTLER.
YOU WERE BIG SINCE YOU WERE BORN.
YOU WOULDN'T STOP CRAWLING WHEN YOU WERE A MONTH OLD.
DON'T BE SILLY.
SHE WAS WALKING AT FIVE MONTHS.
THAT'S NOT POSSIBLE.
You're imagining that.
I WONDER WHAT KIND OF BABY YOH WAS. I WANT TO SEE A PHOTO...
NO. I DON'T WANT YOU TO SEE IT.
I BET HAT'S HAT E'D AY.

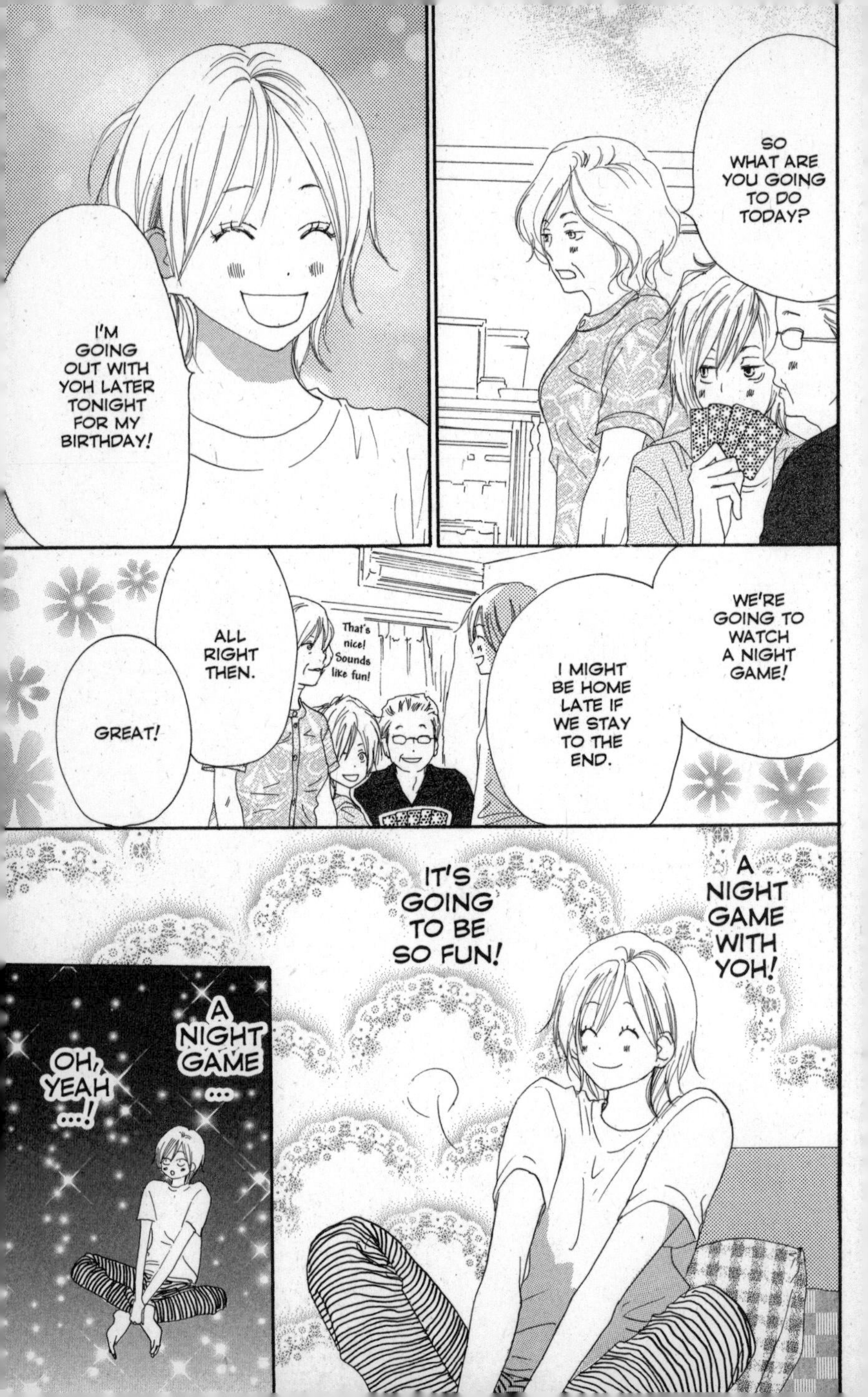
SO WHAT ARE YOU GOING TO DO TODAY?
I'M GOING OUT WITH YOH LATER TONIGHT FOR MY BIRTHDAY!
WE'RE GOING TO WATCH A NIGHT GAME!
I MIGHT BE HOME LATE IF WE STAY TO THE END.
That's nice! Sounds like fun!
ALL RIGHT THEN.
GREAT!
A NIGHT GAME WITH YOH!
IT'S GOING TO BE SO FUN!
A NIGHT GAME ...
OH, YEAH ...!

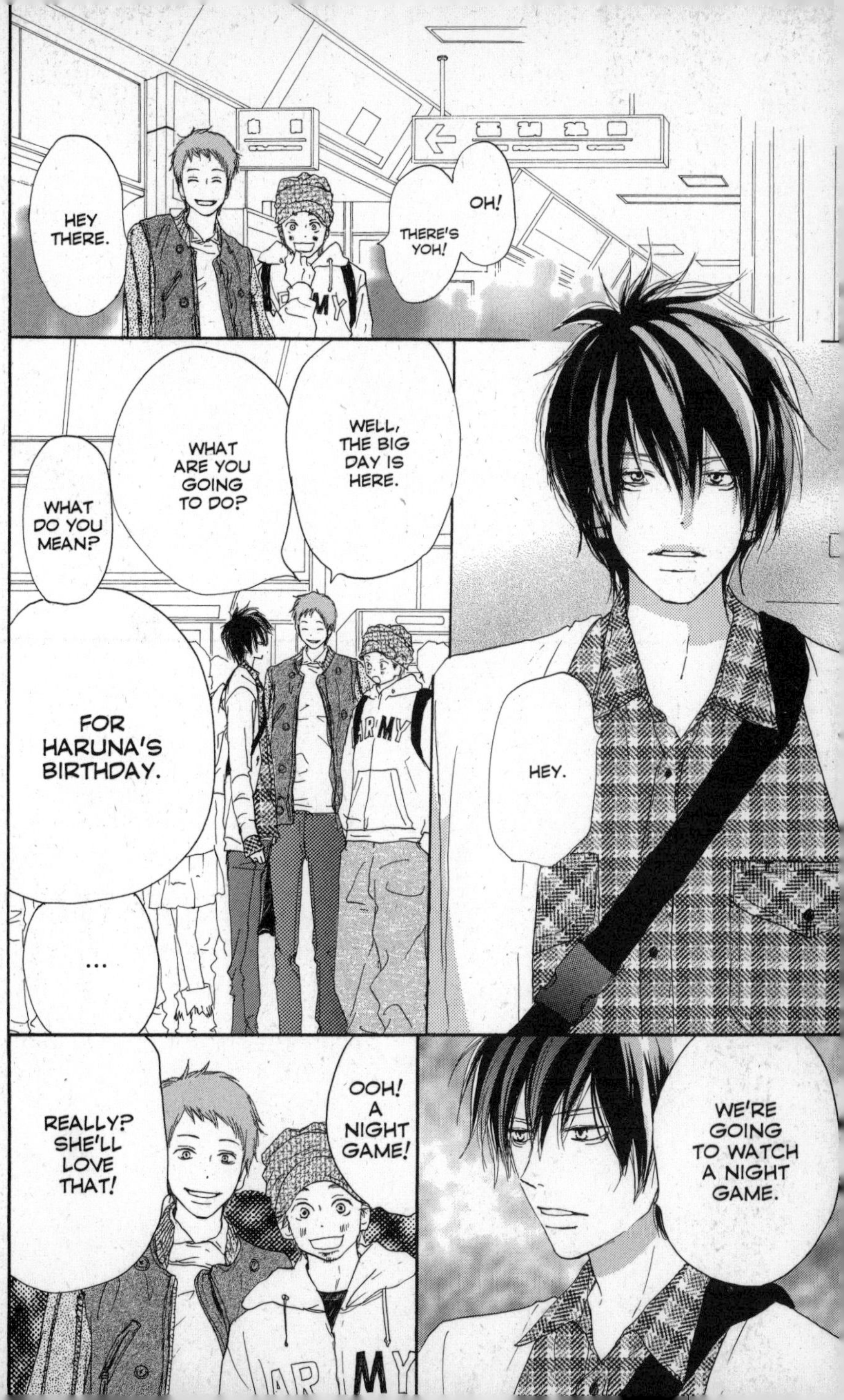
OH!
THERE'S YOH!
HEY THERE.
HEY.
WELL, THE BIG DAY IS HERE.
WHAT ARE YOU GOING TO DO?
WHAT DO YOU MEAN?
FOR HARUNA'S BIRTHDAY.
...
WE'RE GOING TO WATCH A NIGHT GAME.
OOH! A NIGHT GAME!
REALLY? SHE'LL LOVE THAT!

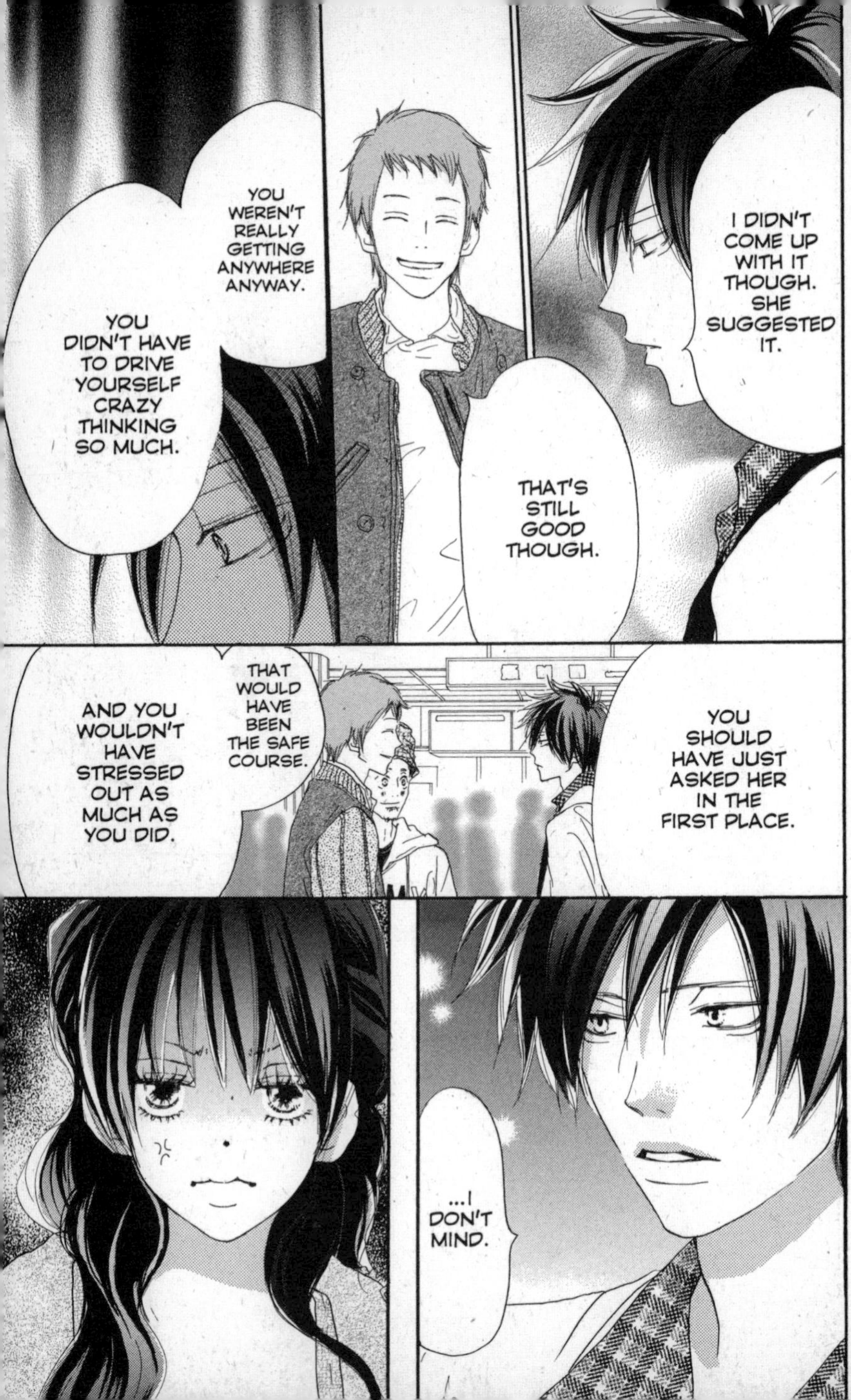
I DIDN'T COME UP WITH IT THOUGH. SHE SUGGESTED IT.
THAT'S STILL GOOD THOUGH.
YOU WEREN'T REALLY GETTING ANYWHERE ANYWAY.
YOU DIDN'T HAVE TO DRIVE YOURSELF CRAZY THINKING SO MUCH.
YOU SHOULD HAVE JUST ASKED HER IN THE FIRST PLACE.
THAT WOULD HAVE BEEN THE SAFE COURSE.
AND YOU WOULDN'T HAVE STRESSED OUT AS MUCH AS YOU DID.
...I DON'T MIND.

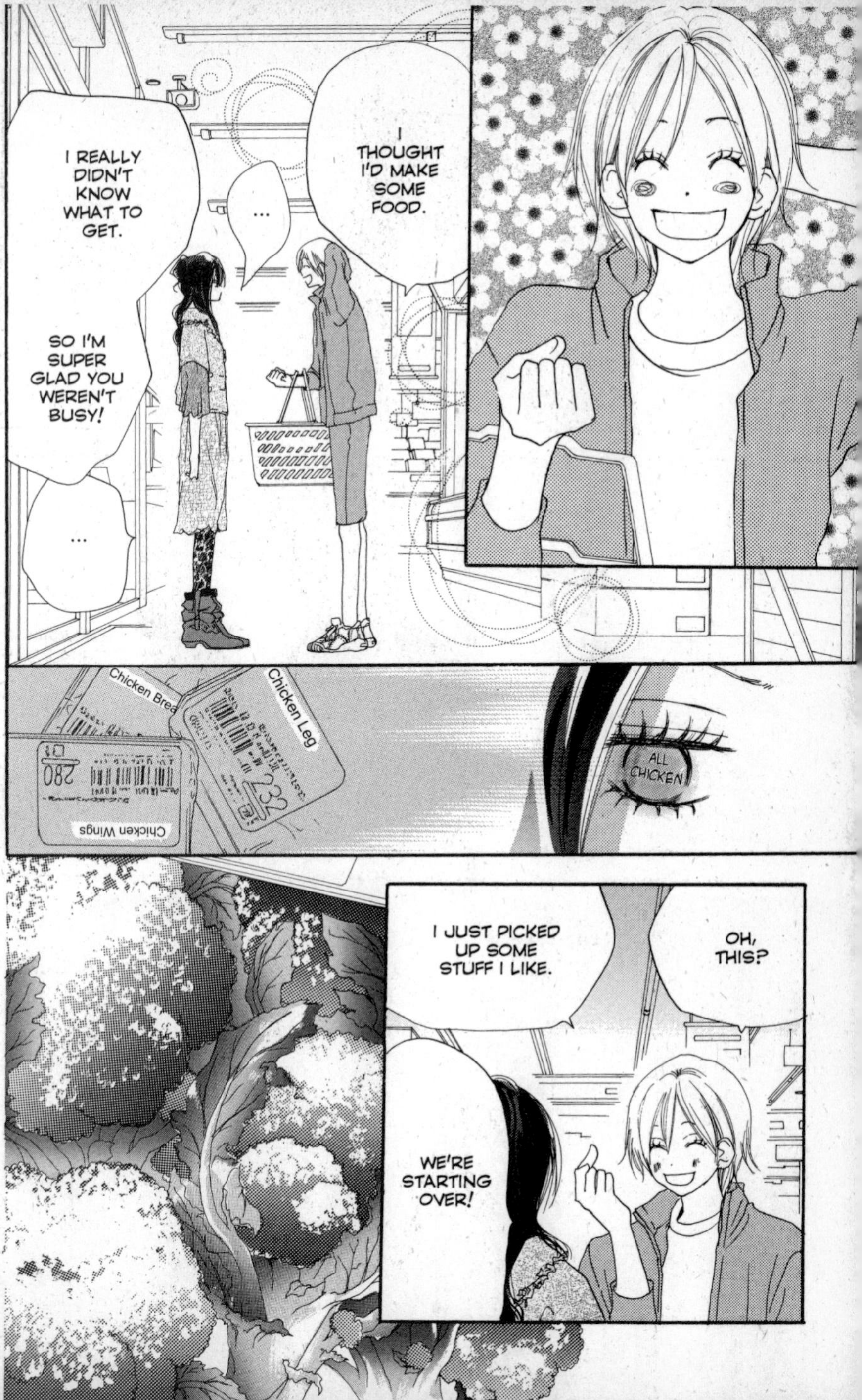
I THOUGHT I'D MAKE SOME FOOD.
...
I REALLY DIDN'T KNOW WHAT TO GET.
SO I'M SUPER GLAD YOU WEREN'T BUSY!
...
ALL CHICKEN
Chicken Leg
232
Chicken Brea
280
Chicken Wings
OH, THIS?
I JUST PICKED UP SOME STUFF I LIKE.
WE'RE STARTING OVER!

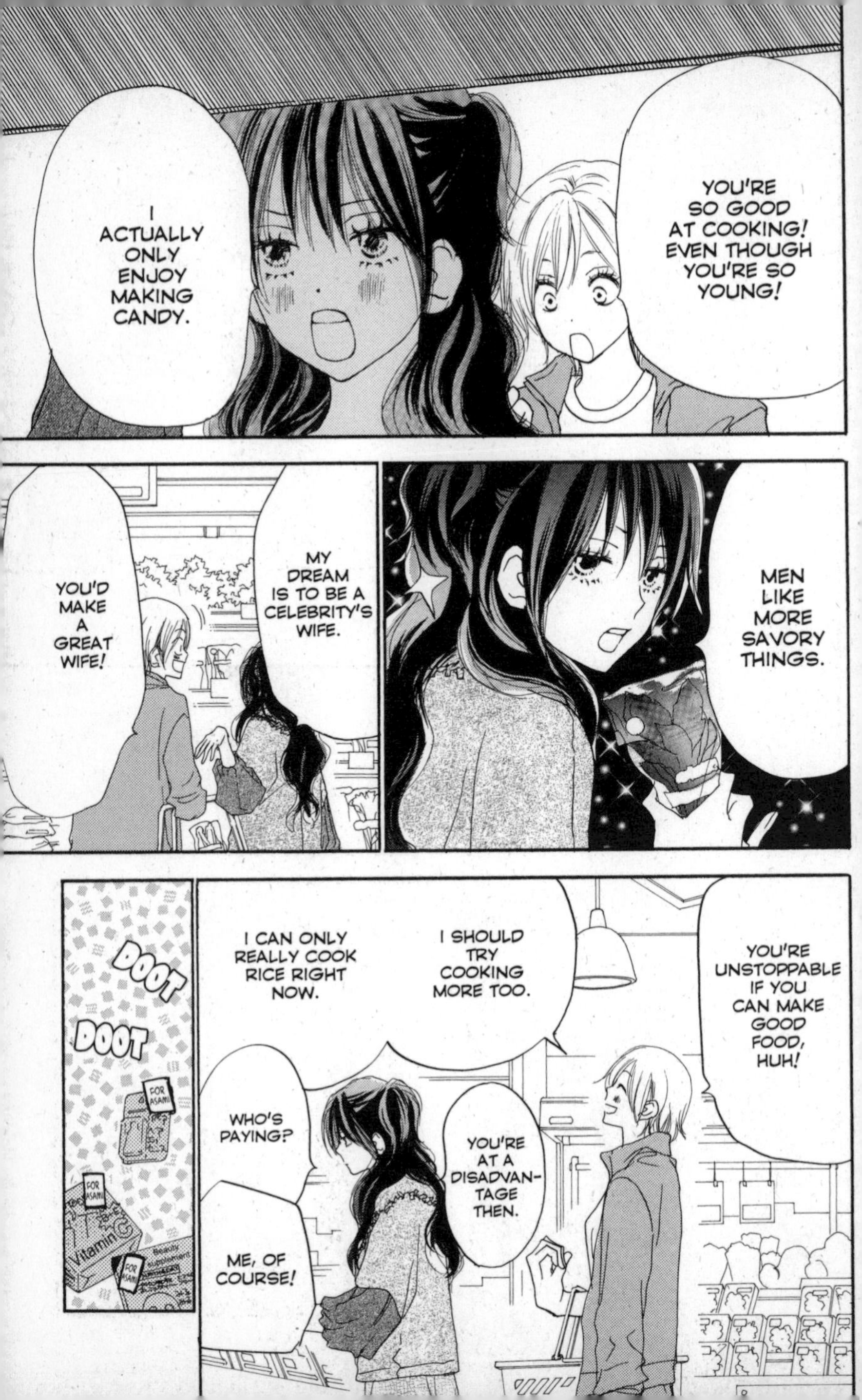
YOU'RE SO GOOD AT COOKING! EVEN THOUGH YOU'RE SO YOUNG!
I ACTUALLY ONLY ENJOY MAKING CANDY.
MEN LIKE MORE SAVORY THINGS.
MY DREAM IS TO BE A CELEBRITY'S WIFE.
YOU'D MAKE A GREAT WIFE!
YOU'RE UNSTOPPABLE IF YOU CAN MAKE GOOD FOOD, HUH!
I SHOULD TRY COOKING MORE TOO.
I CAN ONLY REALLY COOK RICE RIGHT NOW.
YOU'RE AT A DISADVANTAGE THEN.
WHO'S PAYING?
ME, OF COURSE!
DOOT
DOOT
FOR ASAMI
FOR ASAMI
Vitamin C
FOR ASAMI
Beauty supplement

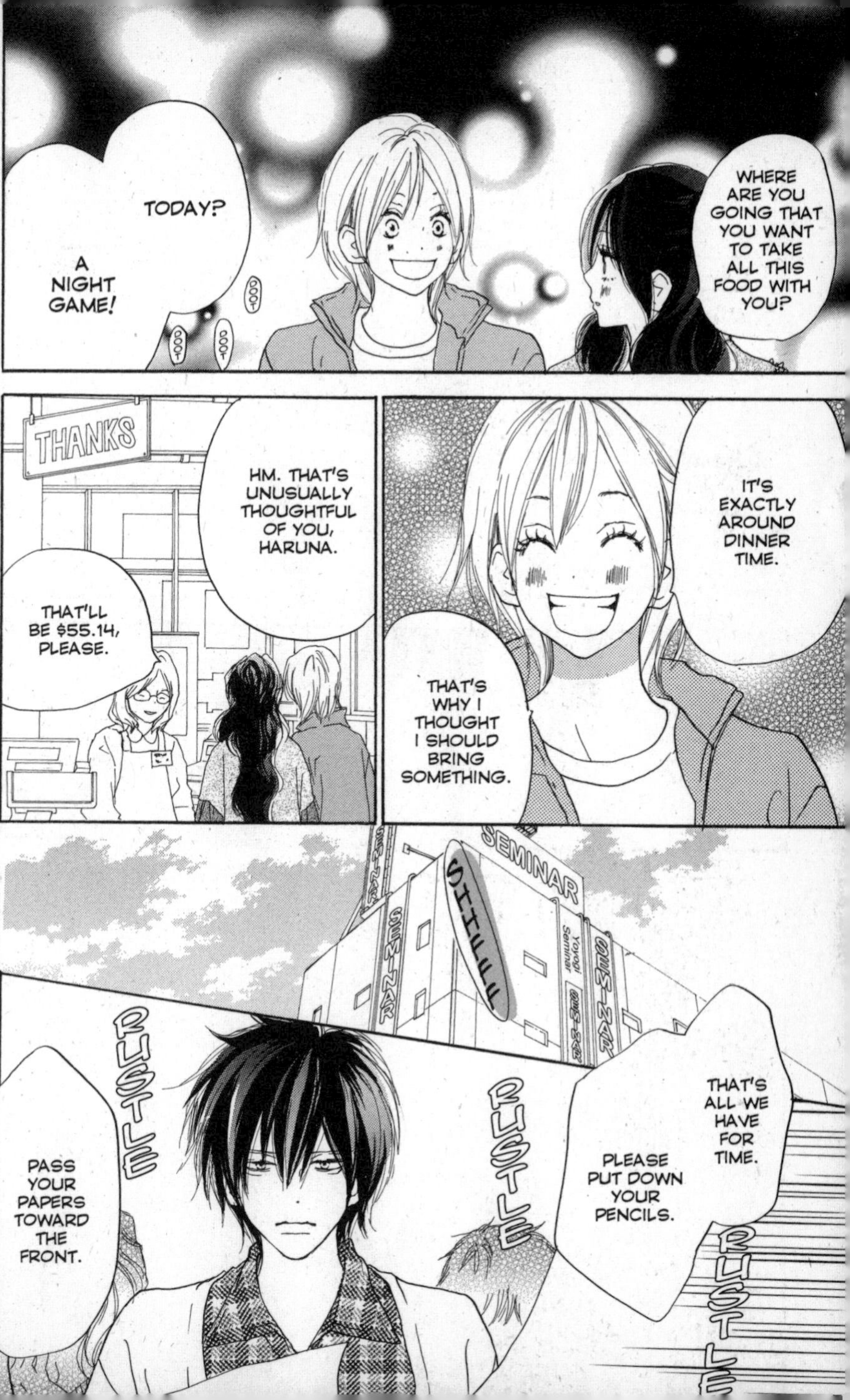
WHERE ARE YOU GOING THAT YOU WANT TO TAKE ALL THIS FOOD WITH YOU?
TODAY?
A NIGHT GAME!
DOOT
DOOT
DOOT
IT'S EXACTLY AROUND DINNER TIME.
THAT'S WHY I THOUGHT I SHOULD BRING SOMETHING.
THANKS
HM. THAT'S UNUSUALLY THOUGHTFUL OF YOU, HARUNA.
THAT'LL BE $55.14, PLEASE.
SEMINAR
SEMINAR
Yoyogi Seminar
SEMINAR
SEMINAR
THAT'S ALL WE HAVE FOR TIME.
PLEASE PUT DOWN YOUR PENCILS.
RUSTLE
RUSTLE
RUSTLE
PASS YOUR PAPERS TOWARD THE FRONT.

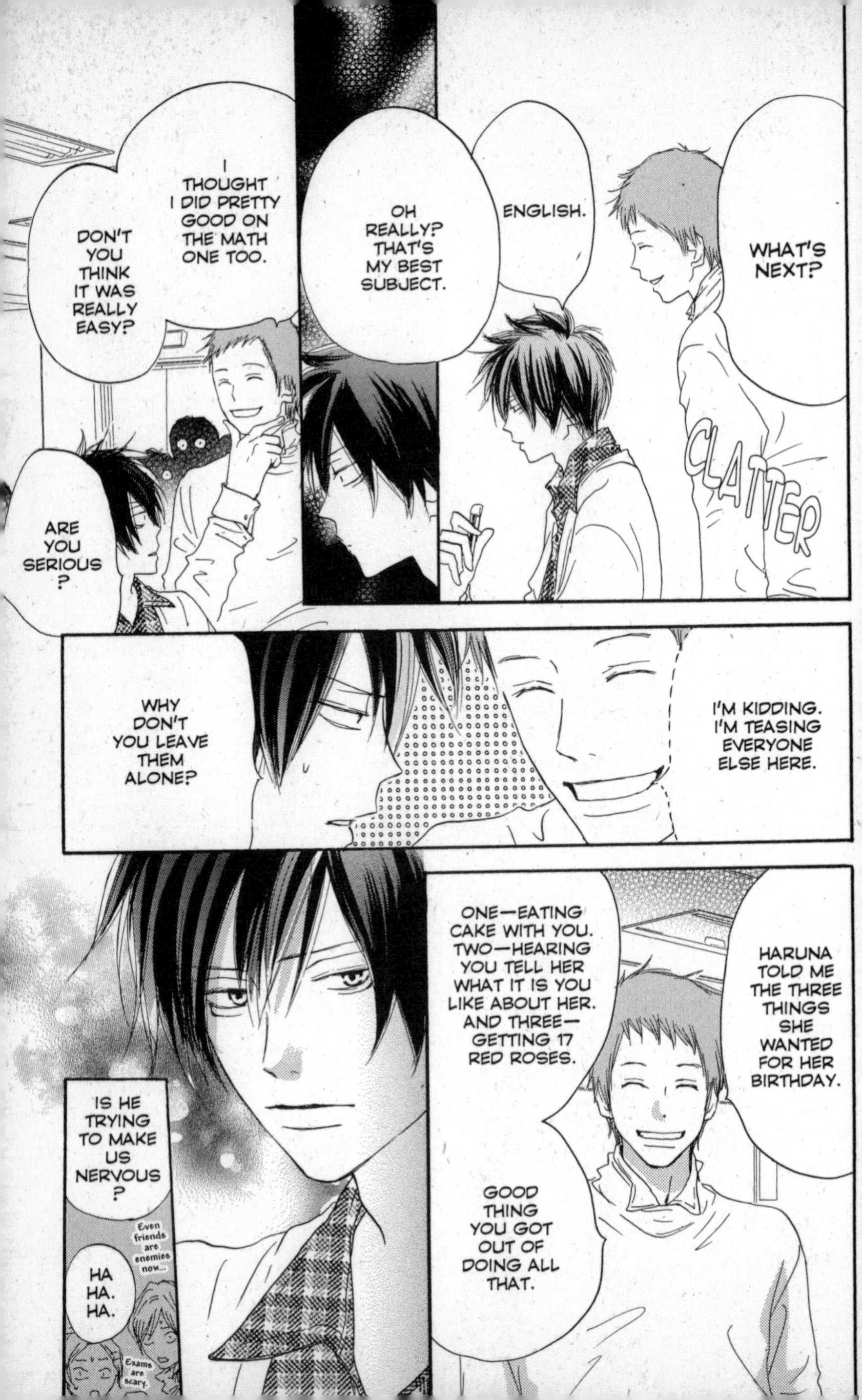
WHAT'S NEXT?
CLATTER
ENGLISH.
OH REALLY? THAT'S MY BEST SUBJECT.
I THOUGHT I DID PRETTY GOOD ON THE MATH ONE TOO.
DON'T YOU THINK IT WAS REALLY EASY?
ARE YOU SERIOUS?
I'M KIDDING. I'M TEASING EVERYONE ELSE HERE.
WHY DON'T YOU LEAVE THEM ALONE?
HARUNA TOLD ME THE THREE THINGS SHE WANTED FOR HER BIRTHDAY.
ONE—EATING CAKE WITH YOU. TWO—HEARING YOU TELL HER WHAT IT IS YOU LIKE ABOUT HER. AND THREE—GETTING 17 RED ROSES.
GOOD THING YOU GOT OUT OF DOING ALL THAT.
IS HE TRYING TO MAKE US NERVOUS?
Even friends are enemies now...
HA HA. HA.
Exams are scary.

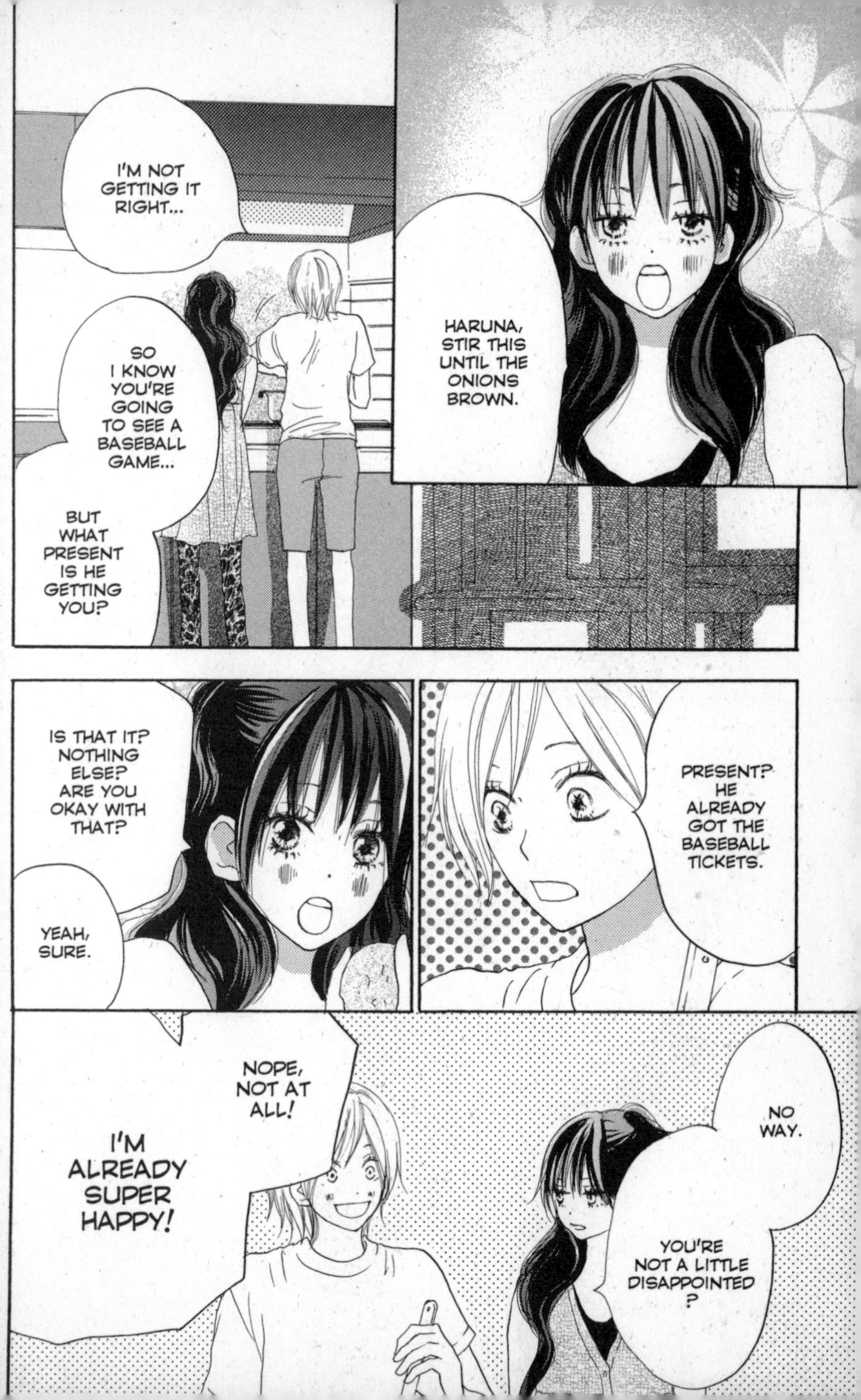
HARUNA, STIR THIS UNTIL THE ONIONS BROWN.
I'M NOT GETTING IT RIGHT...
SO I KNOW YOU'RE GOING TO SEE A BASEBALL GAME...
BUT WHAT PRESENT IS HE GETTING YOU?
PRESENT? HE ALREADY GOT THE BASEBALL TICKETS.
IS THAT IT? NOTHING ELSE? ARE YOU OKAY WITH THAT?
YEAH, SURE.
NO WAY.
YOU'RE NOT A LITTLE DISAPPOINTED?
NOPE, NOT AT ALL!
I'M ALREADY SUPER HAPPY!

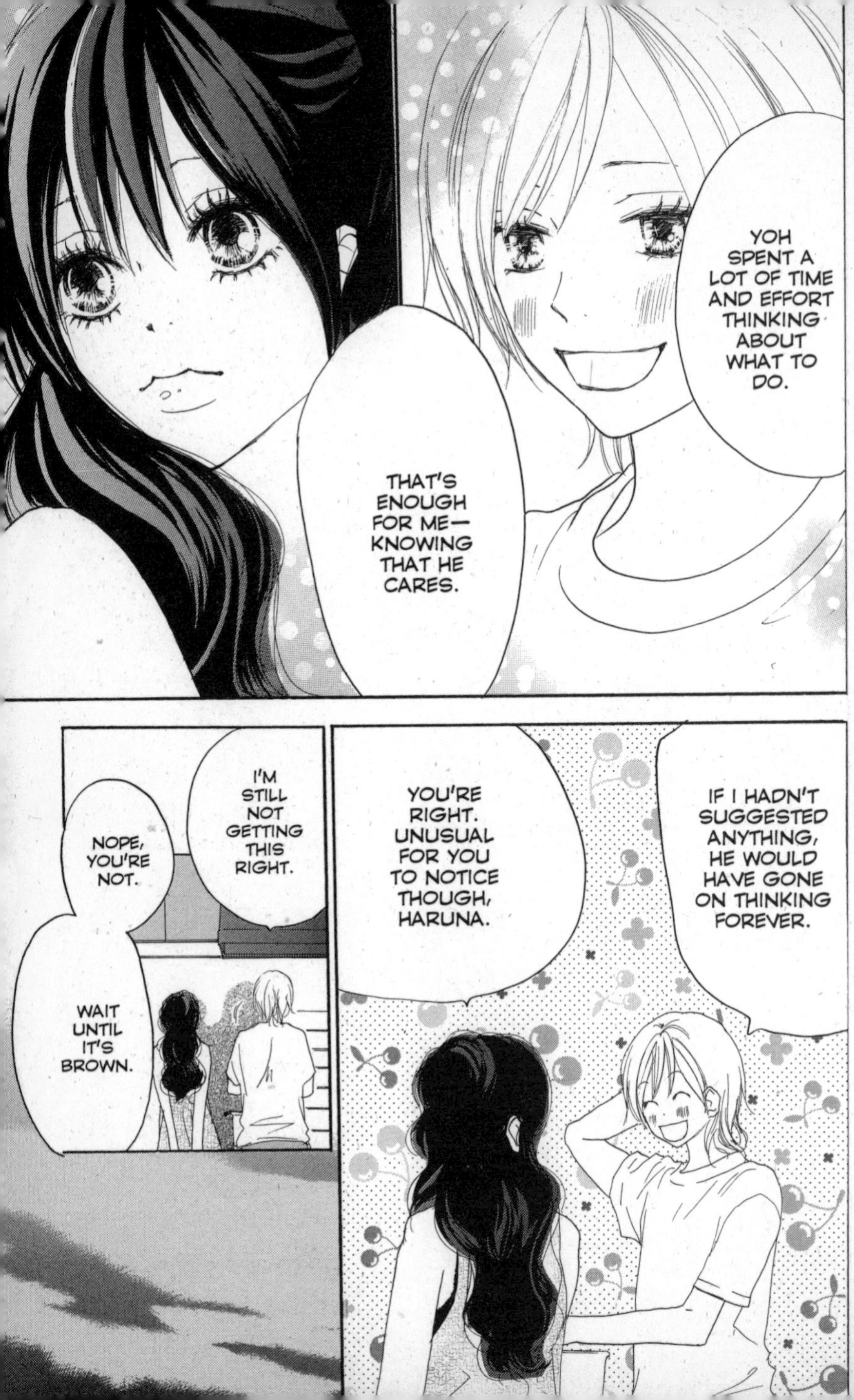
YOH SPENT A LOT OF TIME AND EFFORT THINKING ABOUT WHAT TO DO.
THAT'S ENOUGH FOR ME—KNOWING THAT HE CARES.
IF I HADN'T SUGGESTED ANYTHING, HE WOULD HAVE GONE ON THINKING FOREVER.
YOU'RE RIGHT. UNUSUAL FOR YOU TO NOTICE THOUGH, HARUNA.
I'M STILL NOT GETTING THIS RIGHT.
NOPE, YOU'RE NOT.
WAIT UNTIL IT'S BROWN.

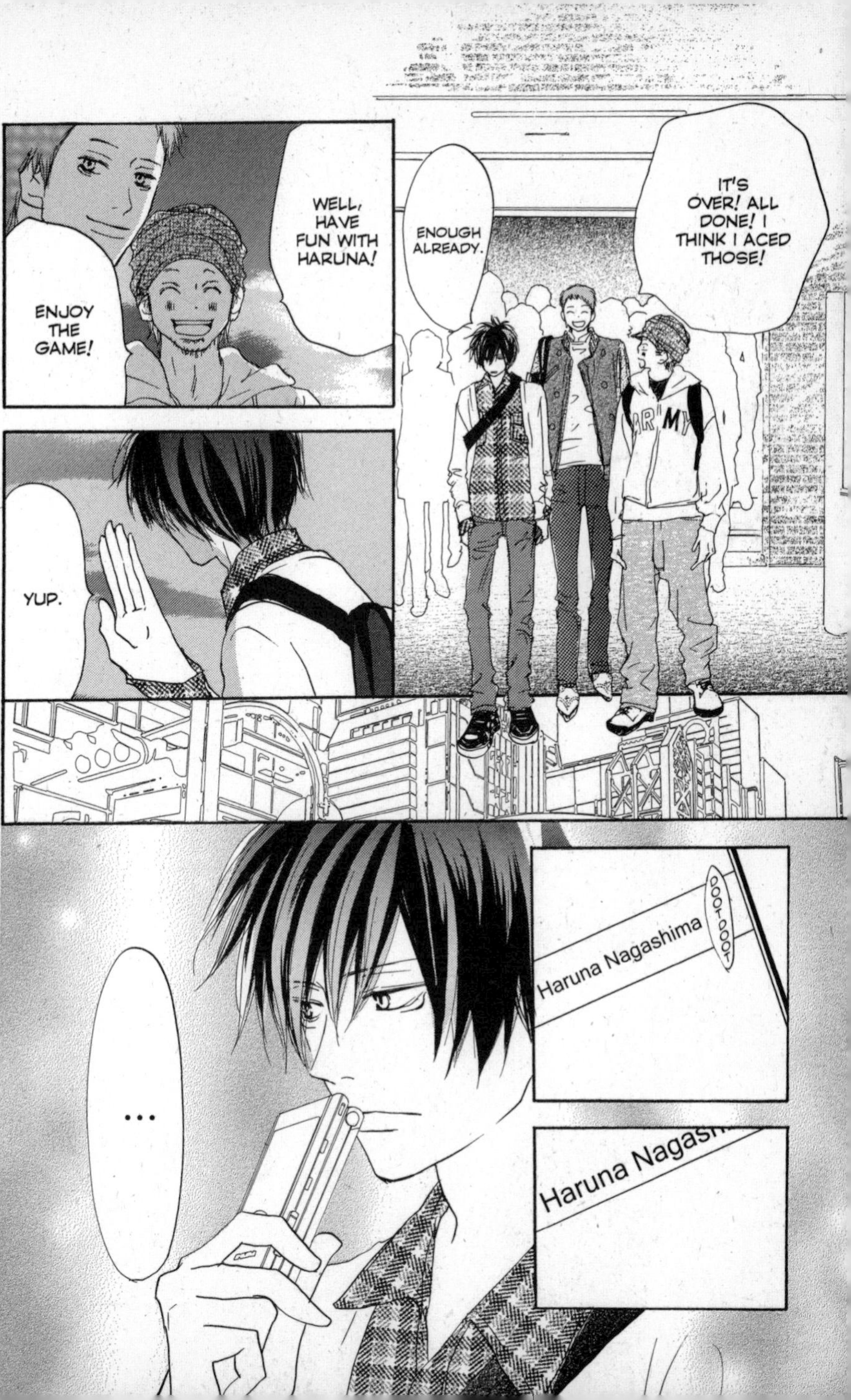
IT'S OVER! ALL DONE! I THINK I ACED THOSE!
ENOUGH ALREADY.
WELL, HAVE FUN WITH HARUNA!
ENJOY THE GAME!
YUP.
DOOT DOOT
Haruna Nagashima
...

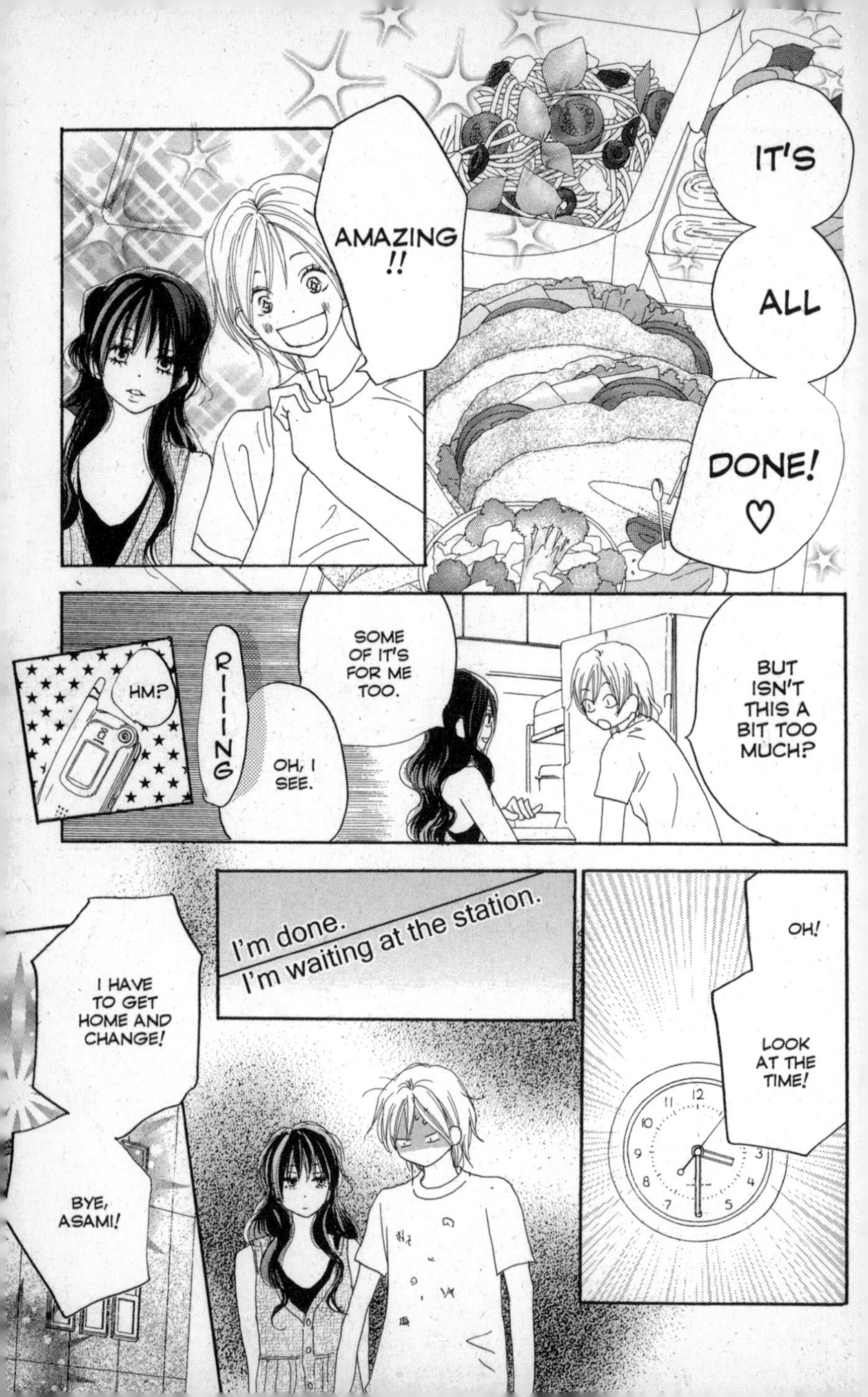
IT'S ALL DONE! ♡
AMAZING!!
BUT ISN'T THIS A BIT TOO MUCH?
SOME OF IT'S FOR ME TOO.
OH, I SEE.
RIIING
HM?
OH!
LOOK AT THE TIME!
I'm done.
I'm waiting at the station.
I HAVE TO GET HOME AND CHANGE!
BYE, ASAMI!

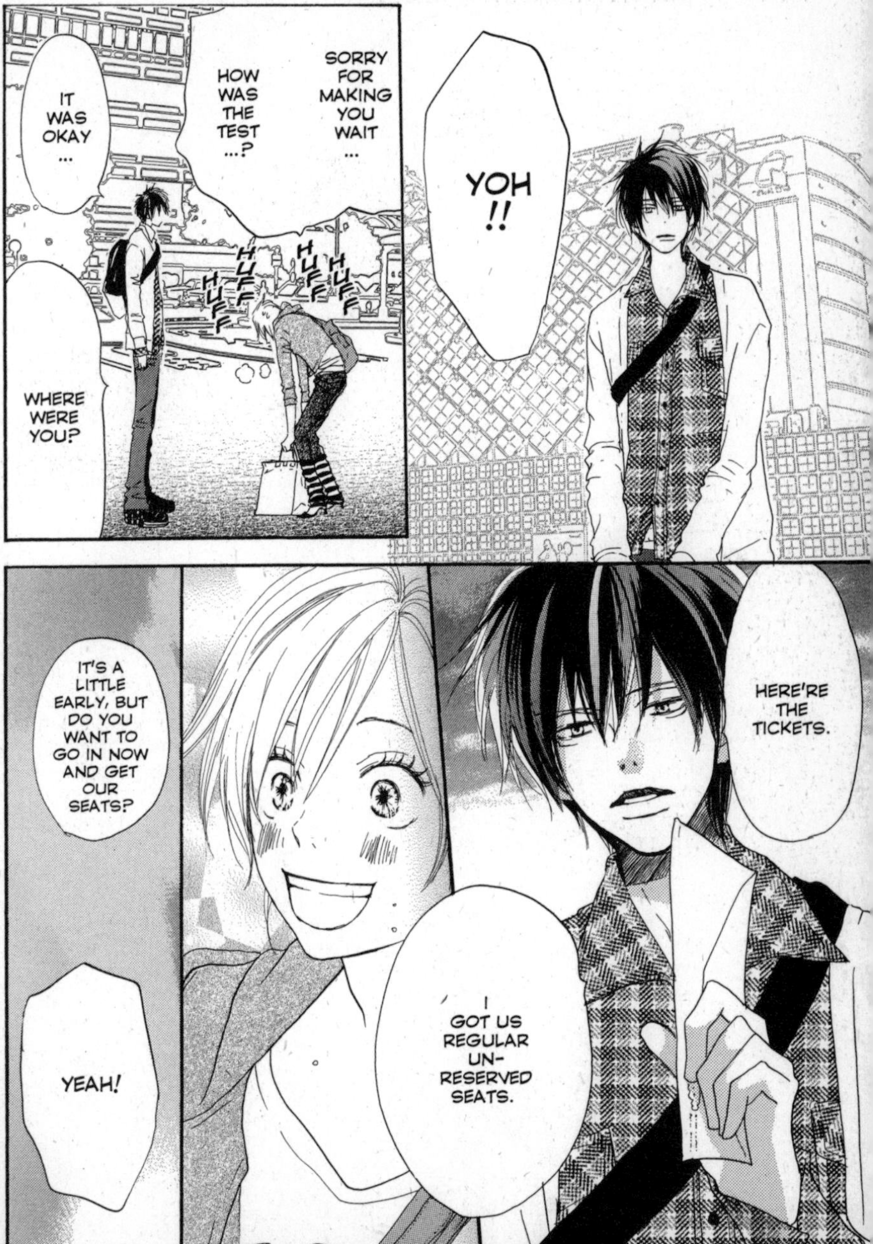
YOH!!
SORRY FOR MAKING YOU WAIT...
HUFF HUFF
HUFF HUFF
HOW WAS THE TEST...?
IT WAS OKAY...
WHERE WERE YOU?
HERE'RE THE TICKETS.
I GOT US REGULAR UN-RESERVED SEATS.
IT'S A LITTLE EARLY, BUT DO YOU WANT TO GO IN NOW AND GET OUR SEATS?
YEAH!

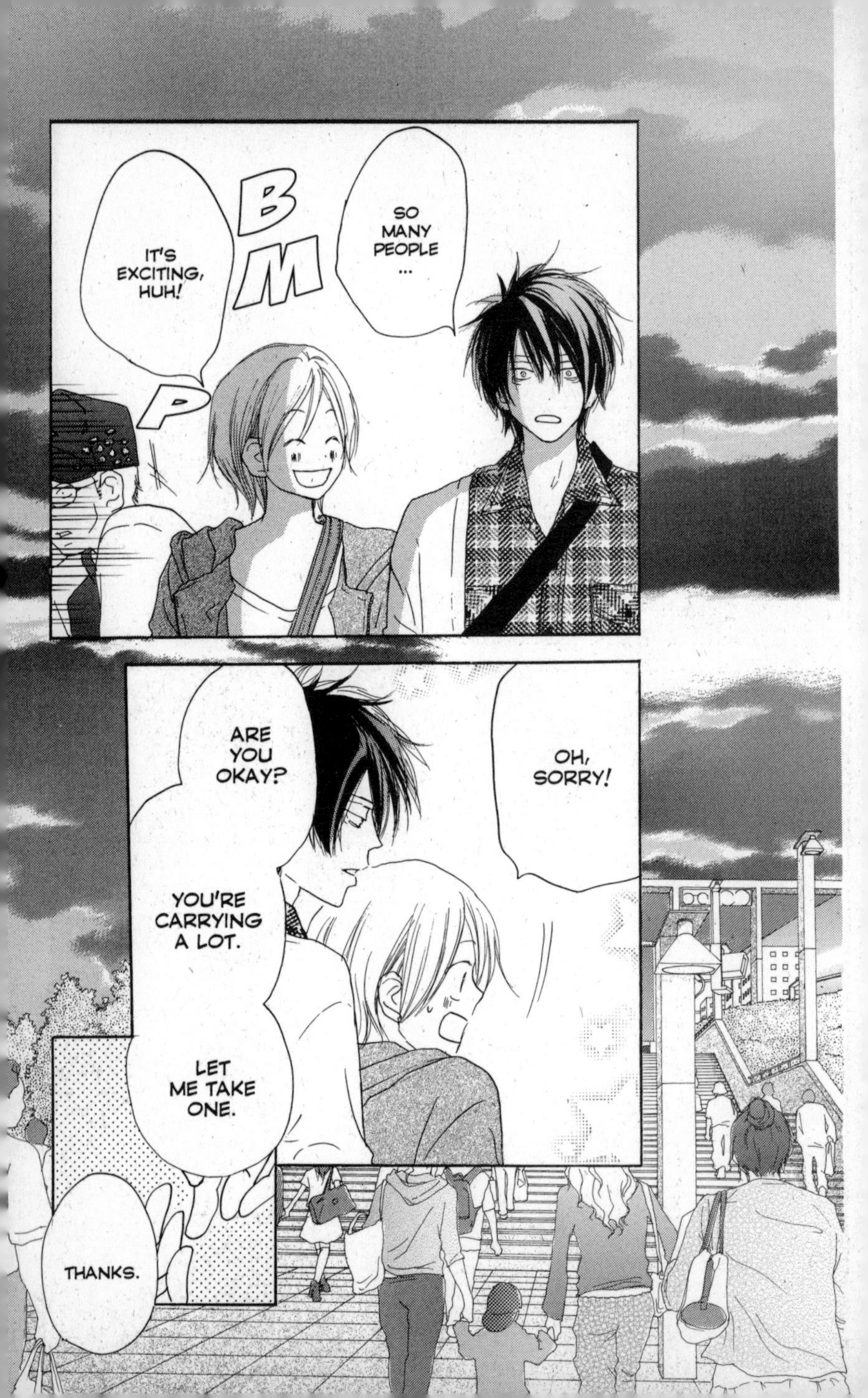
SO MANY PEOPLE ...
BMP
IT'S EXCITING, HUH!
OH, SORRY!
ARE YOU OKAY?
YOU'RE CARRYING A LOT.
LET ME TAKE ONE.
THANKS.

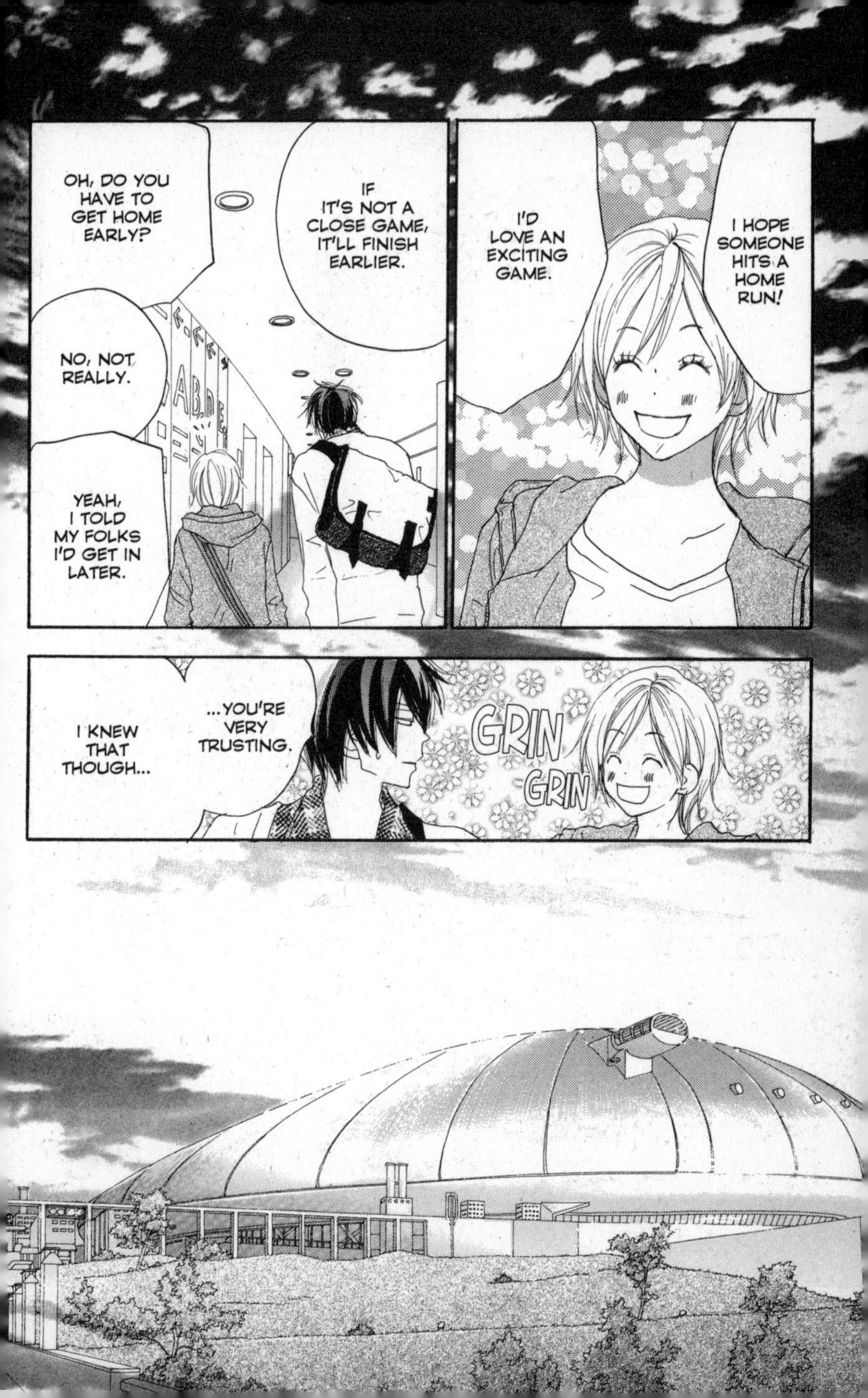
I HOPE SOMEONE HITS A HOME RUN!
I'D LOVE AN EXCITING GAME.
IF IT'S NOT A CLOSE GAME, IT'LL FINISH EARLIER.
OH, DO YOU HAVE TO GET HOME EARLY?
NO, NOT REALLY.
YEAH, I TOLD MY FOLKS I'D GET IN LATER.
GRIN
GRIN
...YOU'RE VERY TRUSTING.
I KNEW THAT THOUGH...

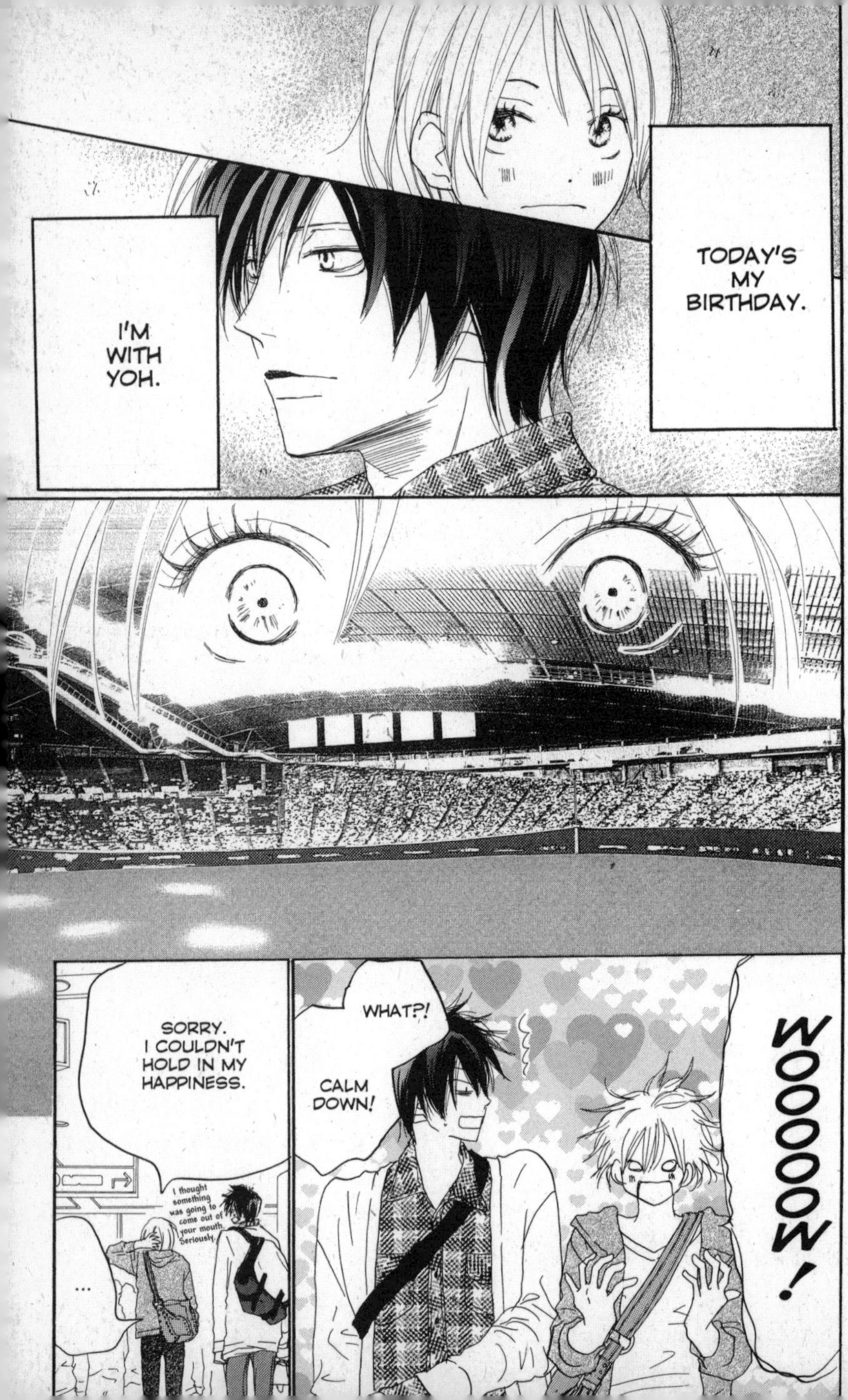
TODAY'S MY BIRTHDAY.
I'M WITH YOH.
WOOOOOOW!
WHAT?!
CALM DOWN!
SORRY. I COULDN'T HOLD IN MY HAPPINESS.
I thought something was going to come out of your mouth. Seriously.
...

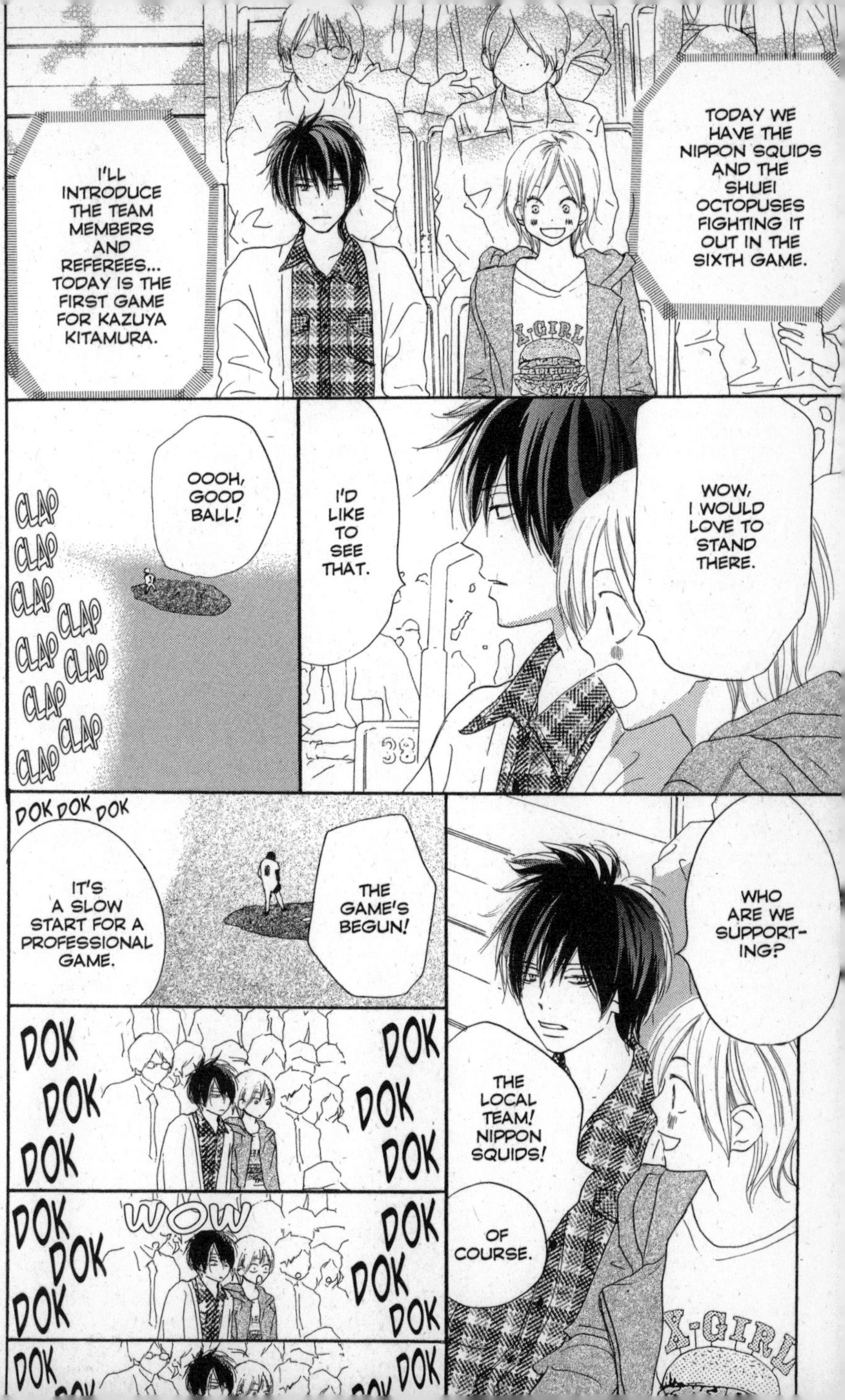
TODAY WE HAVE THE NIPPON SQUIDS AND THE SHUEI OCTOPUSES FIGHTING IT OUT IN THE SIXTH GAME.
I'LL INTRODUCE THE TEAM MEMBERS AND REFEREES... TODAY IS THE FIRST GAME FOR KAZUYA KITAMURA.
WOW, I WOULD LOVE TO STAND THERE.
I'D LIKE TO SEE THAT.
OOOH, GOOD BALL!
CLAP CLAP CLAP CLAP CLAP CLAP CLAP CLAP CLAP CLAP
38
WHO ARE WE SUPPORTING?
THE LOCAL TEAM! NIPPON SQUIDS!
OF COURSE.
X-GIRL
DOK DOK DOK
THE GAME'S BEGUN!
IT'S A SLOW START FOR A PROFESSIONAL GAME.
DOK DOK DOK
DOK DOK DOK
DOK DOK DOK DOK
WOW
DOK DOK DOK
DOK
DOK

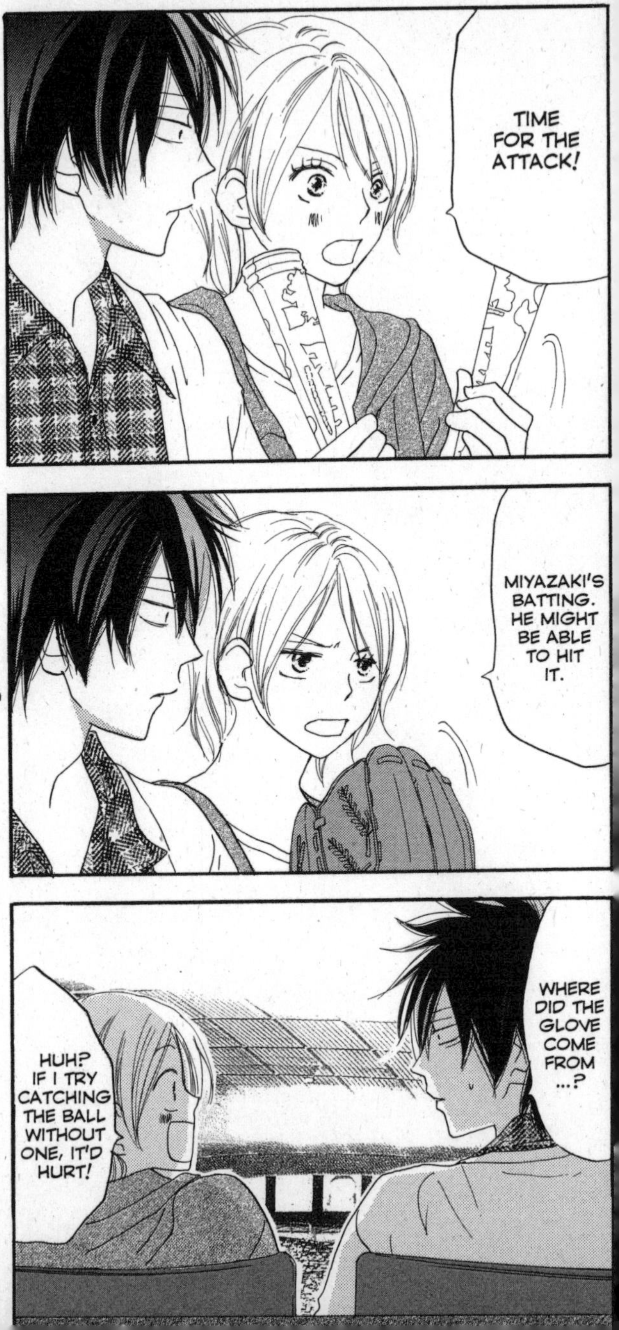
TIME FOR THE ATTACK!
MIYAZAKI'S BATTING. HE MIGHT BE ABLE TO HIT IT.
WHERE DID THE GLOVE COME FROM ...?
HUH? IF I TRY CATCHING THE BALL WITHOUT ONE, IT'D HURT!

3

It doesn't really matter, but my mom's bad at drawing. My niece is only five, but she's already better than my mom. I thought that drawing skills run in my family...but I guess that isn't the case. (Well, not "I guess." I **know** it definitely doesn't.)

Every time I want to draw something I haven't drawn before, I have to put in a lot of work.

The first time I tried to draw a tiger, it came out a bit like this...

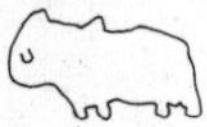

It looks like an alien!

After showing some rough sketches to my editor, I got it to look like this:

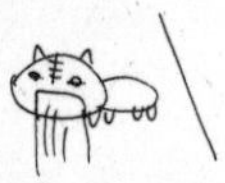

I worked really hard to improve on all the little details and get it just right.

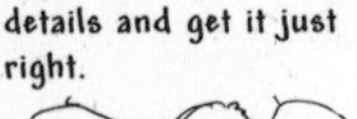
Backbone here...
Hand here...

I tried really hard to perfect it, but...

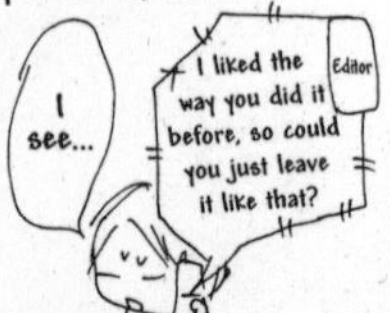
I see...
I liked the way you did it before, so could you just leave it like that?
Editor

I should have just submitted this! →

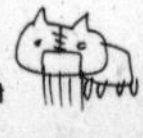

See you in the next volume!

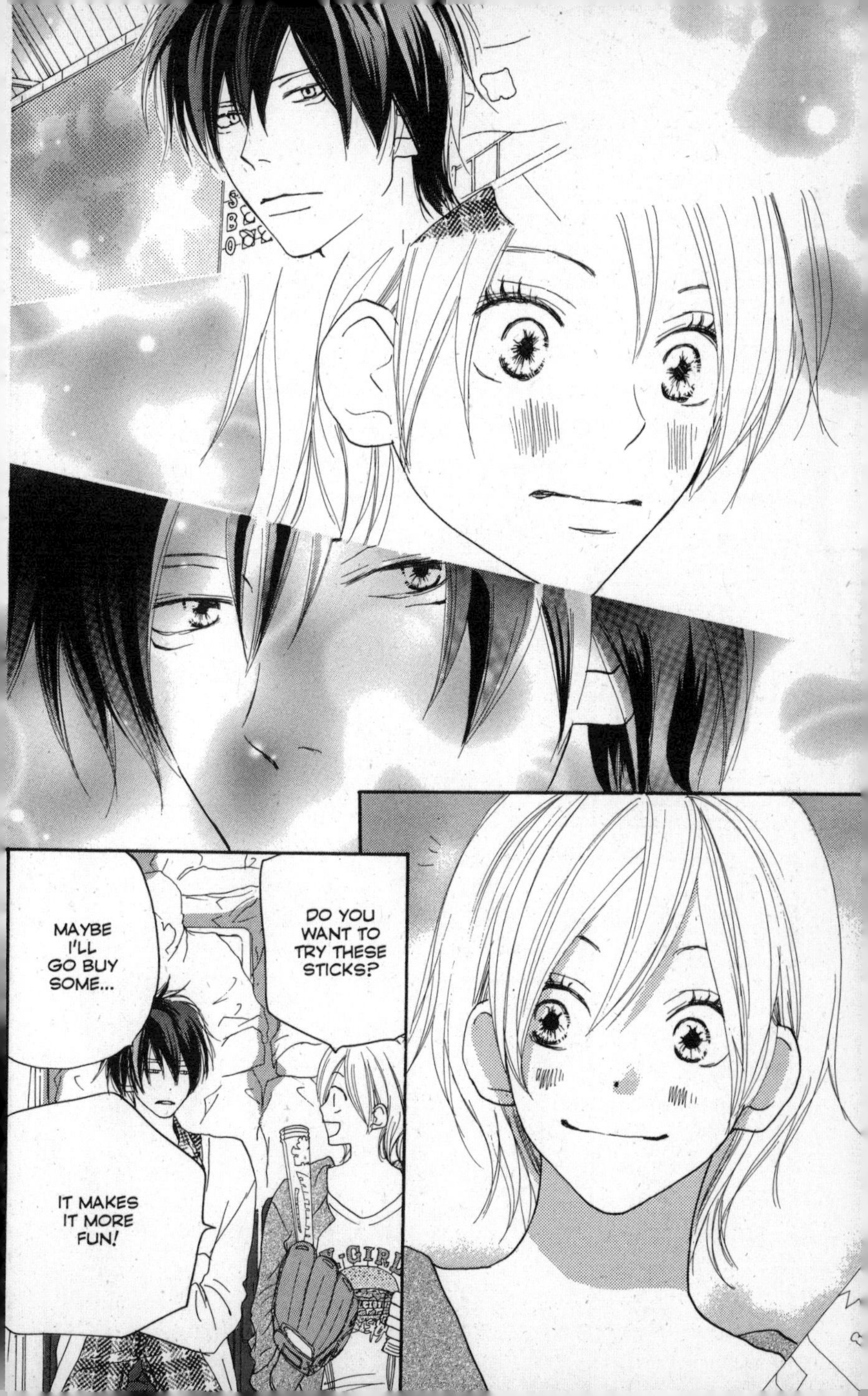
DO YOU WANT TO TRY THESE STICKS?
MAYBE I'LL GO BUY SOME...
IT MAKES IT MORE FUN!

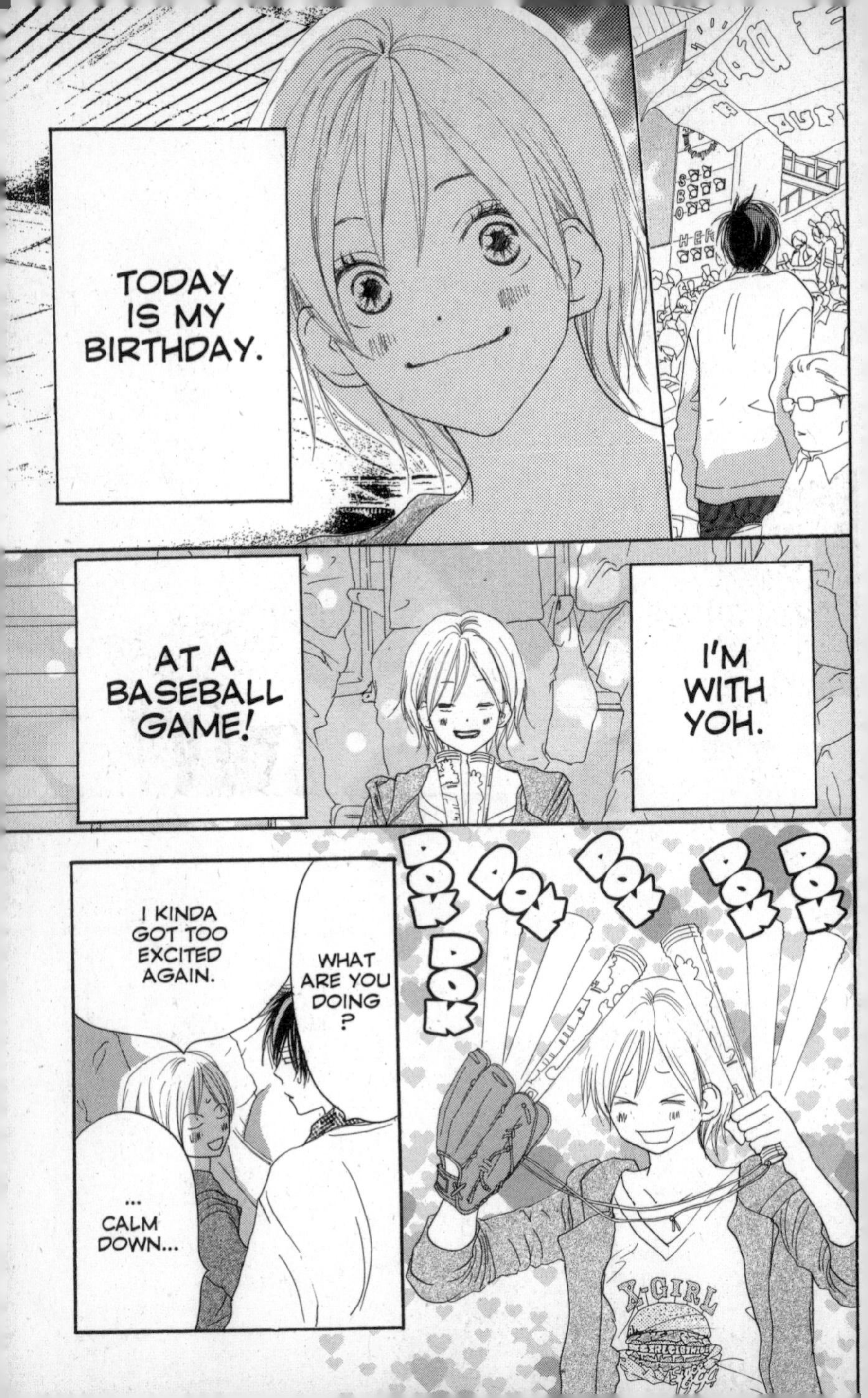
TODAY IS MY BIRTHDAY.
I'M WITH YOH.
AT A BASEBALL GAME!
DON DON DON DON DON DON
WHAT ARE YOU DOING?
I KINDA GOT TOO EXCITED AGAIN.
... CALM DOWN...
X-GIRL

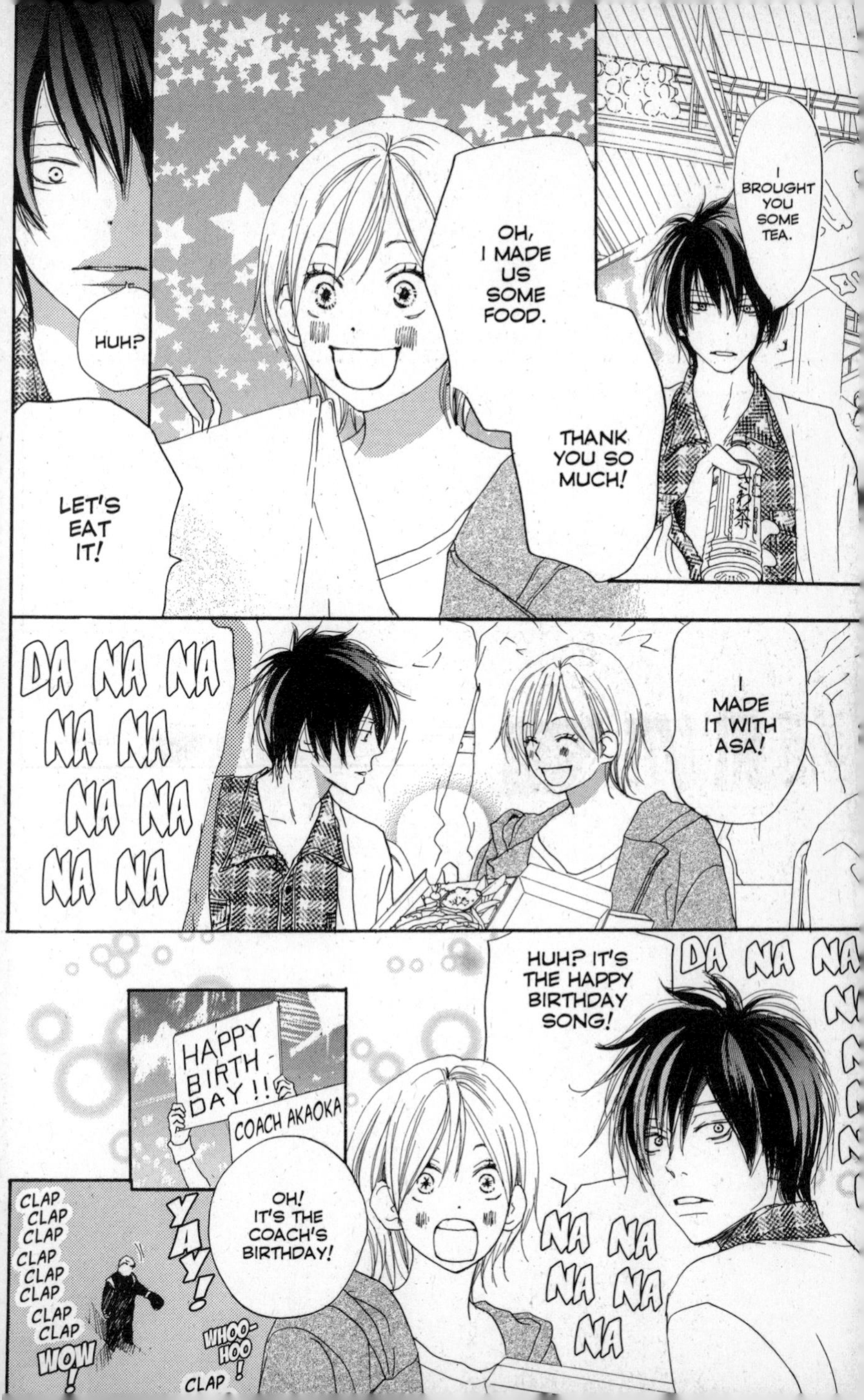
I BROUGHT YOU SOME TEA.
OH, I MADE US SOME FOOD.
THANK YOU SO MUCH!
HUH?
LET'S EAT IT!
I MADE IT WITH ASA!
DA NA NA NA NA NA NA NA NA NA
HUH? IT'S THE HAPPY BIRTHDAY SONG!
DA NA NA
NA NA NA NA NA
OH! IT'S THE COACH'S BIRTHDAY!
HAPPY BIRTHDAY!!
COACH AKAOKA
YAY!
WHOO-HOO!
CLAP
CLAP CLAP CLAP CLAP CLAP CLAP CLAP CLAP
WOW!

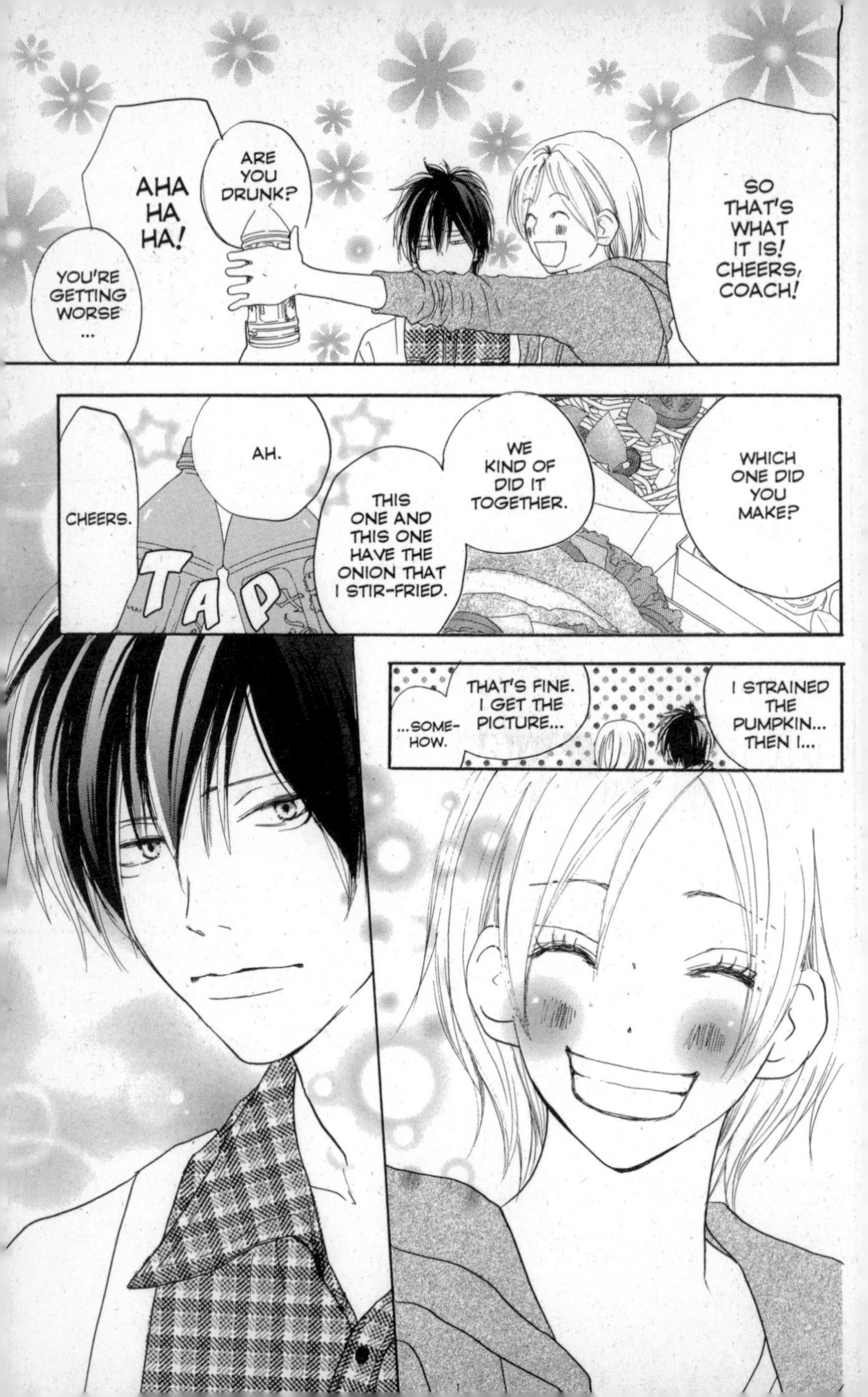
SO THAT'S WHAT IT IS! CHEERS, COACH!
ARE YOU DRUNK?
AHA HA HA!
YOU'RE GETTING WORSE ...
WHICH ONE DID YOU MAKE?
WE KIND OF DID IT TOGETHER.
THIS ONE AND THIS ONE HAVE THE ONION THAT I STIR-FRIED.
AH.
CHEERS.
TAP
I STRAINED THE PUMPKIN... THEN I...
THAT'S FINE. I GET THE PICTURE...
...SOME-HOW.

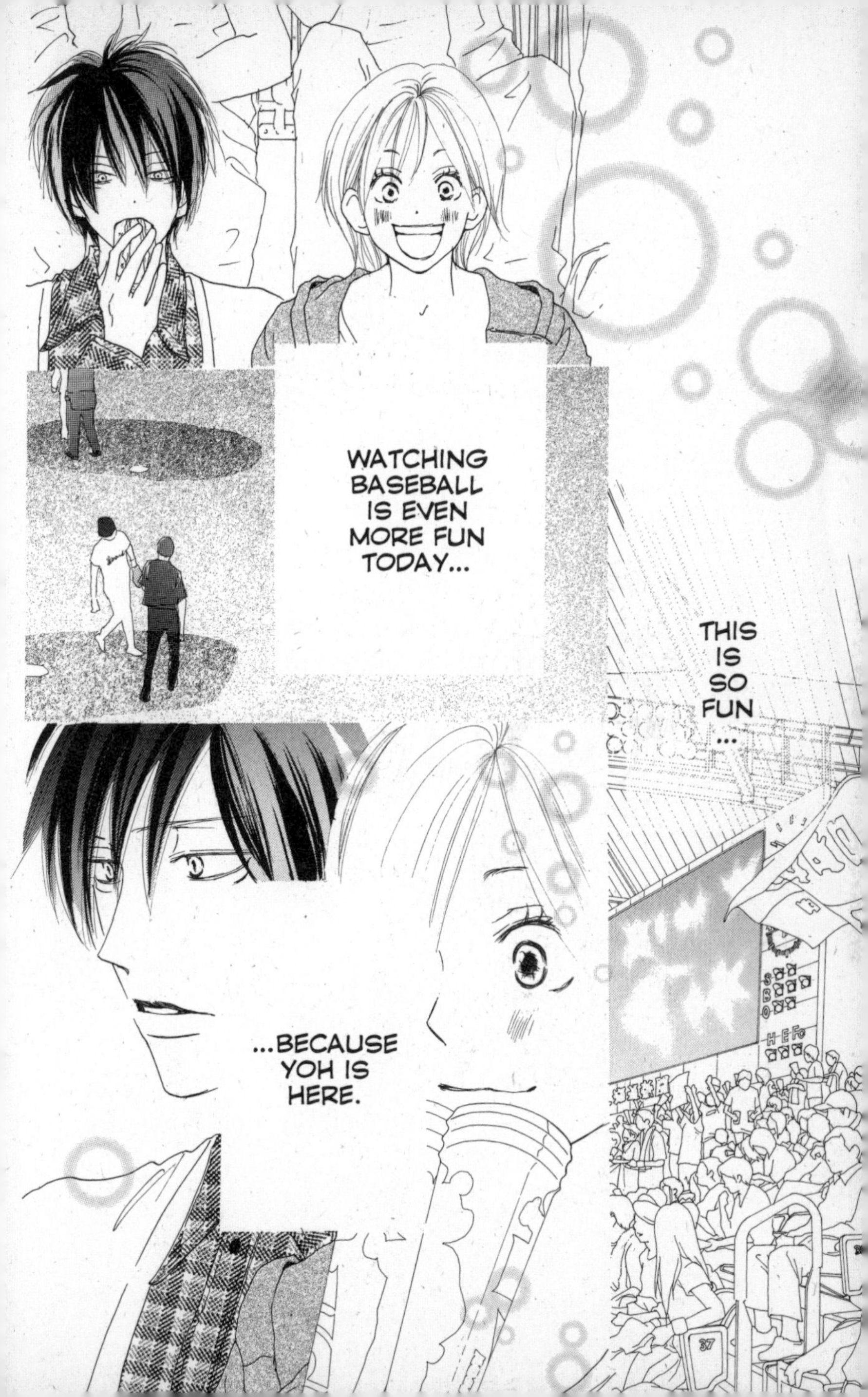
THIS IS SO FUN...
WATCHING BASEBALL IS EVEN MORE FUN TODAY...
...BECAUSE YOH IS HERE.

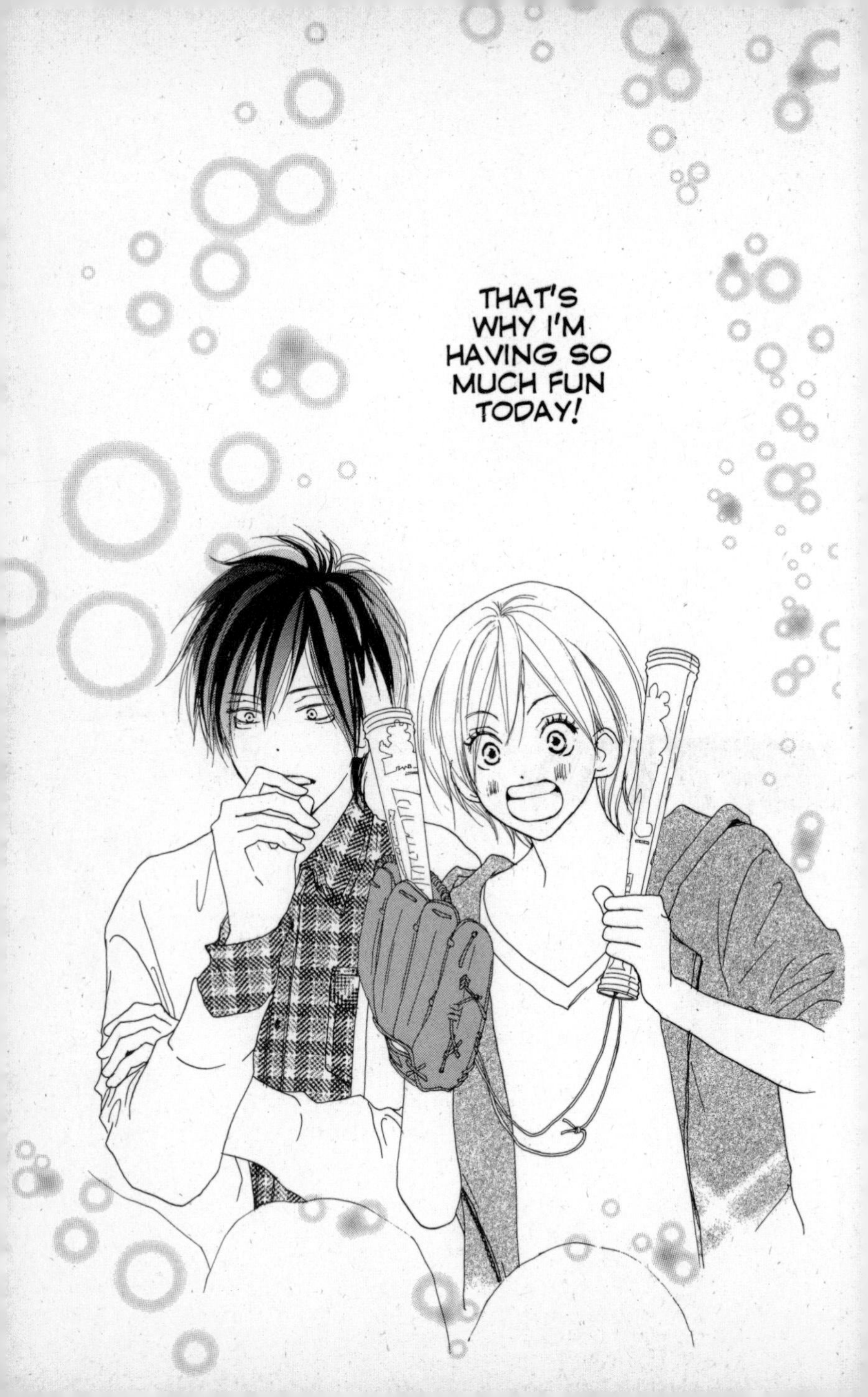
THAT'S WHY I'M HAVING SO MUCH FUN TODAY!

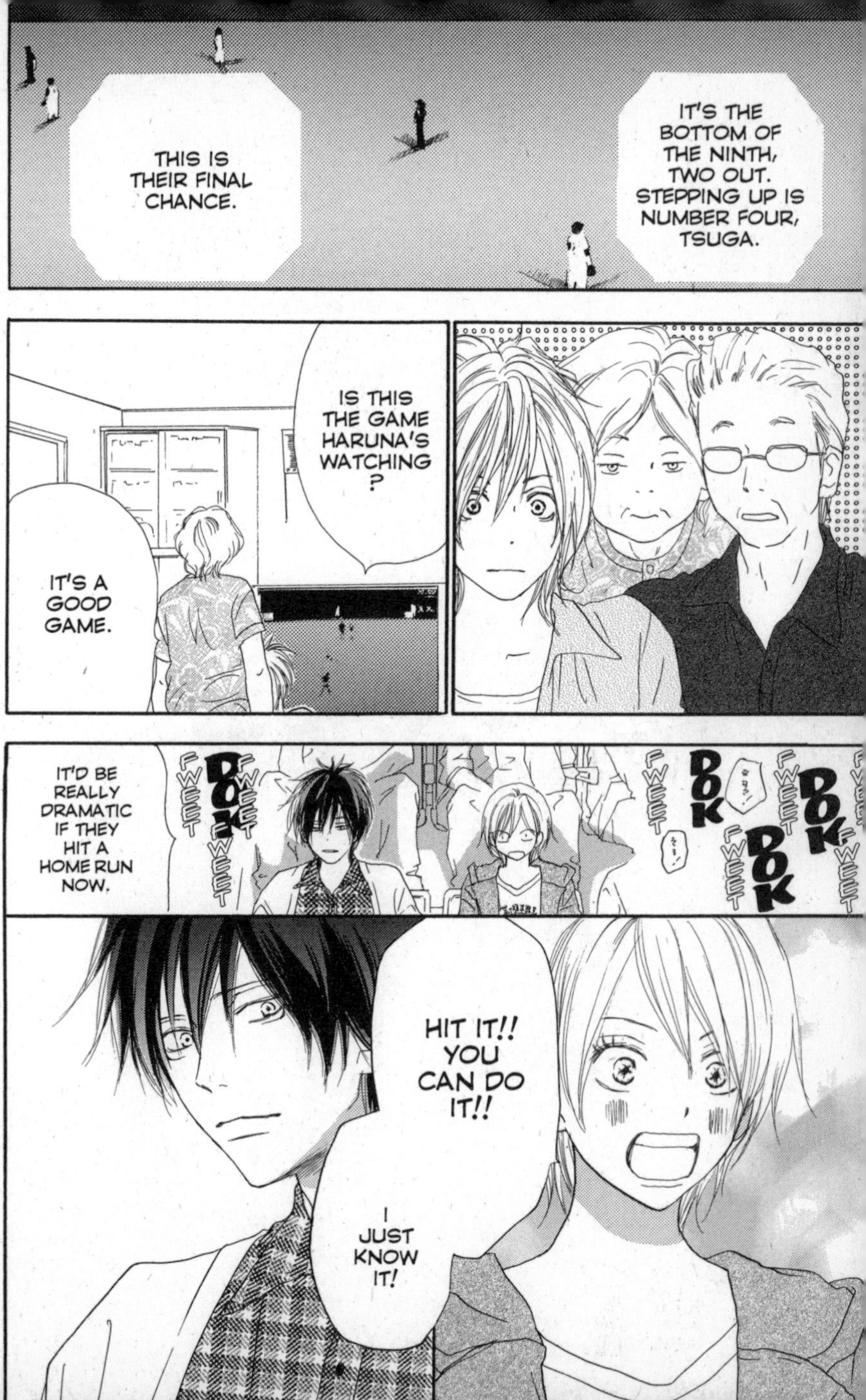

IT'S THE BOTTOM OF THE NINTH, TWO OUT. STEPPING UP IS NUMBER FOUR, TSUGA.
THIS IS THEIR FINAL CHANCE.
IS THIS THE GAME HARUNA'S WATCHING?
IT'S A GOOD GAME.
FWEET
DOK
FWEET
DOK
FWEET
DOK
FWEET
FWEET
FWEET
DOK
FWEET
FWEET
IT'D BE REALLY DRAMATIC IF THEY HIT A HOME RUN NOW.
HIT IT!! YOU CAN DO IT!!
I JUST KNOW IT!

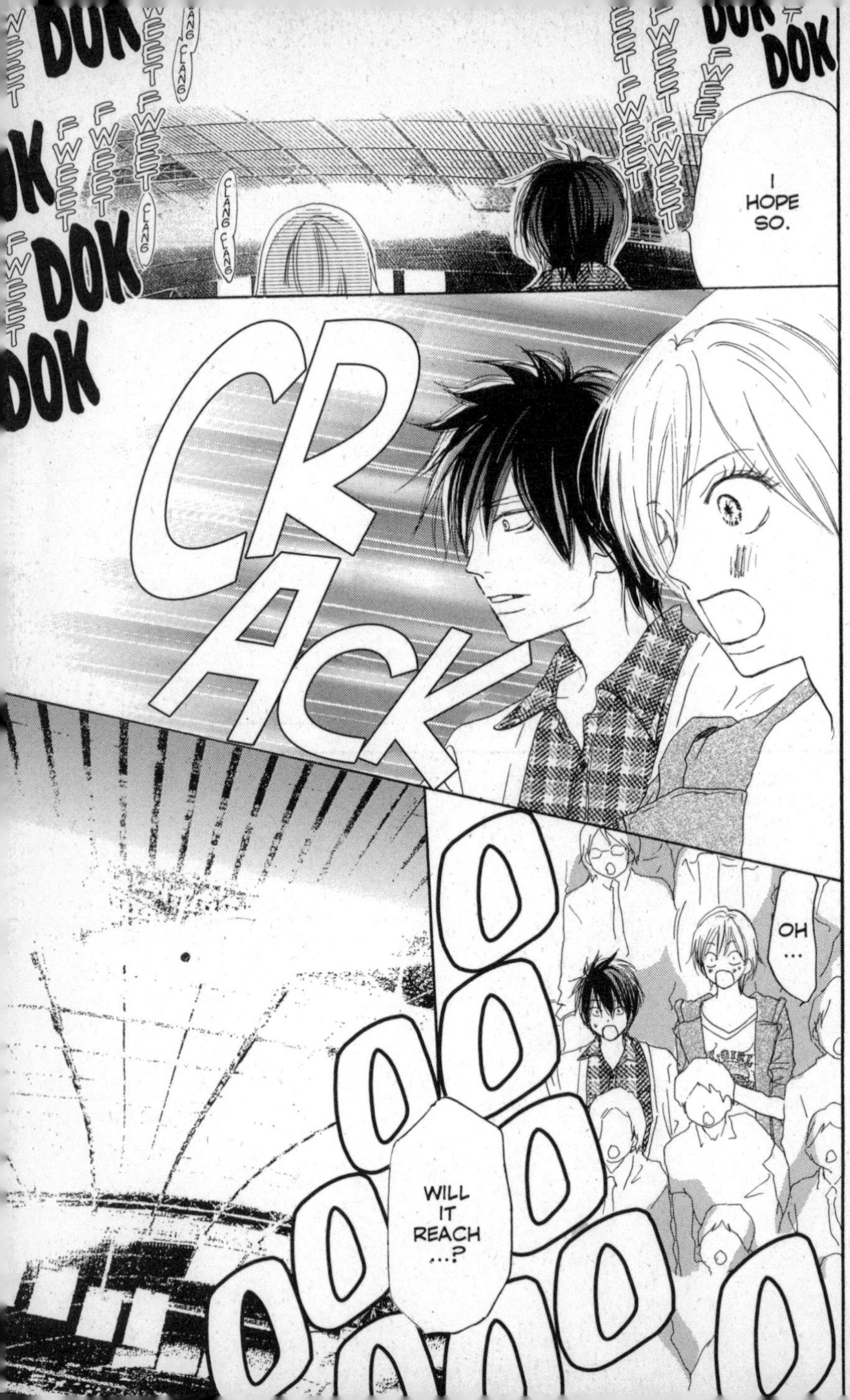
DUR DOK
FWEET FWEET
FWEET FWEET
I HOPE SO.
CLANG CLANG
CLANG CLANG
FWEET FWEET
FWEET FWEET
DUR DOK DOK DOK
CRACK
OH...
WILL IT REACH...?
OOOOOOOOOOOO

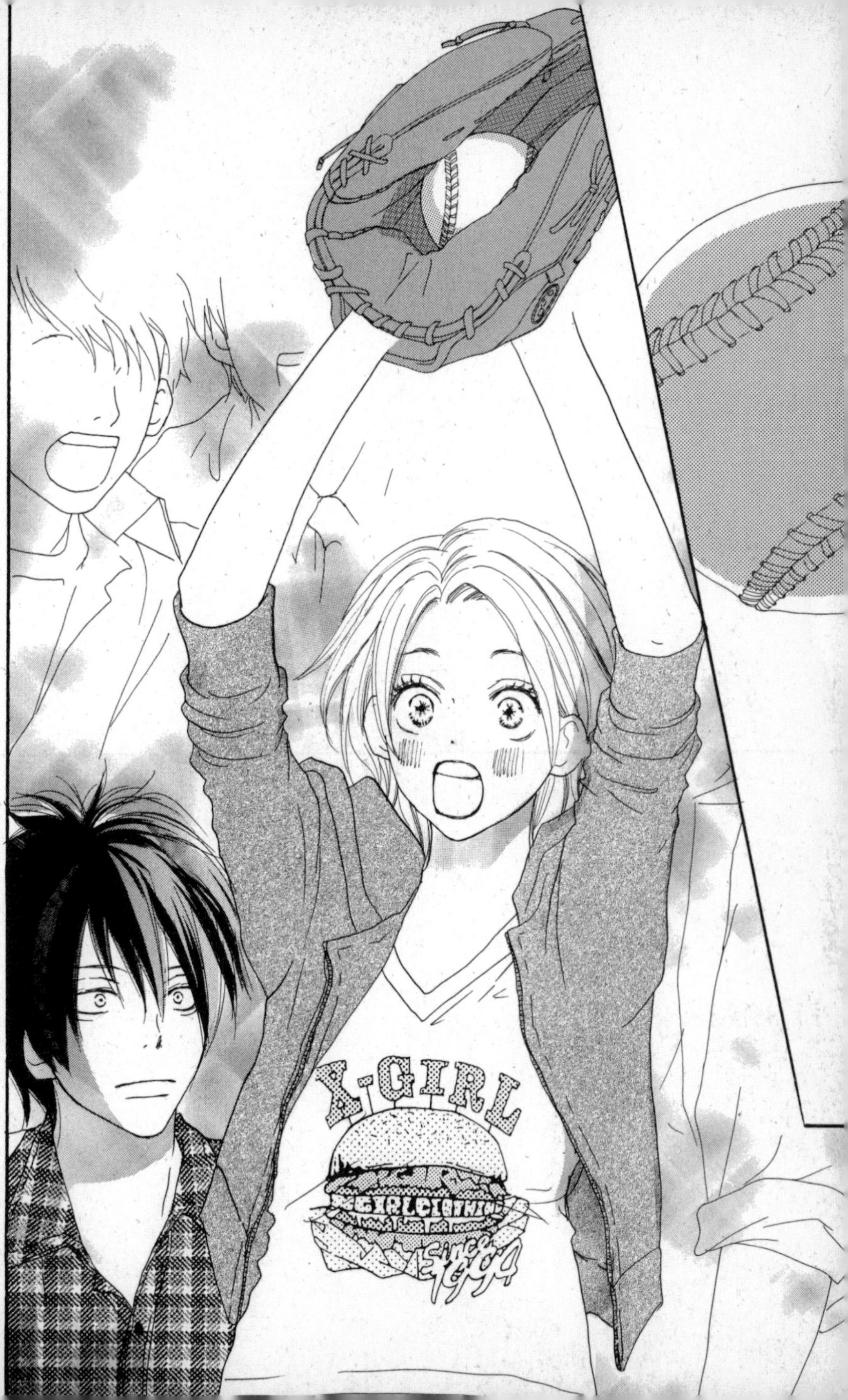
X-GIRL

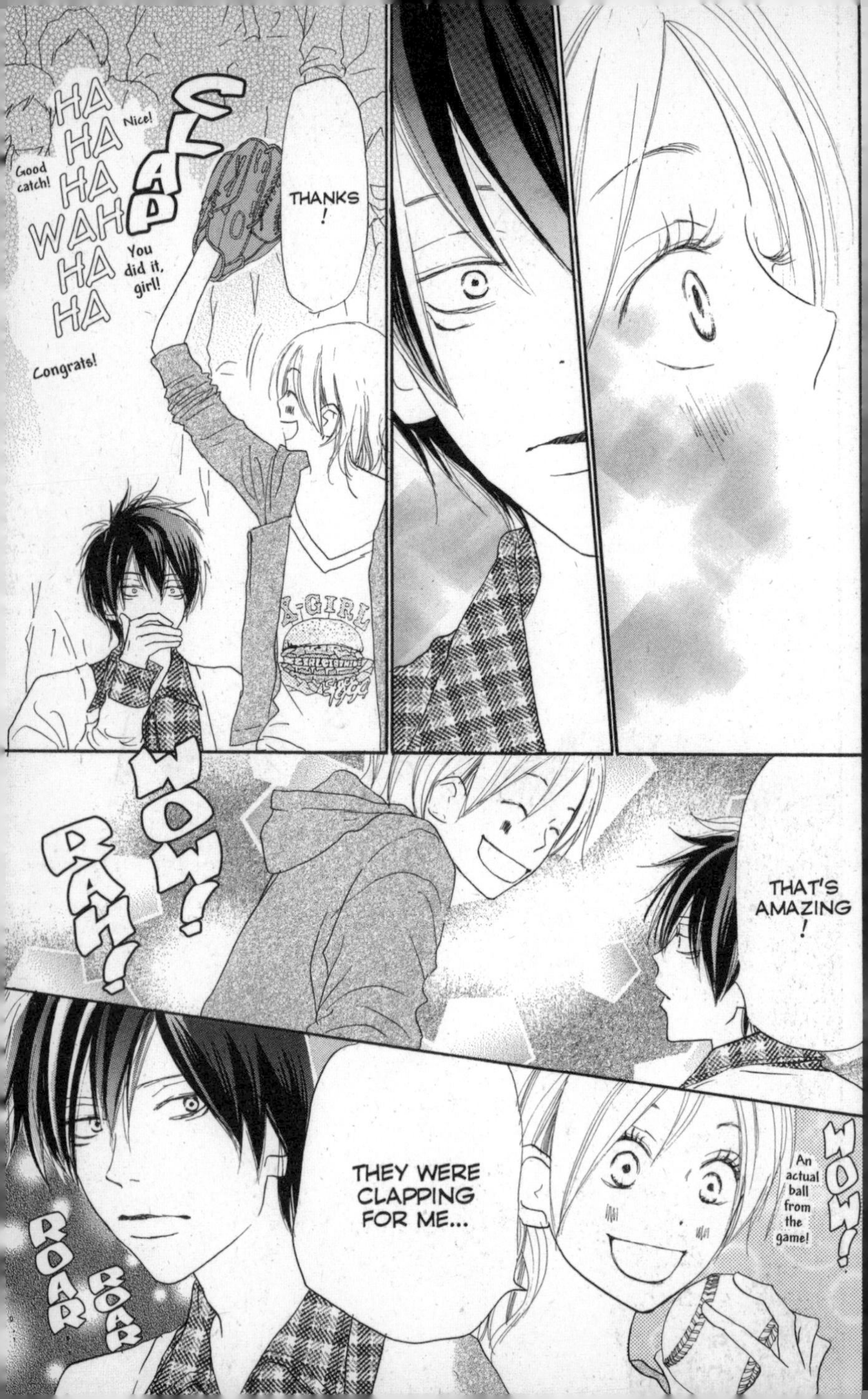

THANKS!
SLAP
Nice!
HA HA HA WAH HA HA
Good catch!
You did it, girl!
Congrats!
THAT'S AMAZING!
WOW!
RAH!
WOW!
An actual ball from the game!
THEY WERE CLAPPING FOR ME...
ROAR ROAR

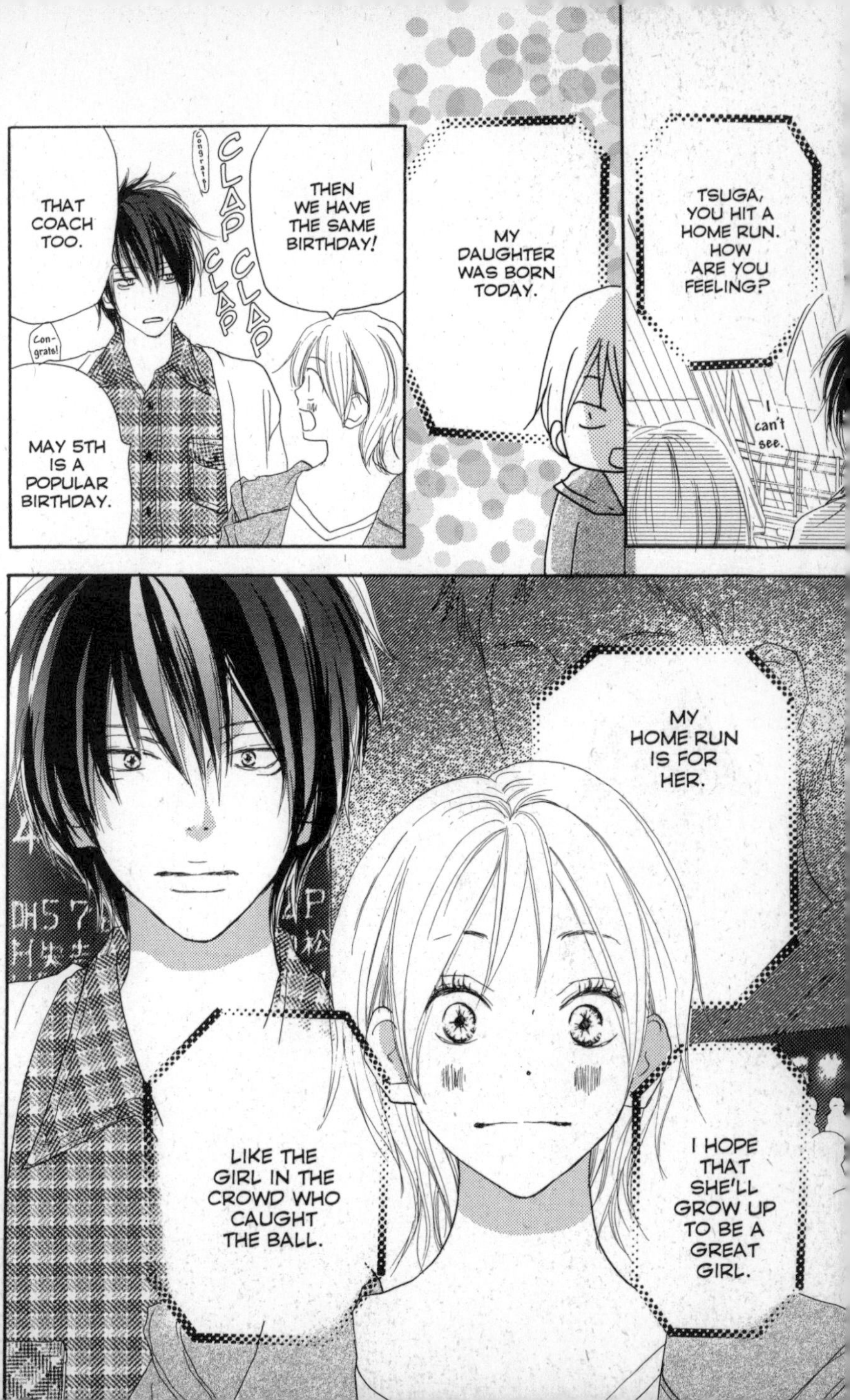
TSUGA, YOU HIT A HOME RUN. HOW ARE YOU FEELING?
I can't see.
MY DAUGHTER WAS BORN TODAY.
THEN WE HAVE THE SAME BIRTHDAY!
Congrats!
CLAP CLAP CLAP
THAT COACH TOO.
Congrats!
MAY 5TH IS A POPULAR BIRTHDAY.
MY HOME RUN IS FOR HER.
I HOPE THAT SHE'LL GROW UP TO BE A GREAT GIRL.
LIKE THE GIRL IN THE CROWD WHO CAUGHT THE BALL.

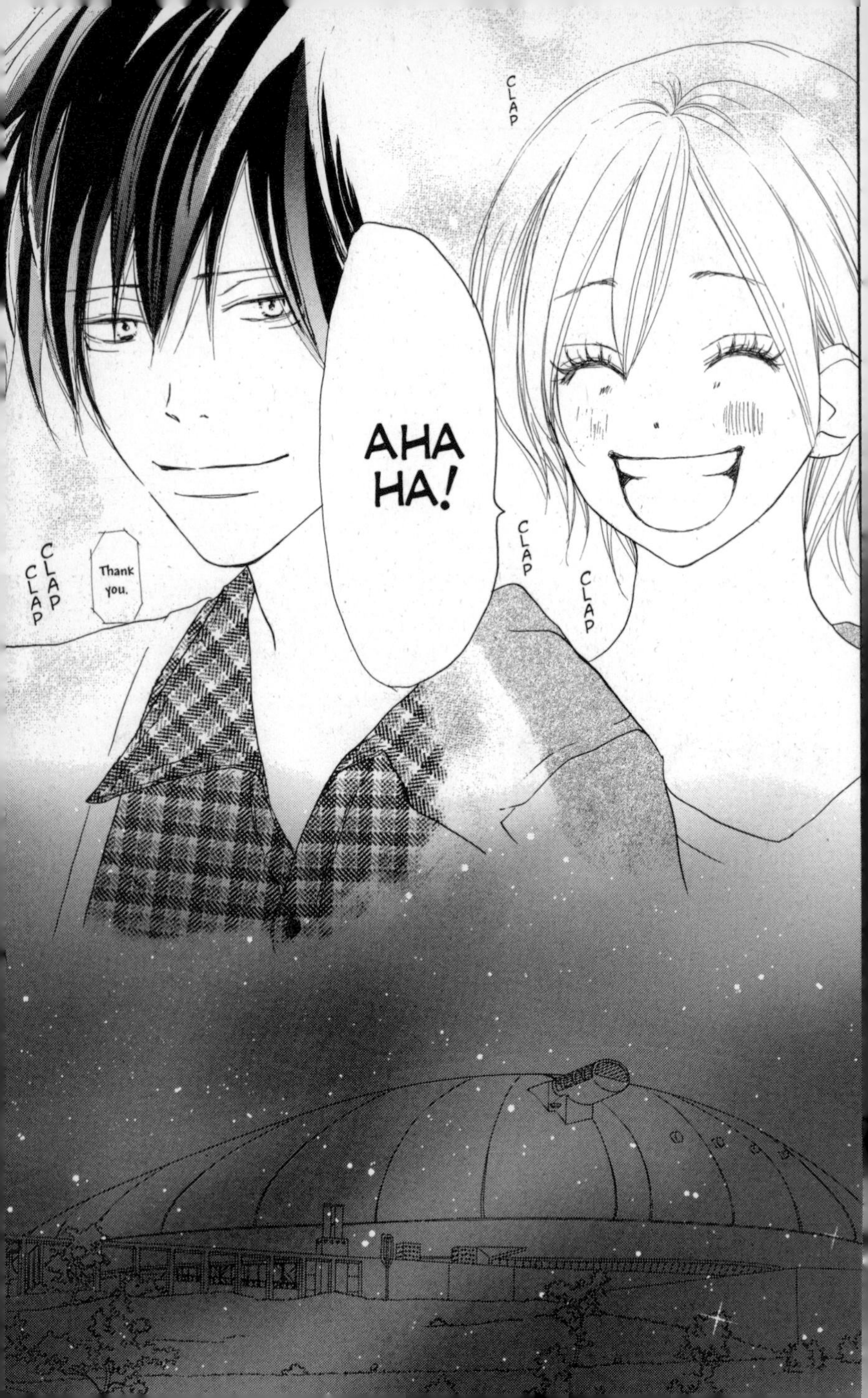
CLAP
CLAP
CLAP
AHA HA!
Thank you.
CLAP
CLAP

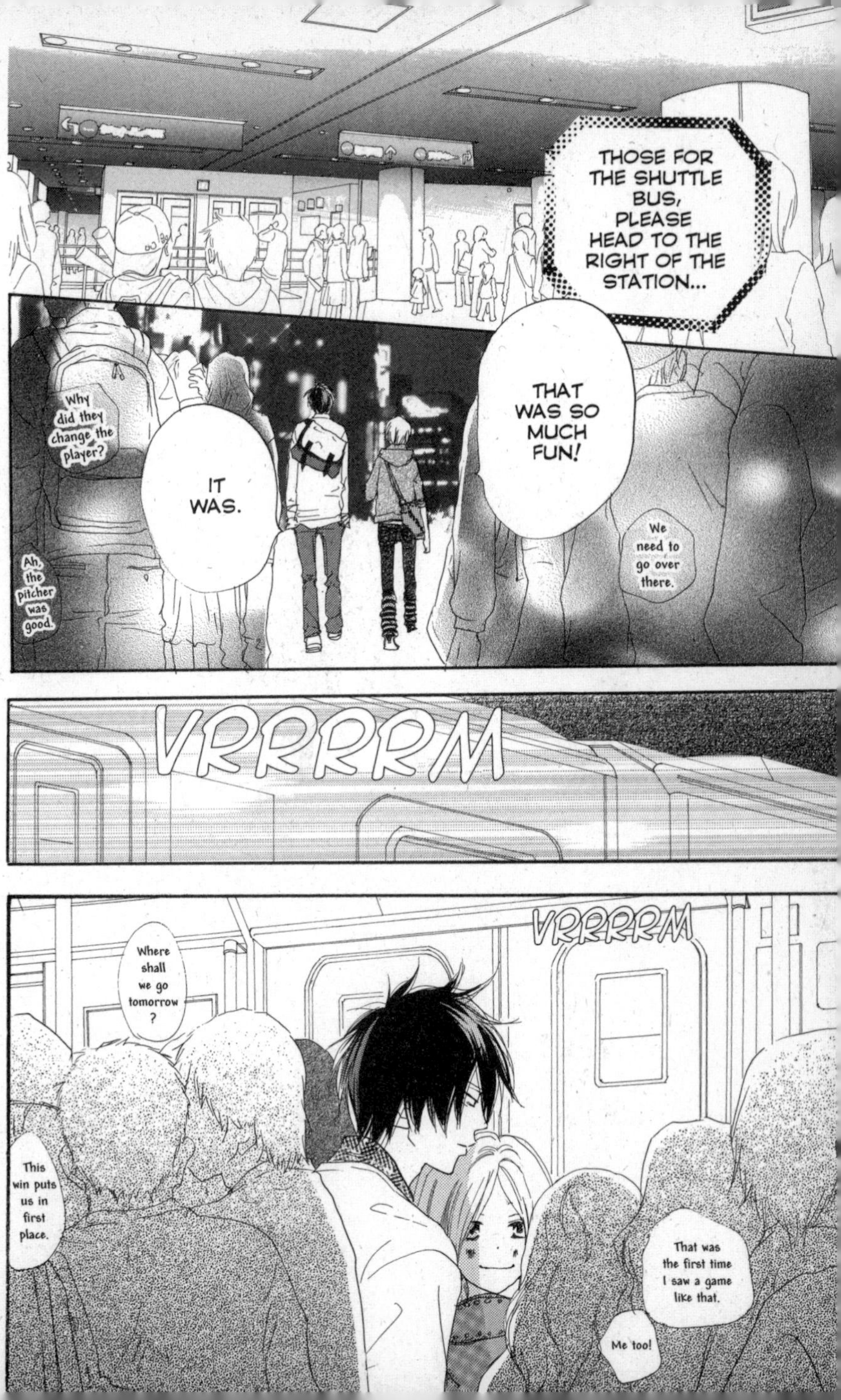
THOSE FOR THE SHUTTLE BUS, PLEASE HEAD TO THE RIGHT OF THE STATION...
THAT WAS SO MUCH FUN!
We need to go over there.
IT WAS.
Why did they change the player?
Ah, the pitcher was good.
VRRRRM
VRRRRM
Where shall we go tomorrow?
That was the first time I saw a game like that.
Me too!
This win puts us in first place.

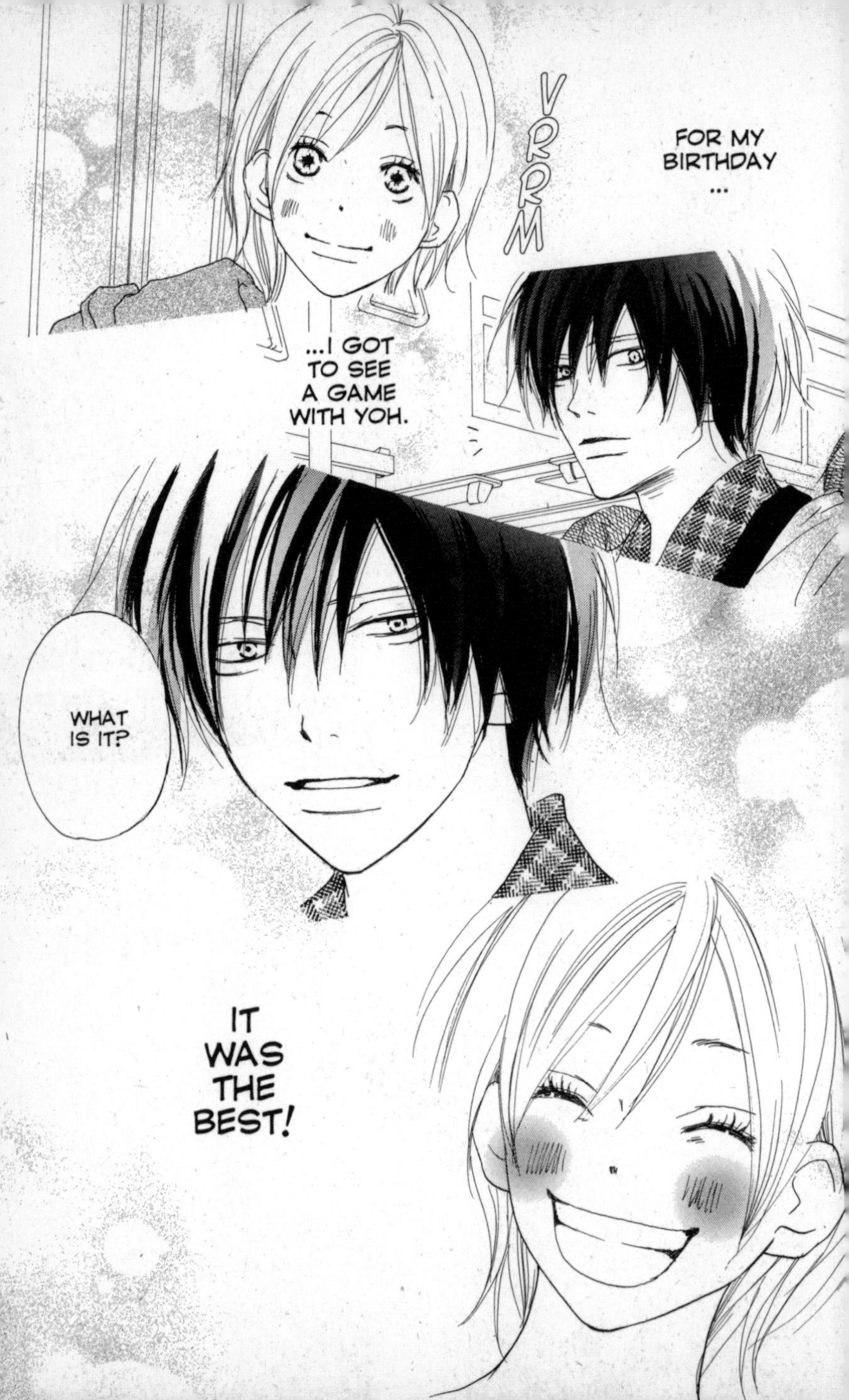
FOR MY BIRTHDAY ...
VRRM
...I GOT TO SEE A GAME WITH YOH.
WHAT IS IT?
IT WAS THE BEST!

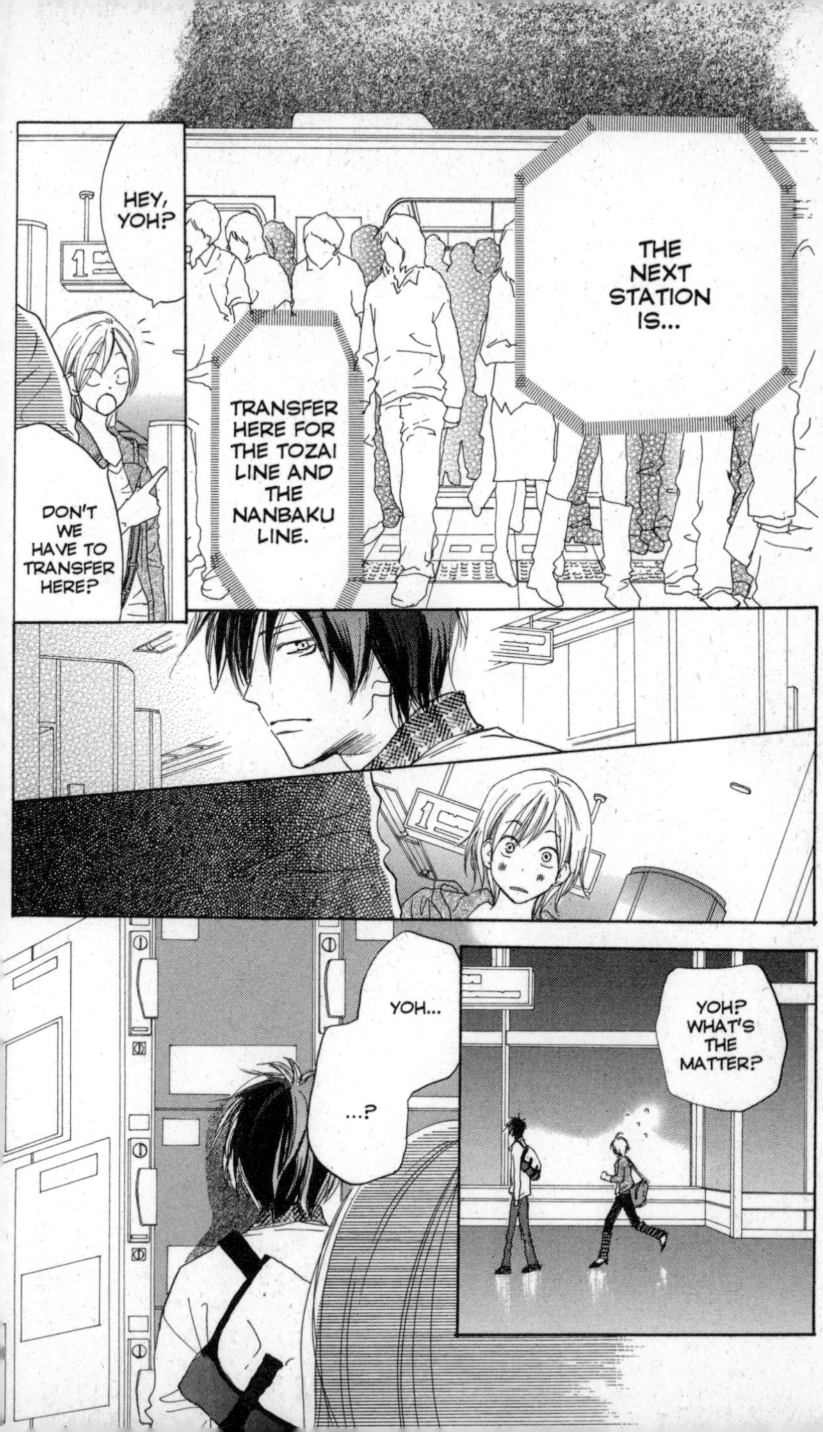
THE NEXT STATION IS...
TRANSFER HERE FOR THE TOZAI LINE AND THE NANBAKU LINE.
HEY, YOH?
DON'T WE HAVE TO TRANSFER HERE?
YOH? WHAT'S THE MATTER?
YOH...
...?

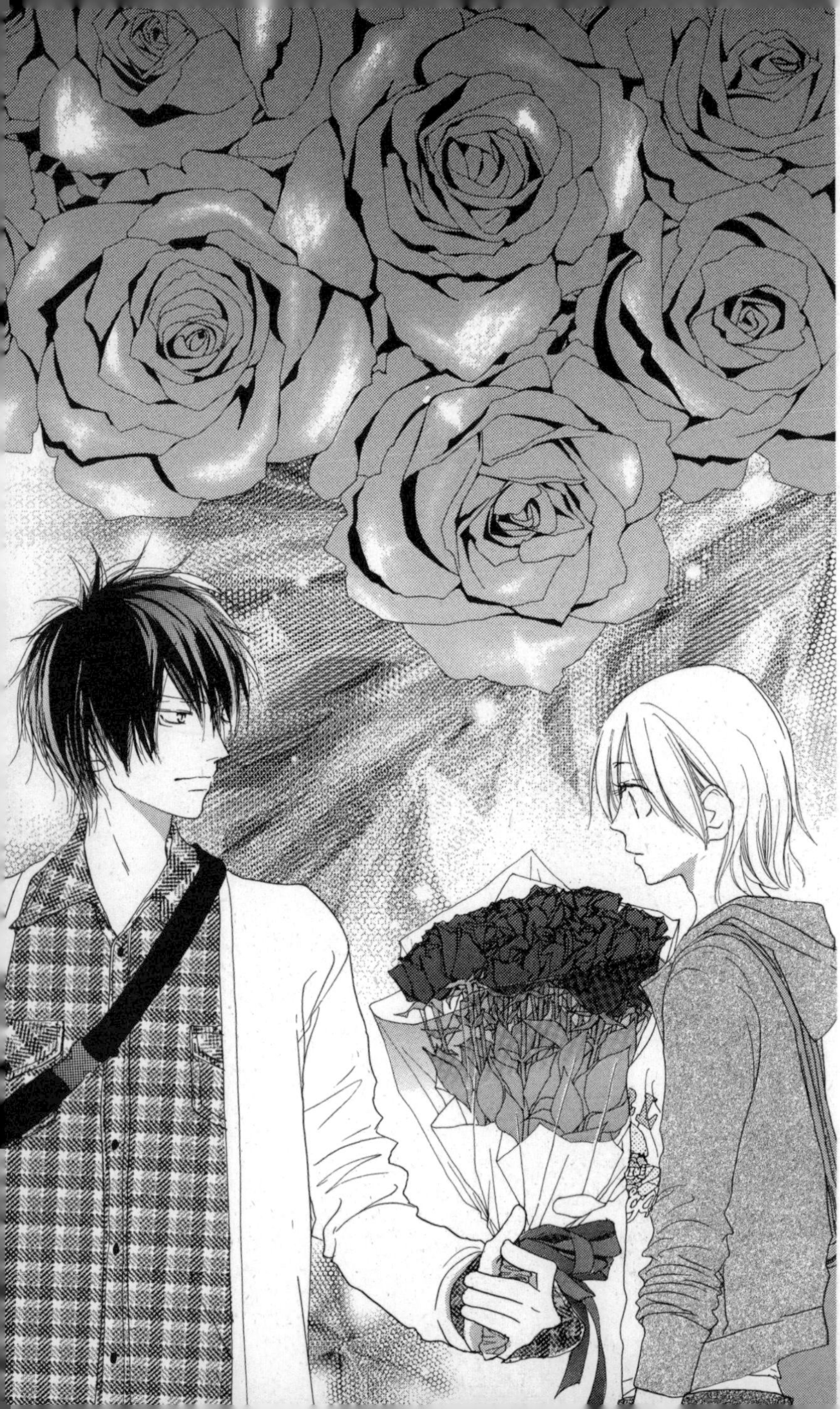

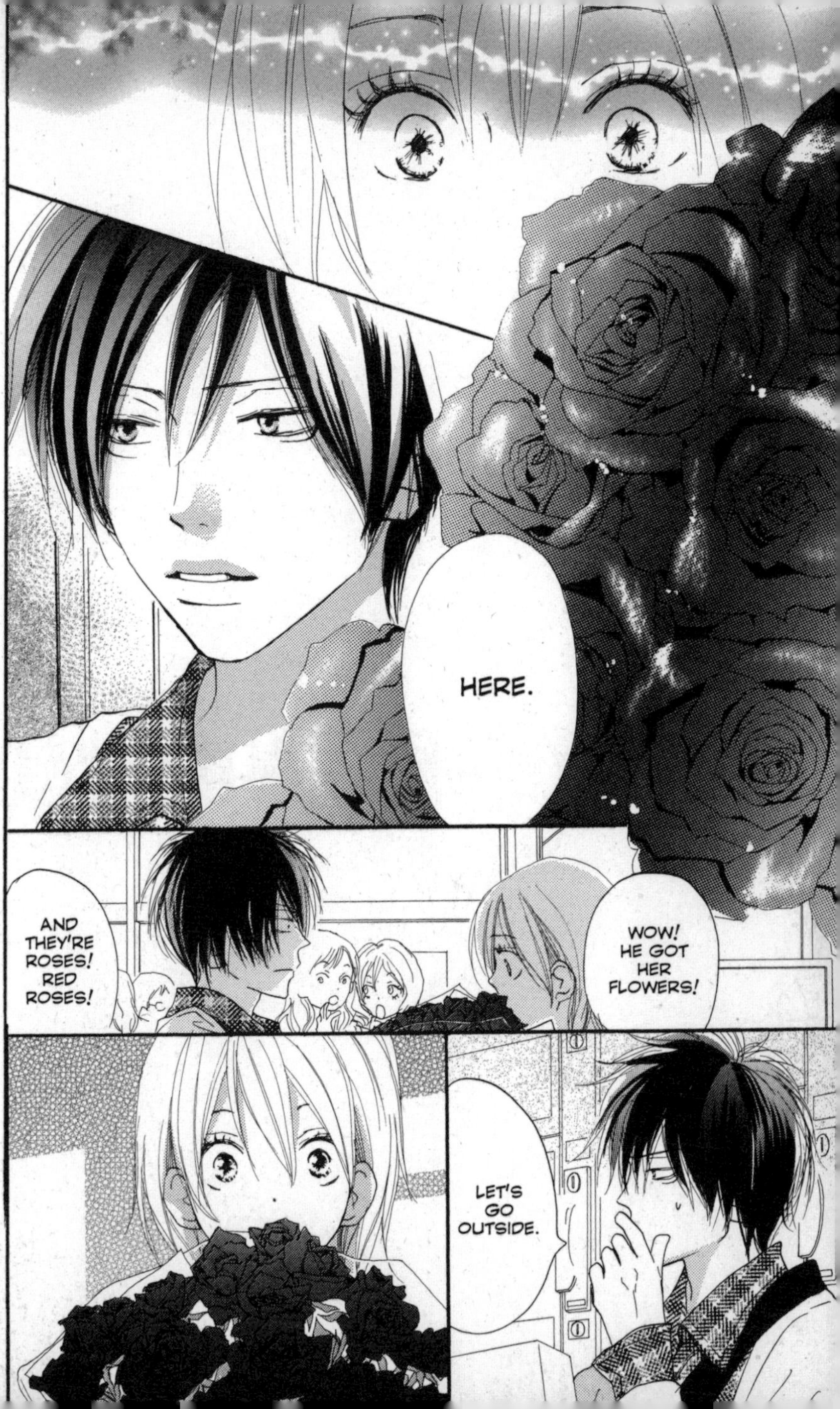
HERE.
WOW! HE GOT HER FLOWERS!
AND THEY'RE ROSES! RED ROSES!
LET'S GO OUTSIDE.

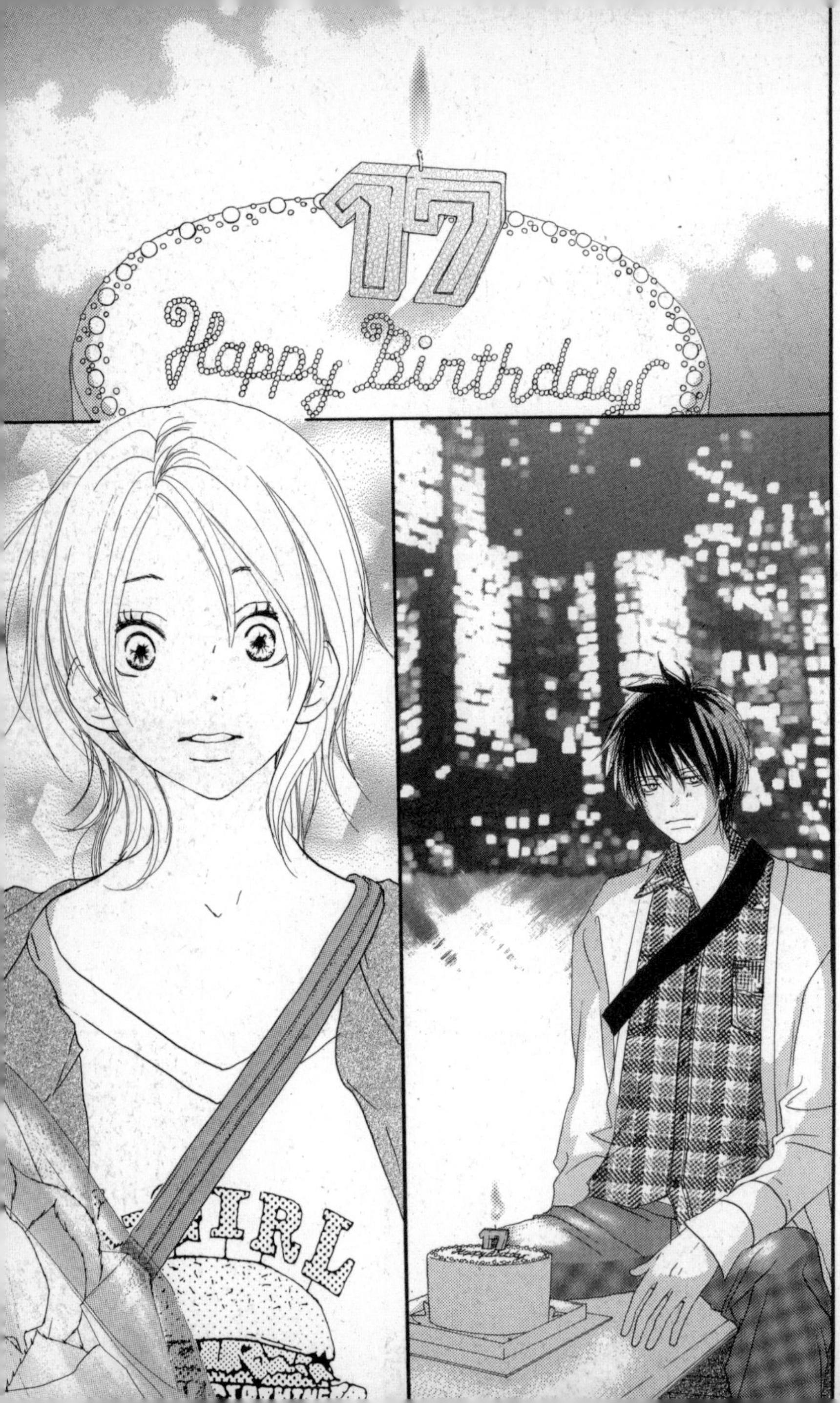
17
Happy Birthday
GIRL

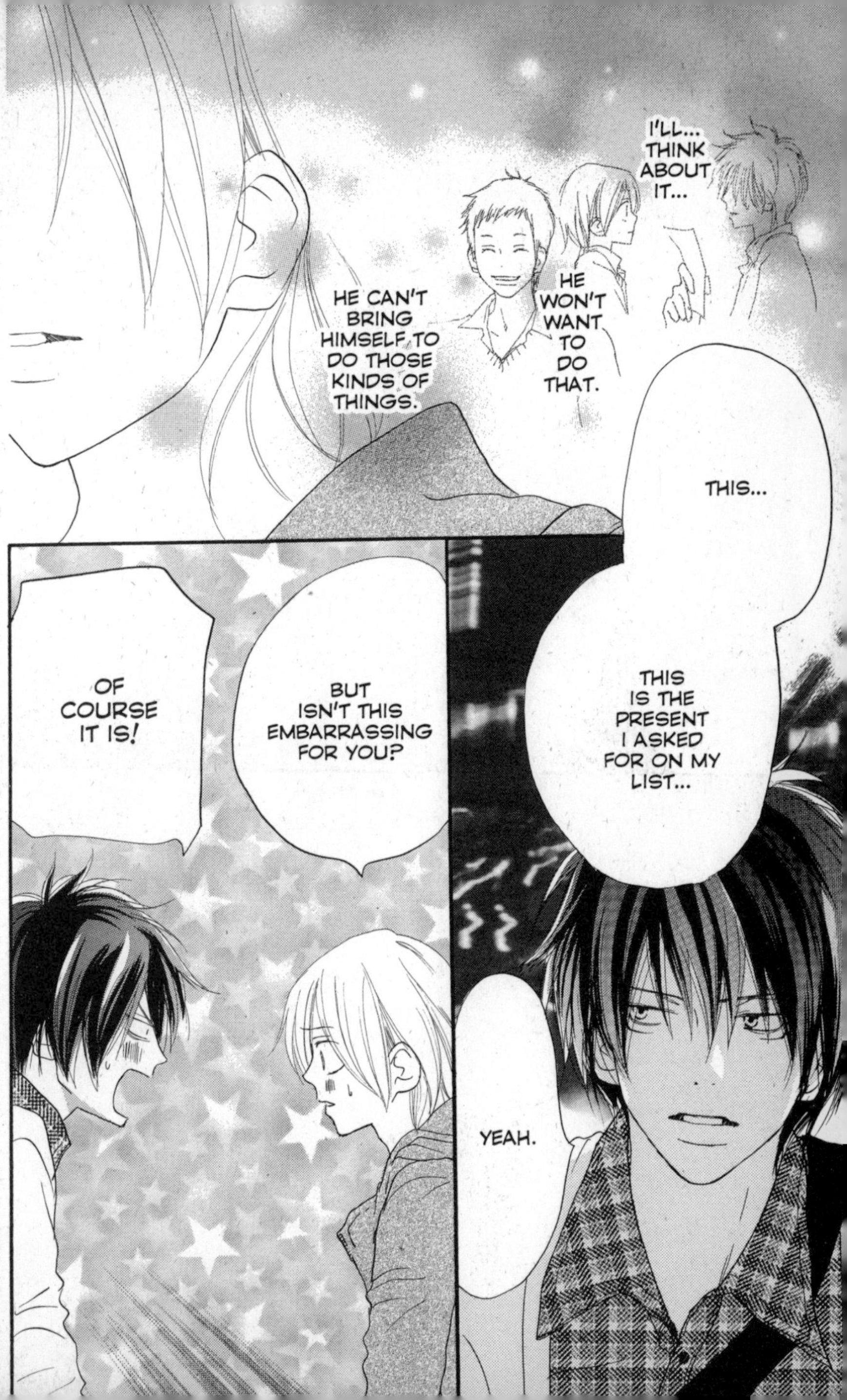
I'LL... THINK ABOUT IT...
HE WON'T WANT TO DO THAT.
HE CAN'T BRING HIMSELF TO DO THOSE KINDS OF THINGS.
THIS...
THIS IS THE PRESENT I ASKED FOR ON MY LIST...
YEAH.
BUT ISN'T THIS EMBARRASSING FOR YOU?
OF COURSE IT IS!

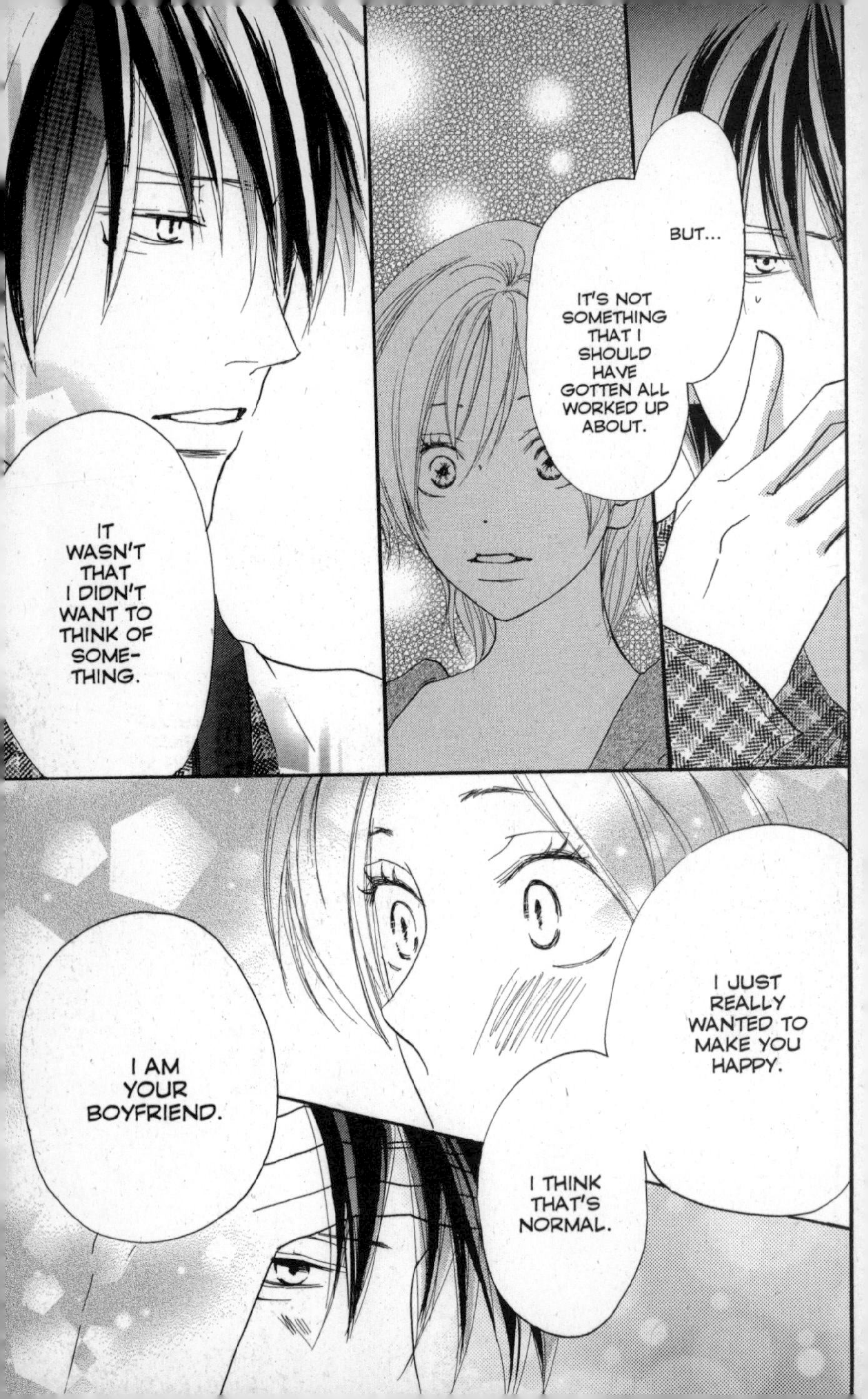
BUT...
IT'S NOT SOMETHING THAT I SHOULD HAVE GOTTEN ALL WORKED UP ABOUT.
IT WASN'T THAT I DIDN'T WANT TO THINK OF SOME-THING.
I JUST REALLY WANTED TO MAKE YOU HAPPY.
I THINK THAT'S NORMAL.
I AM YOUR BOYFRIEND.

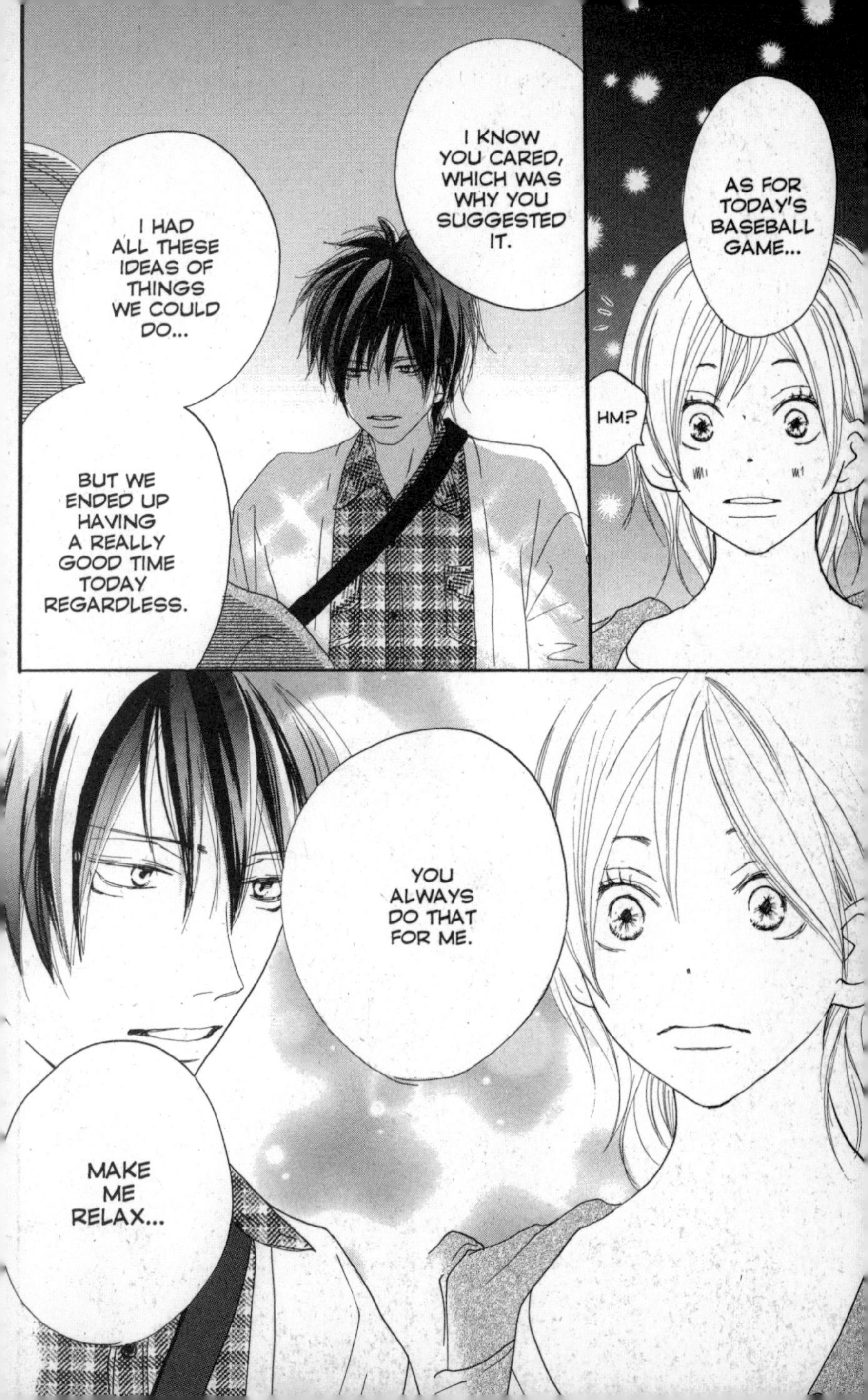
AS FOR TODAY'S BASEBALL GAME...
HM?
I KNOW YOU CARED, WHICH WAS WHY YOU SUGGESTED IT.
I HAD ALL THESE IDEAS OF THINGS WE COULD DO...
BUT WE ENDED UP HAVING A REALLY GOOD TIME TODAY REGARDLESS.
YOU ALWAYS DO THAT FOR ME.
MAKE ME RELAX...

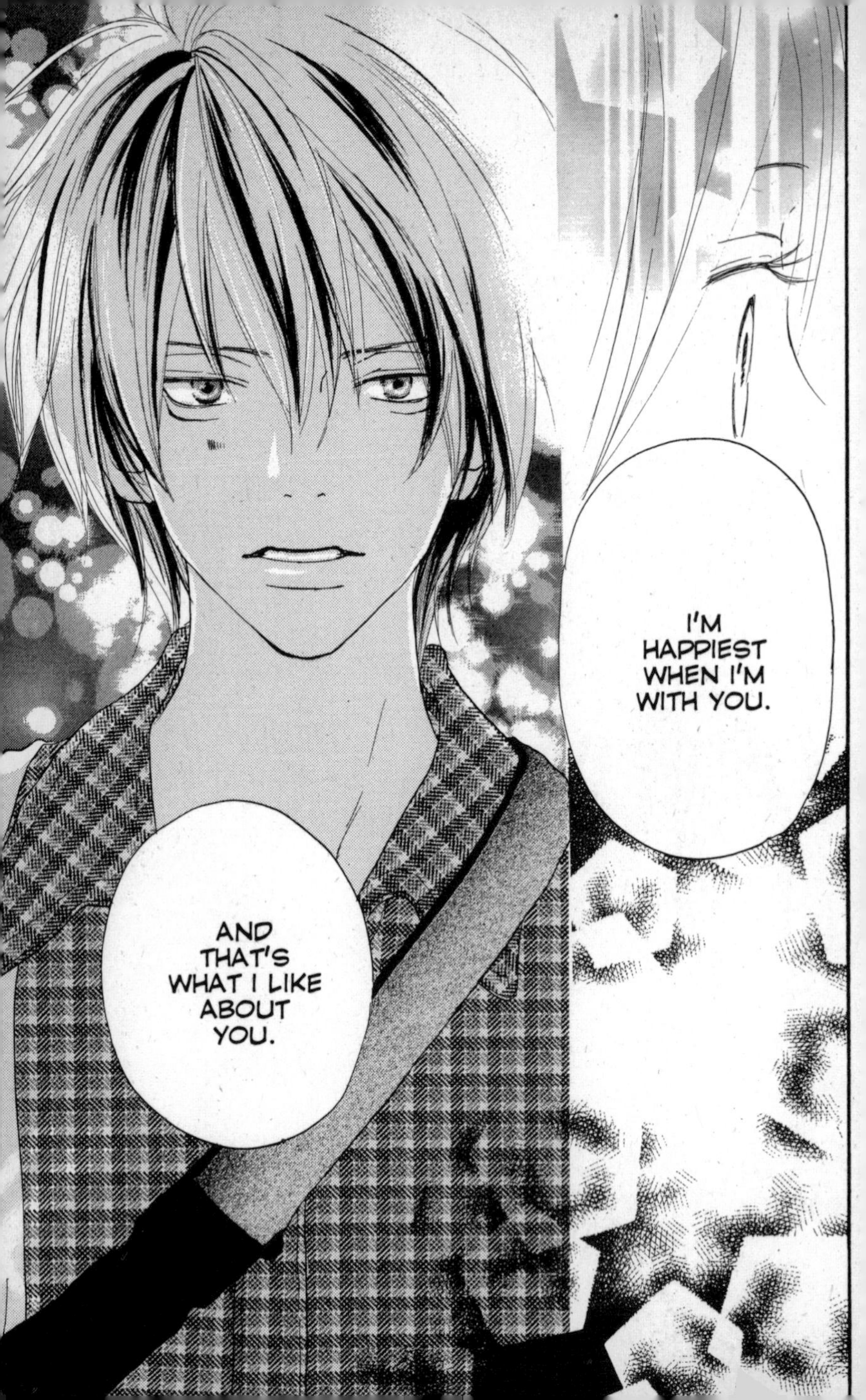
I'M HAPPIEST WHEN I'M WITH YOU.
AND THAT'S WHAT I LIKE ABOUT YOU.

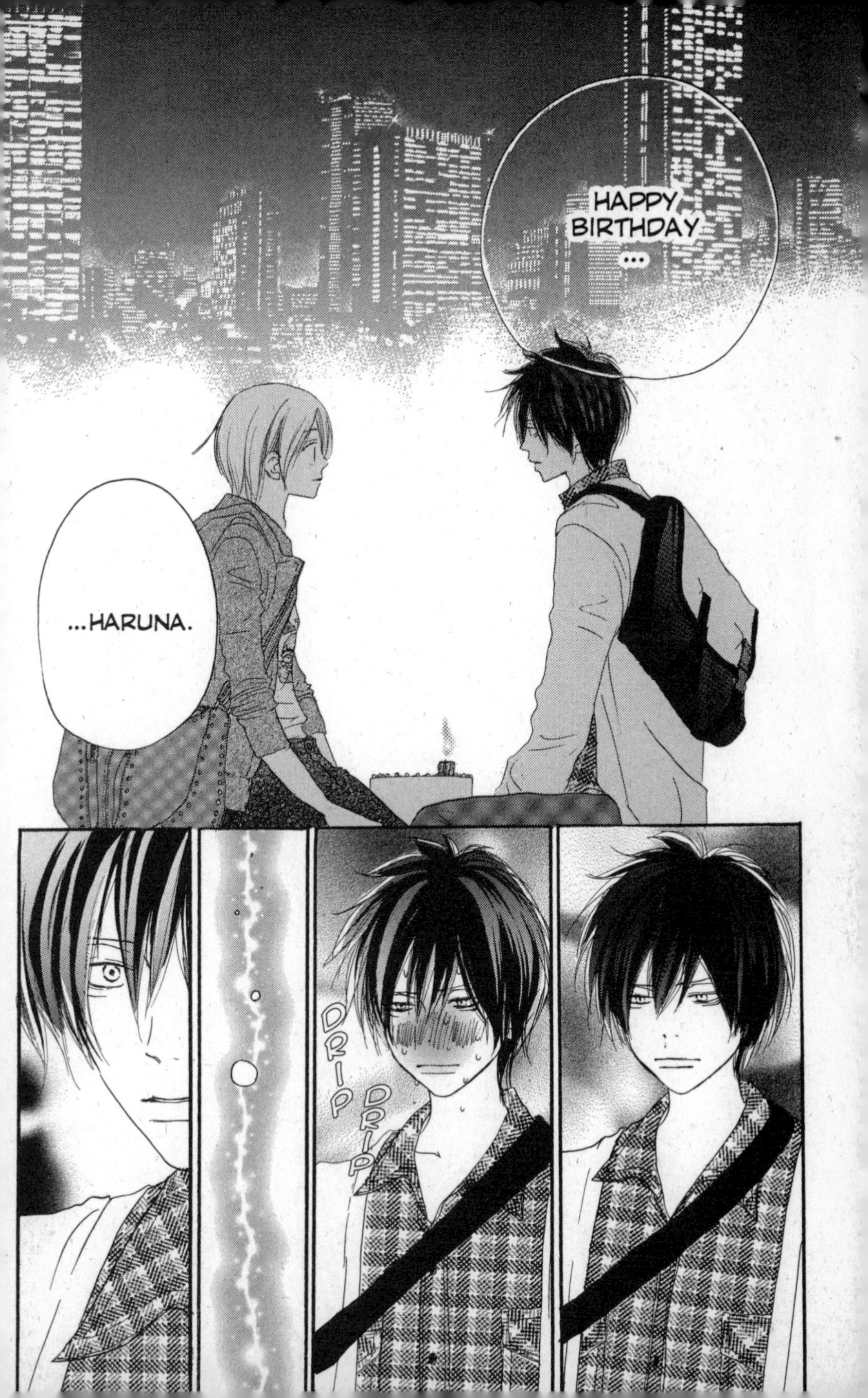
HAPPY BIRTHDAY ...
...HARUNA.
DRIP DRIP

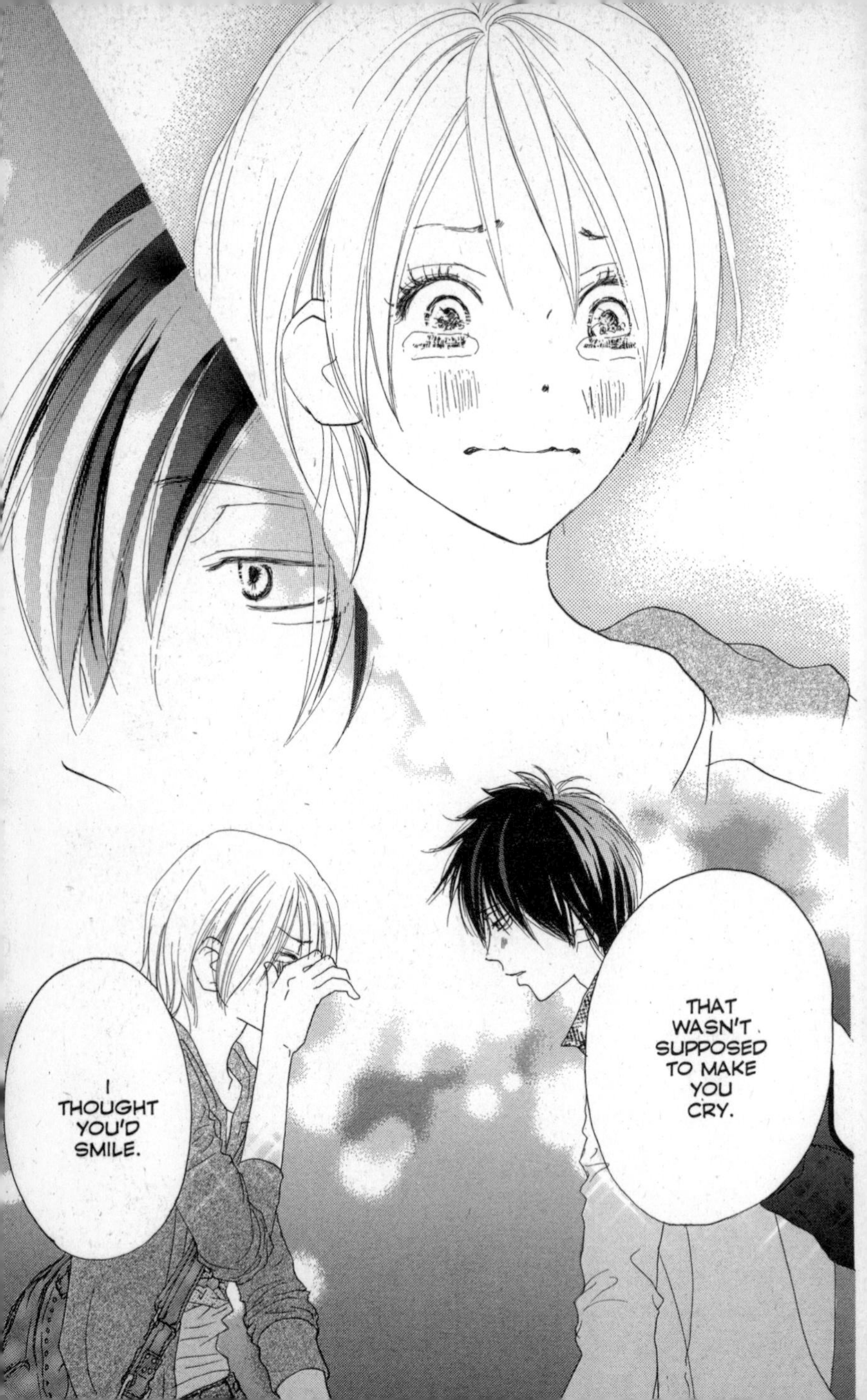
THAT WASN'T SUPPOSED TO MAKE YOU CRY.
I THOUGHT YOU'D SMILE.

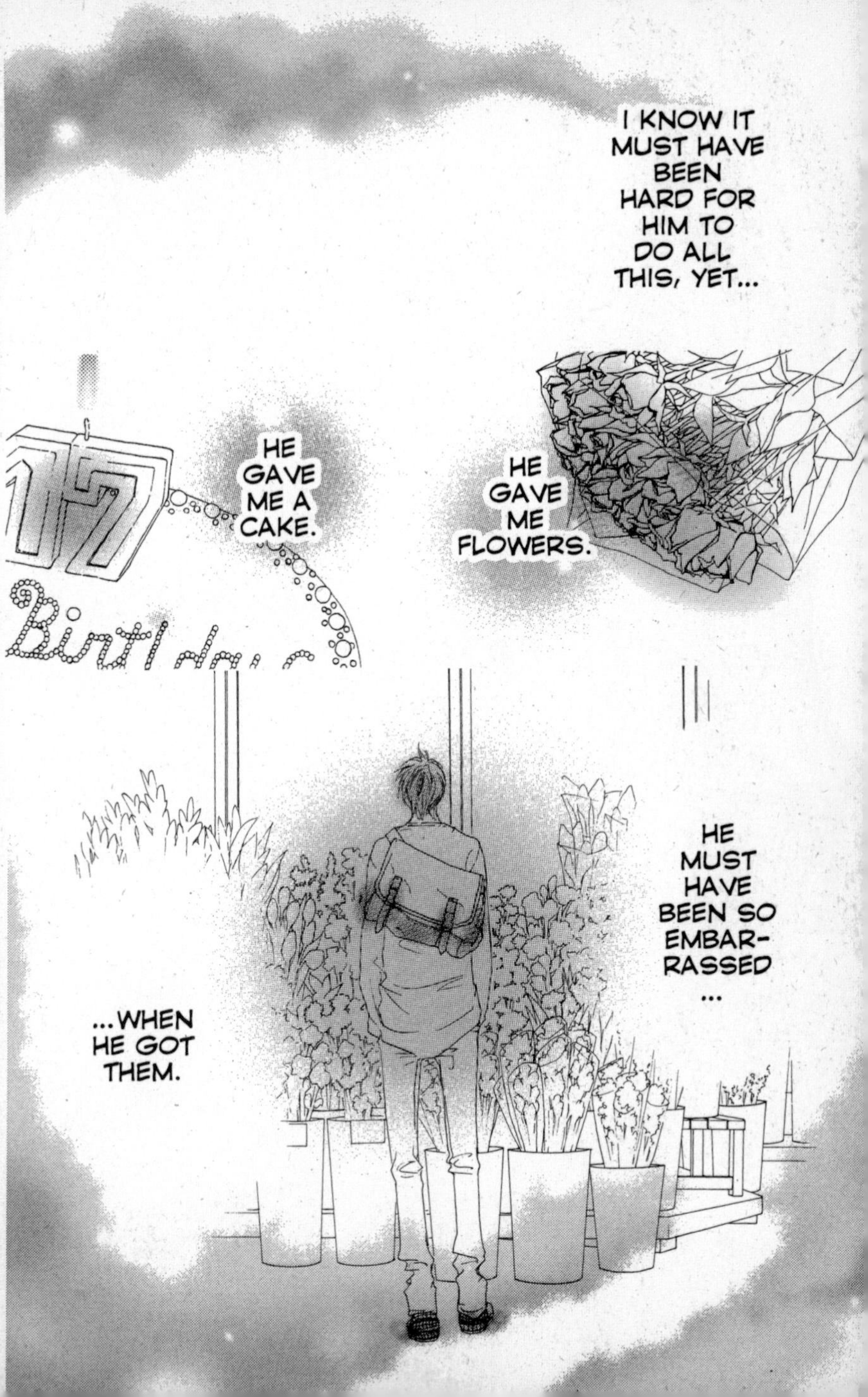
I KNOW IT MUST HAVE BEEN HARD FOR HIM TO DO ALL THIS, YET...
HE GAVE ME FLOWERS.
HE GAVE ME A CAKE.
17
HE MUST HAVE BEEN SO EMBARRASSED...
...WHEN HE GOT THEM.

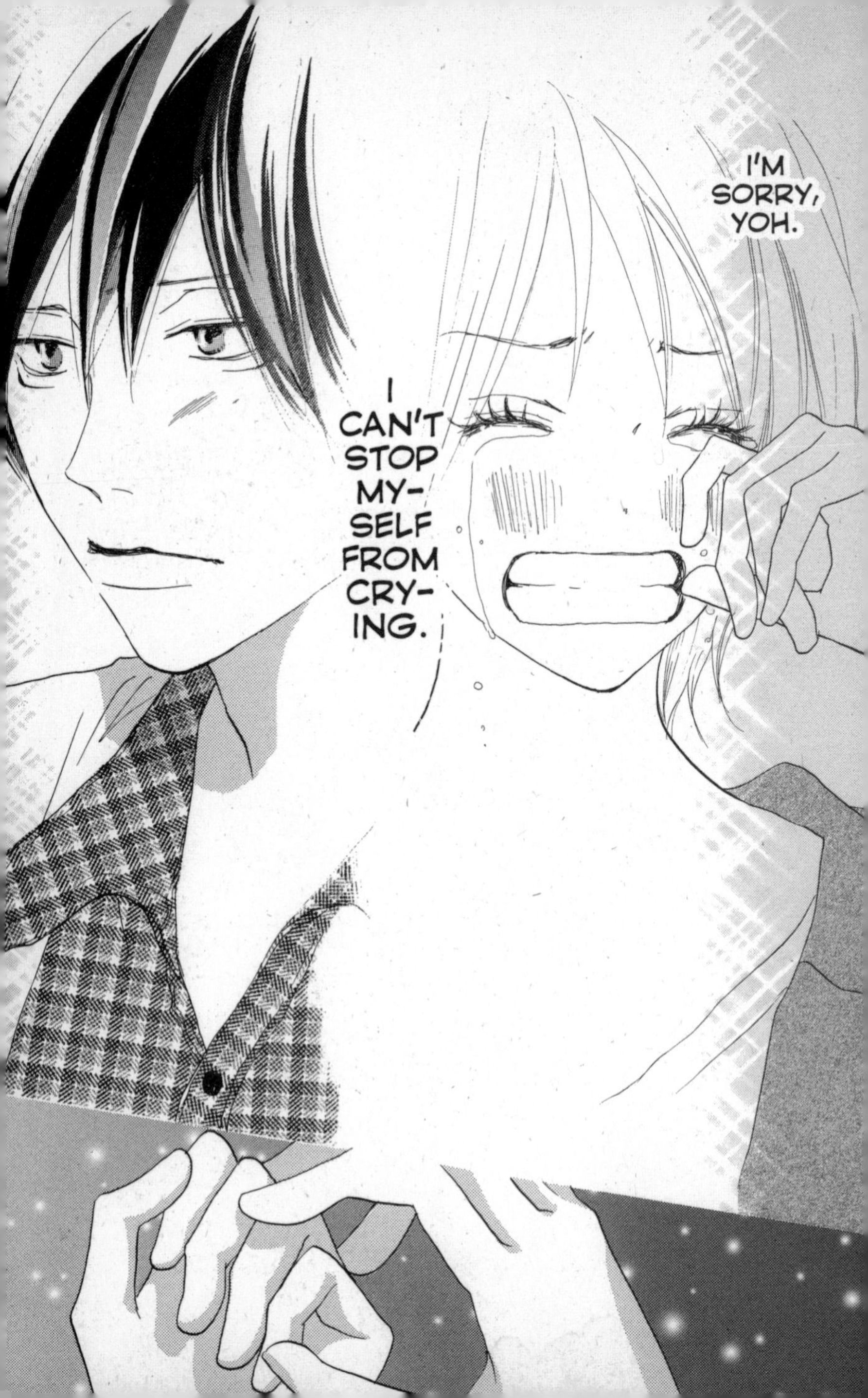
I'M SORRY, YOH.
I CAN'T STOP MY-SELF FROM CRY-ING.

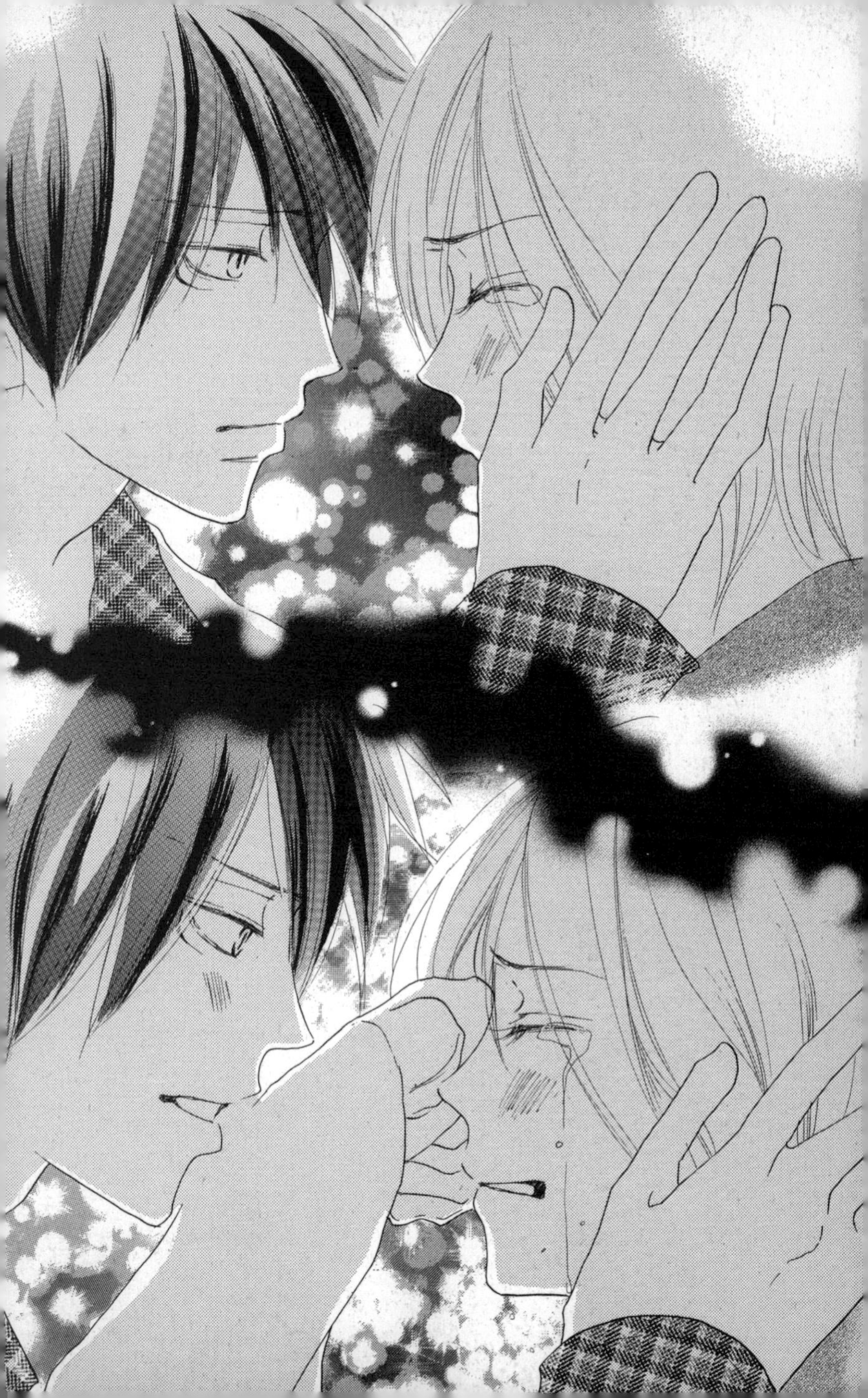

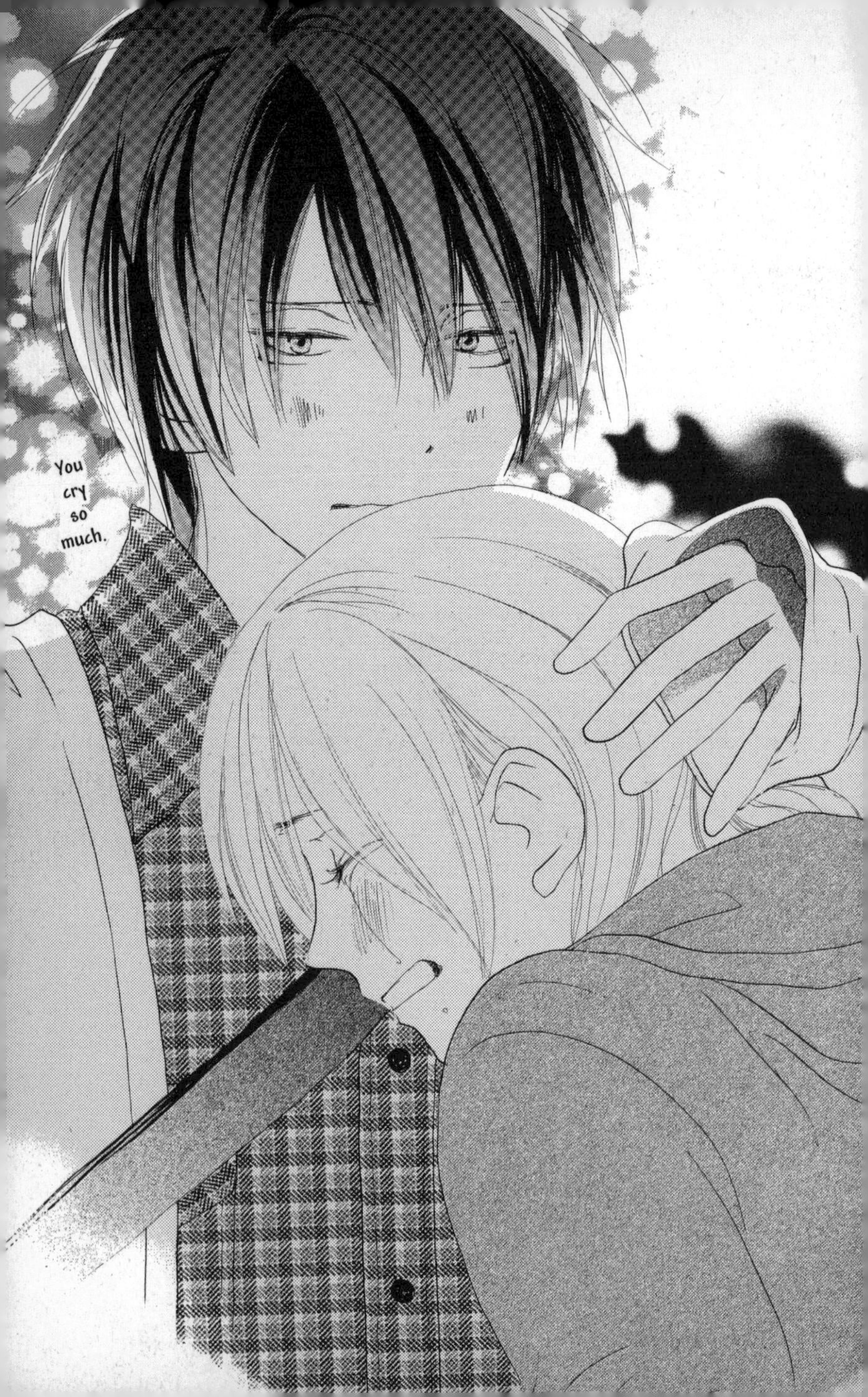
You cry so much.

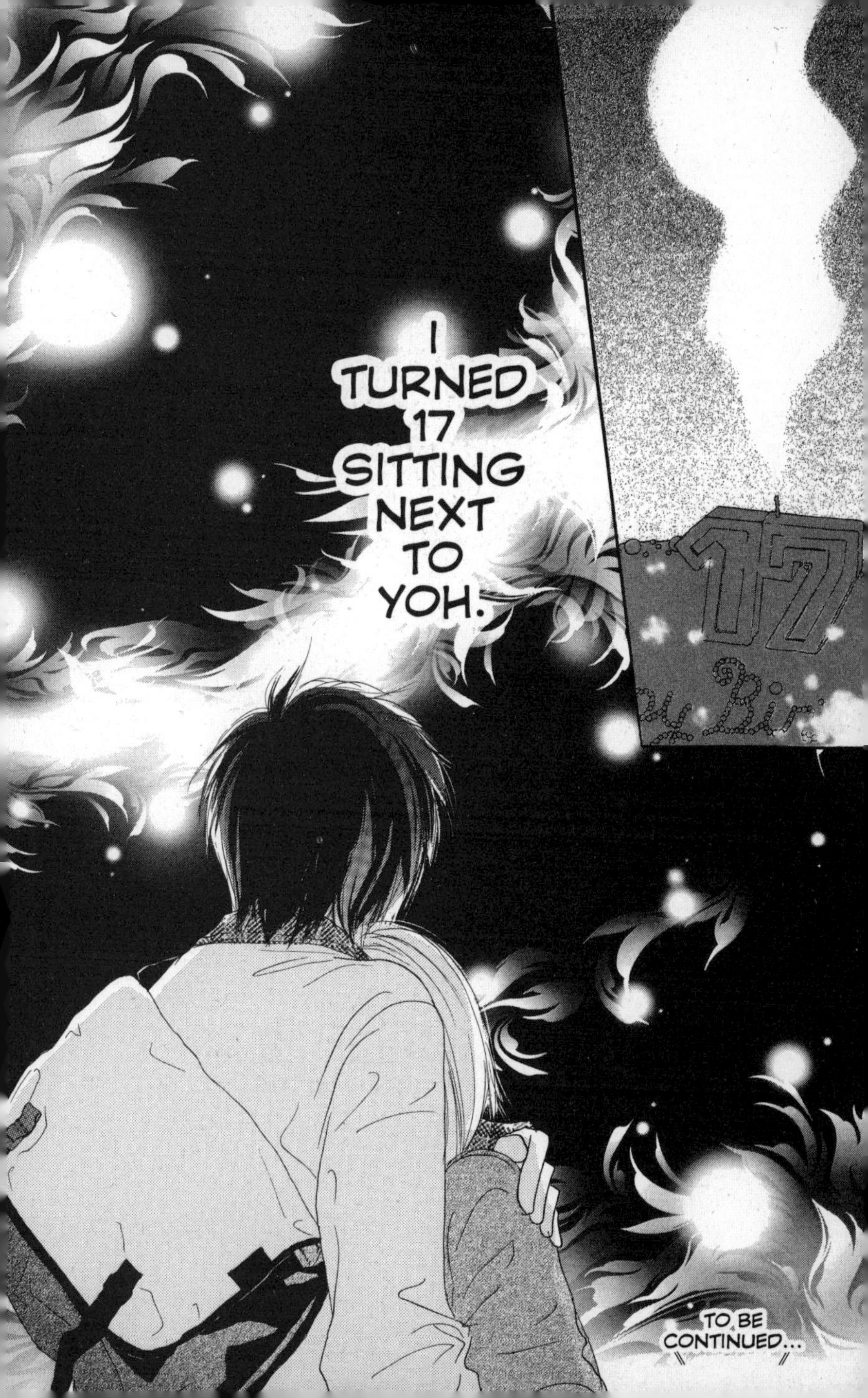
17
I TURNED 17 SITTING NEXT TO YOH.
TO BE CONTINUED...

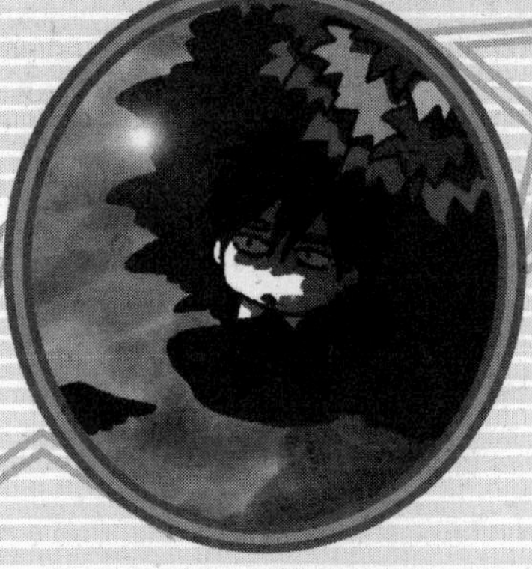

I've been having this neck pain recently. It hurts when I walk. It hurts to lie down, and it hurts to get up. It hurts so much. I wonder what's wrong. My pillow? My sleeping position? Aghhh...

– Kazune Kawahara

Kazune Kawahara is from Hokkaido prefecture and was born on March 11th (a Pisces!). She made her manga debut at age 18 with *Kare no Ichiban Sukina Hito* (His Most Favorite Person). Her other works include *Sensei!*, serialized in *Bessatsu Margaret* magazine. Her hobby is interior redecorating.

HIGH SCHOOL DEBUT
VOL. 8
Shojo Beat Edition

STORY & ART BY
KAZUNE KAWAHARA

Translation & Adaptation/Gemma Collinge
Touch-up Art & Lettering/Rina Mapa
Cover Design/Izumi Hirayama
Interior Design/Courtney Utt
Editor/Amy Yu

KOKO DEBUT © 2003 by Kazune Kawahara
All rights reserved.
First published in Japan in 2003 by SHUEISHA Inc., Tokyo.
English translation rights arranged by SHUEISHA Inc.

Printed in Canada

Published by VIZ Media, LLC
P.O. Box 77010
San Francisco, CA 94107

10 9 8 7 6 5 4 3 2
First printing, March 2009
Second printing, July 2011

www.viz.com   www.shojobeat.com